The Next World War

Also by Peter Apps

Deterring Armageddon: A Biography of NATO

The Next World War

The New Age of Global Conflict and the Fight to Stop It

PETER APPS

WILDFIRE

First published in Hardback in 2026 by Wildfire
An imprint of Headline Publishing Group Limited

2

Cataloguing in Publication Data is available from the British Library

Hardback ISBN 978 1 0354 2485 6
Trade Paperback ISBN 978 1 0354 2486 3

Typeset in 12.5/15.5pt Baskerville MT Pro by Six Red Marbles UK, Thetford, Norfolk

Printed and bound in Great Britain by Clays Ltd, Elcograf S.p.A.

Headline Publishing Group Limited
An Hachette UK Company
Carmelite House
50 Victoria Embankment
London EC4Y 0DZ

The authorised representative in the EEA is Hachette Ireland,
8 Castlecourt Centre, Dublin 15, D15 XTP3, Ireland (email: info@hbgi.ie)

www.headline.co.uk
www.hachette.co.uk

For those I have worked with, served with and loved,
particularly my grandparents and great grandparents
who went through all this before

Contents

Introduction and Acknowledgements

In late January 2024, my flight from Bangkok touched down at Taiwan's main international airport at Taoyuan, just outside the capital. It was a grey and wintry afternoon, and I could just as easily have been in part of Heathrow, Gatwick, Frankfurt or any other major aviation hub. But if war came to the world in the coming years – and particularly if it started with a Chinese attack against Taiwan – then this ultramodern airport and the industrial estates around it might be among the first and most important battlefields.

China's military commanders had already built a giant replica of the airport, the lines of its runways clearly visible at a remote training area in the Gobi Desert,[1] together with other potential targets on the island including the presidential offices. Any such assault would almost certainly be accompanied by beach landings: perhaps the largest amphibious operation since the Allied D-Day invasion of Europe in 1944, perhaps even larger.

Crossing the 90-plus miles of the Taiwan Strait would be no easy matter: between summer typhoons and winter storms, some analysts believed an attack would only be possible in the few normally calm weeks around April or September. As I drove along the coastal road in a wheelchair-accessible minibus a few days later, the storm-tossed waters looked particularly grey and uninviting.

The tiny fishing community at Zhuwei and nearby Chu-wei beach was a brief patch of light and life amid the grey seas, skies, creeks and corrugated iron-roofed buildings that ran down to the foreshore – even if none of the small, brightly painted fishing boats were venturing out to sea. In a small restaurant that still showed its Christmas decorations, family groups clustered around rice, stew and enormous oysters. I chose not to wreck the atmosphere by asking them what might happen if this place became ground zero for an invasion by China's People's Liberation Army (PLA).

In the event of war, these people might be some of the first to suffer but they were unlikely to be the last. Outside, a stallholder who gave her name only as Mrs Chen was open about her worries. Her greatest concern, she said, was for her two sons in their thirties who had done their military service and might well be recalled if an invasion came. She said she did not expect the Americans to intervene to protect Taiwan by fighting, although she thought they might send weapons. As to what she and her community would do: 'We will die or we will flee.'[2]

Earlier that day, I had been talking to other young men and women who might also be doing the fighting: current students and likely future conscripts at the National Taiwan University. Again, they responded in several different ways: the women – not liable for military service unless they volunteered, but often fiercely attached to Taiwan's ideals of democracy and de facto independence – were often the most convinced that the island should fight. Among the young men there were a range of attitudes. 'Some people are determined, and some are scared,' one told me. 'I am one of the scared ones.'[3]

It reminded me uncomfortably of the conversations I had as a young Reuters journalist in Sri Lanka almost two decades earlier, visiting areas that had been on the frontline in previous bouts of the civil war and now faced renewed fighting as its ceasefire unravelled. It was the same feeling of understated, growing dread – but also sometimes a degree of understandable excitement, particularly for those who barely recalled what conflict was really like, either because they were too young, or too powerful or privileged to care.

It was not, of course, an omnipresent feeling. 'You can't think about war the entire time – you simply wouldn't function,' one Taiwanese official told me. There were also plenty of people on Taiwan – perhaps even the majority – who believed that conflict wouldn't happen, or at the very least that officials from the United States were overstating dangers when they warned it might come as soon as 2027. Most people, as always, were simply getting on with life. It was the same a few weeks later in Estonia, where the crowded buses, shops and restaurants felt little like a nation facing an existential threat. People were going about their daily lives – even if some were quietly talking of getting houses in Spain, or other steps to cope in the event of conflict.

US Army reservist and military contractor Rocco Santurri described a similar mood in South Korea: 'It's almost as if the air is slightly heavier. But life goes on.'[4] The same, of course, could be said for those undergoing much worse experiences routinely in Ukraine – just as it was for my two grandmothers, both later conscripted in uniform, as they walked to work through the wartime bombing of Liverpool and the Medway towns.

As recently as the late 2010s, the idea that the world might genuinely be approaching another major war would still have been seen as scaremongering at best. That tensions were rising between the United States and China was by then becoming obvious. It was also clear that Vladimir Putin's Russia was less and less interested in playing by the West's rules. With hindsight, though, the Kremlin's 2014 annexation of Crimea, Beijing's growing assertiveness in the South China Sea and, perhaps most importantly, the indicators of the waning power of the United States should all have been seen as warning signs.

By the start of the 2020 Covid-19 pandemic, it was already clear that things were getting worse – followed briskly in 2021 by the mass-mobilisation of Russian forces along the borders of

Ukraine and the full-scale invasion of February 2022. Soon, the phrase 'Ukraine today, Taiwan tomorrow' was being repeated in Asia and in Washington, while European nations wrestled with how to react to the reality that major land warfare was again a feature of their continent.

As former British Army head and then UK defence chief General Sir Nick Carter put it in an interview in early 2025: 'It's an extremely dangerous decade, reminiscent in some ways of the 1930s – albeit with some differences: nuclear weapons were not around [then] and the world was arguably not as interconnected as it is today. But when you see the nature of the bellicose rhetoric, it seems some people have forgotten the horrors of war.'[5]

Some preparations were already underway as the US and other militaries quietly began to prioritise what they termed 'large-scale combat operations'. From the start of the 2020s, NATO's military planners rebooted Cold War-era war plans into a new concept they called 'Defence and Deterrence for the Euro-Atlantic', setting the tone for the dramatically increased steps that would be taken from 2022.[6] Still, the speed of escalation shocked almost everybody.

In October 2022, US President Joe Biden described the risk of nuclear escalation in Ukraine as the highest since the Cuban Missile Crisis in 1962.[7] Within a year, Jamie Dimon – the legendary chief executive of JPMorgan Chase who had led the bank since 2006 – was also warning the world was entering the 'most dangerous time . . . in decades'.[8]

The modern threat, however, both looks and feels distinctly different to that of what we should probably now call the first Cold War. The prospect of the world being torn apart by multiple atomic blasts is once again no longer unimaginable, although we remain well short of the visceral terror of the most alarming Cold War years. According to analysis of demographic trends, the Cuban crisis was followed nine months later by a mini-boom in the birth rate – but only in those US states within missile range of Cuba. Those expecting to be killed in the opening volley of missiles appear to have been happy to shed their inhibitions – but also in those states further away where people expected to survive the first few days, couples became more reluctant than usual to bring a child into a potentially post-apocalyptic world.[9]

For now, even in most frontline states, few seem to be thinking in terms of such starkly apocalyptic options. With most of the potential conflicts that we see today, the assumption is that they would begin with conventional if perhaps widespread fighting – and that they would most likely stay that way, at least initially and perhaps for weeks or months or even years.

Still, when nuclear rivals India and Pakistan came to blows in May 2025 it took only a matter of days for panic buying to be reported in New Delhi, with some residents talking of fleeing to relatives in the hills in case matters escalated.[10] That fighting was the most serious between those nations since they both acquired atomic weapons; another reminder of how fast the long-standing taboo on nuclear nations fighting conventional wars against each other is breaking down.

As in the early Cold War years, the world looks like it's entering a cycle in which repeated and sometimes overlapping crises can fuel repeated escalation; a more complex counterpart of the series of events from the 1948–9 Berlin Blockade and resulting airlift to the face-off over Cuba of 1962. Only after coming to the very edge of global Armageddon did US President John F. Kennedy and Soviet counterpart Nikita Khrushchev find a way to step back from the brink and usher in détente and more than a decade of talks and lower tensions.

Those who work towards global arms control and to reduce atomic dangers are already waiting for that moment, jotting down potential steps to be used to build confidence after the next crisis. But as US Marine Lieutenant Colonel Brian Kerg – head of planning for the 3rd Marine Expeditionary Force in Okinawa – wrote for the Atlantic Council in early 2024, it is entirely possible that the crisis would instead yield a long and open-ended conflict. 'Everyone loves a short, sharp war,' he wrote. 'They end on time, are won decisively and provide tight narrative completion for the stories we want to tell.' But just as likely, he suggested, was a lethal and frenetic opening stage that could kill tens of thousands across the Pacific and beyond, potentially extending to the use of tactical nuclear weapons by both sides – but which was only the beginning. Providing that escalation could be controlled, the conventional conflict might just keep on going, exhausting high-tech weapons stocks and then reworking economies and societies as all sides commit further to an existential war through conscription, mobilisation and asset stripping of industry.[11]

A July 2024 Congressional report described the US as dangerously unprepared for such a widespread war – particularly if needing to fight China coincided with an attack against Europe from Russia and perhaps also action by North Korea and Iran. 'The US public are largely unaware of the dangers,' warned the report. 'They are not anticipating disruptions to their power, water or access to all the goods on which they rely . . . The nation was last prepared for such a fight during the Cold War . . . It is not prepared today.'[12]

Most other countries are making similar discoveries. From the start of 2025 I was lucky enough to get funding to build the 'Facing Coming Storms: Talking International Defence' podcast for the British Army's think tank, the Centre for Historical Analysis and Conflict Research, probing just these issues for a professional military audience and all others that were interested. Many of the resulting interviews have fed into this book, along with my own travel and reporting as well as that of others (of course suitably referenced).[13]

From the very top of modern militaries to those who will fight the battles on the ground, there are now both active discussions and often simulations of what modern war might look like. 'There is definitely a sobering moment for the marines . . . when they realise that you can have everything done right and unfortunately you still lose some of your people,' US Marine Corps Captain Nicholas Royer told me in spring 2025 as he outlined how his team delivered training. That included simulating the dilemmas junior personnel might face deciding whether to risk detection by flying a small drone, or how to handle a panicked civilian population in the face of an attack. It also included putting personnel in an environment where the rapid helicopter evacuation available throughout much of the 'war on terror' might be rendered impossible by electronic jamming and anti-aircraft systems.[14] Multiple individuals leading large numbers of troops warned me that modern fatalities in a single day of conflict might now extend to several hundred troops, perhaps even more – a dramatic increase compared with Iraq and Afghanistan, where the loss of even a dozen troops in a single day could be seen as a disaster.[15]

In other areas we are now in uncharted territory. While Ukraine offers at least one example of a modern major war on land, as well as the effectiveness of missiles and drones against warships at sea, the world has not seen a real missile-firing major maritime conflict since the Falklands War in 1982. Those who remember that experience describe an atmosphere of deep and sometimes frenetic terror – as well as frantic battles to fight fires and save ships following a bomb or missile impact.

Modern aerial combat – including not just drones and planes but missiles against missiles and electronic jamming – is now evolving at exponential speed, with new technology and tactics every year, and the same is true in space. Cyber attacks and interference in critical infrastructure such as energy facilities, data centres, undersea cables, transport and even sewage all bring different threats, and perhaps huge destruction extending to widespread loss of life. A whole separate book could unquestionably be written on the current 'hybrid' and often hidden conflicts involving sabotage, subversion and other secret acts now constantly underway – with many of the details likely to be revealed years into the future, if they ever see the light of day. Then there is the worldwide battle for resources.

With the return of Donald Trump to the White House in 2025, events have taken yet more complex turns. On the one hand, the new US administration expressed commitment to the maxim of 'peace through strength' and 're-establishing deterrence' with a much more muscular approach to foreign policy and potential foes. On the other, it contained no shortage of 'restrainers' who argued that America was overstretched and must cut back on its commitments. It also appears keen to focus America's military might on homeland defence – something the administration interprets increasingly broadly to include border and missile defence and lethal strikes on drug dealers at sea, not to mention troops policing US cities.

America's allies must now look nervously at the potential fights that they must do more to deter if the US does indeed step back. 'We are at a very dangerous moment because the structures and consensus and the understanding we have of how the world fits together has all been upended,' former British Army officer turned Liberal Democrat MP Mike Martin told British magazine the *Big Issue*, citing conversations with senior officials who believe there is a high chance of a major conflict by 2030. 'If we got into a big war, we would have conscription straightaway.'

It was a long way from where UK defence policy still sat, with talk of building up part-time reserves that could provide another few tens of thousands of soldiers at the very most, while trusting new technology – particularly drones – to fill the remaining gaps. 'We are not at the stage yet where you can replace people with drones,' said Martin. 'You still need people to occupy villages, hold ground and all the rest of it. And that's not going to change for quite some time.'[16]

It was very much a soldier's view – Martin had been one of the most respected experts and critics of Britain's war in Afghanistan, and remained heavily briefed on the fighting in Ukraine. On the far side of the world, at Edwards Air Force Base in California, the base commander Brigadier General Doug Wickert told local civic leaders he believed it was maintaining America's military technical edge that was more important.

Wickert was one of the US Air Force's most experienced test and combat pilots – significant parts of his official military résumé had been redacted to maintain secrecy. The reason the current era was more dangerous than the first Cold War, he believed, was in part because China was able to out-produce the US when it came to warships, planes and missiles. Only a handful of US military capabilities, such as the new B-21 'Raider' stealth bomber being built in nearby factories, were retaining deterrence, he said – and in the event of all-out war, that would likely mean California's air bases and aviation plants would be attacked with missiles, cyber attacks and other means. 'If this war happens, it's going to happen here – it's going to come to us,' he told local government officials. 'The more ready we are, the more likely that we are going to change Chairman Xi's calculus.'

Wickert paraphrased President Dwight D. Eisenhower's maxim that 'the only way to win the next war is to prevent it from happening in the first place'.[17] Others – particularly US Defense Secretary Pete Hegseth – favour the 4th century Roman military writer Vegetius, with his pithy phrase now popularly translated as 'if you wish for peace, you must prepare for war'.[18] In order to support that messaging, the Trump administration would rebrand the Pentagon from the Department of Defense to the Department of War, although any formal change would require an act of Congress – and the official name at the time of writing will be used for the remainder of the book. Trump himself described changing the name and focus explicitly to 'war' as 'much more appropriate . . . especially in light of where the world is right now'. Critics described it as another sign the new administration was tearing up everything achieved since the name had last been changed in 1949, including America's alliances.[19] With his often-quoted saying, Vegetius had been thinking of Rome and the vast armies it retained to protect and expand its borders while keeping down dissent and external attack. But he could equally have been talking about the warlike tribes of Germany and Scandinavia that resisted Roman rule through being just too hard to conquer. Many of Russia's and China's modern neighbours are similarly determined to resist being pulled into the new and growing empires of Moscow and Beijing – but some are much more prepared than others.

In 1939, the combination of Finland's professional soldiers and volunteers held back the Soviet Red Army as it attempted to overrun their nation in the so-called 'Winter War'. They succeeded: a peace deal forced them to surrender whole swathes of their territory, but the Finns retained their nationhood. Throughout the long years of the Cold War, Finland was forced into an awkward position of neutrality – but it had survived.

In the event of a Russian attack, Finland's conscripts are still taught to live in the harsh wilderness, mounting hit-and-run attacks if necessary. The recruits talked enthusiastically of the distinctly Finnish concept 'Sisu', an almost 'berserker'-like rage that could be applied to both fighting a human enemy and surviving in virtually impossible Arctic conditions. All Finnish men aged 18 to 60 have been required to complete their military service, while women had the option to volunteer. 'For me it's because I have a good life,' said female conscript Veera Remes in early 2025. 'That's what this is about, protecting that. The times have changed . . . We grew up [believing] wars were in the past. We have learned that they are not.'[20]

This book argues that Finland has the right approach. The second quarter of the 21st century is likely to be extremely unforgiving for those nations who are not willing and able to defend what they hold dear, whether that applies to territorial integrity or values like free speech and democracy. If Russian and Chinese leaders in the coming years believe that they can take something by force, then they will try to do so – and perhaps unleash catastrophe. Only by making the cost of such actions clear can they hope to be deterred – and the fact that the Trump administration has sometimes flirted with a similar approach in its demands for Panama and Greenland might only encourage such behaviour.

Plenty of better people than me have written more eruditely on deterrence. One of the brightest, Professor Lawrence Freedman of King's College, London, suggested to me that likely answers for the current era come from striking the proper balance between 'complacency and panic'.[21] Still, the quotation I find myself coming back to most often – the one that best captures the duality and doublethink at the heart of modern soldiering – comes from one of my grandfather's senior NCOs during his training back in World War Two. 'What is the first duty of a soldier?' the NCO would bark, to which the desired answer was: 'To keep the peace.' 'What is the second duty?' he would follow. 'To kill the enemy!'

If conflict comes in the current era, those at the sharp end may well find it at least as unpleasant as the global wars that came before. As the coming chapters will show, artificial intelligence and unmanned systems might sometimes reduce the number of people at the front, but they also allow huge numbers of targets to be struck repeatedly. Anyone who has seen videos of drones over Ukraine hunting down their prey will know they bring their own new forms of terror – and there are still plenty of more traditional sources of wartime fear and dread.

Recent wars have already brought back images of families cowering in basements under artillery strikes and bombing, while the supply chain and economic impact of a major global conflict would affect every family on Earth, quite possibly starving the most vulnerable. Not since World War Two have we seen a naval war sinking large numbers of ships, but the advent of new drones and missiles makes this all but inevitable in a major fight, with all the accompanying consequences for an ill-prepared global trading system. Then there are the combat losses, which even within the first hours of a war involving the US, China and many allied nations would go beyond anything those countries have seen in recent memory. Russia's experience in Ukraine suggests some countries can learn to take that on the chin – particularly if those paying the ultimate price of conflict are suitably well paid and come from the fringes of the nation or society. Even there, the Wagner Group's attempted mutiny of 2023 acts as a reminder of the potential fallout.

During the writing of this book, several people have asked me how likely I believe a major war to be. My personal belief is that the risk stands at around 30 to 35 per cent over the coming decade – and the actions that the West and its allies takes in the years to come will dictate whether war becomes more likely or not. I believe that makes the current era already an even riskier time than the beginning of the first Cold War – but the example of that period shows that conflict is avoidable when the right preparations are made, and allies stick together.

Even if the 'next world war' never comes, however, the risk of it and the preparations and actions already being made are shaping the world we live in, and will keep on doing so, most likely for decades and perhaps even for centuries. In time, the main flashpoints may shift from Taiwan, Ukraine and the South China Sea to low Earth orbit or the far side of the Moon, where the West, China and India are already getting started with new forms of high-tech competition. More likely, such rivalry will just add new fronts to existing confrontations.

In terms of when the risk may be greatest, the most dangerous time could well be the start of the next US presidential administration in 2029. This book is neither pro- nor anti-Trump. Indeed, it largely buys his argument that his sheer unpredictability – in his own words: that foreign leaders know he is 'fucking crazy' – may act as an effective deterrent for both Putin and Xi. Those leaders, though, face their own advancing ages – and diminishing opportunity to deepen their legacies – as well as the potential rise of rivals who might see opportunity in conflict. The modern age is clearly shaped by personalities – but we should not fall into the trap of assuming those who are running countries now will be the ones making the decisions in the years to come.

Whatever happens now, I suspect there is a highly credible chance that whoever is in power in Moscow or Beijing may wish to test the next US president as they enter office, whether Republican or Democrat. When Biden's team took office in 2021 it took less than three months for Putin to begin mobilising troops on the border of Ukraine, and it would not surprise me if something similar happened on either or both sides of the world as soon as Trump's successor enters office – and perhaps with each successor after that.

This book examines the fault lines, flashpoints and host of very human influences on where we go from here, also detailing the steady deterioration of the international situation in the months from January 2024 to late 2025. If real-time journalism is the first draft of history, this is perhaps at best a second, written in the moment and rewritten several times as events and trends have shifted.

In some parts of the world – particularly in Eastern Europe – even by the end of 2024 there was a growing view that a new world war had in fact already started, and was already in the process of escalating from Ukraine to spread elsewhere. For now, I instinctively reject that view – firstly because I dislike the idea that endless escalation is inevitable, but secondly because the death, destruction and disruption we have seen so far, horrific though it is, would be dwarfed by the consequences of a true new global conflict. Still, it is increasingly undeniable that a serious battle for the future of the world is already underway.

This book is, I hope, a prequel or a prologue to a war that never happens – but either way, as Eisenhower said to his chief archivist as he built NATO's first military structures in 1951, it is perhaps best that it is written down so it can be read, interrogated and reinterpreted in future.[22] What happens next, after all, will become part of the history that coming generations will look to understand – and even if we avoid outright conflict and disaster, it now looks very much as though international confrontation rather than co-operation will be the order of the day for years if not for decades.

As ever, I'm grateful to the editors and managers at Reuters, to those who have served with me at various points in my army reserve career, those who have facilitated my travel and my writing, particularly my excellent team of personal care assistants, and, of course, my family, friends and loved ones, without whom life would be very different. None of you deserve to face a major global war, and I hope this book is, in its own small way, part of the effort to ensure that we avoid one by being properly prepared.

And with that, like a storyteller of old, I would like to take the reader back to the first days of 2024 in the heart of Scandinavia, where the King of Sweden and the most powerful in that nation have gathered amid snow-covered mountains to discuss how their long years of peace might be coming to an end.

Peter Apps
London, autumn 2025

1

Not this August – But Maybe Next

'Not this August, nor this September . . . Not next August, nor next September; that is still too soon . . . But the year after that or the year after that, they fight – and then what happens to you?'

Ernest Hemingway, 'Notes on the Next War',
***Esquire* magazine, 1 September 1935**[1]

In the first working week of 2024, Sweden's leaders gathered in a ski resort near the Norwegian border to discuss the mounting threat of war. Dressed in camouflage, defence chief General Micael Bydén opened his presentation with images from wartime Ukraine: smashed buildings, destroyed vehicles, industrialised violence on a scale unthinkable in Europe only a handful of years earlier. 'This,' he told his audience, 'is what it looks like when life is turned upside down. I ask each of you: do you think this could be Sweden?'

Few in Sweden had experience of such scenes. The conference guest of honour, Sweden's King Carl Gustav, was 77 years old, born just after the end of World War Two. Sweden had remained neutral in that fight – its last conflict was more than two centuries ago. Now, General Bydén, a former fighter pilot who had led its military for more than a decade but never fired a shot in anger, was telling them the world had changed.[2]

Speaking shortly after, Prime Minister Ulf Kristersson outlined exactly what that meant. 'A country's most important resource in war is the people and their will to defend themselves,' he said, speaking of his pride in Sweden's mixed conscript and professional force, including his own two daughters. 'Ultimately, it is about defending Sweden, our values and our way of life – with weapons in hand and our lives on the line.'[3] Shortly after, it was announced that Sweden's Crown Princess Victoria – the 47-year-old mother of two and heir to the throne – would resume her own military training first started in 2003, including lessons on tactics, strategy and basic soldier skills.[4]

This was a message Sweden's leaders wanted to spread. Much of the annual 'Folk och Försvar' conference – meaning 'Society and Defence' and organised by a Swedish think tank of the same name – was broadcast live, with snippets cut for social media further broadening its reach. The think tank that ran the meeting had its roots in the 1940s when the neutral nation was surrounded by conflict. Carl-Oskar Bohlin, Sweden's first minister for civil defence since 1947, described its audience as 'the whole of Sweden'. Everyone had a responsibility to ensure the country was properly prepared, he said. Civic authorities must build up war plans and ensure the necessary relationships and supplies. Companies and employees should understand their responsibilities, while each household must be ready. 'If you haven't started, you are behind,' he said. 'Whatever can be done quickly must be done quickly . . . Good enough tomorrow is better than perfect in five years.'[5]

The meeting got the headlines that its organisers wanted. According to Sweden's Civil Contingencies Agency, the comments prompted a 3,500 per cent increase in visits to its web-based map of bomb shelters, and a 900 per cent increase in downloads of its information booklet *If Crisis or War Comes*. Child protection charities reported a spike in calls from teenagers and children worried about potential war, while opposition politicians accused the government of talking up the risks in an 'immoral' way – all triggering wider coverage across Europe and beyond. When the Military Committee of NATO – which Sweden was weeks away from joining following Russia's invasion of Ukraine – met in Brussels shortly after Folk och Försvar, its chairman, the former Dutch defence chief Admiral Robert Bauer, was questioned by journalists on whether Swedish officials had been scaremongering or overstating the true danger.[6]

Speaking to Radio Sweden, Prime Minister Kristersson had pulled back slightly on his rhetoric, saying there was 'nothing that suggests that war is at the door' but that the government needed to 'speak clearly' about the broadly rising threat. But military chief General Bydén remained unapologetic. 'We need to realise how serious the situation really is,' he told national television. 'Everyone, individually, needs to prepare themselves mentally.'[7] Speaking at NATO HQ, alliance Military Committee Chair Admiral Bauer encouraged other military chiefs to kickstart similar conversations in their respective nations. For decades, Bauer said, Western democracies had simply assumed that professional military forces could handle 'security issues' through interventions. But that was not enough: in the event of a major war, nations would need a 'whole-of-society' approach, both to generate sufficient troops to fight and the industrial strength to build tanks, ships, aircraft, drones and ammunition – and keep on building them as needed. Households should have battery-powered radios, light and sufficient food and drinking water to survive the first 36 hours of any crisis. 'I'm not saying it is going wrong tomorrow,' he said. 'But we have understood that it is no longer a given that we are in peace, that everything is hunky-dory.'[8]

Throughout the early 2020s it often felt as though things were becoming less 'hunky-dory' almost by the week. Following on from the pandemic and Ukraine invasion, the surprise Hamas attack on Israel on October 7, 2023, killing some 1,200 people in the largest single loss of life for Jewish people since the Holocaust, only deepened global worries. That was followed by yet more bloodshed across the Middle East. To that would soon be added the nerves of US allies as Donald Trump came back to the White House, casting into doubt America's long-term support to allies just as those democracies faced their own political and economic headwinds. Perhaps most serious of all were rising Pacific tensions, with China asserting itself across the region and doubling down on threats against Taiwan, the Philippines and other potential foes.

At the start of 2024 British Foreign Secretary David Cameron described alarm – '[the] lights are absolutely flashing red' – when it came to global instability, and warned that it was 'hard to think of a time when there has been so much danger and insecurity'.[9] Then Defence Secretary Grant Shapps talked of living in a 'pre-war world'.[10] Later in the year, Sir Richard Moore – head of Britain's Secret Intelligence Service, popularly known as MI6 – described the world as the most dangerous he had seen in 37 years of government service,[11] while NATO's new secretary general, former Dutch Prime Minister Mark Rutte, said he had reached a similar conclusion. Both pointed to a Russia and China prepared for a long-term confrontation with the West, now aligned with other authoritarian states to reshape the global order. 'They are testing us,' said Rutte, warning that deterring and restraining them required a 'wartime mindset': 'We are not at war, but we are certainly not at peace.'[12]

'I believe we are living in truly dangerous times,' one British official told journalists on a tour of the vast UK Defence Intelligence base at RAF Wyton outside Cambridge, describing the global situation as closer to a major international conflict 'than any time in recent history'.[13] In its operations room the size of an indoor football field, military intelligence personnel said they had never been busier. While most screens were shut down as the media visited, others showcased a fast-growing range of threats. 'Everybody is incredibly busy,' said one official, pointing to the array of desks across the Pathfinder Building, named for World War Two bomber crews who flew from Wyton and nearby bases. Some were monitoring Ukraine; others

China and Taiwan, the Red Sea, Africa, terror groups and shipping. All it might take, they said, was a 'spark' to set the world ablaze – with little or no time to prepare.[14]

*

In some places, the fire was already burning. Through the first weeks of 2024 Russian forces increasingly outgunned their counterparts from Ukraine, slogging forward agonisingly slowly across a battlefield that resembled the shattered landscape of the First World War. As late as mid-2023 Western officials and pundits had predicted Russian incompetence and growing supplies of Western weapons might allow Ukraine to retake all its captured territory. But by January 2024 Ukraine's embattled frontline soldiers were telling anyone who would listen that the West had missed the boat. 'If our international partners moved faster, we would have kicked their asses the first three or four months,' one Ukrainian soldier complained to a reporter, saying that he and his colleagues would rather be 'sowing fields and raising children – instead it's been two years already'.[15]

President Volodymyr Zelenskyy's government in Kyiv still talked a good game as it worked to maximise support from foreign nations, but Ukraine's fighters at the sharp end were running out of resources. In April 2024, America's top general in Europe, Chris Cavoli, told Congress that Russia was firing five artillery shells for every one from the Ukrainians.[16] Both sides were burning through not just their arsenals but those of their allies. From Pennsylvania to Poland, Ukraine's foreign backers were building up new stocks, but were nowhere close to meeting the demand.[17] Russia had its own much deeper Soviet-era military stores, not just of ammunition but of ageing tanks, artillery and other weapons. From August 2023, the Kremlin was also getting artillery shells by the million across its tiny border with North Korea, part of a deepening relationship that would see North Korean troops themselves thrown into the fight late the following year.[18]

From summer 2024, Ukrainian troops opened up a second front by overrunning Russian territory near Kursk to take pressure from the Donbass front. But Russian forces there continued to push forward. One Ukrainian commander talked of the 'tyranny of time', the mounting strain on limited people, resources and will.[19] Fundamentally, that came down to manpower: with a falling birth rate from the 1960s, Ukraine's population had been shrinking well before the conflict. Now, the flight of refugees and loss of territory to Russia meant one of Ukraine's leading demographers suspected there were as few as 28 million people within Ukraine's current borders, compared to 41 million before the 2022 invasion.[20] This was perhaps the first conflict between countries with shrinking populations since the Black Death in the 14th century – but given plunging global birth rates, such wars might well become the norm.

Still, Russia was by far the larger nation, giving Putin some 130 million people at his disposal – and a brutally simple advantage on the battlefield when it came to enduring greater casualties. By spring 2024, US officials estimated more than 315,000 Russian personnel had been killed or wounded – but with more than 30,000 new recruits each month, the Russian army was 15 per cent larger than it had been prior to the invasion. With the Russian economy prioritised for war, the Kremlin produced more ammunition than NATO's 32 nations combined. In the space of two years, Western military intelligence believed the Russian military had lost more than 2,000 tanks – but by working its weapons factories non-stop and reactivating Cold War stores, it had brought more than that number into service, again, giving it more tanks and armoured vehicles at the start of 2024 than when the invasion began.[21]

To fight that disadvantage, Ukraine would have to innovate. In the skies above the front, a new sound was becoming commonplace: the whine of small propeller-driven 'first-person view' drones, piloted by forward operators whose laptops or virtual reality goggles allowed them to look down on the battlefield waiting for their target. By the middle of the year, this savage high-tech drone war was said to be responsible for the majority of casualties, supplanting artillery, which had held that distinction since at least the US Civil War – although some questioned those numbers. But Russia was also charging forward with military development, the two sides often matching each other within weeks and sometimes days in a way no other global military force, aside from perhaps Israel, had the experience to equal. As George Barros, head of Russia analysis at the Institute for the Study of War in Washington DC, put it at the start of 2025: 'In some ways, the two titans of modern warfare are Russia and Ukraine.'[22]

The conflict kept on escalating – and well beyond its initial borders. Throughout 2024, Western intelligence officials reported a rising tide of sabotage, arson and other suspected Russian-backed 'direct action' across Europe and beyond, ranging from fires in factories and shopping centres to break-ins at water treatment plants.[23] 'I think Russia is on a trajectory to conflict or to war with NATO,' the Czech Republic's Chief of the General Staff Karel Řehka told the *Washington Post* a month before NATO's national leader summit in Vilnius in July 2023, one of the first to make such a suggestion publicly. 'That doesn't mean they're planning to do it. NATO doesn't want to go to war with Russia, just as Russia doesn't want to go to war with NATO. But that doesn't mean it cannot happen. There have been many wars that no one really planned to have.'[24] As 2024 began, such views became more publicly widespread. 'I think the future scenario for Estonia will be very difficult,' Estonia's nominee to become its new military chief, Andrus Merilo, warned in February 2024.[25] 'We should get used to the fact . . . Russia, if it has plans of directing its military aggression in other directions, most probably won't pause to give us time to prepare during these intervening years.'[26]

Those conversations, however, were often far from easy. When NATO's military committee chairman Admiral Bauer echoed

Sweden's calls for significant rearmament and war preparations in early 2024, he too found himself facing public criticism.

'People call me a warmonger, but actually it's the opposite,' he said a year later. 'If you prepare for war in the right way, you will be deterring your enemies better, and the chance there will be war goes down.'[27] Throughout 2023, 2024 and even more so during 2025, events in Europe and beyond only increased the sense of nervousness – particularly as the transatlantic alliance with the United States, arguably the most important single factor in avoiding a major European war since 1945, came under mounting strain.

Meanwhile, across the world in the Pacific, nerves were also fraying.

*

From the northern city of Darwin, the mixed full-time and reservist 'NORFORCE' of the Australian Defence Force was, by the mid-2020s, stepping up patrols along some of the most sparsely populated and dangerous coastlines in the world. Using Zodiac attack boats and fast off-road vehicles for patrols that could last days or even weeks, they watched for drug running, people smuggling or signs a foreign nation might be looking to sneak reconnaissance patrols ashore into this now strategic, savage wilderness.

In more normal times, the greatest threat in northern Australia came from its large saltwater crocodile population, beasts that could grow up to six metres in length and withstand a rifle or shotgun round into their skulls. 'There's a lot of saltwater crocs and inaccessible wilderness,' said Captain Andrew Farrands, recently returned from a two-week patrol in May 2024. 'It would be tough going and you have to remain vigilant.'[28]

Northern Australia's emergence as a strategic hotspot had been a long time coming. As early as 2012, US President Barack Obama had announced America's 'strategic pivot' to the Pacific with the specific detail that significant detachments of US Marines would rotate through Darwin between March and October every year from 2015. Even as those deployments started, Australia still felt able to sign a near $400 million deal with a Chinese firm for the use of Darwin port – something that would be repeatedly questioned in the years that followed, and which the Australian government would soon move to reverse.[29] In 1942, at the start of the last Pacific war, Darwin had been bombed by Japanese carrier-borne planes with considerable loss of life. Now, it looked like it might be in the firing line again if war with China came.

By the time I visited Darwin in late 2023, it was clear the heightened tensions in the Pacific were driving defence interest in the city and its surrounding Northern Territory, including the building of a massive US-funded aviation fuel facility at the city's airport, capable of either refuelling aircraft there or tanker vessels in the harbour.[30] From late 2024, it was announced that Japanese troops would join the annual detachment of US Marines training and conducting regional activities in and from Australia's north.[31] Many of Australia's new F-35s were operating from their northern base at RAAF Tindal, south of Darwin, while the region also hosted major multinational exercises.

Talking to officials responsible for investment in the vast Northern Territory, its importance to the fast-evolving new Pacific geopolitics was difficult to miss. Already, the region's gas reserves were delivering a significant proportion of Japan's energy supplies, with plans for massive solar plants and undersea cables to do the same for Singapore. It was the mounting threat of conflict, though, that meant the usually largely empty harbour was sometimes packed with warships, while fast jets and drones flew in the sky above.

In the first Cold War, giant US B-52s had sometimes flown from Darwin airport – and now the air base and that at Tindal was being readied for their return. Those bases, however, would soon become a target itself if a wider war erupted.

According to a report from military analysts at the RAND Corporation in 2022, China's military expansion into disputed islands in the South China Sea already put Darwin and much of the rest of northern Australia within range of Beijing's long-range DF-22 ballistic missiles. While they lacked the range to strike from mainland China, they could reach Australia from the increasingly militarised People's Liberation Army (PLA) bases on artificial islands such as that at 'Mischief Reef', previously a submerged set of rocks seized from the Philippines in the mid-1990s and gradually militarised in the years that followed.[32]

That threat looked set to rise further in the years to come – and not just because Beijing was ploughing billions into improving its weaponry. Throughout the first half of the 2020s, the PLA, China's coastguard and its maritime militia of fishing boats and other craft intensified their actions around disputed waters across the South China Sea and well beyond, prompting mounting fears of accidental conflict. Among most strategists, however, one flashpoint above all fuelled worries that a major war might be coming closer than at any point since the original Cold War.

By the mid-2020s China's military appeared openly to be preparing for an invasion of Taiwan, and were believed to be working towards a target date of the 2027 centenary of the PLA to be ready to attack. As they watched with growing alarm, America's military chiefs drew up plans to stop them – and if that battle came, it could be enormous.

At the end of 2023, I sailed on a cruise ship through the Malacca Strait – one of the busiest sea lanes in the world between Malaysia and Indonesia. Should conflict come, the ship's captain told me, hundreds of vessels might suddenly swerve out of international waters and attempt to take shelter in the territory of any nation seen likely to stay neutral. Given the events of the decade so far, he said he found that contingency dangerously possible. 'The world is on fire,' he told me. 'We do not know what the next day will bring.'[33] But for some of those driving events, these potential fights had been a long time coming.

*

As Vladimir Putin quarantined himself away from the Covid-19 pandemic in the winter of 2020–21, he appears to have given a lot of thought to Russian and Ukrainian history. For him, Russia's rationale to overrun that nation went back at least as far as the 9th century, when the Viking warlord Rurik expanded his kingdom from the city states that would one day make up the heart of modern Russia to the newly built Ukrainian city of Kyiv – and continued through centuries of wars and clashing empires. His conclusion – in a long and rambling article published on the Kremlin website in July 2021 – was that Russians and Ukrainians had always been 'one people'. Hotly disputed by Ukrainian historians in particular, that article was the start of the final series of self-justifications for the full-scale invasion of Ukraine – and by the time that assault was launched, Chinese leader Xi Jinping had made it clear he was having similar thoughts about Taiwan.

For Xi and those at the top in China, the battle for that island – also known as Formosa – went back almost two millennia, to AD 230 when historian Shen Ying recorded that the ruling Sui dynasty had sent three detachments of soldiers to attempt to secure it. As far as Beijing was concerned, that marked the beginning of its time as Chinese territory – and nothing since had changed that.[34] The historical truth, of course, was hugely more complex – as was the reality of an island that had essentially self-ruled since 1949 and spent the last three decades as a vibrant and enthusiastic technological democracy.

The degree to which Imperial China ran the island had by almost all accounts varied over centuries, with periods of self-rule, European domination and then Japanese occupation from 1895 to the end of World War Two. Then, in the late 1940s, Nationalist Chinese leader Chiang Kai-shek – who only a few years earlier had ruled most of the mainland – fled there at the end of China's civil war to establish his Republic of China (ROC) 'government in exile'.

That, really, was where the modern confrontation started. As soon as the People's Republic of China (PRC) finally evicted the ROC and Chiang in 1949, Mao Zedong and other Chinese Communist Party (CCP) leaders fast began scheming ways of ending Taiwan's existence as a de facto independent state, only to be stopped by the threat of US military force. From the 1990s onwards Taiwan's emergence as a functional democracy – the only ethnically and linguistically majority Chinese democracy anywhere in the world – only further antagonised Beijing.

Taiwan's indigenous population had their own very different histories, sharing their heritage with Polynesian Pacific populations. Indeed, DNA suggested Taiwan might have been the original starting point from which that group spread out.[35] By the 2020s, indigenous Taiwanese made up only 3 per cent of the population, but up to 60 per cent of some of Taiwan's special forces units – and, looking at the fate of China's Uighurs and other minorities, they had more than most to fight for.

Ming Jie, a 43-year-old indigenous Taiwanese former special forces operator turned trainer of civilians in weapons skills and survival, described his community as 'very protective of their people and traditions'. Asighe, another indigenous former operator also teaching at a private defence school warned its students that the lessons would not turn ordinary citizens 'into a hero like in the movies, but I hope it will increase the survival rate on the battlefield'. As talk of a potential invasion hotted up, attendance on such courses grew from the ethnic Chinese majority, including former conscripts looking to make up the gaps left by their military training.[36]

And there were definitely gaps. When I visited the island in early 2024, none of the former conscripts I met had any idea what to do in the event of an invasion. 'I think I might just get in the way,' said one.[37] Taiwan's military – much of it still led by descendants of the Nationalist ROC elite who had established themselves on the island more like a foreign occupation force from 1949 – was both untrusted and unprepared for combat. 'People don't realise the state of infancy [Taiwan's] military is in,' said Kitsch Liao, an expert on the island's forces at the Atlantic Council. 'They have to start training them to do very basic things.' Another military source talked of Taiwan depending on 'one war plan that has remained more or less unchanged for a long time. That's not how this works.'[38] From 2024, the island re-extended its conscript service to a full year in uniform and retooled its training programme, but such actions would take time to have significant effect.

Given the speed of Chinese military preparations, it was not clear that would happen fast enough.[39] Some senior US defence officials pointed to China's lack of combat experience and the arrest of multiple senior officials for corruption as a sign that Beijing's rapid militarisation might be faltering or facing trouble.[40] Still, Biden's Secretary of the Air Force Frank Kendall warned China's military appeared to be working hard to meet Xi's deadline of being ready to invade by 2027 and beat off the United States should it try to intervene. 'I have no idea what Xi Jinping will do in 2027,' he said, 'but I am pretty sure that his military will tell him they are ready.'[41]

Beijing's preferred ambition, most strategists believed, was to seize Taiwan and control over its 20 million people in a single operation, perhaps barely firing a shot – and to have achieved a fait accompli before the US and its allies got their act together and started to intervene. Even a limited conflict, however, might be hugely destructive.

It would certainly also be disruptive. South of Taipei, the factories of the Taiwan Semiconductor Manufacturing Corporation and its rivals continued to churn out roughly 60 per cent of the world's semiconductors – and up to 90 per cent of the most advanced.[42] The waters around the island and immediately beyond also carried a significant proportion of world trade, while any repeat of the kind of sanctions imposed on Russia following the invasion of Ukraine would be hugely more damaging to the global economy if imposed on China. If any war escalated to include the United States and other nations, the shock would be unlike anything seen in recent history.

Nor was there any guarantee such a war would remain conventional. US analysts reported a retooling of China's atomic arsenal: expected to increase from a few hundred warheads at the beginning of the decade to at least a thousand by 2030, including new mobile ground-based rockets and Beijing's first true ballistic missile submarines.[43] China had also limbered up for decades of confrontation in space by becoming the only nation to operate its own sovereign station in Earth's orbit, and with plans to race America to get a manned mission to the Moon.[44]

The most significant preparation, however, appeared to be for war in China's immediate neighbourhood. Throughout 2024, the largest amphibious assault ship in history took shape at breakneck speed in the world's biggest and fastest-growing shipyard, just outside Shanghai. According to imagery from private satellite operator Maxar, the dry dock in which China's first 076 class vessel was being built had been itself only completed the previous September. Within nine months, the main structure of the ship was almost complete – and she was a monster.

The 076 – NATO codename *Yulan* – was roughly 260 metres long and more than 50 wide, almost three US football field equivalents, and considerably larger than the new *America*-class vessels of the US amphibious assault fleet. Like their US counterparts, the new Chinese vessels appeared likely to be able to carry at least 1,000 troops, down-flood their hulls to release landing craft and simultaneously act as mini-aircraft carriers launching helicopters, drones and jets.[45]

For now, that giant assault ship appeared to be the only one of her class – but the People's Liberation Army Navy

(PLAN) also had four slightly smaller, similar 075 *Yushen*-class vessels already in the water, plus access to dozens of other vessels including roll-on-roll-off ferries that could carry troops. But what truly alarmed US and regional naval analysts was the scale and speed with which China was building military capacity, as well as the wider industry capacity that could support it in a war. That included shipbuilding facilities more than 200 times the size of those available to the US Navy.[46] By early 2024, China had two aircraft carriers operational – more than any nation other than the United States, another undergoing sea trials and what looked like more under construction. All that was part of an even broader, larger military effort, one that had seen China's military budget grow as much as fivefold since the beginning of the century, perhaps even more.

According to former head of US naval intelligence retired Rear Admiral Mike Studeman, the most recent – and in many respects the most dramatic – Chinese growth was down to a 2020 order from Chinese leader Xi Jinping to take military growth targets originally intended for 2035 and bring them forward to 2027. Studeman called China's 'hyper-militarisation' the 'greatest build-up of arms since the end of the Cold War'.[47] 'The balance has changed very fast,' one Pentagon official told me recently. 'The US military still has the ability to do things around the world China cannot match. And China has not fought a war since 1979, so there are real questions over the capability. But this is a very different threat to what we have faced in the recent past.'[48]

As the threat to Taiwan grew, the question of whether America would fight to protect the island would become ever more important. Since recognising the Communist government in Beijing as the legitimate rulers of mainland China in 1979, successive US governments had been deliberately 'strategically ambiguous' on that point. It was a position enshrined in law by the 1979 Taiwan Relations Act, which implied but did not state explicitly that the US might come to Taiwan's aid if it was attacked – and demanded that the US military keep up-to-date plans to assist the island if that moment came. But it did not make clear whether those plans would be put into action. Nor did the other handful of binding undertakings the Reagan and Carter administrations had signed with the governments of China and Taiwan, the so-called 'three communiqués' with the PRC and 'six undertakings' with the government in Taipei. They merely guaranteed that the US would pay lip service to Chinese rhetoric about there only being 'one China' but keep up arms sales to Taiwan – and step up its military support if the threat from Beijing increased.

By the 2020s it was clear that risk was indeed rising. As Chinese activity increased further around Taiwan after the Biden administration entered office, it doubled down on messaging suggesting America would fight. In March 2023, the US Navy flew journalists onto the USS *Nimitz* to showcase its readiness. In the event of an attack on Taiwan, US Pacific Fleet chief Admiral Samuel Paparo told the channel's cameras that how US forces would react was a 'decision of the President of the United States and a decision of the Congress'. But should the decision be made to help, he said, 'the bulk of the United States Navy will be deployed rapidly to the western Pacific to come to the aid of Taiwan . . . in thwarting that invasion'.[49] Deterring President Xi and the PLA from launching that assault, US Under Secretary of Defense for Policy Colin H. Kahl bluntly told an audience at London's Chatham House a few months later, was the top foreign-policy priority for the Biden administration. 'Our aim is that they wake up every morning and think: "Not today",' Kahl said.[50]

From early 2022 Biden answered 'yes' on several occasions when asked directly in public whether the US would act militarily to defend Taiwan, unlike in Ukraine.[51] Privately, however, Taiwanese officials noted that other US officials pointedly failed to make the same commitment – it would, they believed, need to be retested with each new US president.[52]

That became even more important as the 2024 US election loomed. There was a growing suspicion that a Chinese attack against Taiwan might be accompanied by Russian action in Europe, particularly given the growing closeness of Xi and Putin in what was described variously as a 'no limits partnership' and 'better than an alliance'. That growing relationship overturned years of Pentagon and associated allied planning working on the assumption of no more than one major regional war at a time, and it also meant that Europe might need to fight Russia on its own as the United States focused on a much more powerful China.

As China, Russia, Iran and North Korea – sometimes referred to as the 'CRINKs' – stepped up co-operation, talk of their growing partnership was stoking worries everywhere. 'I am saying we are not on an inexorable path to war,' said British Army Chief of the General Staff Sir Roland Walker – but he warned the new 'Axis of Upheaval' between authoritarian states meant a confrontation in one part of the world might inevitably 'trigger a sympathetic detonation in another'. 'You get to this point by 2027–2028 [when] this convergence may have reached some sort of mutual singularity,' he said. 'Your ability to deal with them in isolation . . . is significantly diminished.'[53]

It was a concern expressed even more bluntly in public by Walker's predecessor General Patrick Sanders, who stood down as the head of the British Army in 2024 and revealed Whitehall defence chiefs were already wargaming a 'polycrisis' of simultaneous Pacific and European conflict. 'It would start with a large-scale confrontation in the Pacific, like a Chinese invasion of Taiwan, which draws off what remains of US forces in Europe,' suggested Sanders. 'An opportunistic Russia would then get some part of NATO territory where they know they can actually win by achieving local dominance, like the Baltics or somewhere in the High North.'[54] While most analysts believed Putin would hope to seize that ground quickly and then use the threat of Russia's atomic arsenal to deter a NATO counter-attack, not everyone thought escalation could be avoided. At worst, that kind of land grab would trigger long and hugely destructive wars on both sides of the world – a concern that would increase steadily through the first half of the 2020s. The world, meanwhile, continued to throw up unpleasant shocks elsewhere. In the aftermath of the October 2023 Hamas attacks from Gaza on nearby parts of Israel, US Defense Secretary Lloyd Austin reassured a press conference in Brussels that the United States could still 'walk and chew gum at the same time', to tackle simultaneous crises in the Middle East and Europe.[55]

In more normal times, that alone might have been questioned by the foreign policy elites of the US and its allies. By the first weeks of 2024, however, they were distracted by an even more imminent disruption: the increasingly likely return of Donald Trump, this time determined to go to war with the US 'deep state' and throw into doubt the assumptions built up since 1945.

*

Through late January 2024, the Foxhound and Jackal lightly armoured vehicles, Land Rovers and trucks of the Royal Anglian Regiment became a frequent sight in the narrow lanes and villages of Rutland in the English Midlands as they prepped for their departure. They were part of Britain's 7th Armoured Brigade, the 'Desert Rats', part of NATO's Very High Readiness Joint Task Force, about to 'crash out' on a simulated deployment to protect NATO's eastern flank.[56] As 300 Spanish military personnel and 65 vehicles arrived in northern Poland, their commander Lieutenant Colonel Daniel Diaz Simón described the exercise as an 'excellent opportunity' to show that troops as far away as Córdoba and Seville were ready to respond 'at any time'.[57]

Those British and Spanish troops were part of NATO's largest exercise since the end of the Cold War, codenamed STEADFAST DEFENDER and designed to show just how far alliance war plans had advanced since Putin's full-scale invasion of Ukraine in 2022. It was a deliberately ambitious undertaking ranging from the Arctic to the Mediterranean, its schedule of events deliberately rammed with high-profile demonstrations, from German pontoon bridges ferrying tanks across the Vistula River in the heart of Poland to multinational paratrooper drops. According to US Army Europe, of the 90,000 personnel, roughly a fifth were American.[58] As the NATO alliance prepared to celebrate the 75th anniversary of the North Atlantic Treaty in April 2024, the exercise was designed to leave no one in any doubt – not least Putin or any future incumbent of the Kremlin – that the US stood behind its allies and would back them to the hilt.

In reality, even as those troops started moving up, Trump was throwing those pledges into doubt. In mid-February 2024, Trump told a roaring crowd at a campaign rally in South Carolina that when in office he had told an unnamed European leader that he would 'encourage' Russia to do 'whatever the hell they want' with NATO countries that were 'delinquent' when it came to military spending.[59] I was in Estonia when the news of the comments broke, and they dominated news programmes and prompted urgent meetings inside government. 'Such statements are never helpful,' said Estonian intelligence chief Kaupo Rosin diplomatically.[60]

Throughout the first three years of the Biden presidency, many US allies and officials in his administration had seemed psychologically unprepared to consider the prospect Trump might retake the White House. Only as the 2024 election year began did they finally acknowledge it might happen. 'We have been in this situation with him before, and people are trying not to panic,' one European diplomat told me early in the year.[61] Others were much less sanguine. 'We are in a very precarious place,' said one senior NATO official, describing the once and future US president as 'very transactional and ... very narcissistic.'[62] John Bolton, who had served as Trump's national security advisor during his first term, bluntly warned that he believed the former president would quit NATO entirely if returned to office.[63]

Trump's advances in the polls – and his success in apparently banishing the threat of the multiple court cases many of his opponents had hoped might keep him from the White House – had comprehensively overwhelmed any sense of triumphalism in Europe that might have come from the 75th anniversary of the NATO alliance. Instead, the talk was of 'Trump-proofing' as much as possible, including the weapons supplies keeping Ukraine in the fight. What approach Trump might take to that war, no one really knew; but he was promising to 'end it' fast, and implying that he might cut off US weapons shipments as soon as he took office.

Trump was also tearing up Biden's messaging about the US protection of Taiwan. 'Taiwan did take all our chip business,' Trump told Fox News after winning the Iowa caucus. 'We used to make all our own chips, now they're made in Taiwan.'[64] Later in the year, he told another interviewer that Taiwan should pay the US money if it expected to be defended 'as they don't give us anything'.[65] It all fitted the broader message of the Trump campaign: that the Democrats had left America on the brink of disaster. Throughout the last months of the race, Trump and his supporters repeatedly accused the 'failed Biden administration' of squandering America's advantage to leave it overstretched almost to the point of no return.

At the start of 2024, the suggestion that the world might be on the brink of catastrophic conflict had still been controversial. By the time Trump and his team romped to an overwhelming election win in November, it was a mainstay of their rhetoric. 'We stand on the precipice of World War Three,' Republican foreign policy thinker and first-term Trump Pentagon appointee Elbridge Colby – waiting to see if Trump would offer him a role – told right-wing journalist Tucker Carlson three days after the result. 'We need to make a fundamental change before we run right into the iceberg . . . We are on the brink of war in multiple theatres and we could lose them . . . It could be catastrophic.'[66]

Trump and his supporters argued a more realistic, transactional approach to alliances would serve all nations better – but within those who would join his administration, there were already large divisions, soon to become a source of sometimes severe internal tension once his administration entered office.

On one side were a group known as the 'restrainers' – often seen as led by Colby as well as new Vice President JD Vance, who believed the US military were already overstretched and needed to be pulled back from the world. Within a think tank linked to that group known as 'Defense Priorities', there was already talk of pulling at least half of US forces out of Europe, as well as significant withdrawals from the Middle East and even the Pacific.[67]

On the other side were those who felt such an approach might prove disastrous, including plenty of senior commanders and officials who saw America's still hefty presence overseas as central to the network of alliances on which US deterrence had been based since 1945. Even they, however, often acknowledged tough choices must be made, particularly if the growing threat from China was to be the top US priority, as most believed it should. 'The message from the Biden administration was the US would step up in Europe and would always be there,' said Europe specialist Rachel Rizzo, also at the Atlantic Council think tank. 'I think with hindsight that was the wrong message.'[68]

For some of America's allies already under threat, such talk already felt like a precursor to their abandonment. As 2024 drew to a close, Scandinavian newspapers quoted NATO officials warning Russia might be preparing a surprise attack in the coming years that could seize the capitals of Estonia and Latvia as well as chunks of Finland. 'It's not a question of if . . . but when,' one NATO official told a Finnish journalist.[69] In Asia, officials reported a further significant increase in Chinese warships and coastguard vessels practising blockade manoeuvres near Taiwan and harassing ships and outposts of other nations.[70]

Trump and those around him portrayed his unpredictability as a quality rather than a weakness. Speaking to the *Wall Street Journal* shortly before the US vote, he said he did not expect to have to use force to protect Taiwan because President Xi 'respects me and he knows I'm fucking crazy'.[71] 'I'm not going to start any wars – I'm going to stop the wars,' Trump pledged in his first post-election speech.[72] The night before his inauguration, he pledged again: 'I will end the war in Ukraine, I will stop the chaos in the Middle East and I will prevent World War Three from happening – and you have no idea how close we are.'[73]

Ukraine and Taiwan – neither of them formal US treaty allies – were now something of a bellwether of wider US interests, a position neither of them liked. 'If today he could abandon Ukraine – and I don't know if he's really going to abandon Ukraine – then he could also abandon Taiwan.' said Huang Yu-hsiang, a 23-year-old technician in the capital Taipei.[74] That was certainly what Beijing was hoping. By the end of March 2025, Chinese media and associated outlets were pushing a relentless narrative that the United States was abandoning its allies – and that Taiwan would be the first to fall.[75]

2

'Hellscape' in the Pacific

'*No one wants war . . . But peace does not come from the sky, and Taiwan is at the frontlines of the expansion of authoritarianism.*'

Taiwanese President Tsai Ing-wen announcing the expansion of compulsory military service, December 2022[1]

On January 5, 2024 the aircraft carrier USS *Carl Vinson* and her battle group anchored off the Filipino capital Manila. Described by her captain Matt Thomas as '100,000 tons of democracy',[2] her decks were packed with aircraft in an unambiguous reminder of American naval power.[3] It was a display of the 'peace through strength' strategy that would soon be espoused by Trump, but which, in truth, had been at the backbone of US military messaging ever since the last days of World War Two.

The *Vinson*'s visit to Manila was 2024's first US piece of public military manoeuvring – and the initial focus on the Philippines was far from a coincidence. The Philippines was one of America's oldest Asian allies, at one point its only Asian colony – and the fall of much of the Philippines to Japanese forces immediately after their attack on Pearl Harbor in December 1941 had almost swept the US from the whole region. Tens of thousands of US troops – including the father of Biden's Defense Secretary Lloyd Austin – and their Filipino counterparts had spent much of the rest of the war recapturing that territory. The northernmost islands of the Philippines were as strategic for any war with China as they had been against Japan.

US General Douglas MacArthur had once described Taiwan as an 'unsinkable aircraft carrier'. It was also at the heart of what strategists now called the 'first island chain', the closest line of major islands to the Asian mainland, starting with the northern islands of Japan, running down through the Japanese territory of Okinawa to Taiwan and then on and through the Philippines. In the eyes of the People's Liberation Army, seizing Taiwan could open the door to much wider regional domination – including potentially choking off supplies to Japan itself. One textbook – a 2013 Chinese assessment of Japan's military air forces – talked of using such a blockade to inflict 'a famine' on Japan that the government in Tokyo might be powerless to prevent. Taking Taiwan would also make it much harder for the US and its allies to blockade China itself, long a concern for generations of rulers in Beijing.[4]

If China was able to deter the US from intervening in a Taiwan invasion – and that was a colossal 'if' – then it would be a much easier military operation, at least once the PLA had destroyed many of the Taiwanese missile launchers attacking its invasion fleet. Capturing the island itself would still involve a brutal battle, but providing the PLA could keep open supply lines running from the mainland, most believed there could only be one outcome: a full victory for Beijing.

Should the US and its allies choose to fight, it could be a very different matter. Bringing hundreds of thousands of troops across the stormy 90–100-plus miles of the Taiwan Strait would be a massive undertaking. US ships and aircraft – and likely even more importantly submarines, drones and missiles – stood a good chance of inflicting massive losses on Chinese ships and aircraft trying to make that crossing, at least if they could get close enough to launch their drones and weapons.

Few locations in the region were better placed to launch the strikes from than the outlying northern islands of the

Philippines – and the US military was now dramatically stepping up its annual BALIKATAN drills with the Filipino military to integrate them closer into America's war fighting systems, structures and military methodologies. These manoeuvres in the Philippines were now one of the most important moving parts of an enormous biannual military training programme that also integrated Japan, South Korea, Australia and New Zealand, as well as European nations.

The intention was not just to be better prepared – although that was at the core of almost every programme, at least with those US partners expected to be at America's side in any war. It was to ensure that China *knew* the US was prepared for battle – and becoming readier every year. 'We put a lot of effort into deciding what we want to show them and what we want to hide,' one senior US military officer told me. 'And when you see them get upset when we deploy a capability, you know that we are getting through.'[5]

Whether such drills would keep on getting larger, though, came down to the vagaries of US and local politics. As the *Vinson* dropped anchor in Manila at the start of 2024, US and Filipino planners were still putting the final details to that year's coming exercise. Relations between the two nations had sometimes been contentious: throughout much of the first Cold War US financial and military aid had kept in power the notoriously corrupt regime of President Ferdinand Marcos, whose wife Imelda had famously used their position to amass, among other things, the world's most expensive shoe collection. The ousting of the Marcos dynasty in a 1986 popular revolution was followed soon after by the withdrawal of US forces.[6]

The 2022 election of Ferdinand Marcos Jr, son of the former presidential couple, opened the door to much closer renewed relations with the Pentagon, including the reopening of shuttered US bases and a renewed emphasis on the northern Philippines and waters close to China and Taiwan. Soon, the government in Manila was once again being talked of as a linchpin US

Pacific ally, while the number of US troops passing through simply kept on rising – along with important deployments of drones and long-range missiles.

For all that, though, Filipino politics was still a messy dynastic struggle with military and diplomatic implications. From 2016 to 2022, the presidency had been held by the even more controversial Rodrigo Duterte, who attempted to embrace China while clashing repeatedly with the West over his frequent and violent crackdowns, said to be targeting organised crime and drug gangs – but which critics said amounted to a free run to government-backed death squads. Duterte's daughter Sara was now a vice president to Marcos – a relationship that appeared to have completely unravelled by 2024 – and might well be a contender for the next elections in 2028. Nor was her father gone for good – he had just been re-elected as a city mayor despite being imprisoned in The Hague ahead of being put on trial for multiple cases of human rights abuse and murder.[7]

Even more important, though, was what was now happening on Taiwan itself, where the government was working desperately to build up its defences just as Chinese forces across the Strait were stepping up their efforts to persuade the people of Taiwan that resistance was pointless and that they might as well surrender to 'reunification' without firing a shot.

If that strategy didn't work, however, US officials believed Xi and those around him were likely very serious about launching a real invasion. By the early 2020s, China's shipyards were building some 50 per cent of all new worldwide civilian vessels, and there was mounting talk that some of them were being designed to serve military purposes to support an invasion of the island. If the US president gave the order, that invasion fleet would be among the first targets US forces would be looking to destroy – even if that meant starting a hugely wider conflict. The first and perhaps most critical battles on the ground, however, would still likely come down to fights between the PLA and the forces of Taiwan itself – and how they performed in the opening hours and days would be absolutely critical. At one extreme they might hold the forces of the PRC in a way that would mark the greatest challenge yet to China's rise, either forcing the PLA to reconsider its campaign or giving US forces much more time to intervene. At the other, a swift collapse could open the door for Beijing to dominate first the region and then the wider world.

In capitals across the region – particularly Manila, Canberra and Tokyo – quiet discussions had been underway for years on whether it might be better to fight for Taiwan before it fell rather than risk another confrontation as Beijing became yet more powerful still. All that depended, though, on how hard Taiwan itself might be prepared to fight.

*

At the end of January 2024, the 670 officers and soldiers of Taiwan's army 'Batch 2226' reported to their training camps in northern, central and southern Taiwan. Dressed mainly in casual sportswear and almost all wearing surgical facemasks, the young men stood in formation, their bags checked for contraband by a military police dog before they were sent for their regulation haircuts – and a lecture on not using Chinese-manufactured smartphones to avoid leaking military secrets.[8]

Across the Taiwan Strait, the island's 23 million citizens faced down the 1.4 billion of China – both of those numbers starting to shrink as an ageing population and low birth rate worked their inevitable effect. At the very least, Taiwan's conscription programme gave the government a theoretical second army of two million, almost the same size as Beijing's entire regular PLA. Properly trained and equipped, particularly with hidden weapons cachets in the hills, Taiwan's ex-conscripts should be able to make an occupation miserable and perhaps impossible for attacking Chinese troops.

The problem was – as every Taiwanese conscript was aware and tended to tell anyone who asked – that little of that capability

yet existed at the start of 2024. As journalists gathered to watch
the new conscript tranche parade for the first time, a military
spokesman stressed that they would get better, more realistic
training than any of their predecessors. Those joining hoped
that promise would be kept – Taiwanese officials predicted they
would have trained up to 9,000 conscripts by the end of 2024.
'One year of service should be more useful than four months; at
least I should be able to learn some actual skills,' 18-year-old
Huang Cheng-te told reporters as he signed on to join the new
conscript batch. 'They're also raising our pay, so I hope to have
some savings.'[9]

Eight weeks later Taiwan's military brought journalists back
to watch the recruits at the end of their most basic training.
Clad in camouflage gear, the troopers were filmed marching,
fighting through barbed-wire obstacles and assault courses and
firing their ageing M16 rifles. 'The environment on the
battlefield is completely different from the movies,' conscript
Yin Hsin-shih told the running cameras. 'Movies can't convey
all the sound . . . and the pressure.' In fact, of course, they had
come nowhere close to experiencing the reality of combat –
although Taiwanese TV showed one conscript spraying another
with a bottle of fake 'blood' to simulate a casualty.[10]

Ramping up that training was now a top priority – while
Taiwan's full-time regular forces, particularly its special
operations personnel, were working more closely with the US
than ever before. Letting that be known, some suggested, was
itself part of the US strategy to build 'deterrence' and hold
China back from moving to invade. Simultaneously, former
CIA analyst Dennis Wilder noted on social media that the story
was 'sure to get under Beijing's skin'.[11]

Having US special forces on the ground would complicate
Chinese invasion efforts, part of a deliberate plan by US
commanders to 'impose strategic dilemmas' on America's major
foreign rivals. The number of other US personnel passing
through the island would increase further in the months that

followed – by mid-2025, there was talk of as many as 500 US military trainers working on the island, from special forces to reservists and contractors.[12]

In the event of advance intelligence of a Chinese attack, the US might have a window of opportunity to put even more forces on the island – perhaps US marines already based nearby on Okinawa. Whether China would let such reinforcements land, however, was another question – it was far from impossible that even the act of moving such troops into position might prompt Beijing to strike. Within Washington, more cautious voices were already calling for existing US forces to be pulled back from Taiwan, describing their presence as 'provocative' and contradicting prior US commitments not to station forces there.[13]

But even if the US president of the day held back and stopped US forces from intervening, incoming Chinese troops landing on Taiwan expected a hard fight. For all the concerns over Taiwan's military prowess, its most capable forces were well placed to defend the capital and the airport, with such preparations stepped up further during high-profile annual military drills in the 2020s. Even if significant Chinese forces landed, reaching the Taiwanese capital itself would require passing through heavily forested valleys. For a well-motivated defending force, it should be easy to blow up the motorway expressways into Taipei and ambush incoming troops.

One PLA pamphlet on 'Informatized Warfare and Psychological Protection' prepared for military doctors warned that troops arriving on Taiwan would face a 'life-and-death test of ferocious bombing, excessive explosions . . . from start to finish, every moment throughout the landing operation'. In many cases, the PLA warned, personnel might already have been weakened by seasickness and long, uncomfortable and terrifying spells in landing craft or other vessels, or the faster but equally terrifying insertion onto the island by helicopter or transport plane.[14] 'If China does invade Taiwan,' one former Western intelligence official told me, 'they will be taking it extremely seriously and they will not repeat the Russian mistake of believing it will be a walkover.'[15] Still, China's military had not engaged in a major conflict since a brief and unsuccessful war with Vietnam in 1979, and no one truly knew how troops and commanders would react to any kind of fight, let alone one that intense.

Neither, however, had the military forces of the Republic of China (ROC), the official name for the government of Taiwan going back to the Nationalist days of Chiang Kai-shek. In December 2024, when China launched some of its largest unannounced military drills so far, the ROC army swiftly positioned several tanks into locations near the airport and nearby major transport hubs, with armed personnel taking up positions in the streets. It was the first time many civilians in the immediate area had seen such a military deployment outside the heavily promoted drills each summer. Several posted images on social media, while others waved and honked their horns to show their support for the island's troops.[16]

Meanwhile, on the Chinese mainland, satellite imagery strongly suggested PLA fighters were already training for an assault against the capital. During Putin's initial attack against Ukraine, the most important single failure of his attacking troops had been their defeat at Hostomel airport on the outskirts of the capital Kyiv. Had they managed to seize it on the first day as expected – and they threw several dozen troop-carrying and attack helicopters at the airfield in the first few hours of the invasion – then they could have begun landing troop-carrying aircraft almost immediately. Had an airfield takeover been successfully coupled with a decapitation strike against Zelenskyy and his team, that might just have been enough for Putin to win the war outright almost immediately.

Those examining how to defend Taiwan were fully aware of that – and so were those planning an attack. By the mid-2020s, China's PLA had spent well over a decade exploring such avenues in its professional military and training publications, often describing in frank terms both the dangers of such a mission and the huge resources needed. Published Chinese military manuals, and Taiwanese assessments of them, suggest the most likely landing sites would be just south of the Tamsui River that runs into the capital, with Chinese amphibious troops and special forces storming ashore while airborne troops dropped roughly four miles inland to take the international airport at Taoyuan and then the smaller domestic terminal at Songshan, just inside the capital. Follow-on forces would then attempt to force their way inland to seize key road junctions outside of Taipei itself to surround or take the city.[17]

Some Chinese military pamphlets advocated a long naval and air blockade of the island in advance of an assault, accompanied potentially by PLA assaults on Taiwan offshore islands much closer to the Chinese mainland. By the mid-2020s, however, senior US commanders believed Beijing might be much more tempted to launch a sudden lightning operation to decapitate the ROC government before the US was significantly able to respond.

Taiwan's several hundred M60 tanks were relatively ancient by modern standards: their heyday had been in the 1970s when they had garrisoned Germany and helped Israel survive the 1973 Yom Kippur attack. They would still be relatively effective against lightly armed Chinese airborne forces – but only until much more modern anti-tank rockets and drones arrived. At the end of 2024, the Biden administration finally made good on years of promises by delivering the M1 heavy battle tank – still decades-old technology, but considerably more capable.

Taiwan had more than 100 of the long-delayed tanks on order from the United States. The first batch of just less than 40 would be followed by the remainder over 2025 and 2026, Taiwanese media reported. Also arriving were Stinger anti-aircraft missiles and US-made heavy transport vehicles.[18] Alongside a new tranche of F-16 jets, the Taiwanese government was also taking delivery of Javelin anti-tank rockets and a variety of new drones, some already proven in action in Ukraine.

In the event of outright invasion, Taiwan looked to have several cards that it could play. On paper, decades of conscript service had given it a military reserve of perhaps as many as two million – and, it was hoped, more volunteers from the wider population who disliked the idea of Chinese occupation. The island's terrain could also scarcely have been better designed to facilitate resistance: thick forests, plunging hillsides and roadways on tall-concrete legs that would be easy to sabotage.

The question, though, was whether Taiwan was truly ready or capable for the kind of fight that had secured Ukraine's survival. Opinion polls showed support for immediate 'reunification' remained extremely low, ranging from 5 per cent to barely half that.[19] Throughout the 2010s, Taiwan's population watched as an increasingly authoritarian China cracked down ruthlessly on dissent, particularly in Hong Kong. For many Taiwanese previously open to closer relations with the mainland, it became clear that 'reunification' would mark the end of their hard-won democracy and freedoms – and, overall, most hated that prospect. In Nordic states like Finland and the Baltic states, the threat of an overmighty neighbour was enough to drive a degree of enthusiasm for conscript and reserve military service. But Taiwan's famously ineffective training system had already undermined the military's reputation in the eyes of many on the island – and some quietly voiced concerns over the future loyalty of commanders of the island's forces, frequently descended from Chiang Kai-shek's Kuomintang Nationalists who had come across from the mainland in 1949. By 2025, the KMT had become, ironically, the most pro-Chinese of the main parties, with the 2024 elections handing them enough votes to dominate the parliament and frustrate the ruling Democratic Progressive Party (DPP).

With the Chinese threat mounting by the month, that alone was a considerable problem. What worried Taiwan's security services and those who wanted to keep the island effectively independent, though, was that mainland Chinese efforts to recruit supporters within the island appeared focused on the existing military ranks. At worst, a coup d'état at the top of government could hand the island to Beijing – or, failing that, an eventual election victory for the KMT might ultimately do the same, despite repeated proclamations from KMT politicians that they still favoured some form of de facto separation.

More than any other democracy except Ukraine, Taiwan was in the firing line, facing many of the same dangers as those in Eastern and central Europe, but with the downside of being neither a true nation state nor entangled in a formal alliance structure like NATO. By mid-2023, the PLA was sending so many aircraft across the Taiwan Strait that Taipei was forced to stop sending its ageing F-16s to intercept each time in order to reduce pressure on fuel stocks, budgets, pilots and their aircraft, with the 2022 loss of a jet blamed in part on pilot fatigue.[20] Such incursions had by the start of 2024 reached an all-time high, and continued to grow further.

Some suspected Beijing might bet its hand on a blockade to strangle Taiwan's de facto independence without firing a shot. Alternatively, China might embrace a slower strategy of a 'death by a thousand cuts': the gradual cutting of fibre-optic cables; cyber attacks on critical national infrastructure; and subversion of the island's population – or at least enough to assist a takeover.

By the mid-2020s, Beijing appeared to be putting effort into all of those approaches, both in building up its conventional military forces on the mainland for a future assault and waging an intensifying campaign of 'hybrid warfare' against the island and its ruling elements: cyber attacks against the island had roughly doubled every year to more than 2.4 million a day by the end of 2024[21] and near continuous daily Chinese military drills and offers of Chinese citizenship to those on the island showed no sign of abating.[22] Taiwan's National Security Bureau also reported China working through criminal gangs and rogue ROC military – of 64 individuals charged with espionage in 2024, many were serving personnel.[23]

In one such high-profile case, Taiwanese prosecutors announced they had broken up a spy ring led by a former military officer who had recruited at least seven active-duty and three retired service personnel to deliver military secrets – and, in one case, attempted to persuade a special forces pilot to defect to Beijing by flying a CH-47 Chinook onto a Chinese aircraft carrier as a propaganda coup.[24] In early 2025, Taiwanese prosecutors arrested a former ROC general they said had been recruiting an 'armed' group to assist a Chinese invasion, a plan alleged to have involved several trips by him and others to the mainland.[25] 'The threat is not coming just from guns, artillery, rockets, missiles, warships,' Taiwanese General Sun Li-fang told the *New York Times*. 'They are trying to influence our minds as well.'[26]

China was also keeping up its efforts to win the wider population over to supporting reunification. Since the late 2010s, China had offered paid trips for 'village elders' – local elected officials, representing often urban areas of several thousand people – to visit the mainland and make social media posts showing the wonders of Chinese infrastructure projects, pushing forward an argument that Taiwan would be better off joining with the PRC. From 2023, some village elders were encouraged to bring their constituents on similar trips.[27]

Alongside all that, the KMT was making its own political progress – and even though it maintained it was opposed to forcible 'reunification', from 2024 its MPs began taking an increasingly hostile approach to the Democratic Progressive Party government efforts to increase spending on defence. When the Trump administration in Washington began pushing the Taiwanese government to spend much more on defence, the timing for the government in Taipei could hardly have been worse.

Taiwan's 2024 elections had been presented by the government in Beijing as a choice between 'peace and war' – with the KMT implied firmly to be the 'peace' option while a vote for the DPP was presented as leading to inevitable confrontation if not war. With its roots firmly in Taiwan's pro-independence movement, the DPP had by that point ruled Taiwan for just over half the period since its first elections in 1996.

Public talk of independence, however, had been largely stymied by threats from the mainland that made it clear any such declaration would lead to immediate conflict. The DPP presidential candidate in 2024, former Foreign Minister Lai Ching-te, stuck broadly to his predecessors' rhetoric of preserving the 'status quo'. His government, however, was unambiguously committed to building relations with the US, increasing defence spending to at least 3 per cent of GDP and remaining de facto independent. 'China's rise has posed a challenge to the rules-based international order, and Taiwan is a tipping point in the world balance of power,' said Foreign Minister Lin Chia-lung, stressing Taiwan was not just a 'chess piece caught in the middle – we are an actor'.[28]

Beijing's wider programme of expansion across the region, however, was much broader than just the island of Taiwan. Equally importantly, the disputed waters of the South China Sea simultaneously claimed by Beijing and several other nations were now the scene for a bloodless test of strength that might set the conditions for any future conflict.

*

Nowhere was that confrontation more critical or more tense than the disputed and largely submerged reef known on Western charts as 'Second Thomas Shoal'. At the start of 2024 those who watched international tensions closely believed a rusting former landing craft from World War Two deliberately stranded on its beach might be the most likely trigger point anywhere in the world for an accidental war.

Launched in late 1944 on the Missouri River by a United States churning out weaponry at a rate unmatched in human history, the vessel later known as USS *Harnett County* had ferried US soldiers and marines between Pacific islands in the closing days of World War Two. Reactivated in the 1960s to serve in

Vietnam, she acted as a floating helicopter base for a new generation of US forces before being transferred to the government of South Vietnam. After the April 1975 fall of Saigon to the Communist fighters of the Vietcong, she had sailed into Manila crammed full of refugees, then spent a quarter-century in the service of the Philippines as the BRP *Sierra Madre*.

In 1999, the *Sierra Madre* had been deliberately beached on Second Thomas Shoal, known as Ayungin Reef to the Philippines and Rén'ài Jiāo to the Chinese. With hindsight, the Manila government had been smart to make an early move: China's claims that almost the entire South China Sea was Beijing's 'historic waters' had originated with Chiang Kai-shek's Nationalist government on the mainland in the 1940s. Despite their lack of international recognition, by the 2020s such claims were being pursued by China's Communist rulers more ruthlessly each year, keen to lock in potentially vast reserves of underwater energy and minerals as well as fisheries. If the battle over Taiwan – bloodless or otherwise – was the era's defining confrontation, these much smaller South China Sea face-offs (also taking place with Vietnam and Malaysia) were both a parallel opening stage and preparatory test of wills.

By the time the first journalists were allowed on board in 2011, the *Sierra Madre* was already dramatically decayed. Waves sloshed through the inside of the hull and holes gaped even in internal walls, making life extremely tough for the dozen or so Philippine Navy Special Operations Group marines still living aboard. Plastic containers lay on the deck to catch the rainwater for drinking, while smaller pots grew string beans, squash, okra and sweet potatoes.[29] 'It's a lonely place,' Marine Staff Sergeant Joey Loresto told a reporter in the 2010s. 'But we keep ourselves busy.' Fishing lines hung from the decaying superstructure, providing further food, while other stores such as tins, rice, coffee, sugar and toiletries were delivered by small boats sometimes escorted by the military and coastguard.[30]

In 2016, the Philippines had turned successfully to the United Nations maritime court in The Hague to reject China's 'nine-dashed line' that claimed most of the South China Sea, obtaining a ruling that Second Thomas Shoal and most other parts of the Spratly Island chain were part of the Philippines Exclusive Economic Zone. But that did nothing to stop Beijing dialling up its efforts: building increasingly sophisticated military bases on artificial islands such as Mischief Reef, seized in the 1990s, as well as tightening its blockade of the *Sierra Madre*.

Throughout the 2020s – and particularly from 2023 – Chinese efforts to force the Philippines to withdraw from Second Thomas Shoal became increasingly aggressive. These 'salami tactics' – advancing 'slice by slice' through threat rather than actual use of force – saw Chinese patrol vessels attempt to physically block supplies, at times using non-lethal weapons such as water cannon to damage Filipino craft. Mindful of the mutual defence treaty, the movement of Chinese vessels around the *Sierra Madre* was tracked relentlessly by both sides, including US MQ-9A Reaper drones flown from Filipino bases.[31]

In November 2023, US journalists accompanying half a dozen Filipino craft heading to the *Sierra Madre* watched a US P-5 Poseidon maritime patrol plane flying overhead as more than twice that number of Chinese vessels moved to block the Filipino convoy. 'You are a state party to UNCLOS,' an officer on the largest Filipino ship radioed to the encroaching Chinese craft, referring to the UN maritime convention. 'Your actions are illegal. Stop your activity, or face the consequences.' 'Stop the operation and leave the sea area immediately,' replied one of the Chinese officers, turning dangerously close in front of the Filipino vessel.[32]

Time was running out for *Sierra Madre*. According to one former official in the Philippines, an assessment of the vessel suggested it might break up in as little as two years, most likely in a storm. Meanwhile, Beijing kept on tightening its chokehold and its rhetoric. Even as the government of the Philippines tried to strike a deal with China, the confrontation at Second Thomas Shoal risked setting the tone for multiple other maritime confrontations across the wider region. Philippines President Ferdinand Marcos Jr made an effort to lay down 'red lines' at the Shangri-La summit in Singapore at the end of May, but with only limited success. The phrase 'red lines' had become increasingly common to describe one nation outlining actions by another that it would view as unacceptable and likely to prompt military action. In this case, Marcos was threatening even more than that, warning that any deaths of service personnel would be followed not just by Filipino action but a request to Washington for military support under their mutual defence pact with Manila. Shortly afterwards, Chinese patrol boats made their most violent interceptions of a Philippine supply run yet, causing one Philippine marine to lose his thumb.[33]

Next, the authorities in Manila were reported to have struck a deal with Beijing over resupplying the *Sierra Madre*, only for the focus of confrontation to switch to the similarly disputed Sabina Shoal a few hundred miles away. There, Chinese patrol boats blockaded the largest vessel in the Filipino coastguard for five months until it finally headed back to port in September 2024, its air-conditioning and water-purification systems failing and four of its crew requiring hospitalisation for serious dehydration.[34]

Should the Philippines surrender their positions, some US strategists in Washington worried it might send a perhaps catastrophic signal of weakness to Beijing – at worst persuading Xi and those around him that they could move against Taiwan. 'We can't afford to ignore this sort of thing because eventually it sets precedent and shapes perceptions,' said Samuel Byers, a former Pentagon official and now senior adviser at the Centre for Maritime Security. If that meant US helicopters or small boats had to run the gauntlet of Chinese patrol craft to keep the Filipinos supplied, that might be a risk future US commanders would have to take, he warned.[35] In Washington, ambassador of the Philippines Jose Manuel Romualdez predicted Beijing would keep testing its strength. 'The aggression that we are facing is very real,' he warned. 'There can be one major accident and . . . all hell breaks loose.'[36]

*

If 'all hell' did break loose, the US and its allies were determined to be prepared. The man responsible for that at the start of 2024 was Admiral John Aquilino, head of the US Indo-Pacific Command (INDOPACOM). An Italian-American aviator with barely greying hair and chiselled features, he was a graduate of the Naval Academy in Annapolis, the Harvard Kennedy School of Government and the US Navy 'Top Gun' fighter weapons school in California – US Defense Secretary Austin joked he had been hoping to be cast as one of the admirals in the most recent film.[37]

Where Aquilino could have found the time was another question: his diary was a never-ending series of video calls and flights, glad-handing with the top commanders of every ally and most of the neutral nations. While many nations in Southeast Asia were keen to avoid taking sides between Washington and Beijing, most were still keen to retain and grow relations with the US military, sometimes alongside a similar effort with the PLA. Others – particularly America's closest treaty allies: the Philippines, Japan, South Korea and Australia – were knitted much more deeply into the US command chain, keen to be prepared to fight a war if matters escalated beyond the point of no return. The result was a series of partnerships and alliances, some bilateral and others involving several nations. There was the 'Quad' of the US, India, Australia and Japan; then the simultaneous 'Squad' of the same countries plus the Philippines. Japan, South Korea and the US had their own three-way partnership, albeit without an established snappy name, while the US also had its AUKUS partnership with the UK and Australia.

While some saw the complexity of those networks as a weakness, other US officials described the 'latticework' as providing maximum mutual deterrence while retaining flexibility.

'China has a basic premise that they are the rising power, we are a declining power, and either you get in line or you're going to get the Philippines treatment,' said Biden's ambassador to Japan and former Obama White House Chief of Staff Rahm Emanuel. 'Our message is that we are a permanent Pacific power and presence and you can bet long on us.'[38]

Part of that was about ensuring military personnel from different nations were used to working closely together, including fixes to allow previously incompatible computer systems to work together without endangering important data. For the first time, multiple INDOPACOM drills in 2024 trialled 'open architecture' software that allowed them to access information from US military networks without US military devices, with the US controller able to determine and adjust what their partner forces were able to see. Intelligence sharing was critical to ensuring all sides could fight together – but given Chinese efforts to penetrate and spy on every country in the region as well as the US itself, opening up too much could give everything away.

Some shows of force were deliberately dramatic, not least the sinking of a former Chinese-built tanker serving as a Philippines supply ship, sent to the bottom after being hit by multiple bombs, guns and missiles.[39] That was a precursor to an even larger SINKEX at the major RIMPAC (Rim of the Pacific) naval drills a few months later: the destruction of former US Navy assault ship *Tarawa* from a US B-2 stealth bomber, designed to showcase America's ability to sink China's new carriers and assault ships.[40] Inevitably, such large-scale displays of force grabbed headlines – as did air force exercises in northern Australia, described as '*Top Gun* in the Top End', including the Italian aircraft carrier *Cavour*.[41]

By 2024, the US was conducting around 120 exercises a year in the Asia–Pacific region, almost all increasing in size each year. INDOPACOM commander Aquilino described them as 'more complex, less scripted . . . real training for our militaries to be able to come together at any time.'[42] Some, such as COBRA GOLD in Thailand, focused on humanitarian activities for countries that wanted to stay neutral between the US and China.[43] Others focused on the larger-scale fighting that would be central to any major conflict.

A major Pacific conflict would likely involve the largest naval battles conducted since 1945. In that first Pacific war, Japanese and US carrier fleets had launched long-range strikes against each other, almost never coming even close to visual range – but in any new conflict the distances could be vastly greater. Weapons with a reach of several thousand miles could bear down on warships from both sides; a brutal test of dominance and numbers between attacking anti-ship and anti-surface weaponry and the air-defence missiles sent flying up against them. The cost of losing that battle for a warship or ground installation would likely be catastrophic damage or destruction, in the case of naval vessels and aircraft perhaps well beyond the range of rescue.

Still, as US General George S. Patton was once reputed to have said, the purpose of warfare was not to die for one's country but to make sure the other bastard died for his. The key to deterring a Chinese move against Taiwan, in the Pentagon's eyes at least, was the ability to inflict massive potential casualties on Chinese forces as they crossed the Taiwan Strait while – ideally at least – doing anything possible to reduce US losses. The key to that, at least for the 2020s, was drones and long-range missiles – and for the US with its homeland on the far side of the Pacific, that meant finding somewhere further forward that the weapons could be fired from.

*

In April 2024, a US C-17 heavy transport aircraft touched down in the northern Philippines, ground crews working swiftly under floodlights to unload a multi-wheeled missile launcher into the tropical night. It was, a Filipino official later said, a deliberate decision by the two nations to give China 'sleepless nights'. The Typhon system, capable of launching several different missiles, including the SM-6 and Tomahawk, could strike targets almost a thousand miles away, putting the whole island of Taiwan and much of southern China in its range, prompting rapid Chinese anger, notably in public.[44] Initially, the Typhon deployment was expected to be short-term. Every time there was a further incident around Second Thomas Shoal or another disputed island, however, its presence was extended – and by the end of the year, it appeared to be becoming permanent.

Also drawing attention was another much smaller deployment. The Batanes islands, almost within sight of Taiwan itself, became temporary home to a small detachment of US soldiers working from pickup trucks and air-conditioned tents. They operated a lightweight, solar-powered K1000 long-range surveillance drone alongside a range of other systems including high-altitude balloons.[45] Chinese officials warned that the stepped-up US presence was 'playing with fire'. On the Batanes islands themselves, some residents said they felt safer with the US there, not least thanks to new infrastructure such as a new harbour. But others felt it made them a target. 'It is like living in a paradise,' said Basco mayor and former teacher German Caccam. 'We do not like to be disturbed by conflicts.'[46]

Those drones were only the beginning. In mid-2023 the Biden administration announced Project REPLICATOR, a plan to mass-produce unmanned systems including underwater vehicles to make the Taiwan Strait impassable to a naval or invasion force. The aim was to bring those drones into being faster than could possibly be done through the mainstream industrial defence base, which was already struggling to expand. It meant new factories, new techniques, new technologies – and a bonanza for a new generation of defence tech firms.

'The great paradox of military innovation is you're going to have to make big bets,' US Deputy Secretary of Defense Kathleen Hicks told its launch event, saying it was designed to cut through the red tape of normal military procurement to deliver cutting-edge mass-producible unmanned weaponry into service, sometimes in as little as a year. 'Dollars are not the major challenge – getting the production up and running and getting it at scale is.'[47] Doug Beck, director of the Pentagon's Defense Innovation Unit, described the focus as 'combining cutting-edge hardware with cutting-edge software – the capabilities and needs of each pushing the bounds of what is possible with the other'.[48] In earlier decades, something like REPLICATOR might have been announced without specifying its intended battlefield or target. But Hicks went out of her way to explicitly link it to China, and particularly the threat against Taiwan. 'We must ensure the PRC leadership wakes up every day, considers the risks of aggression and concludes: "Today is not the day,"' said Hicks. 'And not just today, but every day between now and 2027, 2035, 2049 and beyond.'[49]

According to Aquilino, his team at INDOPACOM had been experimenting with drones for at least a decade. The scale at which they might now be usable, however, was increasing exponentially. In a major conflict, Aquilino said he wanted to be able to hit as many as a thousand targets in the first hours alone. The aim, he said, was a 'hellscape' of unmanned drones and missiles.[50]

What Aquilino was suggesting was essentially using unmanned drones and submarines to do the job his predecessors in World War Two had been forced to do with America's young soldiers, sailors, airmen and marines – but it would still be a bloody business. If a Taiwan invasion came, the 'hellscape' concept was intended to kill thousands if not tens of thousands of Chinese personnel – and it might well be taking place against the wider backdrop of long-range US and Chinese missile strikes across much of the Pacific.

By the middle of the decade, firms were queueing up to provide the sort of unmanned systems that could make that 'hellscape' not just a reality – US commanders said some of that classified capability was already in service – but resilient enough to last in a potentially long and bloody war. But they warned that Beijing was also getting ready. 'What we all have to understand is we haven't faced a threat like this since World War Two,' Aquilino told the Senate armed services committee in March 2024, warning that China was churning out new ships and aircraft at an unprecedented rate and well on course to be ready to attack Taiwan by 2027. 'Their actions are becoming much more belligerent, their rhetoric is more clear.'[51]

China's wider military capabilities were also becoming more impressive by the month: stealth frigates, mobile landing piers and a host of other technology, almost all of it looking like it was deliberately designed for either landing operations on Taiwan itself or operations against the US and its allies in the surrounding waters. That included hunting US submarines in the relatively shallow waters of the Taiwan Strait, and using long-range missiles to hit US bases as well as moving ships. In China's giant military test areas and ranges in the Gobi desert, enormous mocked-up targets included US *Ford*-class aircraft carriers, destroyers and other warships – one on a moving rail bed to simulate a ship at sea attempting to evade incoming weapons. For some watching US officials, that suggested Beijing was at least considering the option of a massive strike on the first day of war against US targets, likely also using cyber attacks and electronic warfare to spread maximum chaos and confusion.[52]

As former US naval intelligence chief Mike Studeman put it to me, just focusing on the number of Chinese planes, ships and troops was to miss the bigger picture. 'The capability advancements are eye-watering,' he said. 'They have learned the lessons of Ukraine, which is to say that if you hope to actually do something very quick and easy, it may end up being something akin to the old wars of attrition.'[53]

'I can't see the Chinese deciding at that point that they are going to give up,' added former US intelligence officer Lonnie Henley. He predicted that even if an initial invasion of Taiwan was defeated with massive Chinese casualties, the PLA would continue to use its own missiles, drones and overwhelming numbers of small ships to keep Taiwan blockaded. 'If there is a war, there will definitely be a blockade and if there is a serious war, we will lose because of the blockade.'

Even a blockade without invasion could be hugely challenging – Biden administration Asia official Ely Ratner predicted its impact on the global economy or even a limited blockade would likely be much larger than the Covid-19 pandemic. 'The global economy falls through the floor,' he warned.[54] A wargame that examined 26 separate blockade and quarantine scenarios hosted by a Washington think tank in summer 2025 showed that bringing dangers for all sides, with Taiwan particularly vulnerable to having its energy supplies cut off. In multiple instances the US and allies were able to defeat a PLA blockade, but only with substantial casualties, sometimes including aircraft carriers. In a public discussion immediately after, not all US participants believed such a military campaign was in the US interest, suggesting Washington might do better to hold back its forces and avoid intervening militarily.[55]

When it came to confronting China, the US was hugely behind in terms of shipbuilding and repair – and the vast distances US vessels would also need to cover would likely overstretch sparse logistic resources and stockpiles of weaponry and fuel. It was a worry that would grow throughout the Trump administration – and prove very hard to fix.

For others, the parallels to earlier pre-war periods were also unmistakable. On the smaller mountainous island Itbayat, elder members of the mostly indigenous population still remembered December 7, 1941, when the Japanese bombed them the same day as they struck Pearl Harbor, invading the northern Philippines almost immediately afterwards. 'We can help our community and our country,' said 60-year-old Cyrus Malupa, the oldest of more than 100 local volunteers for the Philippines naval reserve. 'China is bullying us too much. But we're not worried because the Americans are helping.'[56]

The key question was how much longer that could be relied on. Even before Trump returned to office in 2025, that was being queried.

In Japan, from September 2024, incoming Prime Minister Shigeru Ishiba suggested the likely return of Trump and US withdrawal from the world meant it was time to replicate in Asia the type of formal NATO-style alliance that had helped keep the peace in Europe.[57] In South Korea there were calls from those close to President Yoon Suk Yeol for the country to acquire atomic weapons.[58]

Without doubt, North Korea was also becoming more aggressive. Under Yoon, stepped-up radio broadcasts into the totalitarian North prompted the government in Pyongyang to load basic helium balloons with rubbish and human excrement, which were then sent drifting south across the minefields and barbed wire into the democratic South. On at least a couple of occasions in 2024, that included such material being dumped on the presidential palace.[59]

The real shock in South Korea that year, however, barely involved the North. About to be impeached by South Korea's parliament that December, Yoon and Defence Minister Kim Yong-hyun appeared to attempt a military coup, claiming – without apparent evidence – that those about to bring down the government were in the pay of North Korea. It proved swiftly unsuccessful, not least because thousands of protesters descended on the building to confront the troops, and led swiftly to the dismissal and arrest of both Yoon and Kim. Nevertheless, the coup attempt left Washington blindsided – despite the presence of more than 28,000 US troops on the Korean peninsula, no one in the Korean military appeared to have been in touch with US counterparts to warn them.[60]

On the other side of the world, other overlapping crises were also now underway in Europe, with the mounting threat of conflict again intermixed with multiple pre-existing political tensions as well as an escalating battle for real-time military supplies. There, they had already sparked a real live shooting war – and some suspected that was only the beginning.

3

The Return of War to Europe

*'We have never fully trusted our neighbour [Russia],
which has been the prudent approach.'*

**Major General Veiko-Vello Palm, Commander,
Estonian Division, February 2024**[1]

The medieval Danish warriors who built Hermann Castle in
what became Estonia's easternmost major city, Narva, could
not have known it at the time, but what started as their wooden
border checkpoint would one day mark the tensest point on the
frontier between NATO and the modern Russian Federation,
perhaps the most likely place in Europe for World War Three
to start.

Since 1492, the smaller Danish-built castle on the Estonian
side of the Narva River – rebuilt by Germanic Catholic crusader
knights in the later Middle Ages – has faced a much larger
Russian-built counterpart on the cliffs above the gorge that
marks the start of Kremlin territory. The Ivangorod Fortress
there – now flying the flag of the modern Russian Federation –
was built by Ivan the Great, also builder of the Kremlin
buildings themselves, the first king of the newly established
Muscovy to style himself 'Tsar of All the Russias'.

Eastern Europe and the Baltic states were used to living at
the 'crossroads of history', said Liis Mure, Estonia's lead
diplomat for defence in Washington DC; according to Estonia's
government and historians, the country had been attacked

more than 40 times by Russia since the early Middle Ages. In 2007 it had also come under suspected Russian cyber attack after a dispute over a Soviet-era war memorial, and by the early 2020s was dealing with an endless Russian 'shadow war' of sabotage and subversion.[2]

But history can cut both ways, particularly here in Eastern Europe where the last major war was still just on the edge of living memory. As far as Russia was concerned, it had also faced catastrophic attacks through the Baltic states at several key points in its history: first by those Catholic Teutonic Knights, determined to convert Orthodox Russians to Roman Catholicism and loyalty to the Pope, then later by Napoleon in 1812 and Nazi Germany from 1941. Like the population of Ukraine – some of whom sided with the Nazis in part as a consequence of Soviet abuses, not least that of a catastrophic famine – the population of the Baltic states would never be trusted by the Kremlin. The newly independent governments of Estonia and Latvia, meanwhile – Lithuania had many fewer Russian speakers – would always be nervous of their own potential 'enemy within'.

Nowhere in the Baltics was this starker than Narva. In 1944, Nazi German troops supported by Estonian conscripts and volunteers held back a Soviet offensive for more than six months from February to August. After the advancing Red Army eventually took the city, Russian troops expelled its previous Estonian population, replacing them with settlers from elsewhere in the Soviet Union – settlers whose children and grandchildren then found themselves within Estonia's borders after independence.

When I first visited Narva, in spring 2017, it was obvious the city felt divided from the rest of Estonia, linguistically and culturally – almost its entire 50,000 population were Russian speakers, and Estonians elsewhere in the country talked of 'going to Russia' on the rare occasions when they visited. Once Vladimir Putin annexed Crimea in 2014 and then moved against Russian-speaking regions of eastern Ukraine, there was plenty of speculation that if the Kremlin ever decided to seize a piece of NATO territory, their target would be Narva.

'Would the US and Western Europe really go to war to defend the territorial integrity of Estonia?' asked Professor Michael Ben-Gad at London's City University. 'I think Estonia has reasons to worry. Narva is the most obvious place.'

'Putin is a judo master,' said a Baltic intelligence official at the time. 'When he sees his opponent off balance his instinct may be to put him on the floor. The best place to try that could be Narva.'[3]

From 2014, the population of Narva and its civic officials were politely irritated by the successive groups of journalists who visited the town to see where the next European war might start. In the short term the Obama administration had moved fast to reassure Estonia and the other Baltic states – all three NATO members since 2004 – that they would not be abandoned. US paratroopers, special operations forces[4] and, later, heavy armour were moved swiftly to all three countries, although the Pentagon insisted their presence was 'persistent' not 'permanent'.[5] As one of the US armoured cavalry officers told me at the time: 'There's nothing like a tank if you want to achieve an effect.'[6] In February 2015, some of those armoured vehicles and heavy artillery paraded through the streets of Narva for Estonia's Independence Day, intended as an unambiguous sign of US and NATO commitment to fight for the town and the remainder of the Baltic states.[7]

Ever since independence in 1991, successive Estonian governments had hoped to tackle Narva and Estonia's broader community of ethnic Russian-speakers with a 'soft touch', investment and the promise of better integration. Aside from that single 2015 display of US and NATO firepower, the Estonia military and its allies kept a much lower profile in the town, with no permanent military base – for now, at least – within the city or its outer districts.

When I visited in 2017, the city's Russian-speaking deputy mayor talked down prospects that many of the population might be sympathetic to the Kremlin. The biggest difference between the Russian-speaking areas of Estonia and their counterparts in Ukraine, he said, was that the Russian-speaking areas of Ukraine had been notably poorer than nearby parts of Russian territory, giving an obvious incentive for people to favour change. Estonian-governed Narva, in contrast, was visibly wealthier than the tower blocks around the Russian fortress in Ivangorod. Russian speakers living in Estonia also had the option of working across the European Union, something several residents cited to me as a key reason – alongside the fear of war – that they would rather not see the city annexed to Russia.[8]

During my 2017 visit, the US tanks were pulling out of Estonian territory to be replaced by what was to be the first of many rotating British-led 'Enhanced Forward Presence' battle groups that also included tanks and troops from France, Denmark and several other nations. The new NATO troops, like the Americans before them, were mainly based in Estonia's largest military garrison at Tapa, more than an hour's drive from Narva and the border.[9]

*

By the mid-2020s, the divisions between the Russian-speaking population of the Baltic states and their compatriots were becoming deeper, manifesting themselves in part through greater numbers voting openly for pro-Kremlin candidates in local elections. Some Narvans were simply leaving the town, either for Russian territory proper or to move deeper into Europe.[10]

For the Russian-speaking population of the Baltic states, the 2022 full-scale invasion of Ukraine marked the beginning of the toughest time since independence in 1991. In Latvia, where roughly 30 per cent of the population were

Russian-speaking, some received official orders to leave the country immediately 'for the sake of national security'.[11] In Narva, Estonian authorities removed a Soviet-era tank serving as a war memorial in late 2022.

While some of the backlash that provoked was almost certainly stoked from across the border, much was clearly genuine: one 19-year-old resident said it made 'her Russian blood boil'. Svetlana, aged 38, said that since its removal she felt she was 'no longer at home in Estonia, but like a guest in a friend's house', and was now more attached to a Russian-speaking identity than ever before. 'They are punishing us,' complained one Narva resident in his early forties. 'It's unfair.' Also unpopular was an order to cease Russian-language education and switch schools to teaching in Estonian. 'We are not ready – there are not enough teachers and many will lose their jobs,' said Anna, aged 26. 'For me, it is obvious that it is because of the war.'[12]

Russia was working to exploit those divisions. On a pro-Kremlin Telegram channel known as 'Grey Zone', heavily read by Russian speakers both in and outside Russia, adverts appeared throughout 2024 explicitly recruiting for campaigns of sabotage. When a think-tank researcher pretending to be a 26-year-old Russian-speaking Estonian responded to an advert, they were swiftly offered money to practise with a Molotov cocktail in a forest. 'Send a video,' wrote their handler. 'The money through crypto after a mission is done.' A 'mission', the anonymous recruiter told Ivanov, could be anything from spying on military bases to setting fire to NATO vehicles – or committing murder at $10,000 'a head'. The researcher ended the conversation.[13]

In spring 2025, Estonia finally bit the bullet and announced it was building a military base in Narva to ensure that there was a permanent armed Estonian presence in the event of an attack. Major General Vahur Karus, head of the Estonian Defence Force headquarters, said the plan was to have roughly 200 to

250 personnel at a time stationed in the city, adding that they would have 'all their weapons with them'. That ongoing presence, he said, would likely include members of allied NATO forces and was intended to 'normalise' the presence of troops within the city and ensure that it remained part of the Estonian state.[14]

How Estonia's NATO allies might respond to such an invitation was not immediately clear. Those forces deployed in Narva would be among the most exposed in Europe – and certainly outnumbered in the event of a major attack from Russia.

The forces the Kremlin could build up in nearby parts of Russia – particularly once the Ukraine war reached its end – were considerably more powerful than the defensive forces deployed within the Baltic states. According to George Barros, lead Russia analyst for the Institute for the Study of War in Washington DC, once it had ceased fighting in Ukraine the Kremlin might have as many as 12 full-strength fighting divisions in its new 'Leningrad Military District' just across the border from Estonia. Each of those divisions amounted to roughly 10,000 personnel and several hundred tanks and armoured vehicles. Estonia's primary fighting force amounted to no more than a division, backed up by thousands of much more lightly armed conscripts. The entire NATO battle group in Estonia led by Britain was approximately 1,000 personnel. Many of those Russian troops would be stationed sufficiently close to the NATO border that they could attack with little warning – while the Kremlin was deepening its relationship with Belarus to keep more troops permanently based there where they could also threaten Poland and Lithuania.[15]

In total, US officials talked of as many as 22 Russian divisions capable of attacking the three Baltic states with relatively little warning from the territory of Belarus and Russia once Ukraine fighting ceased, backed up by strike missiles and hefty air defences around the Russian enclave of Kaliningrad as well as

St Petersburg itself.[16] In the short term, commercial satellite footage of the two-dozen closest major military installations to the Baltic states in Russia and Belarus suggested Putin's desperation to prioritise his army in Ukraine had lowered the immediate danger to NATO's European members. At Pskov airfield, just over 20 miles from the Estonian border, scorch marks were still visible on the tarmac where Ukrainian drones had destroyed two large Ilyushin Il-76 transport planes and forced the Russian military to re-base other aircraft further east.

Other bases, however, already showed signs of rebuilding. At the Luga military centre less than 100 miles from the heartland of Estonia, new trucks, tanks and armoured vehicles could be seen, as well as a brigade of Iskander medium-range rockets capable of striking anywhere across the immediate region. When Estonian journalists showed the images to former military chief Martin Herem, his response was instantaneous. 'This isn't good at all,' he muttered.

*

'I think a Russian attack will be limited,' said Herem. 'They come in, run havoc, create some very grotesque scenes, and while we would not be occupied, we become so terribly afraid of Russia that we would accept conditions. This can be achieved with a military operation.'[17]

This was also what Britain's Ministry of Defence as well as others across Europe were just starting to wargame. The most likely scenario, according to former British army chief General Sanders, was that Putin would move fast, take a patch of NATO territory – and then lean on his Ukraine-era playbook to threaten nuclear response if NATO forces attempted to kick him out again. 'That's very high-stakes,' said the former British general, predicting that a NATO failure to respond would risk the entire alliance essentially becoming worthless. 'But the payoff for Putin would be huge.'[18]

Others feared Putin might go even further – as he had originally hoped to do with his invasion of Ukraine – and attempt to overrun one or more of the Baltic states entirely. 'We lack strategic depth – the Russians could move through the whole country in hours, if not days,' former Lithuanian Foreign Minister Gabrielius Landsbergis complained to Britain's *Daily Telegraph*, warning that a ten-year plan to build up bunkers and defences along the borders was simply not happening even close to fast enough. 'Putin is not going to let us wait those ten years,' he said.[19]

With the Trump administration pressuring both Putin and Zelenskyy to end the fighting in Ukraine, European nations feared time might be running out. In May 2024, head of Polish intelligence Jarosław Stróżyk warned Russia already had enough forces to launch a very small-scale attack against a NATO country – again perhaps to seize, say, Narva – even while fighting continued in Ukraine.[20]

Even without that, multiple intelligence agencies believed the Kremlin was likely to build its military to the point that it could attack Europe within the next half-decade, enough to threaten the outright existence of some smaller NATO nations. 'Within two years, Russia could pose a credible threat to one or several NATO countries if NATO does not build up its own military power at the same rate as Russia,' warned Danish Defence Minister Troels Lund Poulsen, while, in early 2025, French President Emmanuel Macron described the threat as 'existential'.[21]

'The root cause of Russia's aggression against Ukraine is clear – Putin's ambition to restore the Russian Empire,' said Estonian defence minister Hanno Pevkur.[22] From Washington, the incoming Trump administration was soon making it clear the United States would no longer take the lead in preventing that from happening. As things stood, however, the entire NATO alliance that had been built up over more than seven decades continued to be based heavily on US leadership – and if war came to the continent, a US senior commander would be responsible for leading the fight.

*

As a wrecked Europe had emerged from World War Two, there had been a clear feeling that only US military leadership could persuade those nations they could win against a large, determined foe. By 2025, European nations were among the richest in the world, with combined defence spending of NATO alliance states amounting to more than half of all global military spending – more than Russia and China combined. And yet, it seemed, the dependence on US leadership remained, and that was a real problem. If Europe could not find a more sustainable dynamic, it was potentially in a lot of trouble.

US Army General Chris Cavoli took over as head of the US European Command (EUCOM) – and simultaneously as NATO's Supreme Allied Commander Europe (SACEUR) – shortly after the full-scale February 2022 Ukraine invasion, swiftly finding himself facing a planning task on a scale not seen since Eisenhower took the same job in 1951.

Back then, the disastrous opening days of the Korean War had supercharged already serious worries that Western Europe was grossly ill-prepared to meet a Soviet offensive – and Eisenhower had swiftly built the military structures that still run NATO forces today. The aftermath of Putin's full-scale Ukraine invasion delivered a similar sense of alarm if not outright panic, one that the Biden administration moved fast to address, building heavily on initial war plans drawn up since 2020.

Initially, that involved a major NATO reassurance effort: deploying US and European troops to nations along the alliance eastern flank, while simultaneously building extremely fast-growing US and allied support to Ukraine itself. Then, from the Madrid summit in June 2022, it expanded to enlarge and add more forces and much more detailed plans to defend 'every inch' of alliance territory.

The son of an Italian-American US Army NCO who had largely grown up on military posts in Europe, Cavoli spoke German, Italian and Russian fluently and arrived with a reputation for attention to detail, diplomacy and holding the big picture. As a young infantry officer, he had first deployed to Europe in the last days of the first Cold War, and was now returning in command as those dangers returned.

The scale of Russia's attack against Ukraine, he publicly acknowledged, went well beyond anything the US or anyone in recent history had predicted – and that was also true of the sheer resource intensity of the conflict. Soon, Ukraine had exhausted almost the entire Western stockpiles of Javelin anti-tank and Stinger anti-aircraft missiles – and it would go on to burn through years' worth of production of artillery shells in a matter of months.

Initially, the Biden administration went out of its way to use the Ukraine invasion to show the US was again firmly committed to the support of Europe after all the question marks from Trump's first term in office. By the start of 2025, however, with Trump about to re-enter the White House, Cavoli's remit was to demonstrate Europe's ability to do much more itself.

In the immediate aftermath of the Ukraine invasion, the Biden administration moved some 20,000 US personnel to Europe, bringing the total number on the continent to more than 100,000. As late as spring 2024, Cavoli and the Biden administration were suggesting those forces might grow even further, with the general telling a Congressional hearing that the Euro-Atlantic area now faced more 'threats and dynamic challenges than at any time in the past 30 years'.[23] In the event of major conflict, some talked of as many as 200,000 further US forces crossing the Atlantic as fast-moving reinforcements.[24] Those European officers who had served with US forces were keen to warn their colleagues that the US ability to move huge forces quickly took colossal planning, maintenance and other work – almost impossible for anyone else to match without huge military reform.

In addition to co-ordinating Western war plans for the defence of Europe, Cavoli was co-ordinating much of the US and wider Western support to Ukraine in its actual shooting war. Never before had US commanders and personnel been so closely involved in a direct conflict with Russia – and both that conflict and US involvement were broadening and escalating.

*

In a secret operations room at a US base in Germany dubbed colloquially 'the Pit', US, British and other allied military personnel worked daily to track the conflict in Ukraine and find new ways to support the government in Kyiv.

Under stringent controls imposed from Washington, US officials and military personnel were deliberately constrained in what information they could share – something that periodically sparked irritation from Ukrainian counterparts.[25] Still, when authorised to work together, the combined effects of Western and Ukrainian innovation could be remarkable. In mid-2024, US Army Colonel Rosanna Clemente, deputy chief of staff of the US Army's 10th Air and Missile Defense Command, detailed to a military conference how US advisers and Ukrainian operators of a donated US Patriot surface-to-air missile brought down one of Russia's highly valued Antonov-50 early warning planes, almost certainly killing all its crew.[26]

By that point direct US collaboration in Ukrainian strikes on other Russian military targets was relatively common, to the discomfort of some Europeans. 'They are part of the kill chain now,' one European intelligence chief told the *New York Times*. According to what appeared to be extensive briefings by both US and Ukrainian officials to that newspaper, by mid-2024 US officials were frequently passing what they called 'points of interest' to their Ukrainian counterparts, avoiding the phrase 'targets'. Those 'points of interest' were then rapidly hit, often with extensive Russian casualties.[27]

Having US and other Western forces in such close proximity brought with it sometimes unexpected and alarming risks. Among the closest near disasters was what US documents described as the 'near shootdown' of a British RC-135 'Rivet Joint' reconnaissance plane over the Black Sea in October 2022. British officials had initially described the incident, in which a Russian missile was fired from a Russian Su-27 near the UK aircraft, as a 'malfunction' on the Russian side. In reality, it was more serious and dangerous. According to accounts from three different defence sources to the BBC a year later, intercepted radio communications suggested the Russian pilot had in fact fired deliberately, likely having misunderstood a message from his controller saying 'you have the target' as giving him permission to shoot down the plane, which had as many as 25 personnel aboard. The second Russian pilot immediately realised the potentially catastrophic error and swore violently at his colleague, the officials said, while the British aircraft was only saved by the failure of the Russian missile as it fired.

Had the weapon worked correctly, it is hard to say how things might have escalated. Following the incident, RAF reconnaissance flights continued, the BBC reported – but escorted by Typhoon fighters with live anti-aircraft missiles to swiftly engage any Russian jets that tried the same.[28] It all pointed to a wider issue: different nations were showing wildly different appetites for risk.

As allied support for Ukraine increased in the first months of the war, some in Washington and Brussels worried that the Kremlin might choose to further escalate and strike the weapons-delivery sites in Poland and Romania. The fact that did not happen was seen by US and European officials alike as a sign that Putin respected the NATO Article Five pledge that an attack on one alliance member will be treated as an attack on all – and, most importantly, that meant he believed that attacking a NATO member would prompt a devastating US-led conventional response.

But by mid-2024 it was clear that the danger of a military attack – alarming and growing though it was – was not the only threat. When NATO foreign ministers met in Brussels that spring, almost all reported suspected Russian sabotage within their borders. Examples included the disruption of European railway signals, the jamming of GPS civil aviation systems over the Baltic, an arson attack on a warehouse in the UK and others across the length and breadth of Eastern Europe.[29] It was, Western officials believed, part of a deliberate effort to destabilise and spread alarm across Europe, and a reminder of just how much damage the Kremlin could do in the event of war. Kremlin-linked sabotage and associated incidents escalated throughout 2024: magnesium-based explosive devices caused fires at DHL logistics terminals; throughout the first months of the year, border guards in Finland, Poland and the Baltic states complained that migrants from the Middle East and Africa were being pushed across the frontiers from Russia and Belarus; and the last months of the year saw break-ins at water treatment plants from Finland through to Germany. 'It's difficult to tell who is responsible in every case,' one European official told me. 'But the intent is obviously to intimidate.'[30]

Then there were the growing number of incidents involving undersea cables in the Baltic. After several cables were severed in late 2024, NATO launched a mission dubbed BALTIC SENTRY using drones, patrol vessels and aircraft as well as artificial-intelligence surveillance to protect critical infrastructure in the region. Addressing a NATO press conference in January 2025, Cavoli described BALTIC SENTRY as a clear indicator that the alliance could act without significant US forces. The decision to launch the mission had been his as SACEUR, he said, but it involved no US personnel or platforms. 'It would be irresponsible to . . . speculate about what a future administration might do hypothetically,' he said. 'So I won't do that, but I would point out that the [larger war] plans are [also] designed to be flexible and accept the forces that are made available.'[31]

By early 2025, as tensions grew between Europe and the new Trump administration, Cavoli was able to tell Congress that Europe was spending 40 per cent more on defence than it had been prior to 2022.[32] Whereas the US had been the largest single troop-contributing nation to STEADFAST DEFENDER, NATO's largest military exercise for 2024, 2025's STEADFAST DART was led by European troops, particularly the new NATO Allied Response Force led by an Italian general that featured aircraft, special forces and the ground component led by Britain's 1st Division. One of the senior British officers on the exercise described it as the culmination of more than a year's work to bring troops up to the standard where they could deploy quickly to Romania, just on the borders with Moldova and Ukraine.[33]

That location was hardly a coincidence. Like Ukraine, Moldova had spent most of the decades since the end of the Cold War awkwardly trapped between East and West, part of its territory in Transnistria occupied by Russian 'peacekeepers' while Kremlin-backed political parties attempted to wrest control of the rest of the nation from its pro-European government.

Nearby Georgia had thrown off pro-Russian rulers in the early part of the century, infuriating the Kremlin and facing a brief war with Russia that had cost it two Russian-speaking territories. There, a pro-Russian party, Georgian Dream, was already in control and increasingly tightening legislation to push out Western-funded NGOs they claimed were simply trying to drag the country into conflict.

Romania was also very much a frontline nation, home to NATO's newest and fastest-growing air base near Constanţa on the Black Sea coast, from which allied aircraft could easily track fighting in nearby Ukraine.[34] Like a growing number of states across Eastern and central Europe, including Hungary, the Czech Republic, Slovakia and Bulgaria, Romania's own domestic politics were also firmly being shaped by the wider confrontation between the West and Russia. In November 2024, Romanian authorities cancelled the first round of their presidential election after it was won by Călin Georgescu, a previously largely unknown pro-Kremlin figure who had suddenly leapt to prominence in the weeks before the vote, supported by thousands of newly created accounts on the social media platform TikTok. He remained banned from running the following year – but the election suspension had proved deeply unpopular, prompting many to predict that the more mainstream right-wing nationalist George Simion would win in 2025.[35] In reality, he fell just short, a larger than usual turnout delivering victory for the pro-EU candidate Nicosur Dan.[36]

Such complex politics were one factor that persuaded some in the US they wanted less to do with the long-term defence of Europe. Other Americans, however, were getting more involved. Summer 2024 saw billionaire space and electric vehicle entrepreneur Elon Musk throw his weight first behind Trump in the US, then Germany's right-wing Alternative for Deutschland (AFD) – much to the fury of mainstream politicians in Germany and beyond. In France, the right-wing Front National had challenged mainstream candidates several times for the presidency in the century so far, and looked set to be the primary opposition to Macron at the next French presidential vote expected in 2027.

The greatest short-term challenge, though, was the return of Trump. 'If Trump gets elected, if we take what he has said, it would be a total surprise if we were not to see an immediate stop to military support for Ukraine,' Norbert Röttgen, former head of the German parliamentary foreign affairs committee and an MP for the Christian Democrats, told a pre-election event in London at think tank Chatham House. 'That would mean Europe would have to step in . . . we are totally not prepared for that.'[37]

US arms supplies to Ukraine were temporarily halted on several occasions in Trump's first months, although Ukraine did receive most of the supplies signed off in the last months of Biden's term. But the new administration showed little appetite for more unless someone else was paying.

In his first testimony to the Senate Armed Services Committee following Trump's election – and likely his last before retirement – Supreme Allied Commander Cavoli made the strongest case he could for continued US engagement in Europe, including retaining military leadership of NATO. He spoke of the importance of the alliance for tracking Russian submarines in the Atlantic that might threaten US homeland, how European bases were needed for rapid deployment to the Middle East, and the way in which NATO made possible 'nuclear sharing' between the US and European partners (of which more in Chapter 10). Supporting Ukraine in its fight against the Kremlin, Cavoli said, had also provided invaluable intelligence in the event the US had to one day go to war with Russia, but he also acknowledged that the conflict had seen much greater co-operation than ever before between Russia, China, North Korea and Iran – as well as growing Kremlin efforts to destabilise its immediate neighbours in Europe and beyond. US troop numbers had already fallen in Europe to some 80,000, he told the committee, down from more than 100,000 in the immediate aftermath of the Ukraine invasion in 2022.[38]

Within Washington DC, even before Trump entered office, there was talk those numbers were likely to fall further. The question was whether the Europeans could fill the gap.

*

Following Russia's full-scale Ukraine invasion of February 2022, the Baltic states became among the most committed supporters of Ukraine, as did their Nordic allies. All shared a broadly overlapping concept of 'total' national defence that included planning for catastrophe and moving whole populations from Baltic states under attack to safer areas in nearby nations.

'We agreed to hold regional drills to ensure the evacuation of the population, to see how our institutions are prepared to work together . . . what our capacity is to accommodate people, or the capacity of other countries is, whether they are ready to receive,' said Lithuanian Interior Minister Agnė Bilotaitė.[39]

From the very start, many in the Baltics had expected a future confrontation with the Kremlin. As soon as they regained independence in 1991 they turned to nearby Nordic governments, particularly Finland, for inspiration as they rebuilt their militaries. Unlike them, the government in Helsinki had chosen to fight its Soviet invasion in 1939, and while it had lost significant terrain it had kept its nationhood. The Baltic states followed the example of the Finnish and other Nordic militaries with armies built around a small regular element – often lightly armoured, as with Estonia's elite Scout Battalion – and then larger conscript elements feeding a part-time reserve, capable of fighting a long-running and brutal insurgency.

The Baltic conscript training was designed to deliver physical toughness. 'It takes a toll on you,' said 25-year-old Estonian conscript Toivo Saabas, soaked to the skin in a forested military training area in late spring 2024. 'But in the end, it's service to your country. Being prepared for anything is better than kind of sneaking off and trying to evade this service.' Speaking to the BBC shortly afterwards, Estonian Prime Minister Kaja Kallas – soon to become foreign-policy commissioner for the European Union – said she would like to see every other European democracy take the same approach. 'We have a reserve army of 44,000 people,' she said. 'That would equal, for Great Britain, around two million people. Two million people who are ready to defend their country and know what they have to do.'

The fact that Britain had rejected such a plan, she said, was not particularly surprising. As a child, Kallas's grandmother had been deported to Siberia by the Soviets, only to return after several years – and such experience was widespread. 'We have different historical backgrounds,' she said. 'We have lost our independence and freedom once and we don't want to lose it again.'[40]

Under agreements that went back to the aftermath of the annexation of Crimea in 2014, the primary NATO troop contingent in the Baltic states came primarily from the UK Canada and Germany, each leading multinational battle groups usually of just under a thousand personnel including tanks, artillery and armoured personnel carriers. Under the NATO war plans agreed in Madrid in 2022, those forces could be increased to brigades in time of crisis. By the middle of the decade, Latvia and Lithuania had persuaded Canada and Germany to do just that.

In early April 2024, the first elements of Germany's 45th Panzer Brigade landed at Vilnius International Airport, to be greeted by local dignitaries. Ever since 1945, US, British and sometimes other allied troops had lived on German soil, providing permanent protection – now, a German force eventually consisting of at least 5,000 personnel would do the same for Lithuania, with up to a third of the German personnel accompanied by their families.[41] The increased German presence would help plug one of the most vulnerable points on the NATO front: the so-called 'Suwałki Gap', the roughly 60 miles of Lithuanian territory poised awkwardly between the Russian-held enclave of Kaliningrad on the Baltic coast and the borders of Belarus. For years, Baltic defence planners had feared a Russian attack from Belarus might 'close' the Gap and cut off Estonia, Latvia and the rest of Lithuania from resupply from Europe. The increased force – scheduled to arrive by 2026 – would make such an assault notably harder, while, like US and British families in Germany a generation earlier, the commitment of German partners and children to live in Lithuania was another sign the government in Berlin expected the presence to be permanent. The first families were scheduled to arrive throughout 2027, following negotiations over the provision of children's education in either joint or separate schools,[42] plus a pledge that German military families would get 'competitive' local employment opportunities.[43] 'They don't want an isolated environment,' said Lithuanian Defence Minister Laurynas Kasčiūnas in 2024. 'They want to integrate.'[44]

That more assertive German position in the Baltic states was a sign of things to come. In its last year in office, the Social Democratic government of Olaf Scholz dramatically ramped German defence spending to reach 2 per cent of gross domestic product, making Germany for the first time the fourth-largest defence spender on the planet after the US, China and Russia.[45]

Latvia, the Baltic state sandwiched between Lithuania and Estonia, was also getting a heightened military presence. Canada spent much of 2024 being lambasted by allies over falling well behind on its commitment to reach 2 per cent of GDP for military spending but it accepted Latvia's request to increase the size of the multinational battle group it led there for NATO.[46] 'We will be ready,' Canadian Colonel Cédric Aspirault told a Canadian military podcast in summer 2024. 'We cannot say it will not happen,' he said of an attack, but 'the great advantage will be that we are there. The ground on which we train will be the ground on which we fight.'[47]

By far the smallest NATO contingent in the Baltics was now the British battle group based in central Estonia. Its commander, Brigadier Giles Harris – an urbane, well-spoken officer who had spent longer in Estonia than any other senior Briton – had repeatedly promised a much heavier force to be deployed in advance of any Russian attack.[48] Still, whatever the troops and kit available, the required response would be the same: 'NATO's challenge here . . . is to deter Russia without escalating,' he said. 'If Russia invades, then we go east and fight them.'[49]

Those were brave words – and if Russia did indeed cross the border at some point in the future, few questioned the commitment of Baltic and NATO troops to putting up a fight.

The same would go for the US troops on the ground in three Baltic nations – usually a combination of special operations forces, paratroopers and HIMARS long-range rocket troops.

The presence of those forces was important. In the event of a knife-edge confrontation over Narva, most previous US administrations would have wanted hands-on command of forward allied forces to avoid unnecessary escalation and ensure Washington retained as much control as possible. That had proved critical in the highest-stakes ground confrontations of the first Cold War – the movement of allied and Russian forces along the boundary between East and West Berlin during the 1961 Berlin Wall construction. According to later interviews, at one point NATO's Supreme Commander in Europe US Air Force General Lauris Norstad was effectively controlling the movements of individual groups of US tanks – and equally deliberately keeping British and French forces as out of the way as possible for the key confrontations.[50]

Whether any of that would be possible in a face-off over Narva or any NATO territory that might be targeted by Russia was doubtful – and it would become even more so after the Estonia-led 250-person military base was set up near the town. Even more significantly, some other NATO allies – particularly Poland – were expressing their determination to strike back hard at Russia with everything they had from the moment its forces crossed any NATO border.

More specifically, as former Polish Chief of the General Staff Rajmund Andrzejczak told a conference in mid-2024, Poland and other regional militaries now intended to begin strikes with their hundreds of new long-range rockets deep into Russian territory as soon as an incursion happened anywhere in NATO territory. 'We will strike directly at St Petersburg,' he said. Even a limited attack against the Baltic states, he believed, would be seen by the government in Warsaw and several other nations as 'the beginning of total confrontation'.[51]

By mid-2025, NATO Secretary General Mark Rutte was beginning to echo some of that rhetoric in his official statements, talking for the first time of 'deterrence by punishment' – a polite way of threatening what the Polish former general had outlined. More than any nations other than the Baltic states, the Polish national security establishment had been expecting a future confrontation with the Kremlin ever since the Warsaw Pact collapsed. Now they were becoming much more assertive in calling the shots – and despite its stark internal political divisions, no one in the Polish system seemed to have much appetite for compromise or even US-style crisis management. They intended to draw a line in the sand, and threaten hellfire if it were crossed. It was what the Polish state had been unable to achieve in 1939, and they were not risking history or the Kremlin trying to repeat itself.

*

In the third week of May 2024, several very different remembrance services took place on the Italian hillsides beneath Monte Cassino, the medieval hilltop monastery Allied troops had fought for months to seize in 1944. Most were small and focused on the past.[52] The Polish ceremony, however, involved a cast of hundreds and was broadcast live with deliberate reference to much more modern dangers. President Andrzej Duda reminded those attending that most of the Polish troops in Italy had first been taken prisoner by Soviet troops in 1939 after Hitler and Stalin divided their country between them. Deported to Siberia and then to Kazakhstan, they had been freed under a Stalin–Churchill deal to fight with the Western allies – then forced to choose in 1945 between returning to a Kremlin-occupied Poland or exile in the West. Poland's fighters, Duda said, had been betrayed – and no Warsaw government would let that happen again.[53] As Duda – from Poland's right-wing Law and Justice party – spoke in Italy, Prime Minister Donald Tusk made a similar speech in Warsaw. Tusk's more centrist Civic Platform party had ousted Law and Justice from parliamentary power in the previous October elections, taking a very different line on social issues and relations with the European Union. But when it came to building strong defences to hold back Russia in the future, they were united.

Tusk announced the creation of 'East Shield', a $2.5 billion border protection scheme unlike anything seen in recent history. It would, he said, 'make the Polish border secure in peacetime and impassable . . . in war.'[54] It represented by far the largest European fortification programme since 1945, laying down anti-tank ditches and explosive barriers, as well as flooding marshland to make it harder to advance. New roads and reinforced bridges would allow Poland's own forces – as well as those of its NATO allies – to move forward, all informed by a high-tech surveillance system unlike anything else currently in existence. That included US-manufactured 'spy balloons' as well as a network of watchtowers, all backed up with drones.[55] Days later, interior ministers from Poland, Finland, Norway and all three Baltic states met in Latvia to discuss larger regional defences: a 'drone wall' running south from the Arctic to the border of Ukraine.[56]

The number-one priority, Polish Foreign Minister Radosław Sikorski told an audience in Kraków, was to 'do everything necessary' to avoid 'becoming a Russian colony again'. 'We have a saying in Poland: "Every country has an army, either its own or someone else's,"' Sikorski continued. 'In the long run, it's cheaper to keep your own.'[57] To that end, Poland was on course to spend $35 billion on defence in 2024, rising further in the coming years to approach 5 per cent of GDP, by far the highest rate in NATO and well before other nations began to be pushed towards that level. In raw spending, Poland was outspending Italy, with its much larger economy,[58] when it came to operational artillery, rocket launchers and armour – by the 2030s it could have as many as 1,300 cutting-edge main battle tanks. It was also on course to significantly outgun the land forces of France, Germany or Britain, making it the largest army in Europe other than wartime Russia and Ukraine.[59] It was also locking in a powerful trio of military suppliers, drawing tanks, artillery and rocket launchers from Germany, South Korea and the United States.

Even with Poland's history, though, this remilitarisation was not without its challenges. In the Nordic and Baltic states, events in Ukraine in 2014 and 2022 had ramped up support for their various models of conscription – several of those nations ran a lottery or volunteer programmes to fill their conscript slots. But compulsory service remained a far-from-popular option within the Polish population, with more than 40 per cent opposed as late as the end of 2023.[60] Instead, the Warsaw government did everything it could to make volunteer service appealing and accessible, particularly through a popular 'holidays with the army' scheme in which young people spent several weeks in uniform learning basic skills before swearing an oath to defend the nation.[61]

Then, in March 2025, amid the uncertainty and mayhem unleashed by Trump's apparent – if temporary – abandonment of Ukraine, the Warsaw government tore up that approach. Instead of the dramatic voluntary military expansion already planned, they now intended something even larger. We 'will try to have a model ready by the end of the year in which every man in Poland is trained in the event of war,' said Prime Minister Donald Tusk, adding that plans for a 200,000 strong Polish military had been extended to half a million.

A few days earlier, French President Macron had taken the dramatic step of offering to formally extend French nuclear weapons' protection – and even the ability to drop French atomic bombs or fire French nuclear-tipped missiles – to other European allies, although he noted that the warheads themselves would remain under French command. Tusk welcomed that step – but he implied strongly that Poland wanted control of its own atomic arms. Any nuclear deal with France, Tusk said, would depend heavily on how authority to use those weapons operated. 'Today it is clear that we would be safer if we have our own nuclear arsenal.'[62]

As Poland continued to deepen its military and industrial relationship with South Korea, the prospect of the two nations pursuing some kind of atomic project together became quite imaginable. Indeed, in Washington, some sources suggested the incoming Trump administration was quite open to the idea, providing the only nations that went nuclear were judged to be 'responsible'.[63]

It was a wildly different approach to anything the Biden administration would have considered. From the start, Biden's team had proceeded on the assumption that both US partners and potential foes could be persuaded of the benefits of dialogue, even amid a wider tone of confrontation. It had been a brave approach – but it had not proved successful.

4

2024: 'The Hinges of History'

'Our growing problem is simultaneity — so many things happening at once.'

Professor Nikolas Gvosdev, US Naval War College, 2024[1]

If one man could be described as being at the heart of the Biden administration's approach to foreign and security policy, it would be National Security Advisor Jake Sullivan. From sitting through repeated marathon negotiating sessions with Chinese Foreign Minister Wang Yi, or flying out to a US aircraft carrier to welcome back sailors from the Middle East, he could sometimes seem almost omnipresent.

Slim, earnest and voted by his Minnesota high school classmates as 'most likely to succeed', Sullivan's career had taken him upwards at almost unprecedented speed through law school at Yale, a Rhodes scholarship to Oxford and US Supreme Court clerkship to a slot as one of Hillary Clinton's top aides during her 2008 presidential run, then senior roles when she served as secretary of state.[2] Had Clinton taken the White House in 2016 instead of Trump, Sullivan would likely have become national security advisor at the age of 41. Taking up the role for Biden four years later, he was still the youngest in the job since McGeorge Bundy advised John F. Kennedy through Cold War crises in the early 1960s – Sullivan was arguably the most powerful national security advisor since Henry Kissinger under Nixon in the 1970s.

Like Kissinger, Sullivan was no stranger to secret high-stakes diplomacy. Under Obama, he had been one of only a handful of officials in the room for secret negotiations with Iran. Now, while he was on the road less than Biden's Secretary of State Anthony Blinken, he was widely regarded as the principal architect of administration policy – and, unlike the secretary of state, he ran the key meetings at the White House. Indeed, as reports spread that Biden was struggling, Sullivan was increasingly referred to by many in the DC foreign policy community as 'in charge'.

The Biden team, ironically, had entered office in January 2021 believing it had buried Trump. White House Chief of Staff Ron Klain told veteran *Washington Post* correspondent Bob Woodward they had been elected 'to move this country on' and described Trump's ongoing political posturing as a 'sideshow'.[3] They saw their role as one of rebuilding America's relationship with allies, then doubling down to confront and contain autocracies and 'win the 21st century' by staying true to democratic values.[4] While Biden and Sullivan initially hoped the president could build a personal relationship with Putin, they quietly adopted many of the Trump-era package of policies designed to contain a rising China, including efforts to restrict access to raw materials, computer chips and more.[5]

With hindsight, the administration was slow to see where relations with Russia might be headed. When Biden met Putin in Geneva in May 2021, a few months after taking office – and after Russia had already mobilised some 100,000 troops in a clear effort to intimidate Ukraine – the US priority remained persuading the Kremlin to rein in cyber attacks on essential US infrastructure. As the imminence of a full-scale invasion became more apparent, most important of all was avoiding accidental escalation to a US–Russia or NATO–Russia war. 'One thing that was – and still is – on my mind every day is escalation management,' US Chairman of the Joint Chiefs US Army General Mark Milley told Politico shortly before leaving office in 2023. 'Russia is a nuclear-armed state. They have the capacity to destroy humanity . . . Every move has to be consciously and deliberately thought through to its logical extension.'[6]

Once the war began, it consumed much of the energy in Washington. Throughout the first half of 2022, Sullivan described himself as the 'quartermaster' of the Ukrainian military, his small team in the White House hitting the phones to US allies and partners around the world to source artillery shells and other key equipment. Then suddenly fears mounted that Ukraine was doing 'too well', that the Russian frontlines might be on the edge of collapse and that Putin might go nuclear.

From the start, the Biden administration had approached Ukraine with the intention of imposing sufficient diplomatic and financial cost on Russia that it might also help deter Beijing from moving against Taiwan. But summer 2022 saw a new crisis with China that just served to worsen relations. A visit to Taiwan – opposed by the White House – by House of Representatives Speaker Nancy Pelosi that August infuriated the Chinese authorities, prompting a complete suspension of military-to-military direct communication, as well as a level of Chinese military activity around the island on a scale unseen in recent history.

In its aftermath, President Biden appeared, if anything, even more determined to hold firm on his personal pledges to defend the island if attacked – although Taiwanese officials noted that other administration officials almost always rolled back on such rhetoric immediately afterwards.[7] It was the closest any US leader had come since the 1970s to abandoning 'strategic ambiguity' – or perhaps ever would.

By the time Biden and Xi met at the G20 in Bali in November 2022, there was mounting concern that worsening relations with Beijing might increase the chances of an unintended event escalating beyond control – particularly given parallel tensions in the South China Sea. Despite Beijing's fury over US actions on Taiwan, the two superpowers managed to find some common

ground as they both expressed their opposition to the use of
nuclear weapons in Ukraine. In their meeting, Biden and Xi
agreed to set up what they called a new 'strategic track' of
ongoing meetings and negotiations fronted by Sullivan for the
US and Foreign Minister Wang Li for the PRC.

Wider US–Chinese relations, however, looked like they
might unravel fast. In January 2023, a warning from the
head of the US Air Force's Mobility Command to his
subordinates that he expected war by 2025 was widely
covered by US and foreign media. That prompted a
swift Pentagon edict clamping down on that kind of
speculation in official communications – but there was clear
public acknowledgement of the growing risk.[8]

'The geostrategic history of the century will likely be
determined by the United States–China relationship and
whether it remains in competition or tips into a great power
war,' Chairman of the Joint Chiefs of Staff Mark Milley told the
National Press Club in Washington that June.[9] Throughout
2021 and 2022 – the first two years of the Biden administration –
US–China trade continued to increase, rebounding healthily
after the coronavirus pandemic. By the start of 2023, however,
it was in freefall, dropping by 25 per cent in the first six months
of that year, with Mexico replacing China as the largest US
trade partner.

Increased speculation about potential conflict was becoming
widespread – the US was particularly worried by the complete
cessation of military-to-military communications. 'This is
something that we want to solve,' said White House National
Security Council spokesman John Kirby, adding that not to do
so increased the risk of 'miscalculation'. Signs of US outreach
included visits to Beijing by Secretary of State Blinken and
Treasury Secretary Janet Yellen, as well as a visit by Henry
Kissinger himself, now almost a century old and clearly in
the final stages of his life. Still, as architect of the Nixon
administration's original outreach to China in the 1970s – and

with decades of business links with the country through his consultancy – he enjoyed both access and goodwill no serving US official could begin to match.

Kissinger received a direct audience with Xi, and referred to him as 'old friend'. But the breakthroughs were extremely limited – an agreement to increase the number of US–China commercial airline flights between the two nations from 12 to 20 every week was reached. That was a fraction of the number before the pandemic, and another measure of just how disconnected, both economically and diplomatically, the US and China were rapidly becoming.[10] Then Kissinger died in November 2023. Taking things further would be down to Sullivan, with several encounters a year in cities like Vienna and Bangkok setting the scene for direct summits between Xi and Biden in late 2023 and 2024 respectively.

For their meetings in between the national leader summits, Sullivan and Wang would meet for around six hours a day for two days, then fly out again. 'It's pretty barebones,' complained one US official. 'You fly in, you drive to the hotel, you go into the room, you sit there for hours and hours … It's the least glamorous way to see the world.' US officials tried to inject as much spontaneity as possible to allow open discussions, sometimes even shifting the topic to travel, sport or culture before returning to the tougher issues.[11] Just keeping the conversation going was an achievement in itself. But that could take hours of listening to endlessly repeated Chinese talking points.

The man across the table, 'Director Wang' – his position as director of the Chinese Communist Party (CCP) Central Committee Foreign Affairs Commission was theoretically senior to his simultaneous role as foreign minister – came from a very different generation to Sullivan and those around him. Born in Beijing in 1953, he had been forced to work as a farm labourer during the Cultural Revolution before marrying into elite diplomatic circles. As ambassador to Tokyo from 2003, he had presented himself as a freethinker who enjoyed smart suits and golf. But in the years that followed, with China growing more assertive and Xi Jinping more powerful, Wang had re-engineered himself as a nationalist 'wolf warrior' diplomat whose loyalty was unquestioned.[12]

It was a reputation that had made him China's top official dealing with Taiwan, then foreign minister from 2013 and finally taken him to the top CCP foreign policy directorship nine years later. The man who replaced him at the foreign ministry, former Washington DC ambassador Qin Gang, had survived barely nine months in the role. A one-time favourite of the Chinese president, he had vanished from public life in July 2023. Within China, rumours variously described him as imprisoned, executed, held drugged in a hospital for the top elite or demoted to obscurity to run a party bookstore.[13]

What Qin had done wrong remained opaque – there was talk of an affair with a glamorous TV star (also now disappeared) said to have been a Western spy, while others said Xi felt Qin had become self-centred and outspoken, damaging US relations.[14] Whatever the truth, Wang – like other Chinese top officials – knew that he could not take risks: if he upset his master in Beijing, he might not be seen again.

Sullivan was no stranger to such tactics – nor the very different blame games of Washington. From the chaotic withdrawal from Afghanistan to Ukraine's struggles on the battlefield, he was the one most often on the receiving end of public criticism when things went very wrong. To an extent, it was part of his job. In 2012, barely four years into his career at the very top of government, he told students at the University of Minnesota that when he first began attending meetings in the Supreme Court or White House situation room, he felt both he and those around him were something of a fraud. 'There must be another room, somewhere down the hall, where the real meeting is happening, where the real experts are, making the real decisions,' he said. 'Because it can't just be us. It can't just be this . . . Turns out that it is.' Public policy, he said, was a 'study in imperfection. It involves imperfect people, with imperfect information, making imperfect choices – so it's not surprising that they're getting imperfect results.'[15] Those results would get even more imperfect in Biden's final year in office.

As Sullivan sat down with Wang in an air-conditioned Bangkok room in January 2024, the administration believed they might have another presidential term to come. At 81, Biden was the oldest to ever hold the office, let alone seek re-election – but he was determined to have another go.[16] It was a decision that would contribute to disaster for the Democrats, and usher in a very different era of US foreign policy.

*

While it would be an overstatement to describe the Hamas attack on Israel on October 7, 2023 as the straw that broke the camel's back of US global military dominance, the conflict that followed showed the growing limits of that military power, and the increasing vulnerability of US forces to both ever-deadlier new technology and more capable hostile forces.

The Hamas onslaught had – like all major flashpoints of the era – been a long time coming. The battle for what some still called the Holy Land had been raging for millennia, nudged into an even higher gear by the establishment of the state of Israel in 1948 following the Nazi Holocaust in Europe. What felt almost miraculous for the arriving and often traumatised Jews of Europe was a disaster for the Palestinians who had dwelt there for centuries. More than seven decades later they still refer to it simply as the '*Nakba*': the 'catastrophe'.

No sooner had Israel come into existence than it faced repeated attempts to destroy it from most of its Arab neighbours. In fact, those conflicts only led to its expansion: by the time the guns fell silent, Israel's borders had expanded into areas including the old city of Jerusalem and the Golan Heights that once belonged to Syria. The Palestinians, meanwhile, found themselves either in refugee camps or in what had become the two 'Palestinian Territories' of the West Bank and Gaza. In 2004, Israeli troops and settlers who had been occupying much of Gaza were withdrawn as part of an internationally brokered peace deal, followed by elections that led to a messy power-sharing deal between the moderate Fatah and much more Islamist Hamas. The latter surprised the West, Israel and Fatah by winning elections in Gaza – and, having been frozen out of power, Hamas fighters seized the Strip from the Fatah-run Palestinian Authority in a lightning five-day military assault in June 2007.

By the summer of 2023, 16 years after the initial takeover and a series of bloody military interventions, the Israeli military and intelligence establishment believed they had the Gaza situation finally controlled – not to mention subject to high-tech surveillance that could detect and destroy any new threat. In late September, barely a week before Hamas launched its surprise attack, Israeli officials took Chairman of NATO's Military Committee Dutch Admiral Robert Bauer on a tour of the frontline there, showing off the high-tech operation centre, automated weapons systems and artificial intelligence programs.[17] In fact, those very same command centres were about to witness one of the most devastating systemic intelligence and military failures of the modern era.

It was an example that would give those responsible for defending Europe, Taiwan or even the US mainland sleepless nights for years to come. To make it all the worse, it soon transpired after the assault that there had indeed been warnings, but they had been ignored. Israel was one of the very few countries to conscript women in the modern era – something multiple European nations including Britain, Russia and Nazi Germany had done during World War Two. The duty of some of those young women was to watch the surveillance feeds from Gaza from bunkers and control rooms sometimes within sight of the border. For many, it was the first time away from their families, and they would bond through dance routines, cooking and their shared focus on the footage they watched every day for hours.

By late September 2023, their WhatsApp group chat recorded a sense of growing worry. 'What, there is another event?' asked one. 'Girl, where you been?' replied another. 'We had one every day for the past two weeks.' One female conscript would later recall watching Hamas fighters training along the border. 'They even had a model tank that they were practising how to take over,' she said. The reports were logged and sent on to more senior commanders, but they were ignored. When the attack came, some of their patrol bases were among the first to be overrun.

At least one Israeli former major general would tell the BBC he believed 'chauvinism' might have been a factor in failure to act. But an overreliance on technology almost certainly contributed, as well as 'groupthink' within the Israeli security establishment that Hamas had been ground down by years of blockades and strikes, and had abandoned ambitions for a large attack.[18]

Israel's high-tech systems should have delivered one final warning of the attack. A later investigation by the Israeli army revealed the sudden activation of several hundred Israeli mobile phone SIM cards by Hamas fighters, the last stage of preparation before the assault was launched. Instead, the frontier was under-garrisoned during an Israeli holiday, and Israeli commanders did not have a full picture of the battlefield until midway through the day. By then most of the 1,200 Israeli victims of the attack had already been killed, while its 'Iron Dome' air defences were briefly overwhelmed by the sheer number of rockets fired from Gaza.[19]

Within days, Israel was calling up reserves for its largest ever assault into the Gaza Strip, the start of a campaign that would kill more than 55,000 Palestinians in the first 18 months alone and leave the enclave in ruins.[20] Over the following

weeks and months, Iran's regional proxies began their own
response, including rocket and drone attacks on US outposts
in Iraq and Syria. Without the rapid presence of America's
newest aircraft carrier the *Gerald Ford* in the Mediterranean,
US Defense Secretary Lloyd Austin later told reporters he
believed the immediate regional escalation could have been
much worse.[21]

He may well have been right. The overwhelming US
military presence in the region almost certainly acted as a
deterrent to Hezbollah in Lebanon, persuading them not to
attempt to take advantage of the situation by launching their
own attacks on Israel. But that did not stop escalation further
south from Yemen, where Iran-backed ethnic Houthi militants
who ran much of the country were soon launching long-range
rockets at not just Israel but also nearby cargo vessels.

It was a fight that soon brought the US Navy into one of its
most intensive periods of action since 1945, burning through
missile stocks at an unprecedented rate and supercharging
existing worries that the US lacked the necessary weapons
stocks to sustain a major war.

As the crew of the carrier *Dwight D. Eisenhower,* her
accompanying cruiser and four destroyer escorts of Carrier
Strike Group Two prepared to leave the Eastern Seaboard in
October 2023, they expected to head for Europe for months of
NATO drills, including STEADFAST DEFENDER, and
to replace the *Ford* so she could return to the United States. In
the words of *Eisenhower* captain Christopher 'Chowdah' Hill,
that 'all went out the window' after the surprise Hamas attack
from Gaza.[22]

In early November, *Eisenhower* and escorts passed south
through the Suez Canal and entered the Red Sea.[23] By the end
of December there had been more than 20 attacks on shipping,
largely on vessels linked to Israel but also against US warships,
most beaten off by the missile defence destroyers operating
around the *Eisenhower* as well as aircraft from the carrier itself.[24]

The Biden administration was at first reluctant to respond. But with US troop detachments in Syria and Iraq also being hit by Iran-backed militia, from January the White House authorised strikes against Houthi targets in Yemen, joined initially by a couple of British warplanes flying from Cyprus supported by aerial tankers for refuelling.[25]

For those in the *Eisenhower* battle group, this became a round-the-clock confrontation until they left the region six months later. 'This was the first time we've seen ballistic missiles shot [at ships] in combat, the first time they've been shot down by our ships,' said Hill. 'We knew drones would be coming – we've been talking about this for decades – and now we saw them. One of the things that I was challenged with was making sure people were getting the right amount of sleep so they could perform well, that they had good reaction times.'[26]

Modern warfare was a sleep-depriving business, particularly at sea: on their own eight-month deployment, the 4,000-strong crew of USS *Ford* consumed well over 150,000 cans of the energy drink Red Bull.[27] On some occasions, Hill said he found himself on the *Eisenhower* bridge during an engagement wearing his pyjamas – and accepting that would happen was part of adapting to the tempo. So was keeping a relentless eye on his crew morale – the average age was less than 25, and he would pull as many as possible of his crew through his personal briefing room for small group discussions.

One of the advantages for this deployment, Hill later recalled, was that the carrier now had continuous satellite Wi-Fi connectivity except for periods when it was turned off for operational necessity. That allowed crew members to communicate with loved ones back home – and for the captain himself to become an unexpected star of social media. On his personal feed on X, previously Twitter, Hill posted throughout the ongoing fight, often showcasing how life continued normally on board. Among the most popular features were images and quotations from individual crew members called to the bridge to be given a cookie for their service and a message from their families. Others featured the 'morale dog Captain Demo', or the popular Mexican food-themed 'Taco Tuesdays'. But it was the fact that the ship was doing something to 'make a difference in the world', he said, that provided the greatest engine for morale. 'We felt like we had mission and purpose,' Hill said later. 'We were affecting the enemy . . . [and] showing American resolve.'[28]

The day before the ship re-entered harbour in July 2024, journalists were flown aboard to watch senior US officials praise the battle group and its personnel. 'Our job is to preserve the peace, respond to crises and, if necessary, fight and win decisively, and you delivered on all of those objectives,' said Chief of Naval Operations Lisa Franchetti, America's most senior admiral. Navy Secretary Carlos Del Toro told the battle group its success against the Houthi missiles offered a 'valuable lesson' of the power and reach of US carriers.

Sullivan, who also flew out, told the crew that he had kept the president updated on their actions. 'What stories I got to tell,' he said.[29] Still, when the *Eisenhower* returned to the US, the Red Sea was left without a carrier while attacks on civilian shipping continued unabated. With the *Eisenhower* headed for the dockyard after its extended mission, five of America's 11 carriers were now in some kind of maintenance. Those who staffed the 'aircraft-carrier shuffle' and its equivalent for other US forces described an endless, unforgiving process. As regional headquarters, staff officers, civilians and contractors worked continuously to get aircraft, troops and other resources to the scenes of headline-grabbing crises while also maintaining presence elsewhere to keep allies reassured and enemies deterred.

'There really just aren't enough ships to go around,' said Bradley Martin, a former US Navy surface warfare officer, now director at the RAND Corporation. 'It's a problem of capacity.'[30] As conflict flared and Israel and Iran exchanged missiles later in the year, the US moved two carriers – the *Lincoln* and *Roosevelt* – to waters near Iran, leaving the Pentagon without a carrier in Asia for the first time in decades.[31] Much broader capacity issues were also becoming clear: America's defence industrial base, used to providing the relatively small quantities of weapons needed for the 'war on terror' of the 2000s, was proving comprehensively unable to meet the demands of the modern era. Ukraine had exhausted stocks of artillery, anti-tank and smaller anti-aircraft missiles, and now the fight against the Houthis was chewing through considerably more land-attack and anti-aircraft missiles than were being made.

In the first day of strikes on Yemen, the US Navy said it fired more than 80 Tomahawks – the ultra-accurate long-range cruise missiles that had been at the centre of every major US intervention since the Gulf War in 1991 – considerably more than the 55 it had purchased in the whole of 2023. Over the last decade, the US had procured only just over 1,200 Tomahawks, which suggested even a relatively small campaign might exhaust them completely – and just as new deployments like the 'Typhon' to the Philippines were driving up demand.[32] By the end of the year, Ukraine was also requesting Tomahawks to deter Russia, while the planners at US INDOPACOM likely wanted hundreds to strike targets in China if it came to war.

Air-defence missiles proved another pinch point. The multipurpose US Standard Missile 6 (SM-6) – which could hit air, land or sea targets when fired from a warship – were again fired by the dozen by US vessels in the Middle East in early 2024, almost certainly outstripping the mere 125 individual missiles manufacturer Raytheon said it could produce each year. Stocks of the Patriot air-defence rocket – another weapon first fired in the 1991 Gulf War but which had been considerably improved in later decades – were further in demand, with talk they might also be fitted to warships to make up for a lack of other missiles. How deep Western Patriot stockpiles really were was a closely guarded secret – but they were being dragged into almost every available theatre of operations.[33] In Ukraine, Zelenskyy's government had put further Patriot systems at the top of their wishlist to protect their major cities from aerial attack, while other European nations also wanted more of them. Manufacturer Lockheed Martin declared it would increase production of the most advanced PAC-3 Patriot variant by 70 per cent by 2027 – but with only 380 rockets produced in 2023, that still wasn't very many.[34]

The bottom line was simple: America's three most militarily committed regional combatant commands – INDOPACOM in the Pacific, EUCOM in Europe and CENTCOM in the Middle East – were chasing the same weapons stocks, and the US defence industrial base was not building enough to even come close to meeting the fast-growing need.

That was also now feeding a shortage of warships, including those most critical to any future conflict. The next carriers due to enter service, the *Ford*-class *Enterprise* and *John F. Kennedy*, were running ever further behind when it came to entering the fleet due to problems in construction.[35] Submarine construction was if anything even worse performing, in part the consequence of a lack of skilled engineers and welders to build such hugely complex vessels – including the *Columbia* class that would carry the next generation of US ballistic missiles to deliver a deterrent from the early 2030s.[36]

Beyond that were broader worries over the stability of supply chains often relied upon for decades – not just microchips from Taiwan but a host of critical minerals and components, many currently supplied from China. A review of such dangers ordered by the Biden administration in its last months in office concluded perhaps a touch self-servingly that matters were better than in 2021, when the aftermath of the pandemic showed just how strained some supply chains were. But it also flagged ongoing and growing geopolitical risks – and acknowledged the next administration would likely need to do much more.[37]

Squaring many of those circles would be the responsibility of the Pentagon – and it would prove a messy balance of trying to fix problems in the face of a growing maelstrom of headlines and threats, together with the gradual unravelling of the Biden administration's hopes of re-election.

*

As 2024 began, the secretary of defense – often known as 'SECDEF' – was Lloyd Austin, a towering African-American former infantryman who described the military machine he led as the 'strongest fighting force in human history', often adding 'and make no mistake, we're going to keep it that way'. He also frequently quoted a phrase from Biden's inaugural address that described the 2020s as the 'decisive decade' that would determine whether the century would be dominated by democracies or autocrats, before adding his own rather blunter warnings.[38]

Austin took both US military power and deterrence seriously – and, like other SECDEFs both before and since, often gave the impression that he viewed himself as its personal primary messenger. According to multiple sources, in late 2022 he told Russian counterpart Sergei Shoigu that if the Kremlin used a tactical nuclear device against Ukraine, as US intelligence believed it was considering, the US would 'reconsider' all the restraints it had been operating under in that war so far. It was a warning that if the Kremlin 'went nuclear' in any way, America's conventional military would devastate Russia's forces in Ukraine, and possibly beyond. 'I don't take kindly to being threatened,' Shoigu is said to have replied. Austin's response was tougher still: 'I am the leader of the most powerful military in the history of the world,' said Austin. 'I don't make threats.'[39]

Austin had the background needed to make that kind of warning, particularly to someone like Shoigu, who was essentially a bureaucrat and had never served in action. As assistant commander of the US 3rd Infantry Division in the

2003 invasion of Iraq, Austin had become one of only three US generals to win a 'silver star' for combat leadership in the 'war on terror'. As US troops advanced towards Baghdad, he was frequently the farthest forward senior officer, directing the overwhelming firepower the official record described as 'saving the lives of countless soldiers while inflicting catastrophic damage on the Iraqi forces'.[40]

As much as any previous SECDEF, Austin knew the forces and structures that he led. After 2003 he had led a brigade in Afghanistan, a division in Iraq, then commanded the Joint Staff within the Pentagon itself. Between 2013 and 2016, he had commanded CENTCOM against Islamic State. More than six foot three inches tall, and prone to talking of himself in the third person, Austin had come out of his wars with a reputation for being tough and effective – and for not talking to the media. He was both a savvy operator and a practising Roman Catholic, attending services in Iraq in 2008 alongside Joe Biden's eldest son Beau, at the time serving on active duty there as a military lawyer. When Barack Obama selected the older Biden as his running mate later that same year, Austin's already strong reputation was suddenly enhanced with powerful political connections.

When Biden himself took the White House in 2021, Austin was his first pick to run the Pentagon, easily gaining the Congressional waiver he needed to bypass US law requiring secretaries of defense to have spent seven years out of uniform after leaving high military office.[41] In many respects Austin was a master communicator, his frequent speeches mixing policy talking points with personal references and a sense of fun. His discomfort with the press and desire for personal privacy, however, continued throughout his time as secretary. He avoided question-and-answer sessions in the Pentagon briefing room when possible, and frequently ignored the Pentagon press corps who flew with him on his foreign trips.

That desire for privacy would get him into trouble. As 2024 began, the man responsible for the 'most powerful military in the history of the world' was not at his desk in the Pentagon but lying in an intensive care bed at Walter Reed military hospital where he had been taken on New Year's Day following complications from prostate cancer surgery in late December. It was a hospitalisation that would last two weeks – and while by the end of it Austin was working from his bed and taking calls, for the first few days of January he was completely out of action.

That, in itself, was not so serious: Austin had a deputy, Kathleen Hicks, and the US system, like most other forms of government, has multiple ways in which authority can be shared or shifted. But Austin had not shared the news of his hospitalisation, neither with the White House nor apparently with Hicks. For several days at the start of 2024, the entire command structure of the US military was effectively out of joint, something even those at the very top of government only became aware of days later.

Austin apologised, ascribing the failure to his reluctance to 'burden' others – including a 'busy' president – with his medical condition. But the failure of Austin's aides and office to inform the necessary channels pointed to wider problems within the Biden administration that would soon become much harder to ignore. Over the weeks and months that followed, stories would grow of an ageing president losing his grip, those around him attempting to carry on regardless. In time, it would help propel Trump back into the White House.

By the middle of 2024, the Biden team were also highly aware of the challenges facing the US defence industrial base, and the need to build military capability in a hurry. For several years, Navy Secretary Carlos Del Toro had been pushing for the US Navy to reload its warship missile tubes at sea rather than having to sail all the way to port every time their stocks were exhausted. The situation in the Middle East had further flagged that need, with warships sometimes needing to sail hundreds of miles if not more to rearm at bases in Europe or beyond. Throughout 2024, engineering teams worked on the capability to physically lift missiles from offshore barges into warship vertical launch tubes with specially adapted cranes. It was an idea first discussed in the 1990s, but it had taken the threat of real war in the Middle East, and growing fears of even larger Pacific conflict, to deliver the necessary urgency to finally make it happen.[42]

That still left the underlying problem of the missiles themselves – together with plenty of other items of weaponry, ranging from handheld rockets to ballistic missile submarines – that were simply coming off the production line much slower and in lower numbers than needed. Speaking to defence reporters shortly after the November 2024 election, National Security Advisor Jake Sullivan acknowledged that the Biden team had entered office without truly realising just how overstretched the defence industrial base was. 'It was really [in] the lead up to the war in Ukraine . . . that I began to recognise that, in many respects, the cupboard was bare,' he said, adding that the more he dug into the problem the more serious it looked. 'People would produce charts for me – basically going back to 1990 – [showing] the workforce challenges, the supply-chain challenges, the underinvestment. And it became clear to me that this has been a story that I don't think has got the attention it deserved.'[43]

When it came to production of items like artillery shells, the plant producing them had barely been updated since the Korean War in the early 1950s. With hindsight, that was not surprising – America's modern wars had consumed much less ammunition than those that came before, particularly for heavy weapons. Even the first Gulf War in 1991 had left the US with vast amounts of unfired ammunition stocks left over after its conclusion – and, in the era since, the false assumption had quietly grown that items could be ordered and replenished largely based on short-term need.

The return of an era of hugely destructive and potentially long-term military campaigns such as Ukraine – let alone a larger Pacific war – suddenly made that approach look extremely foolish. 'I remember getting lectures about this – that we needed to adopt just-in-time delivery, minimise inventories and drive costs down,' Biden's Undersecretary of Defense William LaPlante told a symposium in 2023. 'Well, that's great until something bad happens. And we've paid a price for it.'[44]

As the new head of INDOPACOM, Admiral Samuel Paparo, assumed command from May 2024, he put 'magazine depth' – stores of sufficient weaponry for war – at the top of his list of worries.

But what type of weaponry? In the Indian Ocean, the US Navy was now trialling crewless wind-powered surveillance drones that could cruise for days or weeks without human intervention, scrutinising passing vessels with both cameras and a range of other sensors. That information was then analysed by algorithms aboard the unmanned ship that could do most of the work identifying them as a potential tanker or small trading craft, and then make its own decision over whether that information should be relayed back to humans at headquarters.

This was 'edge computing', cutting-edge use of artificial intelligence on a weapons system or other platform, bringing the world of Silicon Valley into the defence sector on a scale never seen before.[45] Even more was expected from the Pentagon's ability to build massive secure data 'cloud' networks in conjunction with both established civilian technology firms including Microsoft, Amazon and Google as well as a new generation of high-tech defence contractors. Almost all had advanced technology, its usage dramatically increased during the four years of the Biden administration, and many believed it would accelerate from there.

'Generative AI . . . is probably one of the most disruptive technologies and initiatives in a very long, long time,' US Defence Information Systems Agency director Lieutenant General Robert Skinner told an audience in 2023. 'Those who harness that [and] that can understand how to best leverage it . . . [are] going to be the ones that have the high ground.'[46]

By the time it left office, the Biden administration was predicting more technological change in the coming decade than seen over the 50 years that came before.[47]

America's new top commander in the Pacific wanted all of that technology, and he wanted it as fast as possible. But he also wanted more traditional ships, bombs and missiles – and he was worried that he did not have enough.

Like EUCOM commander Chris Cavoli and INDOPACOM predecessor John Aquilino, Admiral Samuel Paparo came from Italian-American East Coast roots, in his case Pennsylvania. Again like Aquilino, he had been a fast jet pilot and former Top Gun student and instructor who also served tours with the air force in the Middle East and army in Afghanistan. 'It's all been leading up to this,' US Defense Secretary Lloyd Austin told him as he offered his congratulations.[48] Outgoing commander Aquilino described the US Indo-Pacific team as 'the best of the best, in the most crucial theatre, against the most challenging threat. They will serve you well.'[49]

Unlike many other US admirals, Paparo had not come through the Naval Academy at Annapolis, instead gaining his commission through the Reserve Officer Training Corps at Villanova Catholic University. He remained openly religious, telling the *Hawaii Catholic Herald* shortly after his appointment that he listened to a Bible podcast every morning and used specific verses for calm, wisdom and strength.[50]

His worries in the office, however, were deeply worldly. Summer 2024 would see the largest ever Chinese exercises across the Pacific region. At one point, that would include at least 200 combat ships – roughly three-quarters of China's entire amphibious force – and some 43 brigades of troops, including engineers for breaching obstacles and units optimised for fighting in urban areas. As Paparo later told a think tank in Washington DC, he believed that was not just an exercise: 'That is a rehearsal.' As far as Paparo was concerned, arguments over whether or not China would be ready to blockade or overrun Taiwan by 2027 risked missing the point. 'We need to be ready now,' he said.[51]

At the annual Shangri-La Dialogue international relations meeting in Singapore at the start of June 2024, organised by the International Institute for Strategic Studies, US Defense Secretary Austin, describing the world as being at a decisive 'hinge of history', pledged that the US was 'all in' and talked of a convergence on both sides of the world between democracies determined to maintain the rule of law. With Zelenskyy also speaking at the conference, Austin warned that the Ukraine invasion offered 'a preview of the world that none of us want[s] ... where tyrants trample sovereign borders, where peaceful states live in fear of their neighbours and where chaos and conflict replace rules and right[s]'.[52]

The Chinese had also upped their game rhetorically. In the Q&A session after Austin spoke, a PLA colonel compared Austin's talk of growing partnerships to NATO expansion in Eastern Europe, something the Chinese officer then blamed for the conflict in Ukraine. 'I respectfully disagree with your point that the expansion of NATO caused the Ukraine crisis,' said Austin, to applause from other gathered delegates. What the US was building in Asia, he said, was not a formal structure like NATO but a collection of 'like-minded countries with similar values and a common vision of a free and open Indo-Pacific ... working together to achieve that vision.'

Austin also outlined a range of new defence industrial partnerships, including work with India on jet engines and Japan on an interceptor missile to counter hypersonic threats such as the Chinese 'carrier killing' DF-26. America's approach, he said, '... isn't about imposing one country's will. It's about a sense of common purpose. It isn't bullying or coercion.'[53]

Although he did not reveal it at the time, the US admiral had another move up his sleeve he hoped would deepen US deterrence. On the sidelines of the conference, he sat down with *Washington Post* columnist Josh Rogin, one of the best-connected foreign policy journalists, who had started out as the DC stringer for a Japanese newspaper at the start of the 'global war on terror'. To Rogin, Paparo outlined in more graphic detail than anybody had before INDOPACOM's plan to save Taiwan.

The PLA's aim, he predicted – as he had during his confirmation hearing at the Senate – would likely be to grab control of the island as swiftly as possible before significant US forces arrived to intervene. The 'hellscape' concept outlined by his predecessor offered the US and its allies a solution to that problem, a way of fast deploying – or pre-deploying – enough autonomous weapons systems to ruin Beijing's plans, either by stopping an invasion force or cutting it off from resupply. 'I want to turn the Taiwan Strait into a hellscape with a number of classified capabilities,' the admiral told the reporter. 'I can't tell you what's in it,' he said, when pressed about details of the plan. 'But it's real and it's deliverable.' What that meant, he said, was making life for Chinese commanders 'utterly miserable for a month, which buys me enough time for the rest of everything'.

Elements of that story had been told the preceding summer – but the *Washington Post* piece blasted them to a wider audience.[54] Indeed, some in China now suspected America's heightened talk of how ready it would be to protect Taiwan in a few years' time might be a deliberate gambit to make the PLA attack before it was truly ready. According to a subsequent *Financial Times* story citing European sources, China's president had suggested to President of the European Commission Ursula von der Leyen that he believed the US was trying to 'goad' Beijing into moving quickly against Taiwan, something he said the PRC would not do. If anything, that only served to deepen worries in Washington about decision-making at the top in China. 'If Xi genuinely believes that the US actively seeks conflict with China over Taiwan, then concerns that Xi has created an information vacuum, or is otherwise getting poor counsel from subordinates, are worryingly true,' said China expert Jude Blanchette.[55]

But the Biden administration was almost out of luck and time. The July 2024 gathering of NATO leaders in Washington DC had been intended to seal the lasting impression that the Biden administration was leading a successful global team of democracies to confront the autocrats. Instead, it was refocusing on efforts to 'Trump-proof' the alliance, such as transferring elements of the US-led process managing weapons supplies to Ukraine to be run through Europe and NATO. If that was not enough to show power slipping from the White House in the aftermath of the president's poor debate performance, the moment he called Ukraine's President Zelenskyy 'President Putin' by mistake arguably sealed his fate. By the end of July Biden had backed out of the race in favour of Vice President Kamala Harris.

Even after the election loss, what was left of the administration kept trying to shore up the 'international consensus' it hoped would be its legacy. Visiting the Pacific for the last time in December 2024, Defense Secretary Austin met Australian and Japanese counterparts in the northern Australian base where Japanese troops would now be trained for part of the year alongside the US Marine detachment who had rotated through annually for almost a decade. Visiting the Philippines shortly afterwards, he signed a deal to provide its military with reconnaissance drones to keep up surveillance on disputed reefs and potentially resupply its outposts, such as the *Sierra Madre*.

In the last weeks of the administration, it poured additional US weaponry into both Ukraine and Taiwan, including multiple systems previously held back – in the case of Taiwan, sometimes for several years. In Ukraine, some restrictions previously imposed on long-range missiles to strike deep into Russian territory were also finally eased. But there was an awareness that the era was changing. On his last visit to Kyiv before the US election in October, Austin had again used his phrase from the Shangri-La Dialogue in Singapore – 'the hinge of history' – to describe the moment. 'For anyone who feels that American leadership is expensive,' he had warned, 'consider the price of American retreat.'[56]

It was strong rhetoric – and it could have come from almost any US defense secretary back to Truman's day, including those who had served under and so often clashed with Trump in his first term. The incoming administration would face the same and growing threats, and would sometimes make not-that-dissimilar choices. But in other ways it would be very different, and it was about to take every opportunity it got to show the world just that.

5

Trump Shakes the World

It was January 20, 2025, just over four years since pro-Trump protesters had stormed Capitol Hill in Washington DC – but the scene could hardly have been more different. Alongside the Trump dynasty sat the heads of the largest US and global tech firms. Between them, Amazon founder Jeff Bezos, Google CEO Sundar Pichai, Facebook founder Mark Zuckerberg, Apple CEO Tim Cook and Elon Musk of Tesla and SpaceX were valued at more than $1 trillion. Their highly public presence – closer to Trump than his incoming cabinet members' – suggested the returning president was doubling down on embracing power and money, both his own and other people's.[2]

'My proudest legacy will be that of a peacemaker and a unifier,' said Trump, pledging to control America's borders, put tariffs on its rivals and ensure a new era of 'peace through strength'. At the heart of the speech were two words barely used by US presidents since the 19th century – 'manifest destiny' – and an eye-catching pledge to not just rebuild America but 'expand its territory'. The inaugural address explicitly promised to return the Panama Canal to US control 'from China', and raise the US flag on Mars. America's alliances and partnerships simply went unmentioned.[3]

In the weeks before and after his inauguration, Trump and those around him unleashed a deliberately overwhelming barrage of domestic and foreign policy suggestions, announcements and executive orders. During his first term, the president and his supporters had believed large elements of the federal government – and also US foreign partners – had worked to hold back his agenda. They were determined there should be no chance of that this time around – those in top jobs were chosen first and foremost for their loyalty and commitment to the president and his platform. They would put 'America first' above all else, and had no objection to public rows with enemies or allies.

Within days, the first of these had erupted over Trump's ambitions to make Greenland part of the United States, much to the immediate frustration and nervousness of Denmark, which had administered it for centuries – and that was just the start of the relentless news flow.

There was, in some quarters at least, still substantial belief that Trump's sheer unpredictability might deter foreign aggressors from taking risks for as long as he remained in Washington – and that the US president might be correct when he argued that Putin's invasion of Crimea would not have happened had he occupied the White House. As long-term backer Senator Lindsey Graham put it less than a month into the new term: 'I'm tired of worrying about being provocative to bad guys – I want them to fear us . . . I think if you don't fear Donald Trump, then you're a little crazy.'[4]

Anyone who had hoped the new administration would supercharge the cause of Western capitalist democracies against a Moscow–Beijing-led autocratic alliance was set for rapid disappointment. Even more than during his first term, the new president and those around him were determined to entrench their power – and in their early months they often appeared more comfortable dealing with autocrats than those in democracies. At the very least, the new administration was more openly transactional than anything seen before.

As former British Foreign Secretary David Miliband put it, 'Trump was elected as a disruptor. The message is: "buckle up". They don't buy the argument that America benefits from its global stabilising role. One should respect the electoral mandate he has, but also understand that he's not kidding.' Speaking to personnel at the US State Department, new Secretary of State Marco Rubio told them US foreign policy would be '. . . focused on one thing: the advancement of interest. Anything that makes us stronger or safer or more prosperous, that will be our mission.'[5]

It was an approach that would bring a very different foreign policy and a very different Pentagon, but also an even more eccentric team around the president. 'Trump prizes loyalty above all,' observed my Reuters White House press corps colleague Jeff Mason shortly after Trump fired Chairman of the Joint Chiefs US Air Force General 'CQ' Brown, Chief of Naval Operations Admiral Lisa Franchetti and several other senior military officials, including the head lawyers of each service. 'He has no qualms whatsoever about appointing who he wants and getting what he wants.'[6]

Unsurprisingly, some talked of the beginnings of an 'imperial presidency' – and certainly, at least until the midterms in 2026, Trump had the votes in Congress to appoint who he might wish.[7] When it came to foreign affairs, however, it increasingly seemed as though he was hoping to build one kind of 'imperial America', a sphere of unchallenged influence from the Panama Canal to Canada and Greenland, while pulling back elsewhere – at the cost of tearing up the 'Pax Americana' of US global influence built up over decades.

It was a worldview that flirted with outright isolationism and initially espoused a much less interventionist approach than the US had pursued in decades. Speaking at the swearing-in of Defense Secretary Pete Hegseth, Vice President JD Vance said that what separated Trump from past presidents was his belief that, 'We should be sparing in how we deploy our most precious resource . . . the men and women who are willing to put on the uniform and put their life on the line for this country. We shouldn't send them everywhere.' Hegseth – already, like his predecessor Austin, getting well-drilled in his talking points – put it slightly differently, but with the same underlying sentiment. 'We don't want to fight wars, we want to deter them . . . and end them responsibly . . . But if we need to fight them, we are going to bring overwhelming and decisive force . . . and bring our boys home.'[8]

Vance and Hegseth were both veterans of the 'war on terror', and such sentiments were entirely understandable. Almost eight decades earlier another American soldier considering a switch to politics had admitted similar feelings to his diary. 'God knows, I personally would like to see the United States sit at home and ignore the rest of the world,' Dwight D. Eisenhower wrote in March 1951, shortly after becoming NATO's top commander. 'What a pleasing prospect, until you look at the ultimate consequences: disaster.'[9]

Running for the presidency a year later, Eisenhower had done more than any other to lock in decades of US commitment on both sides of the planet. But even as he wrote those words, a young Donald Trump was approaching his fifth birthday. As he entered adulthood and gained fame and fortune, he would come to look at the Cold War not as a series of lines that must be held to avert catastrophe, but an opportunity for 'a deal' – with him as the top US negotiator.

*

The world in which Trump first built his reputation in the late 1970s and early 1980s was perhaps uniquely open to his kind of relentless self-promotion – but it was also in its most perilous state since the Cuban Missile Crisis in 1962. The most dangerous point, with hindsight, came through the winter of 1983–1984, as the paranoia of a declining Soviet empire led to officials, commanders and spies there wrongly interpreting the deployment of short-range US missiles and the most realistic

NATO drills in years as a genuine threat and precursor to a real strike.

An April 1984 profile in the *New York Times* by journalist and broadcaster Bill Geist described Trump as the 'man of the hour', quoting various fans describing him as an 'unbelievable negotiator' and 'mad and exciting'. But, Geist noted, Trump's bombastic mood was occasionally interrupted by moments of introspection in which he mused that his power, money and profile – and that of the buzzing city round him – might be gone at any moment. 'But what does it all mean?' Geist reported Trump saying more than once. Pressed on what he was thinking, Trump said that what really worried him was the risk of catastrophic atomic war. His solution, though, was simple: let him negotiate a way out of the nightmare as America's arms envoy.

That suggestion produced by far the most negative paragraphs of a broadly friendly profile: the idea that Trump might be allowed to negotiate for the United States, Geist wrote, would 'seem the naive musing of an optimistic, deluded young man who has never lost at anything he tried'.[10] But Trump wasn't giving up – interviewed for his first profile in the *Washington Post* later that same year, he pitched that idea again. 'Some people have an ability to negotiate,' Trump said. 'It's an art you're basically born with ... It would take an hour and a half to learn everything there is to learn about missiles ... I think I know most of it anyway.'[11]

When the hoped-for call from President Reagan did not come, Trump took matters into his own hands. In 1986, he approached Nobel Prize-winning cardiologist Bernard Lown, who had shared the prize with a Soviet doctor and met with Mikhail Gorbachev the previous year. According to Lown, almost four decades later, Trump asked him to facilitate a meeting with the Soviet leader – and talked again of reaching out to the administration to become the top negotiator for US–Soviet nuclear disarmament.[12]

What the Russians made of this is anybody's guess – and there are plenty of theories. What we do know is that with the Cold War coming to an end, Gorbachev – still expecting to be in power for years, and for the Soviet Union to remain intact – was reaching out across the board to help build what he hoped would be a very different US–Soviet dominated world. In early 1986, by Trump's own account, he was invited to Moscow to discuss hotel investments, and finally won his meeting with Gorbachev.

What happened there – and on the rest of the trip – remains shrouded in mystery, but on his return to New York Trump gave several hints he was preparing to run for president. He spent almost $100,000 of his own money taking out adverts in the *New York Times*, *Washington Post* and other papers declaring that the country just needed a little 'backbone' to fix US defence and accusing US allies of freeloading. Then, despite speculation he might run in the New Hampshire primaries with the encouragement of a local businessman, he seemed to drop the idea entirely.[13]

At roughly the same time, Trump's ghostwriter on his 1987 bestseller *Art of the Deal*, Tony Schwartz, concluded Trump had an overwhelming and continuous need to be seen as 'strong' and 'winning' – something he attributed in part to a distant and demanding father who Trump found he could only interact with as a 'businessman'. Throughout the writing process, Trump would call Schwartz most evenings to recount his latest exploits. Only years later would Schwartz discover The Trump Organization had been skirting the edge of bankruptcy. 'He lied as easily as he breathed . . . and without a hint of a guilty conscience,' he wrote in 2024. '[But] what struck me from the first day I met Mr Trump was his unquenchable thirst to be the centre of attention. No amount of external recognition ever seemed to be enough.'[14]

Trump was easy to mock – but even easier to underestimate. When he proposed again, in mid-2015, that he might run for the White House, some suggested it was simply a publicity stunt. Instead, he upended US politics and set history on a different path.

Before he entered the presidential race in mid-2015, most Americans had expected their next president to be either Hillary Clinton or Jeb Bush. It was, many conceded, an uninspiring choice: either the wife of the man who had left office in 2000 or the brother of the one who had left in 2009. By July 2015, the star of *The Apprentice* had demolished the younger Bush's ten-point lead in the Republican primaries and was headed for the White House.[15]

Trump's return in the 2024 election again guaranteed him the attention that he craved – but he was coming back with not just an agenda but a praetorian guard of senior 'Make America Great Again' (MAGA) figures determined to support him even as they pursued their own agendas.

That was what had some of America's allies most concerned. Unlike in the first Trump administration, this time much of the heavy lifting was being done by a much smaller and ideologically committed group of individuals, some of whom might well be around for years, particularly if the Democrats continued to struggle to get their act together. 'There are only 12 people who count in this administration, and six of them are Steve Witkoff,' Alex Ward, senior national security correspondent for the *Wall Street Journal*, told a think tank event early in the new administration, only half joking. He was referring to Trump's friend, former business partner and now envoy to the Middle East who frequently also inherited other issues including the Ukraine war.[16]

The result would be particularly infuriating for Washington's think tank and journalist community: policymaking tightly held among a handful of individuals, most of whom were themselves continually working to assess what the president himself actually wanted them to do. It made a dramatic contrast to the more traditional approach inevitably favoured by the

Washington 'machine', in which large circles of advisers and those who worked to influence them helped 'create consensus' around policy proposals, then took them to the decision-makers who would put them into practice.

For the ideologues around the president, the next step was obvious: dramatically shrink the remainder of the government, including elements seen as vital to foreign and defence policy, now all part of a campaign initially driven by Elon Musk before his own dramatic fall from favour. Among the first to go was America's humanitarian aid agency USAID, now folded into the State Department which would itself soon see a cull of more than a thousand diplomats. Atop that sat Rubio as Secretary of State, the former Florida senator whose reputation working across the aisle had seen him confirmed into that office by the Senate by 99 votes to none now working furiously to promote the Trump agenda. 'The Marco Rubio that used to talk about the importance of democracy and human rights, freedom of speech as part of American foreign policy has disappeared,' protested Maryland Senator Chris Van Hollen, complaining of what he called a 'MAGA brain transplant'.

One Rubio aide told the *Washington Post* that those who had hoped he would be the 'adult in the room' had neglected to remember that the purpose of cabinet appointees was to support the decisions of the democratically elected president. Certainly, Trump himself appeared initially impressed. 'When I have a problem, I call up Marco; he gets it solved,' he told reporters later in the year. Such comments did nothing to cool speculation that Rubio – who had first run for president in 2016 – still held those ambitions, and hoped his support for Trump and MAGA – and reputation as an 'adult' – might yet take him to the top.[17]

For now, however, the presumed front runner in that race was Vice President JD Vance, whose behaviour in the first weeks of Trump's new term in office would do more than any other to upset US allies and convince them that their world had changed. If he was successful in gaining the Republican presidential nomination in 2028 and then took the White House, he could be in power until January 2037.

Those at the very centre – particularly the president – were now more powerful than ever, while those in positions down a rung or two found their voices silenced. Some personnel within the US military – such as regional combatant commanders – found themselves dissuaded and then apparently outright banned from many of their prior engagements including with think tanks where they might have talked on policy. 'It is absolutely to control who says what, where and when,' one US official told Politico.[18]

*

Like Trump, Vice President JD Vance was easy to underestimate. Aged just 40 as he took office as vice president, he now had access to both power and financial backing, and clearly intended to use his office to shape the agenda like no vice president before him. His background – both his childhood and military service – was unlike that of anyone who had held real power in recent US history. As became clear, that had shaped his worldview and his temperament – and that combination would have significant effect.

Vance hailed from a mixed Irish–Scottish ancestry and had grown up in searing intergenerational poverty in the poorest of white communities in Ohio. Like the generations of poor from such a background who had filled the ranks of the US and also British armies going back to the US war of independence, he saw enlisting in the US Marines as a way out and up. Serving in Iraq as a photographer and journalist with the marines but never seeing combat, he used his 'GI Bill' funding to get into Ohio State University, opening the door to a law degree at Yale – and a host of other opportunities: that included meeting US tech billionaire Peter Thiel who helped back his political career and election to the Senate in 2022.

It was a meteoric rise – but, by his own admission in the bestselling autobiography that had helped bring him to power, the challenges of his background had left him with, like many of the leaders of the 2020s, a visceral aversion to showing weakness, and an instinct to react overwhelmingly to perceived or actual slights. In his book he noted one occasion in which his new wife Usha had been forced to talk him down from beating up a driver he felt had wronged him on the roadway – something he acknowledged made him sound 'like a lunatic'.

'I see conflict and I run away or prepare for battle,' he wrote, noting that 'the very traits that enabled my survival during childhood inhibit my success as an adult'. His wife, he added, had to remind him that not every 'perceived slight' was a reason for a 'blood feud'.[19] Even more than Trump, Vance preached that America should prioritise its own people and interests first before it tried to fix anything overseas – and he also had a long tradition of railing against what he saw as excessive Islamic immigration into Europe. In mid-2024, he had suggested a Muslim-dominated Britain might become the first 'Islamist nation' with an atomic bomb.[20]

Such comments – and that temperament – augured an almost immediate row with Europe. Visiting the Munich Security Conference for his first big foreign policy speech in mid-February 2025, Vance chose a topic that he knew would shock, grab headlines and infuriate his European hosts: attacking European nations for their immigration policies over decades in what was almost a full-throated endorsement of the right-wing 'Alternative for Deutschland' party barely a week before German elections.

Attending the same event the previous year as a freshman Ohio senator, some in the foreign policy community recalled that Vance had been treated as something of an 'oddity' – and certainly not treated with the respect that he believed he deserved.[21] If this was his revenge, then it was a deliberate display of political firepower designed to infuriate Europe's political establishment, particularly in Germany where he criticised the 'firewall' agreement between more moderate parties to keep the far right out of coalitions.

Pouring salt on the wounds already opened up by Elon Musk, Vance also laid into European nations for their efforts to limit the spread of suspected online disinformation, as well as the recent decision to suspend and then postpone Romania's presidential election after reports of Russian interference. 'In Britain, and across Europe, free speech, I fear, is in retreat,' claimed the vice president, accusing authorities in Germany, the UK, Sweden and beyond of imposing 'thought crime' restrictions on citizens who opposed them on anything from abortion to migration. 'If your democracy can be destroyed by a few thousand dollars of digital advertising from another country, then it wasn't very strong to begin with.'[22] That line was one of the few in the speech to win him some applause – but, by the time he finished, Vance had established himself as something of a hate figure among not just a whole generation of European leaders but many others on the continent.

The visit by Ukraine's President Zelenskyy to the White House at the end of February 2025 would cement that reputation – as well spook many of America's closest allies more than anything seen in recent history.

*

According to multiple accounts, the US–Ukraine relationship was already in trouble when Zelenskyy arrived in Washington on February 29. Despite that, what was expected to be a short chat in front of the press corps began relatively well. In their opening statements, Trump praised the bravery of Ukraine's troops and Zelenskyy talked of the importance of US support, as well as the prospect of collaboration on drones and other fronts. Zelenskyy's comments were less focused than they might have been, bouncing through various talking points, including prisoners, captured Ukrainian priests, a need for long-term security guarantees and for occupied territory to be restored. Matters remained broadly good-natured as the press questions began, although the Ukrainian leader – who had pointedly worn only military-style fatigues since the first day of the invasion – did not conceal his irritation when asked why he did not wear a suit.[23] According to several US sources, Trump's envoy on Ukraine Keith Kellogg and Senator Lindsey Graham had both lobbied Zelenskyy to turn up in more formal clothing.[24] Even after that question, however, the discussion remained friendly.

In more normal times and with more traditional leaders, the press would soon have been removed and the real discussions commenced in private. To the reporters there and those watching on TV, it was unclear why this did not happen, or why neither team did not bring things to a close. Given the style of the two leaders perhaps no one could have done so.

Roughly 30 minutes in, Zelenskyy said that he would take one more 'serious question' – but ten minutes later, the discussion was still going and Trump too was getting testy, particularly when criticised for talking to Putin. 'If I didn't align myself with both of them [Ukraine and Russia], you would never have a deal,' he snapped. Then, almost exactly 40 minutes into what should have been a short press conference, JD Vance stepped in. His opening comment was relatively bland compared to what followed, criticising the Biden administration for 'thumping our chest' and praising Trump for 'engaging in diplomacy'.

Then things unravelled fast, as Zelenskyy said Putin could not be trusted and talked of a decade of failed diplomacy from 2014 – including during the first Trump administration. 'What kind of diplomacy are you talking about, JD?' asked the Ukrainian president. 'I'm talking about the kind of diplomacy that is going to end the destruction of your country,' replied Vance. When Zelenskyy said that Vance should visit Ukraine, the vice president dismissed such trips as 'propaganda tours' and accused Zelenskyy of disrespecting Trump by attempting to 'litigate' in front of the assembled press. As Zelenskyy folded his arms and Vance jabbed his finger at him, some of those watching online believed they saw the Ukrainian president mutter the word '*cyka*' – roughly meaning 'bitch'.[25]

Another photo shared by CNN reporter Kaitlan Collins showed Ukraine's ambassador to Washington Oksana Markarova with her head in her hands, while a nearby Secretary of Defense Hegseth looked forward with the most neutral expression he could muster.[26] Zelenskyy, Trump and Vance were now talking furiously across each other in an exchange unlike anything broadcast from the Oval Office before, to the generally appalled fascination of those watching. Vance kept up the offensive, accusing Zelenskyy of campaigning for the Democrats in the 2024 election and demanding that he publicly thank Trump and the current administration for the ongoing US support to Ukraine. Trump himself kept on telling Zelenskyy that he did not 'have the cards' to succeed in the current negotiations without strong US backing. 'You're gambling with World War Three,' Trump told him. 'What you're doing is very disrespectful to this country.'

By the end, Trump appeared to be praising Putin for sticking with him through a 'phony witch-hunt' around allegations of Russian interference in the 2016 election, while doubling down on Vance's warnings that Zelenskyy was not being grateful and risked losing his war. 'I will say this,' said Trump as the ending finally came. 'This will make great television.'[27]

The US and Ukrainian delegations were supposed to head on to lunch, and then conduct the signing of a mineral deal. Instead the Ukrainians were bundled into the Roosevelt Room for almost an hour before Secretary of State Marco Rubio and National Security Advisor Mike Waltz told them they were being thrown out altogether.[28]

*

While there were plenty who felt Zelenskyy might have handled the encounter better, the sheer number of statements of sympathy and support for Ukraine that followed were remarkable. It was Putin, French President Emmanuel Macron said, who was 'playing' with a new world war, not Zelenskyy. It was an implicit rebuke to both Trump and Vance, the latest of a growing number from European leaders that had begun even before the Munich speech, which intensified dramatically thereafter and continued to for months after. Even Britain, which was bending over backwards to avoid any use of words that might be seen as critical of the new US administration, put a still-visibly shaken Zelenskyy in an RAF Puma helicopter as soon as his meetings with European leaders were complete and sent him to see King Charles. The photos of a smiling monarch with Zelenskyy – still wearing his utility fatigues – appeared to be as close to the wind as Britain was prepared to go with Trump for now.

In fact, despite the clear potential for a further breakdown in relations, European leaders continued to push the line that they could only send forces to stabilise Ukraine if there was some kind of US guarantee to intervene if Russia broke its word. It later transpired other conversations were taking place behind the scenes as some Europeans pushed for US military action in Yemen to reopen the Red Sea to international shipping.

None of this went down well in Washington – not even after Trump ordered the carrier *Harry S. Truman* to 'reopen freedom of navigation', in the words of his administration's top officials, as they discussed the strikes on the messaging application Signal. They were unaware that National Security Advisor Waltz – a former Green Beret turned Congressman who should certainly have known better – had apparently inadvertently invited one of Washington's best-connected journalists, *Atlantic* editor Jeffrey Goldberg, to the group chat and he was seeing everything.

Presumably, the Signal chat had been set up to co-ordinate what in Washington was known as a 'principals committee' – as well as perhaps to have covert conversations that would not be added to the long-term presidential archive and declassified in future. Instead, of course, the chats became public within weeks – causing no small amount of embarrassment to the administration and nearly costing Waltz his job. They would also deepen the existing concern among America's closest allies, who could see first-hand the terms in which they were discussed and the transactional thinking of at least some members of the administration.

'Team, I am out . . . doing an economic event in Michigan,' wrote Vance, warning he believed the US was making a mistake by yet again doing what should be Europe's work. '3 percent of US trade runs through the suez. 40 percent of European trade does [capitalisation and formatting as original]. I am not sure how the president is aware of how inconsistent this is with his message on Europe.'

Waltz responded first by quietly questioning Vance's figures – roughly 15 per cent of global and 30 per cent of container traffic passed through the Red Sea before the Houthi campaign, and that contained plenty of components and other materials that were then repackaged or sent onward to the United States. The bottom line, he said, was that 'we have a fundamental decision of allowing the sea lanes remain closed, or to reopen them now or later . . . we are the only ones with the capability unfortunately'.

That, so far, was an exchange that could have occurred under any presidency. What was much more unique, though, was Waltz's further comment that 'per the president's request we are working with DOD and State to determine how to compile the cost associated and levy them on the Europeans'. In case there was any doubt on that, another official on the chat – most likely White House Deputy Chief of Staff for Policy Stephen Miller – talked of the requirement for Europe to 'remunerate' the US or otherwise ensure 'some further economic gain' be extracted in return.

It was Defense Secretary Hegseth's endorsement, however, that seemed to carry the greatest weight. 'If you think we should do it let's go,' Vance typed. 'I just hate bailing Europe out again.'

'I fully share your contempt for European free-loading,' replied Hegseth. 'It's PATHETIC. But Mike is correct. We are the only ones on the planet (on this side of the ledger at least) who can do this. No one else comes close. Question is timing. I feel like now is as good a time as any, given POTUS [President of the United States] directive to reopen shipping lanes. I think we should go; but POTUS still retains 24 hours of decision space.'

In any normal circumstance, a US official or military officer sharing the fact that the president might be 24 hours away from ordering a set of strikes on an unclassified social media channel might have been punished severely if they had been caught. The same was even more true for the information Hegseth shared the following morning, on the likely timing of incoming strikes, some details on the targets and the aircraft types involved.[29]

Any junior official or ordinary military service member who shared data like that could expect immediate punishment, perhaps even dismissal or imprisonment. Those towards the top of every command chain, however, had often played by somewhat different rules. In 2021, a senior British diplomat had left a 50-page classified dossier in a south-east England bus stop that was handed to the media and found to include secret material including the locations of UK special forces in Kabul – and despite being publicly named, he continued to be promoted through the years that followed to increasingly vital roles.[30]

Admittedly, the US did have more of a reputation for removing senior leaders for mismanagement or errors, particularly within the military – but under the new administration, such decisions would become ever more political. When National Security Advisor Waltz was fired a few weeks later – or more specifically, appointed US ambassador to the United Nations – there were plenty who viewed 'Signalgate' as the most likely cause. It had irritated the president, insiders said, but it was not the only factor: one White House source said what had truly sealed his fate was pushing opinions that opposed those of the president. They also accused the former Congressman of acting too much like a 'principal' rather than a loyal adviser.[31] Hegseth too faced mockery but not immediate sanction: he had the president's ear and perhaps – initially, at least – what looked like his personal affection. Even more importantly, he had the critical role of interpreting Trump's instructions, worldview and assumptions and implementing them through a Pentagon that was deeply enmeshed with almost every international ally, and had proved remarkably resistant to taking more isolationist direction during Trump's first term.

*

When Trump announced Hegseth's nomination as the next SECDEF back in December 2024, some in Washington who did not watch Fox said they had never heard of him – and his appointment came as even more of a surprise to US allies.[32] But by mid-February he was on his way to Europe to tell NATO's other members the world they knew had changed. Within hours of landing at a German airbase, Hegseth was conducting physical training with US special forces there.[33]

A pair of meetings of defence ministers in Brussels in mid-February – less than a month after the inauguration, and just before the fireworks of the Munich conference – was the first direct interaction many of the attendees had with the new Trump administration, and Hegseth set a polite but resolute tone. Almost all the details had been trailed well before he arrived in Europe – and yet for many in the room, the content still felt shocking. Hegseth made it clear that the administration was determined to end fighting in Ukraine, viewed NATO membership for that country as 'unrealistic' and believed that European nations should increase their spending to as high as 5 per cent of GDP. 'We are also here today to directly and unambiguously express that stark strategic realities prevent the United States of America from being primarily focused on the security of Europe,' he told defence ministers. The need for the Pentagon to focus on US border security and the China threat, he said, all meant European allies must 'lead from the front' – including arming Ukraine and delivering its security in the aftermath of any deal.[34]

Just how seriously those at the top of European defence took that warning we may never know, but the following events in Munich and then Zelenskyy's meeting in Washington dramatically ramped up their worries. These were exacerbated further by the US suspension of support and intelligence sharing with Ukraine in early March, temporary though it proved to be.

For all that, much of the pre-planned defence activity in the rest of Europe continued largely uninterrupted. At the end of March, for example, a press release from US Army Europe noted that US forces had worked with Norwegian and Belgian counterparts to practise the rapid and unannounced deployment of a HIMARS rocket battery into Norway. The missiles themselves were guided to their destination by a Norwegian F-35 and maritime patrol plane as well as by Belgian special forces, exactly the kind of multi-ally operation the Biden administration had made central to its planning. The operation, said one officer involved – part of the Fort Bragg-based US 18th Airborne Corps – showed just how fast an air-deployed missile battery could engage distant targets and then move to another new location before an enemy knew that it was there. Such a capability, he noted, was much more potent if you could also wrap in data feeds and targeting from allies.[35]

Hegseth was proving similarly difficult to pin down – perhaps unsurprisingly, as he came with both a very different background and somewhat divergent character to anyone who had run the Pentagon before him. He was also from another generation. Whereas his predecessor Lloyd Austin had already been a one star general at the time of 9/11, Hegseth had been at Princeton University, gaining his commission through the Reserve Officer

Training Corps (ROTC) program that provided part-time military training and financial support for his degree. Afterwards, he chose to join the reserve National Guard rather than the regular US Army – but he had volunteered for full-time tours in Guantánamo Bay, Iraq and Afghanistan.

In his book *The War on Warriors* – which accused the US military of 'going woke' and abandoning effectiveness – Hegseth described those wars as 'killing Islamists in shithole countries'.[36] It may be how some US military personnel spoke to each other – but it was not the way the Pentagon's top ranks were supposed to talk or think. It was rhetoric Hegseth honed as he carved out a new career for himself as a Fox News presenter on his return from war – but it had sat awkwardly with his military superiors.

After commanding his troops on the DC streets during the 'Black Lives Matter' protests, particularly watching the abuse his African-American soldiers suffered, Hegseth was angered by what he saw as his own military command chain adopting the protest rhetoric. Hegseth was then removed from duty during the 2021 Biden inauguration over a tattoo he had of a 'Jerusalem cross', an emblem once used by Crusader knights which was now judged a right-wing emblem. Both incidents only served to deepen his opinion that the US military and government was fast losing its way.

Hegseth clearly saw himself as a 'soldier's soldier'. When military lawyers lectured his troops on rules of engagement and the Geneva Convention, he took his soldiers' side, later writing, 'America should fight by its own rules and we should fight to win, or not go at all.'[37] 'Lots of people need to be fired,' he wrote, pointing to the growing China threat. 'They have a full-spectrum, long-term view of not just regional but global domination and . . . we have our heads up our asses.'[38]

Not everyone believed that was the right attitude for a job as demanding and sophisticated as running the Pentagon. 'He would make a great company commander,' one serving army officer told Military.com. 'But that's not the job he's in right now.'[39]

In the first weeks of the Trump administration, Hegseth and his team said they had clear priorities from the president – and the first was to secure the southern border. Another was to remove all remnants of 'DEI' – 'Diversity, Equality and Inclusion' – from the Pentagon and its subordinate elements. Throughout the new administration's first weeks in office, artificial intelligence-enabled algorithms took down photographs and posts seen as elevating or highlighting one minority group above another – an imperfect process that at one point included as many as 100,000 images and posts, inadvertently removing content such as references to the wartime bomber *Enola Gay* that had dropped the first atomic bomb on Hiroshima.[40]

'This DOD moves fast on the orders of the president,' Hegseth told personnel at Guantánamo Bay on a February visit, as the first migrants were deported to the base being used for those deportees judged 'high risk' for cartel or other links. Another high priority, he said, was the new US missile defence system Trump first announced at his inauguration, initially named 'Iron Dome' after the Israeli system and then 'Golden Dome', possibly because the Israeli name was discovered to be trademarked by its manufacturers.

The 'Golden Dome' proposal – not particularly trailed to allies or elsewhere – raised immediate eyebrows, particularly as it became clear that it would be likely rather different to 'Iron Dome', which was primarily employed to protect against short and medium-term threats from Israel's neighbours across the Middle East, and more to protect against long-range ballistic missiles. That made it much closer to the Reagan-era 'Strategic Defense Initiative', which had deeply alarmed US allies in Europe and beyond. Then UK Prime Minister Margaret Thatcher had been one of several concerned that if the US could protect itself from long-range Russian threats, it might withdraw from Europe and leave the continent to its fate. Only when she concluded the system would not work with the technology of the time did her worries ease.

This time, with talk that the US would spend $100 billion or more on the system and the Pentagon already setting up a new organisation to spearhead the project, its feasibility was less clear.[41] As Trump announced Boeing had been awarded the contract for America's next-generation fighter aircraft – named the F-47, apparently after the 47th president himself – those close to Trump warned that only a toned-down version of the aircraft would be offered to US allies, 'which probably makes sense, because someday, maybe they're not our allies'.[42]

Alongside the temporary shutdown of support for Ukraine, this had allies spooked. The new administration was still trying to pressure US partner nations to dramatically increase their defence spending – but their growing success, perversely, was not because allies were being convinced by the US arguments, rather, they were simply concluding that Washington might no longer be worth trusting. 'It is very hard to say that you could definitely rely on the US now, and as soon as you allow that thought to exist, you have to admit that Japan needs to do a lot more to defend itself,' one Japanese official told the *Financial Times*.[43]

This was just the start of nervousness among US Pacific allies. Most serious strategists believed the confrontation with Beijing might define the Trump administration even more than those with Russia. In those first few weeks – particularly after the Zelenskyy meeting – there was some excited talk in Washington of the president achieving a 'reverse Kissinger' by winning over Putin and shifting Russia away from China. By the end of March 2025, however, the Russian leader's increasingly apparent intransigence when it came to US-led peace negotiations appeared to start infuriating Trump, and he was talking in terms of new tariffs and sanctions to bring the Kremlin to the table.[44]

If that was the direction of travel, though, it would take some time to take effect. In the meantime, the future of US military policy was being quietly debated within the Pentagon, with the majority of the most important discussions taking place primarily at the very top. At the start of April, the Senate finally confirmed Elbridge Colby as undersecretary for policy, the number three official at the Pentagon – and like Hegseth himself, his appointment was sufficiently controversial that it required Vice President Vance to exercise his tie-breaking vote to get it through the Senate.[45]

By then, it was clear that Hegseth himself would keep embracing controversy, perhaps whether he wanted to or not. When it came to strategically important statements on where the US sat on major issues such as the Middle East or Europe, his talking points were almost always as tightly formed, clear and steadily repeated as those of Lloyd Austin, his Biden-era predecessor – sometimes saying more or less the same as Austin, sometimes something very different. But they were coupled with repeated rows with journalists, diatribes on 'wokeness' and broadsides against the prior administration, often delivered with a tone of open anger.

Elbridge Colby's brand – he was almost always known as 'Bridge' – could hardly have been more different to Hegseth's: not least because he had spent years of the Biden administration travelling the world and talking repeatedly in Washington and beyond to diplomats, journalists and the global foreign policy elite. Well-groomed and with a reputation for politeness even when criticising others, he was the grandson of a former CIA director – and even much more liberal Democrat foreign policy thinkers were often at pains to point out not just that they knew him, but they respected his intellect and views.[46]

Almost all agreed with the basis of his diagnosis: that the US faced a threat from China that it must prioritise. But many from the foreign policy mainstream disagreed with the strength of his prescription: a much more significant pullback of US forces in Europe and the Middle East than most considered wise, and perhaps even so in Asian allies closely facing China if they could not step up more in their own defence.

That included Taiwan, where 'Bridge' was as aware as anyone of the deficiencies in the islands' military and defences. A year before he entered office, he had written in the Taiwan press that the islands needed to dramatically increase their defences or face the US pulling back.[47] 'We are watching Elbridge very closely,' one Taiwanese official told me before the US vote.[48]

Several months into office, where the administration itself stood remained deliberately opaque. When a Chinese delegation led by former senior diplomat Cui Tiankai visited Washington in the first weeks of the new presidency, they struggled to get meetings with current or likely members of the administration because no one yet knew what to say.[49] As the administration began to increase tariffs against both friend and foe alike, the Foreign Ministry in Beijing released a more aggressive statement: 'If war is what the US wants, be it a tariff war, a trade war or any other kind of war, we are ready to fight until the end.'[50]

In a more normal world, such words might have attracted greater concern. Meanwhile, as Russian state-backed media outlets remained unusually subdued, China's state-run media outlets – particularly those reaching Asian and European audiences – were pushing the relentless message that a chaotic America was abandoning its allies, and a rising PRC was ready to fill the resulting gap.[51]

Not all of that messaging came through media. In early February, Australian maritime surveillance detected a Chinese warship transiting the Torres Strait north of the Australian mainland. But it was a civilian airline pilot who made the most alarming discovery on February 21, intercepting English-language warnings from a three-vessel Chinese fleet that the PLA Navy was conducting live fire drills in the Tasman Sea to the south of Australia, a direction from which it had previously not been so directly threatened.

The Chinese flotilla proceeded to sail the entire way around the Australian continent, unleashing a furious debate not just about Australia's defences, but its relations with the United States. The government in Canberra had just paid half a billion dollars to the Pentagon as part of the AUKUS deal to procure *Virginia*-class atomic submarines for the Australian Navy. But the US made no public comment at all on the Chinese vessel presence, despite it being the dominant news story in Australia and coinciding with a visit from a US submarine and a US admiral. There was increasing speculation that Australia might not get the submarines at all – *Virginia*-class production was well behind schedule, and there was plenty of talk in Washington that the US might choose to prioritise the vessels for its own use instead.[52]

Quietly, Australia joined the list of other countries – including South Korea, Poland, Ukraine and even Germany and Japan – where talk of a national nuclear weapons programme was subtly gaining traction. Among almost every major democracy, there was a feeling of crisis and looming dread about the future. The question was: what were they prepared to do about it?

6

The Challenge for Democracies

'You must know that we're not ready?'

**BBC Defence Correspondent Jonathan Beale
to UK Secretary of State for Defence
John Healey, December 1, 2024**[1]

At the start of December 2024, a British government Jaguar limousine and its Range Rover escort pulled into the Honourable Artillery Company (HAC) reservist military base in the heart of London. On the parade square, a few reporters huddled against the cold alongside a handful of soldiers and contractors, a camouflage-netted lightly armoured vehicle and several lightweight drones.

Out of the limousine emerged a tall, thin man with a serious but friendly expression and no hat to protect his bald head against the cold. At Cambridge University, Defence Secretary John Healey had briefly joined the RAF University Air Squadron for basic pilot training. But he then cut any military ties, becoming a trade union official, MP and then a minister under Tony Blair and Gordon Brown.[2] Now, after 14 long years in opposition, Labour was back in office with a parliamentary landslide – but also heavily indebted post-pandemic public finances. That left Healey fighting for yet more money from the Treasury as the global situation worsened while Britain attempted to stabilise Ukraine and maintain relations with both the US and European allies. It was less than a month since Trump's overwhelming win in the November 2024 election, and Britain and Europe were still digesting the news.

The firm exhibiting its drones for him, Helsing, was barely three years old – but its latest crop of investment put its overall worth at more than $5 billion. Its founder, Gundbert Scherf, was a former German defence official who believed, like many others, that Ukraine was the 'defining conflict' when it came to the emergence of artificial intelligence and unmanned systems.[3] Under the camouflage netting, Helsing's black fleece-wearing technicians and sales personnel showed Defence Minister Healey footage of autonomous weapons launching from woodland and slamming into target vehicles. Enough of the drones, one technician said, could give a country an 'invasion-busting' capability, breaking up and destroying enemy formations.

This was the kind of technology Poland already hoped to use in its 'East Shield' frontline protection. It was also, the Helsing presentation heavily suggested, just the sort of weaponry Britain might procure to meet its NATO obligations in Estonia and send to Ukraine so the government in Kyiv could survive the winter. Speaking with journalists shortly after the demonstration, Healey praised Helsing for its 'China-free' supply chain. A more resilient defence industry that could survive major geopolitical and other shocks was a top priority, he said; as well as the prospect of being outgunned by Russia, any major Asian conflict could devastate Britain's long-distance and almost entirely undefended trade routes. As Healey prepared to brief journalists in London, a tabletop 'wargame' involving major defence firms was underway at the UK Defence Academy in Shrivenham, near Swindon. He described the exercise as pushing industry 'to be capable of innovation at a wartime pace' when 'we may be faced with protracted fighting (and) severe disruption in the established supply chains and our processes'.[4]

Strikingly, however, there was no promise of new purchases, whether from Helsing or any other company.

Even given the rising need, defence industry insiders complained contracts were still a long time coming – enough to threaten the existence of some firms. Nor were supply chains the only likely issue. As BBC defence correspondent Jonathan Beale – tall, hawk-like and ruthless when it came to puncturing what he saw as lazy rhetoric – was quick to point out, an earlier US Army wargame had shown the British Army running out of artillery shells in days – and suppling Ukraine had degraded such stocks further. Then there was the question of what to do next about the conflict in that country, where the incoming US administration was already making it clear that it saw a role for European troops. 'Our duty now is to stand with them as they fight, as we are doing now,' Healey said after I pressed him on the prospects for any potential post-war Ukraine UK troop deployment. 'If and when there is some kind of settlement, there will be a period where Ukraine will require support in its security.'

As Healey moved on to his next meeting, the press pack hastily compared notes and interpretations of what his noncommittal comments had and had not meant. 'He didn't deny they might send ground troops,' said one journalist. 'I'm not going to write that the government is considering it – but someone is going to,' said another experienced correspondent. 'Then we will be in yet another war,' warned another Fleet Street veteran.[5]

As Healey and his team faced their shorter-term decisions, a three-person panel with experience of some of the most decisive moments in modern military history raced to complete Britain's latest Strategic Defence Review on the bigger picture. As NATO Secretary General in September 2001, the review's chairman Lord George Robertson had taken a huge diplomatic gamble in ordering a vote on NATO's Article Five 'self-defence clause', in which the entire North Atlantic Council agreed to treat the 9/11 attack on the US as an attack against themselves. A single veto might have marked the end of the most successful alliance in military or diplomatic history – but he had got away with it, and the fact NATO had rallied to America's support had been endlessly referenced by its officials and supporters ever since that moment.

That had been particularly true in the first Trump administration, as European officials had sought to remind the president of NATO's prior commitment. That first term had also seen Robertson's co-reviewer Fiona Hill – who still retained her distinctive British County Durham accent despite being a US citizen for decades – as lead US National Security Council official for Europe and Russia. Her criticisms of Trump after leaving office were widespread and highly public, but she remained highly respected on both sides of the Atlantic, now often working remotely from her US home on the UK review. The last member of the trio, retired British General Richard Barrons, had led troops in Afghanistan, Iraq and the Balkans, loyally defending all those deployments while still in uniform. Since leaving the military, however, he had become one of the louder voices calling for much greater reliance on technology to fill existing gaps.

UK military history from the fall of the Berlin Wall had proved a messy business, and previous defence reviews had often been criticised for making matters worse. But building up armed forces larger than it could adequately sustain had long been a British habit, as with other European armies. Getting a British armoured division to the Gulf in 1991 meant cannibalising the rest of the British Army, with many Cold War units abolished in its aftermath. Sending a similar force in 2003 for the US-led invasion was, if anything, even harder, with the UK force lacking logistics to make it beyond Basra, the closest Iraqi city. There, British troops initially donned berets and lectured US counterparts on their 'Northern Ireland experience' before losing control of the city. From

2006, the British Army looked to re-establish its reputation in Afghanistan, but its initial deployment into Helmand saw small detachments of troops pinned down in remote locations, devastating the surrounding areas by calling in overwhelming firepower – and, it later became clear, tricked into fighting battles for certain local warlords against their nearby foes.[6] In both Basra and Helmand, UK troops ended up pulling back as US counterparts took over, a prelude to the eventual withdrawal of US troops themselves.

More recent deployments, particularly for the army, had been notably more limited: primarily supporting NATO activity in Europe and much smaller counterinsurgency operations in Iraq and Syria, while warships, including a carrier battle group, periodically sailed for the Gulf and Pacific. In all three services, personnel complained simultaneously of overwork and lack of worthwhile action or activity, as well as poor food and housing – and some were voting with their feet. According to official figures, by late 2024, 300 more staff were leaving every month than joined.[7] Other estimates showed the RAF recruited 1,800 people over a 12-month period but lost 3,000 – a rate British military blogging site the Wavell Room calculated would leave Britain's air force with no personnel at all by 2048. Similar figures for the army – already well below its target level of 70,000 – meant it would run out of troops by 2055, with the Royal Navy losing its last sailor in 2065.[8]

As Barrons and Robertson briefed the House of Commons Defence Select Committee at the start of December 2024, they acknowledged that tackling recruitment and retention would be one of their priorities. A call for evidence earlier in the year had produced more than 8,000 responses, many from serving personnel, now being scoured and repackaged for analysis by an artificial programme from Palantir, one of the largest and fastest-growing defence technology firms to emerge from Silicon Valley.

Using AI to crunch through defence review submissions was hardly the most controversial thing those firms were doing – but it still provoked a backlash: 'It's just going to be a word cloud,' one defence expert complained.[9] In reality, it was a necessary step – the trio had only a limited time on their contracts to complete the review, slated to come out in 2025 not long after Trump's new administration entered office. The review team had also been given clear guidelines by both Healey and Downing Street: to offer their views on the most effective way to spend 2.5 per cent of gross domestic product on defence. That was very different to what a lot of people, including backbench MPs, wanted them to do, which was to look at the range of threats and advise on what the UK should be spending in response.[10]

The actual fighting in Ukraine, meanwhile, offered a savage reminder of just how bloody modern war might be. Former UK Defence Secretary Ben Wallace said he doubted any democratic nation would tolerate losing as many as what he estimated could be 250,000 Russian dead in Ukraine so far. 'This is the big test for the West,' he warned. 'It's about resolve. What are we going to do in a world where the dictators have no regard for their own population – and they believe that that is how they win?'[11]

In February 2024, Britain's Chief of the Defence Staff Admiral Tony Radakin used a major speech to hit back at what he called 'sensationalist' headlines on the risk of war with Russia and prospects for conscription. Neither, he said, was a serious possibility. 'We are safe because we are in NATO, the largest and strongest alliance in history, and also because we are a responsible nuclear power,' he asserted, although he added that a range of other threats remained: from cyber attacks to attacks on national infrastructure.[12]

A major architect of the modern Royal Navy, with its carriers and ambitions to operate as far as the Pacific, Radakin had also been one of the key drivers of Britain's Ukraine support, referred to by Zelenskyy simply as 'the Admiral'.[13] He firmly believed the ability of NATO nations to strike deep into Russia if war came still deterred the Kremlin from attacking alliance nations, while pushing for the long-range drones and rockets that had devastated Russia's Black Sea Fleet and largely driven it from the combat zone.[14] Under his direction, a small British team known as Task Force 'KINDRED' had built a reputation for speed and originality in taking existing weapons stocks, repurposing and rebuilding them – strapping what had been Soviet-era air-to-air missiles to trucks to deliver badly needed ground-based air defences.[15]

But worries were now deepening in the MOD itself. 'In a war of scale – one similar to Ukraine – our army, for example on the current casualty rates, would be expended, as part of a broader multinational coalition, in six months to a year,' one of Healey's subordinate defence ministers, Alistair Carns, told a London conference later that December. The result was a blizzard of headlines from almost every major news outlet predicting the British Army would be 'wiped out in months'.[16] According to reports, those headlines sparked new anger in Downing Street – but the drip of bad news about the military continued to be relentless, including the revelation that up to a fifth of UK Armed Forces personnel had medical issues that meant they could not deploy.[17]

Carns was not a man to make such a warning lightly. When he resigned his regular commission to seek election as a Labour candidate at the 2024 election, the 44-year-old white-haired Royal Marines colonel was weeks away from becoming one of the youngest brigadiers in recent UK history, having spent much of his career on operations with UK special forces. In one interview, he recalled one of several near-death experiences: falling from a tanker his team was boarding in the Gulf, sinking down beneath the propellers of the ship, with the risk of sharks, before finally being rescued by his comrades.[18] Five months after his election, Carns re-enlisted in the part-time Royal Marine Reserve, saying he wanted to be ready to return to uniform if war broke out in Europe.[19] In fact, he was already being talked of as a potential defence secretary if a major conflict came and more mainstream politicians proved unable to meet the moment.

In the run-up to the two world wars, Britain's part-time reserves had seen huge numbers of young men volunteering in the hope of getting training and perhaps even some promotion before the conflict started. Britain's military leaders were now rather hoping the same might happen again. 'If we aren't prepared to fight for our freedom and our way of life as we have always done, then we will become prey in the world of predators,' said General Sir Patrick Sanders, head of the British Army until 2024. So far, however, there were few signs of such enthusiasm. One poll by *The Times* showed only 11 per cent of 18-to-27-year-olds would give a blanket pledge to fight for their country, half the level of 2004. Another 37 per cent said they would fight if they agreed with the cause, down from 57 per cent two decades earlier – 41 per cent said they would not fight at all under any circumstances.[20]

Britain's support for Ukraine and membership of NATO was still proving popular – but only as long as the UK avoided being pulled into the actual fighting. One opinion poll in mid-2024 showed only 9 per cent of British parents would be prepared for their child to fight in the British Army to defend Ukraine from Russia. Scarcely more – 15 per cent – said they would be more willing if another NATO member such as Poland was attacked. Even when the scenario was Britain itself being invaded the number was only 21 per cent.[21]

While many countries complained they were in a uniquely challenging position, this problem was in fact becoming increasingly ubiquitous. Australia[22] and Germany, both looking to grow the number of individuals in their forces, found their numbers actually contracting,[23] while French service personnel were on average leaving a year earlier than previously in the century. 'These conversations now exist in all capitals, all democracies that have professional armies without conscription,' said French Armed Forces Minister Sébastien Lecornu.[24]

Mick Ryan, a former Australian major general who had made hefty studies of both Ukraine and Taiwan, argued that having a credible national system for conscription in a major emergency was now a critical part of deterrence, and something most major nations should look at doing.[25] The world's democracies, however, were increasingly betting that technology was about to solve that problem, and finally free them from the awful sacrifices of previous great wars. The conflict in Ukraine, they hoped, was about to point the way.

*

Within days of the full-scale Ukraine invasion in February 2022, emissaries of the fastest-growing US defence tech companies of the modern era arrived in Kyiv at the invitation of President Zelenskyy and his government. 'People in Kyiv had the look as if they'd had a close shave, a near-death experience,' Louis Mosley, Executive Vice President of Palantir, recalled later. 'When you talked to government officials, they looked traumatised. They'd been hours away . . . from losing everything, their lives, their families.'

Founded in 2003 by PayPal founder Peter Thiel and others, Palantir took its name from an 'all-seeing-stone' in J. R. R. Tolkien's 'Lord of the Rings' fantasy trilogy – and had spent the subsequent two decades supporting the Pentagon, CIA and others, including Israeli military intelligence, through using high-tech 'data mining' to help them hunt their targets. Now, their friends in Western intelligence had recommended that Zelenskyy use their systems to tie together multiple sources of intelligence to help generate the targets and decisions that would win the coming fight. 'He made a very compelling pitch,' Palantir executive Mosley said of the Ukrainian leader. 'They'd identified us as the best "miltech" company in the world and were very eager for access to our technology.'[26]

By the time of the Ukraine invasion, artificial intelligence and 'machine learning' technology – as well as the range of other 'data-crunching' tools refined by firms like Palantir – were allowing huge quantities of data to be sorted and interrogated. For Ukraine, that was particularly important: its US and European allies were not always happy to share their raw intelligence. The US officers sitting in 'the Pit' in Germany often had much better insights into the battlefield than those commanding in Ukraine – but with both 'the Pit' and Ukraine's analysis systems running on Palantir and similar technology, the Ukrainians were soon able to piece together their own targeting information rather than being forced to rely on the bowdlerised version they received from Western partners.

Next through the door when it came to tech firms with a high tolerance for danger was Anduril, another taking its name from 'Lord of the Rings', for 'Flame of the West'. Anduril's founder, Palmer Luckey, took that ambition seriously. At the age of 23 he had sold his virtual reality start-up Oculus Rift to Facebook in a deal that *Forbes* magazine estimated took his personal net worth to some $700 million. Two years later, in 2017, he founded Anduril with some former Palantir executives with the explicit intention of becoming the leading Western – and ideally global – producer of a new generation of drones and autonomous weapons systems. The Ukraine war, they believed, was the perfect chance to test them. 'We were there not before the invasion, but basically from the moment it kicked off,' Anduril Head of Strategy Chris Brose told me almost three years later. 'We have people who are spending a significant amount of time . . . at the frontline with the kind of elite drone units that are using our technology, and they're really harvesting the lessons and building that back into the system.'[27]

Other European firms such as Germany's Helsing and Estonia's Milrem were also on the ground. The first weeks and months of fighting saw strong performance from the Turkish Bayraktar TB2 drone: bulky, slow and already almost a decade old, but critical to striking slow-moving Russian columns as they attempted to close in on Ukrainian cities. The Ukrainians themselves were also proving highly innovative, often through small firms working out of garages or even frontline units. Deborah Fairlamb, a former Boston management consultant who relocated to Ukraine, described an 'entire ecosystem' of technology entrepreneurship based in Kyiv and Ukraine's western city of Lviv over the first three years of war. That included Ukraine-specific funds investing in high-tech defence – former Google CEO Eric Schmidt was a key investor in one of the largest, D3, standing for 'Dare to Defend Democracies'.[28]

'This really is a weapon we have that our enemy does not,' Eveline Buchatskiy, managing partner at D3, said of the venture capital base and Silicon Valley links.[29] In truth, however, some parts of the Ukrainian system were proving much more capable than others when it came to innovation. Among the most successful were Ukraine's security services and special forces, building on close connections to US and British counterparts fostered since Russia's 2014 annexation of Crimea. By the end of 2024, their maritime Sea Baby and Magura unmanned attack boats had forced Russian warships from much of the Black Sea, and were also carrying remote-controlled machine guns capable of engaging and apparently damaging Russian attack helicopters that tried to intercept them.[30]

Ukraine had also made huge leaps forward when it came to utilising artificial-intelligence data-crunching algorithms to detect Russian drones and aircraft by mounting microphones on every cell-phone tower in frontline regions and triangulating the sounds of their engines. On occasions, that simply meant guiding ground machine-gun fire or even another drone armed with nothing but a stick to knock them from the sky. According to reports, the system had been designed by two Ukrainian engineers in their garage – but this was technology no Western state could match, although US officials said they were working swiftly to make something similar. As one Ukrainian drone operator told a conference in Warsaw: 'We do in three days what NATO does in three months or three years.' A report from Georgetown University noted that innovation at the frontline was not particularly co-ordinated – but that might be a strength rather than a weakness. As one source put it, 'Ukraine is a testbed, not a moneymaking opportunity.'

A testbed, however, was exactly what those companies needed – and they were soon learning even more from their failures than they were from their successes. Within months, Russian electronic warfare and much better anti-aircraft weaponry rendered many of the first generation of drones, including those from Turkey, all but obsolete.[31] According to several sources, one cutting-edge Western drone taken to Ukraine for trials initially failed to take off at all, likely the result of Russian jamming.[32] Russian interference with GPS systems also rendered the supposedly 'cutting-edge' 'Excalibur' guided artillery shell no more accurate than its less sophisticated counterparts, prompting the US to suspend deliveries.[33]

Both Anduril and Palantir had been among the greatest beneficiaries of a Pentagon project known as 'Maven', designed to use technology to speed up targeting, which had grabbed the headlines in 2018 when Google abruptly ceased involvement after protesting letters from many of its staff. According to reports at the time, the firm became concerned such direct engagement in a military programme might damage not just its brand, but its ability to recruit cutting-edge talent for its business.[34] In the aftermath, other major tech firms such as Microsoft showed similar reluctance to work on military technology, while major traditional 'defence primes' such as Boeing and Lockheed Martin lacked the innovation speed for the most cutting-edge technology.

By the mid-2020s, almost all the major tech firms like Microsoft and Google were back working on defence projects, particularly on 'cloud computing', secure networks and more – but their temporary pullback had left the field open for firms like Palantir and Anduril to thrive and begin to dominate. The former carved out space in a host of intelligence agencies and military formations, including delivering systems designed to give commanders the best possible information for making decisions. Anduril, with its focus on actual unmanned weapons, was soon pushing into the area of undersea naval vehicles that would be vital for any future war in the Pacific, something that would involve much greater distance and hugely larger platforms. According to Brose, one of the largest unmanned projects – an autonomous submarine known as *Ghost Shark*, for the Royal Australian Navy – was the 'size of a (US) school bus'.[35] At the other end of the size spectrum, Anduril munitions – already being mass produced in the US as part of the Pentagon's Project Replicator – were being sold directly to Taiwan, seen as an essential weapon to break up a PLA invasion.[36]

As Russia was showing in Ukraine, however, the drone revolution cut both ways – and the Kremlin's manufacturers were matching Ukrainian and Western developments at a speed unparalleled in recent history. When it came to drones, both Ukraine and Russia were relying heavily on components shipped from China – while the Kremlin was also increasingly reliant on Beijing for parts for its long-range missiles and much other military hardware.

Within the US, there were also growing worries over how fast China was progressing technologically. Just how advanced its mainstream AI platforms had become soon became apparent when Chinese firm DeepSeek – a start-up with less than 200 staff – launched an AI 'large language model' chatbot in January 2025 that quickly proved a rival to much more established US-owned platforms such as ChatGPT. That alone – together with the fact it appeared to have been built without dependence on some of the high-end fast-processing microchips previously judged necessary – was enough to prompt a months-long sell-off in US tech shares, undermining the US stock market just as Trump re-entered the White House. What was at least as striking, though, was how fast it was being taken up by China's government organisations. Within months, DeepSeek was reportedly being used for everything from determining divorce settlements to suggesting treatment plans in hospitals – despite warnings that it might generate false results or make up information.[37]

PLA documents suggested the Chinese military was similarly willing to take even bigger bets on AI. This was the PLA equivalent of Palantir-assisted targeting or the even more sophisticated systems that might be required for a major naval battle or missile defence shield. But Beijing – like the Kremlin – was a lot less squeamish about putting the algorithm in outright control without a 'human in the loop', and the West was being put under pressure to do the same.[38]

Anduril founder Palmer Luckey – who described himself as occasionally 'hitting up' Trump from time to time to talk – argued the Pandora's box of AI was already open, and there was no choice but to push forward with development. 'People say it's really spooky to have these autonomous weapons,' he said. 'I say: you know what's spooky? Having to fight the Third World War with dumb weapons. That's the thing that is going to result in far more collateral damage.'[39]

More specific concerns over how AI actually worked were now starting to emerge. Brigadier General John Cogbill, deputy commander of the US 18th Airborne Corps, one of the most enthusiastic early adopters, described AI 'hallucinations' in which the software literally made up information, making its introduction into service 'tricky' and requiring ongoing human checks. 'Every time we get better, but we can never take that for granted,' he said, describing the 2024 performance of the Maven targeting system as a 'a "C" at best'.[40] But progress was now relentless. In Ukraine, multiple companies were already mass-producing 'first-person view' drones in which AI could replace the pilot, or in which one pilot could control multiple drones in a 'swarm' simultaneously. Long-running discussions over building an international legal framework to control 'killer robots' through the UN or other systems were seen as basically hopeless – the only apparent area of agreement between the US and China was that AI should not be used in nuclear launch systems. 'The geopolitics make it impossible,' said Alexander Kmentt, Austria's top negotiator on autonomous weapons at the United Nations, talking about the kind of wider ban on machines making decisions to take human lives that human rights groups had been pushing for years. 'These weapons will be used, and they'll be used in the military arsenal of pretty much everybody.'

'Data ... is the oil, the oxygen we will need to have a decisive advantage,' head of US Special Operations Command (SOCOM) General Bryan Fenton told a trade gathering in 2023, adding that his command was 'harnessing data like never before'. By then, the US military was already trialling pilotless F-16 jets flown by artificial intelligence in mock dogfights with each other.[41] Within two years, those with awareness of operations in Ukraine talked of unmanned vessels 'in control' of the Black Sea, largely evicting Russian warships.[42]

But while drones often took the headlines, they were just one part of the high-tech military ecosystem the US was constructing with its defence and technology firms and its increasingly overt policy of pushing allies to integrate ever closer. Then, only a few weeks into Trump's new-term in office, his administration cancelled intelligence and security assistance to Ukraine with apparently no warning, suddenly turning off huge swathes of its targeting capability as well as air defences.

*

Among America's allies, the shock was palpable. Through the summer of 2024, US troops at Fort Sill, Oklahoma, had trained several dozen of their Taiwanese, Estonian and Romanian counterparts on the use of the US-manufactured HIMARS rockets on which all three of their militaries intended to rely in the event of an enemy invasion.[43] Now, they suddenly faced the prospect that the US might be able to abruptly turn off that support – and, as in Ukraine, force their governments to move towards a peace deal with the nation that attacked them.

Across Europe, Asia and beyond, senior officials and governments worked to gauge the long-term implications – including whether or not the US could ever be trusted to be consistent or reliable in the future. 'It changes with every news cycle,' said one UK official.[44] 'Everything is up in the air, or whatever phrase you want to use,' another European defence official told me.[45]

'The Europeans are discovering that if the US doesn't want to back their forces, they are quite vulnerable,' said Sten Rynning, a visiting lecturer at the NATO Defence College and professor at the Danish Institute for Advanced Study. 'Almost all allies have bought a lot off the shelf from the United States to tie themselves into the alliance and show solidarity,' he continued '[but] if the US wants to turn off, to disable European equipment, then it can. It can refuse to send the software upgrades . . . It can refuse to send the spare parts. It can refuse to send the intelligence on which they depend.'[46]

America's allies in Asia were more diplomatic but, if anything, even more concerned – Trump's pick as US ambassador to Tokyo was already making noises about making Japan 'pay more' for US forces even as he talked of a 'new golden era' in relations.[47] Japan's Prime Minister Shigeru Ishiba was extremely circumspect, saying he had 'no intention of taking sides' between Trump and Zelenskyy. Anonymously, however, MPs from his own party worried that Japan might find itself in the same position as Ukraine. 'What Japan has learned . . . is that the era when we could rely entirely on the US is over,' said another former senior Japanese official.[48]

Worries about future US reliability struck at the heart of the new US-led models of the emerging battlefield on which sustainable communications and the necessary bandwidth to analyse information was increasingly important. A target might be identified by an artificial-intelligence algorithm from satellite and communications data, then passed through several headquarters and targeting hubs to a ship, submarine, aircraft or ground-based missile battery. That weapon might then be guided to the target – or even have its target changed – over secure communications links to multiple other ships, planes, drones and military units, including soldiers on the ground. A more autonomous weapon might be able to guide itself completely to the target – including making course corrections and determining its own final approach – using its own onboard software and intelligence. But almost all of those systems relied on elements of American technology.

The money piling into non-US defence manufacturers fast became remarkable, too. South Korea's Hanwha, which sold artillery systems into Europe and was also benefiting from rising Asian spending, saw its stock price double in the first three months of 2025. Germany's Rheinmettal had also doubled in value over the previous year, and expected to see orders rise by as much as 25 per cent by the end of 2025, with talk of taking over car plants from companies such as Volkswagen.[49] Another expected likely winner was drone and AI start-up Helsing, now opening its first factory in Germany and in negotiations with multiple other nations. Each Helsing factory and the drones that it produced, the company stressed, were 'sovereign by design' – in other words, the technology was entirely usable by that nation and the data, details and often even software could not be shared without that nation state's permission.

From the Munich conference in February 2025 – and specifically the speech from Vance – European leader after European leader committed themselves to greater military spending and a foreign policy much more independent of the United States. In particular demand was Friedrich Merz, chairman of Germany's Christian Democrats and the expected incoming chancellor, now explicitly positioning himself and a more muscular Germany as the continent's co-ordinator for defence and diplomacy.

At 59 years old, Merz had been knocking around at the top of German politics for more than two decades, losing the leadership of his party to Angela Merkel in the early 2000s before dropping out of politics to work as a lawyer for finance firms including BlackRock. Now, the man once described as among the most pro-US leaders in Europe was advocating the urgent message that Washington must no longer be relied on. As soon as his election victory was confirmed, Merz said his 'absolute priority' was to create unity in Europe as fast as possible so that 'step-by-step, we can achieve independence from the US. I never thought I would have to say something like this'.[50]

Soon, Germany was talking of removing its 'debt brake' to allow much greater spending on weaponry, a move that could rapidly make it the third-largest defence spender in the world after the US and China. When it came to leadership on European defence and military matters, though, the incoming government in Berlin had several rivals – and the vagaries of the German coalition negotiation meant it took months to even get the Christian Democrat-led government properly into office.

As always vying for leadership and influence in Europe was France, with President Macron giving speeches and convening meetings both on the broader future of the defence of Europe and the specifics of handling Ukraine. Ever since Charles de Gaulle in the 1960s, a significant element of French opinion had predicted that the US would one day turn against or just abandon the European continent, and in many respects the French leadership had been waiting for this moment ever since.

Macron, quite reasonably, grabbed every opportunity to bang the drum furiously for European weaponry in general and French arms in particular. In an interview with several French newspapers, he said his intent was to go and win over

'European states that have been accustomed to buying American', continuing, 'Those who buy Patriot [air-defence missiles made by Lockheed Martin] should be offered the new generation Franco-Italian SAMP/T. Those who buy the F-35 should be offered the [less sophisticated but independently French-built] Rafale. That's the way to increase the rate of production.'[51]

In a separate broadcast, Macron announced that he had decided to 'open the strategic debate' on the nuclear protection of the continent. What that might mean is examined in Chapter 10 – but the fact it was on the table at all spoke to the sense of crisis and strategic need. When it came to mainland Europe, that empowered another player: the European Union. For years, the EU had been forced to play second fiddle to NATO when it came to military thinking, with nothing to equal the long-running command structures and exercises of the older military alliance with the US at its core.

What the EU did have, however, was the ability to set budget rules across the bloc – and that allowed it to open the door to much greater military spending, as well as considerable ability to drive its own investment. 'We need to see not only Russia as a threat, but also more global geopolitical developments and also where the Americans will put their strategic attention,' the EU's new defence commissioner Andrius Kubilius told reporters as the bloc unveiled its defence 'white paper' that might open the door for up to €800 billion worth of spending. As well as relaxing budget rules for four years to allow countries to spend much more on their militaries, it also pledged to push them to work together more closely rather than using different systems from their national companies.[52]

The problems of countries relying solely on their individual 'national champions' were becoming ever clearer. According to NATO officials, the race to supply Ukraine with shells had demonstrated awkwardly and quickly that 155-millimetre diameter ammunition from one nation often did not fit the weaponry of another; something common NATO standards had been supposed to fix back in the time of Eisenhower.[53]

Lack of spare parts was another consequence of this. In 2025, the crew of UK carrier *Queen Elizabeth* found themselves going without reliable water for hot showers for more than six months as the necessary components could not be found to fix it.[54] Similar issues were said to have delayed the repair of the 'submarine lift' at the Scottish submarine base of Faslane that moved the giant vessels in and out of maintenance, complicating efforts to maintain Britain's nuclear deterrent.[55] Stores to keep the UK's domestic-built Challenger 2 tanks and Warrior vehicles running were also notoriously sparse, one of several factors that rendered the UK's 3rd Division – theoretically its most capable and heavily armed fighting force – effectively unable to deploy.

Such choices helped explain why Britain managed to combine having one of the largest defence budgets in the world – until Russia's invasion of Ukraine ramped up its government spending, the UK was frequently described as the third-biggest spender after the US and China – with such limited capability. It also explained why the UK's 2025 announcement that it would increase spending to 2.5 per cent of gross domestic product by 2030 bought similarly limited capability – almost all that money was immediately absorbed by existing projects that had been commissioned but were either underfunded or already well exceeding budget.

By the mid-2020s, Britain could mobilise substantially fewer troops than Finland and had less artillery than Estonia, a consequence, in part, of giving weaponry to Ukraine – and while it was capable of sending a carrier to the Pacific, if it came to an actual war in Europe it would struggle to protect its own airspace from Russian missile attack. Part of that was down to deeply flawed assumptions: most importantly that the UK homeland was not at particular risk from foreign state attack. 'The systems we have are good,' one former officer told me. 'But there simply aren't enough of them.'[56]

More hybrid threats were still firmly on the increase – both sabotage and political interference. Throughout 2024 and 2025, the European Union External Action Service tracked several hundred attempts at manipulating information and social media environments across the continent, with Ukraine, France and Germany all quite predictably among the most targeted nations.[57] The US presidential election in 2024 saw US spies tracking Russian efforts to inflame discussion on topics like immigration that were seen as helping Trump and his campaign for re-election.[58]

The fact that the US president was openly aligned to some of the right-wing political forces in Europe that the existing establishment firmly believed were Kremlin-backed was a challenge Europe's leadership found almost impossible to sensibly engage with. It was made even harder by the purges the new US administration soon began launching within the military and federal government, not least dismantling many of those bodies that tracked potential interference by hostile foreign states.

Throughout the first half of 2025, the publication of the UK defence review was repeatedly delayed. Its initial completion in February had awkwardly coincided with Trump's first weeks in office and the potential overturning of decades of assumptions on the defence of both Europe and Britain itself. Even without that, though, the politics were challenging, both internationally and domestically, in almost every nation. In the UK, Starmer exerted much of his effort in the first half of 2025 in keeping open a good relationship with Trump while working with Zelenskyy, Macron and the Europeans to maintain common ground. The US administration, however, was determined to push ahead with its Ukraine negotiations with almost no reference to Europe.

If America was to turn isolationist and pull back its support from Europe – particularly if that included intelligence sharing with its 'five eyes' partners – the UK, Australia, Canada and

New Zealand – Britain had more to lose than most. In Canada and Australia, Liberal and Labor Prime Ministers Mark Carney and Anthony Albanese had both been re-elected in part on rising local feeling against Trump – although both also made it clear had no intention of abandoning their long-running US ties.

Each democracy was having to reappraise its own priorities. Alex Younger, former head of the UK's Secret Intelligence Service, argued that Britain had become 'infantilised' by its post-war US dependence. Going forward, he said, it would need to make its own priorities – and make tougher decisions about its own use of 'hard power'. For Europe more generally, he argued, that meant both deterring Putin and rebuilding Europe's technological edge to avoid losing out to China. 'It will be hard but it will be good for us,' he said. 'And, actually, it will be good for our relationship with the Americans.' Then there was Ukraine – which Younger described very much as 'Europe's problem'.[59]

In late March 2025, staff officers from some 20 nations gathered at the UK's Permanent Joint Headquarters (PJHQ) in Northwood in suburban north-west London to be briefed on a potential peacekeeping mission to Ukraine. European nations were still being firmly frozen out of the US-run negotiations, but Starmer and Macron had agreed to gauge what a European-led force might look like.

As Trump's relationship with both Europe and Ukraine became rockier by the day, Starmer's diplomatic star had risen. One French official described the British prime minister as doing 'a great job' while managing 'to stay true to himself' and simultaneously handling Trump, a 'very complicated man with polar-opposite values'. Starmer's first eight months in office had not been seen as particularly successful – indeed, his popularity had slumped at almost record speed. Now, one of his Labour MPs described fixing the transatlantic split – or, more accurately, keeping it at least partially bridged, most importantly on Ukraine – as a new 'galvanising purpose'.[60]

Getting a conversation going on Ukraine – building understanding, structures and relationships that allowed Europeans to work together with much less US input – was certainly an achievement in its own right (as a traditional British military phrase puts it, 'The plan is not as important as the planning'). Still, plenty of European nations, including Poland, were outright reluctant, ruling out their own troops for fear of becoming overstretched. European nations were already struggling to deliver enough troops for NATO's eastern flank, and putting another 10–20,000 personnel in Ukraine would potentially remove many of NATO's only just allocated rapid response troops. In the Baltic states there was some rare open frustration at Britain for offering more troops for Ukraine just as the UK-led Enhanced Forward Presence force in Estonia was actually shrinking, despite the UK's prime responsibility for defending arguably the most exposed nation on the eastern flank.

Even with talk of European aircraft conducting strikes in the event Putin breached any ceasefire and moved further into Ukraine, there was also plenty of scepticism in Kyiv and beyond about how credible such a force might be. Igor Novikov, an adviser to Zelenskyy, told Times Radio that unless such troops were prepared to fight, there was not a lot of point in their coming to Ukraine, even following a truce – and if they were prepared to fight they might as well arrive before the war was over.[61]

As in Britain, recent French military history further stoked wider European worries. The French had spent decades fighting Islamist insurgents across the West African Sahel before pulling out after a series of Russian-backed military coups. If the UK and France sent troops to Ukraine and then pulled them out a few years later as soon as things got sticky, that might well be taken by the Kremlin as the green light to move elsewhere in

Eastern Europe.[62] By the middle of 2025, the diplomatic gossip was that the idea was quietly being shelved. 'It isn't going to happen,' said one military source.[63] Still, ideas continued to be shuffled around both in and out of government, including options such as using US contractors to deliver a degree of US 'boots on the ground' and the associated deterrence value they might bring without a direct US military presence beyond airpower in nearby countries.[64]

Certainly, rhetoric was getting considerably stronger, particularly from Paris. French defence chief General Thierry Burkhard warned that 'a weakened Europe may find itself tomorrow as a hunted animal, after two centuries of the West setting the tone'.[65] So were much more serious commitments from Berlin. 'The sums Germany is investing are so considerable they are about to change the balance of power,' said one European diplomat. 'Today Germany is the economic leader and France the security leader. Tomorrow France will be a follower on both counts.' Former UK General Richard Barrons described the looming debate in almost every nation as 'welfare versus warfare', though there was more to it than that.[66] But even as more European nations began to pull together, there was a significant chance that the current French and German governments would not survive their next elections in 2027 and 2029 respectively – with the far right still gaining in almost every nation.

As European nations pondered their response to Trump in the spring of 2025, the US administration also found itself forced to embark on its own similarly urgent efforts to placate worries among its Asian partners and shore up their support, not just for any fight over Taiwan but also for America's own struggling defence industrial base.

Like its friends in Europe, the US in the Pacific was increasingly aware that only by being ready to fight and win a long war could they deter even a short conflict. And they were still very far from confident that they had prepared enough to do so.

They should not have been surprised. All of the confrontations and flashpoints of the 2020s had been growing in plain sight for decades, some since the messy breakup of the Soviet Union and the end of the Cold War, others since the height of World War Two as the Allied powers had looked to shape the current war and build a future peace.

7

Countdown to Confrontation – From Churchill to Covid

*'With hindsight, we were looking in the wrong
direction and distracted by other things.'*

Former Western intelligence official, 2024[1]

April 2020 began like no month in the prior history of the world.
As the Covid-19 pandemic death toll soared in Italy and Spain –
and then a host of other nations including Britain and the
United States – more than half the world's population were
living under some form of enforced 'lockdown'.[2] Global military
forces too found themselves affected. The US announced it
was dramatically scaling back plans for DEFENDER 2020, a
major deployment of troops and equipment from the continental United States that would have been NATO's largest
exercise in Europe since the end of the Cold War. In the Pacific,
the last days of March had seen a worsening Covid outbreak
aboard the carrier USS *Theodore Roosevelt*. The start of April saw
her tied up alongside the US naval base in Guam as the virus
swept through the cramped quarters on board, infecting hundreds of crew who were forced into shore-based isolation tents.[3]

As the rest of the world was going into lockdown, however,
China was coming out; a consequence, Chinese officials believed,
of the success of their tactics in the city of Wuhan where the
outbreak had started. By the start of April, with the rest of the
world almost entirely paralysed – including rival militaries –
they had a unique opportunity to make a show of force.

Japan's alarmed military forces tracked China's first and so far only working carrier, the *Liaoning*, heading through the Miyako Strait around 205 miles from Taiwan towards the Japanese island and US base of Okinawa. It was an assertive and deliberate military manoeuvre, guaranteed to grab headlines and the attention of commanders. With the troubled *Roosevelt* still stuck in Guam and America's other regionally based carrier *Ronald Reagan* now docked in Japan and struggling with yet more Covid cases, *Liaoning* was the only operational carrier in the Western Pacific – and everybody knew it.[4]

It was an achievement Chinese commanders had dreamed of for generations – and while if initially overshadowed by the wider effects of the pandemic, it would prove the start of the sustained campaign to increase pressure on Taiwan that would escalate throughout the decade.

The story of China's first aircraft carrier had begun more than three decades earlier and half a world away in a shipyard in Ukraine – while the modern Taiwan face-off could be traced back another half a century to a dusty, heavily defended hotel on the outskirts of wartime Cairo.

*

Almost captured by advancing German troops in 1942 before they were halted at El Alamein, 1940s Cairo was an edgy, sometimes violent place whose streets, bars and endless, often crumbling buildings had seen the birth of Britain's Special Air Service (SAS) special forces as well as much of modern Arab nationalism. As British Prime Minister Winston Churchill and US President Franklin Delano Roosevelt headed there in November 1943 to meet with Chinese Nationalist leader Chiang Kai-shek, their aim was to negotiate not just the next stages of the current conflict but also to begin to build lasting post-war peace.

Having now faced global conflict twice in less than three decades, Churchill told his colleagues that it was their responsibility

to deliver a settlement that would hold for at least 50 years; anything less, he said, would be a betrayal of the soldiers still fighting
and dying. From Egypt, the US and British leaders would fly
to meet Soviet leader Josef Stalin in the Iranian capital
Tehran – a meeting that would set the wartime victors on the
path to dividing up the coming Cold War world.[5] For those in
attendance, by far the most important discussions were those
deciding the next steps of the war, particularly the D-Day invasion of Europe scheduled for the coming June. Already, however,
both Stalin and Chiang had their eyes on long-term spheres
of influence. As the allies met, Soviet forces were seizing back
Kyiv from its Nazi occupiers, determined to reclaim the whole
of Ukraine and then push west until they reached Berlin. In the
process, they would reoccupy all three Baltic states and overrun
Poland, Hungary, Romania, Czechoslovakia and finally East
Germany. Neither Britain nor the United States would welcome
that at all. But an exhausted West was not prepared to fight to
free those territories – their fate would not come up for grabs
again until the 1980s.

Already struggling to manage their relationship with Stalin,
Britain and the US now embraced a degree of wishful thinking
when it came to post-war Asia. In Cairo, Churchill and
Roosevelt intended to treat Chiang and the KMT Nationalist
movement that he led as though they were the effective
government of all of China, hoping that might prove a self-
fulfilling prophecy. In fact, much of what was already the
world's most populous nation was either occupied by Imperial
Japan or by Mao and his Communist guerrillas. Still, in the
words of Churchill's doctor Lord Moran, the Americans
believed Chiang represented the future Chinese nation of
'400 million people who are going to count in the world
of tomorrow'. What happened in China remained vital to
the still-raging Pacific war, and the other allied leaders also
needed Chiang's signoff on the war plans they were about to
take to Stalin.[6]

Even eight decades after Cairo and five decades since his death, Chiang remains a hugely divisive figure, much as he was in life – and not just on Taiwan. US General Joe Stillwell once described him to Roosevelt as a 'vacillating, tricky undependable old scoundrel who never keeps his word', while another senior US figure described him as 'one of the two or three greatest military and political leaders in the world today'.[7] Britain's General Sir Alan Brooke, attending the conference in Cairo, described him as 'shrewd but small . . . determined to get the best of the bargain . . . very successful at leading the Americans down the garden path.'[8]

Chiang came from an austere militaristic background, and his English was never good – but he had a not-so-secret weapon in wife Soong Mei-ling, daughter of a Chinese businessman who sent her to America for her education. With her southern US accent and shrewd political sensibilities, she helped ruthlessly push the Chinese Nationalist cause, editing her husband's writing for a western audience to remove more authoritarian material and becoming the first woman to address the US Congress. Even against the backdrop of Cairo, she appeared both glamorous and exotic – at least according to the diary entries and recollections of almost every member of the male-dominated US and British delegations. Churchill described her as 'most remarkable and charming', while General Brooke the noted her high-slit dress and 'most shapely of legs'.

In fact, US intelligence believed both Chiang and his wife were having affairs with other people – but that their marriage remained ruthlessly strengthened by shared political agenda. In Cairo that won the Chinese Nationalists more Allied weaponry to fight against Japan – and, even more importantly for the future, agreement that Taiwan, then known as Formosa, should be redesignated Chinese territory once the war was over.[9]

How much those at the table in Cairo knew about the island is difficult to judge – intriguingly, the minutes of the key meetings with Chiang that week are missing from the normally thorough US diplomatic archive, or perhaps were never kept. In any case, the island was under Japanese control and had been since it was seized from China in 1895. While many of those living there were of Chinese ethnic origin, most, by the 1940s, spoke Japanese as the result of a re-education campaign intended to make them permanently loyal.

That indoctrination had indeed proved thorough: fighters from Taiwan had been in the vanguard of the Japanese Imperial offensive through Malaysia and the Philippines from 1941, defeating both the Americans and British. Given the rugged terrain across the island, Allied forces did not move against it during the remainder of the war, with US forces landing after Japan's 1945 surrender. Chiang's Republic of China forces began their own move to the island in the months and years that followed, accelerating dramatically as they were finally evicted from the Chinese mainland by Mao's Communists in 1949.

Chiang's determination to secure the island – and then to enforce his rule there – would shape the 2020s and beyond. Modern President Xi and other mainland Communist Party leaders would claim the so-called 'Cairo Declaration' 'affirmed Chinese sovereignty over Taiwan', something firmly disputed by the Taiwanese authorities.[10] On the island itself, the legacy of Chiang and his family would remain hotly debated, his giant monument continuing to overlook Taipei even as successive DPP governments removed other statues. As already noted, the years immediately after 1945 were brutal for those nations in central and Eastern Europe now under Soviet occupation – and things were not much better in Taiwan under Chiang and his Republic of China government in exile. On February 28, 1947, Nationalist troops and police fired into a crowd of demonstrators that had gathered after officials pistol-whipped a woman accused of smuggling, leaving her unconscious. It was the start of Taiwan's so-called era of 'white terror' as Chiang's Nationalists imposed brutal martial law.[11] Those events and their immediate legacy would be remembered very differently by the majority population compared to the traditional ROC/KMT elites who had arrived with Chiang.

From the start, some in the US expressed their own worries over KMT excesses – even suggesting the KMT should be removed and Taiwan allowed to proceed as an independent nation or US protectorate – but the North Korean invasion of South Korea in June 1950 further pushed Washington into backing Chiang and his still sometimes brutal government. Having nearly lost Korea, the Truman and then Eisenhower administrations could not afford to let the same happen on the island. It had swiftly become clear that Mao and his Communists, after taking the mainland from the Nationalists, had simply taken on Chiang's territorial claims as their own, including Taiwan and much of the South China Sea. When it looked as though Mao might move against the Taiwan-run 'offshore islands' within sight of the Chinese mainland in 1954 and 1958, Eisenhower sent US warships, including two aircraft carriers, while US jets and even nuclear weapons were moved to Taiwan itself.

These were sweaty, high-stakes crises, compared by those involved with the face-offs over Cuba and Berlin that followed not long after. The Taiwanese islands closest to China were almost indefensible – indeed, the US persuaded the government in Taipei to withdraw entirely from a few of the most vulnerable. On the Kinmen archipelago, within sight of the mainland Chinese city of Xiamen, a US-brokered deal saw the Nationalist and Communist sides shelling each other on alternate days to avoid casualties, a bizarre situation that continued until the 1970s.[12]

While much of Europe recognised Mao's Communists as the legitimate government of China in the 1950s and 1960s, Washington stuck with its recognition of Chiang's KMT-run ROC until 1979. By then, however, the first secret and then highly public diplomatic rapprochement between Richard Nixon, Henry Kissinger, Mao and his successors had made the direction of travel very clear: both the US and Beijing expected

Taiwan to eventually return to China, but they did not expect it soon. According to US diplomatic archives, as recently as the 1970s Mao had told Kissinger: 'I would say we can do without Taiwan for the time being and let it come after 100 years.'[13]

By then, though, the ROC government in Taipei was entrenched not just on the island but also as a powerful lobbying force in Washington DC – and both elements resisted the downgrading of US–Taiwan relations. But the subtly brokered switch of China from the Soviet orbit to one much closer to the West was seen as a major and long-considered US strategic victory. At the start of the 1950s, Stalin, Mao and North Korean leader Kim Il Sung had been able to co-ordinate their actions on something like the Korean War in a way that genuinely threatened to overwhelm the US and its allies – and had only truly been contained by the threat of US atomic bombing bringing about an armistice. As the Cold War again intensified in the early 1980s, Beijing was effectively a US ally in all but name – and for US military planners, that made the world much simpler.

The Soviet Union, meanwhile, appeared at the height of its power, even as unrest began in Poland and Czechoslovakia that would ultimately bring down first the Communist governments of the Eastern Bloc and then the USSR itself. The Soviet military, forging ahead with a new generation of technology and weaponry, was blindsided by the speed of the collapse – including the way in which it left some of their most valuable military technology inside the borders of foreign and potentially hostile states.

That included the Soviet Union's first two full-size aircraft carriers under construction in the Ukrainian port of Mykolaiv, named the *Tbilisi* and the *Riga* for the capitals of Georgia and Latvia.

For the Soviet commanders who aimed to use those vessels to confront NATO fleets at sea, the idea that by the end of 1991 Georgia, Latvia and Ukraine itself might all have left a collapsing USSR would have been unthinkable. They would have been even more surprised to see the not-quite completed *Riga* find her way to China through a series of improbable events, to be rebuilt as the *Liaoning*, the first carrier in the People's Liberation Army Navy, opening the door for other larger ships to come.

First, however, the Soviet empire would unravel, China's own Communist rulers would face down and crush the threat of rising protest, and a young Donald Trump would again find his hopes of becoming a global statesman publicly frustrated – all with their own implications for today and well beyond.

*

As late as December 1988, as Soviet leader Mikhail Gorbachev prepared to visit the United States to address the UN and meet President-elect George Bush Sr, the USSR itself was expected to remain a major global player. Already, Poland and other members of the Warsaw Pact were starting to break free, but Gorbachev intended the Soviet Union to endure as a powerful democracy embracing open markets.

Few were more enthusiastic about this new world order than a still young Donald Trump, who had finally got his first meeting with Gorbachev in Moscow a year earlier and now told journalists he looked forward to showing him New York, particularly Trump Tower. 'I hope he's going to find it special,' Trump told the *New York Times*, losing no opportunity to describe the greatness of the building and its luxury suites. Several articles mentioned Trump's own presidential ambitions, implying that the meeting with Gorbachev might be a step towards a White House bid as soon as 1992.[14]

Instead, Trump found himself humiliated after the much-touted Trump Tower dinner was dropped from the agenda by the Soviets, his embarrassment compounded when he raced downstairs to greet a man he was told was Gorbachev 'dropping by', only to discover he was an impersonator.[15]

Trump would not throw his hat again into serious US politics for almost 30 years. Gorbachev's own humiliation would follow shortly after – but for a few months in late 1988 and early 1989, the Soviet leader was fêted as a global political superstar. In New York he was lionised by crowds as his speech to the UN General Assembly – in which he outlined a global role for a democratic Soviet superpower – was compared by some to the eloquence of John F. Kennedy. It was a moment that helped deliver particularly unintended consequences in mainland China, where students also inspired by unrest in Eastern Europe took to the streets in protest in early 1989.

As Gorbachev visited Beijing that May, pro-democracy activists welcomed him as a sign of things to come. Many expected ageing Chinese leader Deng Xiaoping and those around him to swiftly be ousted, while Gorbachev expected the Soviet Union to be around for decades.[16] But China's rulers sent tanks into Tiananmen Square almost as soon as Gorbachev had left – and the collapse of Soviet-dominated rule across much of the rest of Europe followed by the end of 1989. But it was the eruption of unrest in the still-Soviet-run Baltic states that really sealed the fate of USSR itself, and with it that of Gorbachev as leader.

Those leading the resistance movement in Latvia, Lithuania and Estonia watched the Tiananmen crackdown with outright alarm – and concluded they now faced a once-in-a-lifetime chance to escape the Kremlin's grip. 'We knew that if we didn't get free then we never would,' one former activist, later a senior Baltic diplomat, told me decades later. Once Nordic nations – starting with tiny Iceland – recognised the Baltics as independent states the momentum became unstoppable, bringing with it support including Norwegian oil and gas and the first military, financial and technological advice from Finland and Sweden.

For a few weeks, the survival of the Baltic states looked desperately in the balance as Soviet troops tried to reclaim control. But by mid-1991, it was clear the Baltics were out of Moscow's grip and already scheming their way to what would eventually become NATO and EU membership. Even then, though, Washington hoped the rest of the Soviet Union would somehow hold together, reform under Gorbachev's increasingly fragile grip and somehow embrace democracy. At the start of August, Bush visited Ukraine – where pro-independence sentiment was also on the rise – and gave a speech so negative to independence for more Soviet nations that it was dubbed the 'Chicken Kyiv'.[17]

In fact, the USSR was already well past saving, its final death delivered not by the West but the desperate attempted coup that August by Soviet diehards trying to hold the monolith together. It backfired catastrophically: multiple Soviet republics that had tolerated Gorbachev had no intention of coming back under the rule of a hard-line Moscow, declaring independence immediately following the coup.

From the start, Russia's new leader Boris Yeltsin made it clear that he was not happy with the borders of these new post-Soviet independent nations, nor that remnants of the USSR's military forces were left stranded outside the territory that he controlled. As soon as he had secured power, Yeltsin ordered the most complete of the two aircraft carriers still in Ukrainian ports – the former *Tbilisi* now renamed *Admiral Kuznetsov* – to sail for Murmansk in northern Russia so Ukraine could not seize her.[18]

The partly completed *Riga*, now renamed the *Varyag*, however, reverted to Ukraine – and within the Chinese military, there were soon voices calling for the PLA to buy her.

Sometime in 1992, Major General Zheng Ming, until recently head of armaments for the People's Liberation Army Navy, boarded the three-quarters-built vessel in Mykolaiv. The new Ukrainian state was almost bankrupt, in desperate need of foreign currency. 'It was a brand-new ship,' Zheng told a Chinese TV documentary years after the event. 'Everything was completely new, from the armour plating to the other parts. So I suggested the [government] buy it and take it home.'

Zheng found his Beijing superiors feeling less adventurous. It was, they told him, too soon following Tiananmen Square.[19] Already, the Communist authorities were doing everything they could to make the world forget, working to ensure the Chinese Red Cross estimates of more than 2,000 dead never made the official histories. Beijing was also negotiating the 1997 return of British territory Hong Kong, keen to look like a responsible international player rather than a rising military power bent on regional domination.

But within the corridors of power, the idea would not go away. As Chinese officials watched the US dominate the world as an unchallenged superpower – and then use those capabilities to protect an emerging democracy in Taiwan – its time would come again.[20] And with those in power in China now pursuing economic growth and a globalisation strategy that would maximise both their own productivity and access to resources, Beijing would have a lot more money in the future to support whatever strategy it chose.

With hindsight, what became known as the 'Third Taiwan Strait Crisis' of 1996 did more than any other single event to shape the confrontations of the coming century, not least those of the 2020s. For those in charge in Beijing, it demonstrated all too starkly the ongoing dominance of the US across the region, supercharging the desire of Chinese military nationalists to do something to change it. But even more seriously, in Chinese official eyes at least, was Taiwan's emergence as a democracy, a model wildly at odds with the autocratic vision pursued by Beijing.

Lee Teng-hui, succeeding Chiang Kai-shek's son Chiang Ching-kuo in 1988, was a very different figure from his predecessors: he had been born on the island before the KMT arrived, fighting for Japan in World War Two. While a member of the KMT, he was much more interested in democratising Taiwan than maintaining its control, and doubled down on that approach after the Tiananmen Square massacre in 1989. When Taiwan saw its own pro-democracy protests the following year, he invited representatives to meet him at the presidential palace, setting the island on course for its first free elections in 1996.

US-educated Lee was also a master lobbyist, paying millions to firms in Washington to further grow Taiwan's influence on Capitol Hill and beyond. When the Clinton administration denied his request to spend the night on US soil in Honolulu when returning from a trip to Latin America, Taiwan's supporters in Washington responded furiously, forcing the administration to reverse its previous rejection of a visa for him to address his old university at Cornell the following year. That in turn infuriated China, and the stage was set for the most serious confrontation in the Taiwan Straits since the 1950s.[21]

In December 1995, the US sent the carrier *Nimitz* on its way from the Pacific to the Gulf through the Taiwan Strait, a decision US military officials described as 'weather-related' – a claim Beijing did not believe. With Chinese officials now talking in terms of a 'timeline' to follow the return of Hong Kong from British rule in 1997 with something similar for Taiwan itself, one PLA officer told the *New York Times* that time was running out.

China was infuriated by a combination of US weapons sales to Taiwan and the rising popularity of the opposition Democratic Progressive Party – which Beijing appeared to fear might win those first elections and declare immediate independence. Even as officials at the top of the Clinton administration claimed there was no evidence Beijing was planning any action, a Chinese official made the threat explicit. 'We have been trying to do all we can to avoid a scenario in which we are confronted in the end with no other option but a military one,' they told the *New York Times* on condition of anonymity. Unless Taiwan changed its course, they said, 'then I am afraid there is going to be a war'. Former US officials and academics visiting Beijing received a similar message.[22]

As Taiwanese voters prepared to go to the polls for the first time in spring 1996, China stepped up its military posturing to its most aggressive level since the 1950s. The dramatic series of exercises and missile drills around the island in early 1996 prompted the Clinton administration to deploy another two aircraft carriers to the nearby waters, intended as a clear signal to Beijing that Washington was prepared to fight if needed to protect the island. The mismatch in forces was enough to persuade China to stand down – although it was a humiliation Beijing would not forget.

Shortly afterwards, officials within the PLA appear to have reached a simple decision: they were going to buy that Ukrainian aircraft carrier after all.

*

Ukraine in the mid-1990s was scarcely in better shape than it had been upon independence, passing through a series of unpopular governments frequently accused of widespread corruption and subject to continuous pressure from the Kremlin. In the West, Yeltsin was seen first as a champion of democracy then something of a comic character, often drunk in public, a sign of how far his nation was falling. From the very start, however, he and those around him repeatedly suggested the borders of both the Baltics and Ukraine might be open to renegotiation, potentially by force.[23]

While the initial confrontations of the 1990s were not particularly serious, they highlighted fault lines that would again bring bloodshed in the decades that followed. For a while in 1992 it looked as though Russia and Ukraine might fight over the ethnically Russian-dominated Crimean Peninsula, particularly the key naval base at Sevastopol that housed the Black Sea Fleet, while other conflicts flared across the former Soviet Union, including in the eastern Moldovan Russian-speaking Transnistria region as well as between Azerbaijan and Armenia over Nagorno-Karabakh.[24]

Most would become 'frozen confrontations', like in Georgia where Russian-backed separatists abruptly seized control of South Ossetia and Abkhazia, setting the stage for Putin's eventual invasion of them in their entirety in 2008. But for US officials and their Western allies an even greater worry was that the USSR's vast atomic arsenal that was spread over several new and chaotic nations might be up for sale.

Once the Yeltsin government had swiftly removed its small nuclear devices from Kazakhstan over fears they might fall into the hands of Islamic fundamentalists, the greatest worries centred around Ukraine: if the new government in Kyiv was willing to sell its only aircraft carrier to the highest bidder, there were obvious questions over what else might also be on offer. The US pushed Ukraine into a settlement with the Kremlin, including giving up the Soviet nuclear arms stationed on its territory in return for foreign security guarantees – and allowing Russia's Black Sea Fleet to operate from Ukrainian territory in Crimea.

Between 1992 and 1996, the US and West pushed Ukraine into agreements culminating in the Bucharest Memorandum in which its borders were – theoretically at least – guaranteed by the US, UK and Russia. But it was not a formal binding treaty – in the US, most importantly of all, it was not ratified by the Senate because the Clinton administration did not believe that it could win that vote.[25] It was a failure of both diplomacy and imagination.

Through all this time the *Varyag*, rusting at anchor, was believed to be even more deteriorated. Still, the Chinese doubted they could simply buy the ship unchallenged. Instead, they turned to an improbable, somewhat roguish frontman, six-foot-tall former People's Liberation Army basketball star turned flamboyant Hong Kong businessman Xu Zengping. According to his own account, Xu was approached by Chinese military officials in mid-1997. Within weeks he had determined that the Ukrainians were not prepared to sell the craft if it was to be explicitly used for military purposes, and so set up a shell company in Macau to claim the vessel was being purchased as a casino. In January 1998 he flew to Ukraine himself. 'It was the first time I had ever been on a carrier and I was overwhelmed,' he later told the *South China Morning Post*. 'I told myself that I should buy it at all costs and make sure that it became part of our navy.' For reasons that remain unclear, the purchase was to be carried out without government funds, so Xu borrowed money from other Chinese businessmen. He engaged in marathon drinking sessions with Ukrainian officials, and eventually secured the ship for a 'bargain' $20 million.

Xu believed there were forces preparing to block the deal, with an unidentified helicopter landing on the ship's deck the day before the signing. As soon as the ink was dry, he packed the vessel's classified blueprints into sealed trucks and sent them overland to China. To facilitate the story that the ship was a useless hulk, he spread rumours the engines had been removed – although, in fact, they were packed in grease and suspected to still be powering the ship three decades later.[26]

Getting to China would prove a messy process – and much more expensive than actually purchasing the ship. Not until June 2000 did the *Varyag* leave Ukrainian waters, pulled behind a Dutch tugboat with no crew at all aboard the carrier itself. That immediately caused problems – authorities in Turkey refused to allow the ship through the Bosphorus to the Mediterranean, claiming that if the vessel broke free from its tugs the waterway could be blocked entirely.

For almost a year and a half, the tugboat pulled the moribund vessel around the Black Sea at a crawling pace after Ukraine declined to let the vessel back into its waters. Chinese officials – who still maintained the ship was being exported to serve as a casino – were furious then forced to negotiate with the Turkish authorities to get it into the Mediterranean and beyond. 'We were cheated by Ukraine,' one Chinese official complained to the *Washington Post*. 'Ukraine does not want to get involved at all. They got the money, so they are happy.' Aboard the tugboat, the bored crew of mostly Filipinos nicknamed the rusting warship they were towing as the '*Alcatraz*', climbing aboard once a week to check her condition. At one point, another helicopter landed on the deck, leaving behind the enigmatic graffiti: 'The French was here.'[27]

Not until November 2001 did the ship finally receive permission to sail through the Bosphorus into the Mediterranean, before being towed all the way around Africa and across the Indian Ocean to reach Dalian military port in China seven months later. By then, a war in Europe and aerial confrontation over the South China Sea between US forces and the PLA had seemingly set the tone for the confrontations of the coming century – only for matters to be overshadowed by the events of 9/11 and the 'war on terror'.

*

As the *Varyag* – still maintaining the cover story she was a future casino – disappeared into a Chinese naval dockyard in 2002, her future captain Zhang Zheng was getting his first close-up experience of an aircraft carrier in Portsmouth dockyard, part of a visit as he attended Britain's Joint Services and Command Staff College.[28] With the UK and the US now focused on a global counterterrorism campaign, both Moscow and Beijing were seen as potential partners. But some in Chinese and Russian corridors of power were still smarting from face-offs and humiliations almost immediately forgotten by the West, and by the start of the 2000s the resulting tensions were beginning to seep into public consciousness.

Some were more serious than others. In May 1999, a B-2 bomber flying all the way from Missouri to Serbia in support of the NATO campaign in Kosovo dropped several high precision bombs on a building marked on maps by CIA analysts as 'Belgrade warehouse one'. In fact, as a CIA internal investigation later revealed, that building was several streets away. Instead, they hit the Chinese embassy, whose position was wrongly marked on outdated maps.[29]

Conspiracy theories would swirl for years to come – but what does seem clear is that many at the top in China did not believe it was an accident, a belief that intensified throughout the years that followed. The B-2 was America's most advanced strategic bomber, capable of dropping atomic weaponry as well as conventional bombs such as those which hit the Chinese embassy. From the perspective of a Chinese national security establishment never lacking in paranoia it was not difficult to view the US bombing as a deliberate warning from Washington to a rising China.

The 1996 Taiwan crisis had sent Beijing's military leaders looking for an aircraft carrier – and now they wanted stealth technology. When a first-generation US F-117 Nighthawk stealth jet had been shot down by Serbian air defences a month earlier in April 1999, there were reports that Chinese engineers were among those that searched for wreckage in nearby farmland, and may have acquired other parts of it from the government in Belgrade.[30]

Meanwhile, Russian leaders were still nursing their wounds from what they saw as their nation's humiliating decline in the early 1990s, with financial and political chaos leaving it largely impotent in world affairs. The successive crises and conflicts in the Balkans seemed to deepen that frustration, with Russian hard-line nationalists keen to voice 'Slavic brotherhood' and limit Western action.

Initially, Yeltsin's Kremlin looked to position Russia as a genuine partner, supporting first UN and then NATO peacekeeping missions in Bosnia in particular. By the time of the Kosovo war in 1999, however, the Kremlin was outright opposed to further actions, blocking a Security Council resolution along with China. But that was largely ignored by the US and NATO as it began its air assault. Only as Serb forces withdrew from Kosovo and Western troops moved in did an opportunity present itself to show some Russian muscle.

As NATO troops prepared to move on the morning of June 12, footage suddenly appeared on Yugoslav TV showing Russian troops theoretically attached to the force in Bosnia driving armoured vehicles through Serbia and heading for Pristina airport. When British troops arrived a few hours later, America's top general in Europe, NATO Supreme Allied Commander Wesley Clark, ordered them to seize the airport and block the runways to prevent further reinforcements. Even at the height of the Cold War, no US or senior Western officer had ever ordered their subordinates to take such direct action against Russian troops – at least, not according to any account that has ever been declassified (as already noted, at the riskiest moments in Berlin in 1961, the top US commanders in Europe had worked hard to micromanage movements to the tiniest degree).

This time, it seemed, both Clark and the Clinton administration in Washington believed the most important thing was to regain the initiative and seize the vital ground. But the US had also proved unwilling to send ground troops into Kosovo – and they were about to discover that they could not expect the same unquestioning response to US orders, even from America's closest military ally. In a verbal exchange that has gone down in the history books, British Lieutenant General Mike Jackson told his US superior General Clark he would not 'start World War Three' for him. Clark reportedly told Jackson he would have to resign for refusing a lawful order.

In fact, Jackson had already escalated the matter to his military bosses and political leadership in London, who had similarly decided attacking the Russian troops was a bad idea and backed him up. They went over Clark's head to the professional head of the US military, Joint Chiefs Chairman General Hugh Shelton, and got the US to step back.[31]

In the years to come, what happened at Pristina airport would be interpreted very differently in Washington and Britain. In the UK, it would be seen as a sign of British common sense triumphing over an overbearing US commander – the junior officer heading up the lead British armoured reconnaissance troop, future pop star James Blunt, has repeatedly gone on record saying he would not have attacked Russian troops, regardless of his orders.[32] British Brigadier Adrian Freer, commanding the UK paratroop Brigade, also judged the UK position of avoiding direct confrontation as 'absolutely right'. 'It would have been a disaster,' he said in 2024.[33]

Within the US command chain, though, it was a savage reminder that when the chips were down, only US troops could be relied upon to follow US orders. Three months after the incident, US military chief Shelton publicly described Jackson's refusal as 'troubling' during a military operation where discipline could be a 'matter of life and death'.[34]

In reality, matters with the Russians at Pristina were smoothed out relatively quickly – struggling for supplies, the Russian troops were soon dependent on their NATO counterparts for food and water. Whoever was calling shots in the Kremlin, however, was clearly keen to make one last show of force. In the last week of June, Russian nuclear-capable Bear and Blackjack bombers flew their first long-range missions since 1991, along the Norwegian coast and out past Iceland to North America, to be intercepted by US fighters.[35] Less than eight weeks later, Vladimir Putin – appointed head of Yeltsin's National Security Council as the NATO bombing began in March – was appointed prime minister and Yeltsin's heir apparent. He would be sworn in as president in the first moments of the new millennium.

In the South China Sea, again first claimed by Chiang and China's Nationalist rulers in the 1940s, escalation had taken decades – but was now also quietly accelerating. In 1974, China had attacked and seized the Paracel Islands from South Vietnam in a skirmish estimated to have left around 100 Vietnamese dead. Several dozen more military personnel from a now-unified Vietnam were killed in another skirmish over Johnson

South Reef in March 1988, an engagement both sides kept largely silent on but which left the People's Liberation Army and PLA Navy personnel occupying fragile man-made platforms on the shoal.[36] By 1995, the government in Manila reported China building basic wooden structures to house troops on Mischief Reef, the first signs of what would one day become a massive base.

On April 1, 2001, a US Navy EP-3 spy plane took off from the Japanese island of Okinawa to fly over the South China Sea. It was intercepted by Chinese fighters which had been becoming more aggressive in recent months, but the crew – led by pilot Lieutenant Shane Osborn – had no particular reason to be worried. 'It's pretty amazing what you get used to,' he said a few months later. 'As much as you can get used to something like . . . having two or three armoured fighters off your wing, well, we were used to it.' But as two Chinese jets closed on his aircraft about 70 miles south-east of Chinese territory on Hainan Island, he decided this felt different. 'They had been closer and closer, but they never been that close . . . he was, like, ten feet away.' As the Chinese pilot began his third approach, shouts from the back of the US plane alerted Osborn the two were about to collide. 'The plane shook violently and kind of pitched up. I heard a pop, and that was his nose hitting ours.' The Chinese jet plunged towards the sea in at least two pieces. Within seconds, the US plane was upside down and not responding. 'I was pretty certain we were dead,' Osborn later said.

As he regained some control, Osborn concluded the only way he could keep his crew alive was to conduct an emergency landing on the Chinese base at Hainan – ironically, the same facility that was home to the Chinese interceptor he had just collided with. In the back of the plane, the crew began attempting to destroy classified equipment. Chinese officials at the base refused to acknowledge their distress calls, and as soon as they landed they were surrounded by armed troops who took them into custody.[37]

It took 11 days and a formal partial apology from Washington to get the 24 personnel returned – US officials expressed that they were 'sorry' over the death of the Chinese pilot, and also apologised for the aircraft landing at Hainan without Chinese permission. The authorities in Beijing refused to allow the aircraft to be fixed and flown back home, so it was dismantled by US technicians and sent back in bits.[38]

Throughout the following decade, US ships and aircraft would continue the 'freedom of navigation' patrols across the region largely without incident, while small detachments of Filipino marines on the *Sierra Madre* – beached in 1999 as the government in Manila looked to lock in possession of that shoal – and a handful of other tiny outposts in the Spratly Islands continued their long vigil.

In the meantime, however, China was growing its military spending by as much as 10 per cent each year – and making it clear diplomatically that it had no intentions whatsoever of relinquishing its ambitions to dominate Taiwan. At the start of the new century, the assumption had been broadly that whatever Taiwan's future, it would most likely be handled peacefully. Initially, there was talk on the island of independence being declared in the run-up to the 2008 Olympics, those who favoured that option suggesting that Beijing would be unwilling to ruin its 'coming out party' as a major power by intervening militarily.

China was determined to stamp out such talk. The result was China's 'Anti-Secession Law' passed in March 2005, which made any declaration of independence by the island a cause for immediate war. It provoked widespread protest and outrage in Taipei, but it was enough to banish talk of independence.[39]

At the end of 2012, as Xi consolidated his power as president, Communist Party chairman and the most powerful man in China, the reconditioned *Liaoning* entered Chinese naval service after a decade in the dockyard, prompting a flurry of headlines on Beijing's heightened naval hopes.[40] From 2014, as the US found itself also racing to respond to Russia's annexation of Crimea, China's 'island building' campaign in the disputed waters of the South China Sea dramatically intensified, as did the operations of its 'maritime militia', thousands of fishing and other craft that could be readily mobilised to harass those of other nations or even nearby warships. By now China's naval-building was the fastest in the world, with its second carrier *Shandong* launched in 2017.[41]

With his own military heavily rebuilt on the back of post-9/11 oil sales, Putin had begun to assert his anger at the West relatively early in his term of office. Infuriated by pro-Western 'colour revolutions' ousting pro-Kremlin politicians in Georgia and Ukraine in 2003 and 2004, he responded to the admission of the Baltic states into NATO later that same year by sending warplanes to harass their borders – immediately prompting NATO's first 'air policing' deployment to the region.

At the Munich Security Conference in 2007, Putin shocked delegates by launching into a diatribe of complaints against the West, accusing it of 'interfering' in Russia and beyond by backing the 'colour revolutions' and threatening military regime change like that against Iraq. Accusing the US of trying to set itself up as 'one master' for the world, Putin also railed against US missile-defence plans, which he said would completely upset the global balance of atomic power – and also what he called Western aid to political opposition groups within Russia itself. 'What is democratic about this?' he said. 'This is not about democracy, this is about one country influencing another.'

A spokesman for the George Bush Jr White House declared the administration 'surprised and disappointed' by the comments – but the West grossly underestimated to what extent they were a declaration of intent.[42] Cyber attacks against Estonia followed within weeks, while the decision of NATO's Bucharest summit in 2008 to deny Ukraine and Georgia – already theoretically on a path to membership – a clear route into NATO was followed by the swift Russian war against the latter.

With hindsight, that proved something of a precursor to Putin's much larger 2014 action to finally take Crimea.

By the end of the 2010s, both Russia and China were taking a much more assertive approach in support of what they wanted than would have been conceivable at the start of the millennium. Few signs of that were more apparent than the brief maritime face-off between China and Japan over disputed islands in the second half of 2010, in which Japan's high-tech industry was briefly brought almost to its knees by what appeared to be a deliberate if temporary suspension of Chinese 'rare-earth' exports.[43]

It may, however, have been the so-called 'Arab Spring' of 2011 that really sealed the deal, and set what would one day become the loose but real 'Axis of Upheaval' on a collision course with the US and its allies. 'We are next,' Russian President Dmitry Medvedev – theoretically senior to Putin, who was serving as prime minister, but in practice nothing of the kind – is said to have suggested after watching the video of Libyan leader Muammar Gaddafi's death, at least according to a rumour in Western intelligence circles.[44]

Whether or not that was true was not the point: the fear within autocratic governments was genuine. As unrest spread to Syria, the Kremlin and to a lesser extent Beijing made it clear they would support Bashar al-Assad's government almost regardless of what it did – while the US under Obama said it would not intervene unless chemical weapons were used against ordinary people. It was a 'red line' that was practically an invitation for the Syrian regime to test – and it still remains unclear whether or not they had the support of their Russian backers in doing so. After the Obama administration prevaricated and failed to respond militarily to an August 2013 sarin gas attack estimated to have killed almost 1,500 people[45] – preferring instead a messy Russian-brokered deal that theoretically removed Syrian chemical weapons stocks – Kremlin support to Assad simply kept on rising.

From 2014, the Western response to Crimea and the start of fighting in eastern Ukraine was also relatively mild – even after a Russian missile battery brought down Malaysia Airlines Flight MH17. The years that follow provided a light drumbeat of escalation – although Obama was credited with scoring one win over Xi, persuading him to hold back from building an artificial island on Scarborough Shoal, which had been seized from the Philippines. According to the *Financial Times*, Obama explicitly stressed that the US was in an election year – with the apparent implication that the Democrats could not afford to look weak if their candidate Hillary Clinton was to beat Donald Trump, and might therefore be readier than usual to consider military action.[46]

In the run-up to his first inauguration, Trump went further than any recent US president in embracing Taiwan, throwing away the rule book by taking a direct congratulatory call from Taiwanese leader Tsai Ing-wen in December 2016. According to those around the incoming president, the move – which produced a predictably furious response from Beijing – was deliberately planned, intended to showcase the president as someone who would not be bound by normal US protocol.[47] In that sense, it set the tone for the remainder of his term, which also saw both sky-high tensions and face-to-face talks with North Korean leader Kim Jong Un, volatile relations with European partners over military spending, and the assassination by drone of Iranian Revolutionary Guard Commander Major General Quassem Soleimani following militia attacks on the US embassy in Baghdad and military outposts that killed a US contractor.

On other fronts – particularly with both China and Russia – Trump in his first term was also unpredictable, sometimes embracing dialogue and concessions in a way that alarmed the mainstream foreign policy elite. According to his Russia adviser Fiona Hill, he was still 'stuck in a 1980s mindset' when looking at Russia's near abroad, not really viewing Ukraine – or perhaps other post-Soviet states – as truly independent countries.[48] Speaking to Volodymyr Zelenskyy for the first time by phone in

2019, Trump seemed preoccupied by persuading the Ukrainians to prosecute Biden's son Hunter for his business dealings in Kyiv, even appearing to imply that a Ukrainian prosecution might be a precondition for US arms.[49]

It was a call that would lead to unsuccessful Congressional attempts to remove Trump from office through impeachment. Still, as Trump would later remind Zelenskyy in the Oval Office, his first administration did eventually authorise the sale of Javelin anti-tank rockets, many of which proved critical when the invasion came. Indeed, 2019 and 2020 saw the government in Kyiv building up its direct Western military links, with US B-52 bombers flying to the very edge of Crimean airspace and British paratroopers dropping into central Ukraine to link up with Ukrainian counterparts.

As Chinese forces stepped up pressure on Taiwan during 2020, the US administration also increased its diplomatic support to the government in Taipei, sending Health Secretary Alex Azar in the highest-profile official US visit to the island since the 1970s. But as Xi and Putin sheltered from the first full winter of the Covid-19 pandemic, and Trump was pushed from office by the November 2020 presidential vote, both Russian and Chinese leaders clearly decided to keep up the pressure. Within three months of Biden entering office, Russian troops were heading to the borders of Ukraine in their tens of thousands.

That summer, most returned to barracks – although they left much of their equipment in position. August 2021 also saw the chaotic unravelling of almost 20 years of US-led efforts in Afghanistan: the dramatic collapse of the Western-backed government in Kabul and the humiliating final withdrawal from the international airport. By the early autumn, US intelligence was convinced that this time Putin was seriously preparing to launch the largest military assault in Europe since 1945. On that, they were proved entirely correct. On how the Ukraine conflict would develop, though, they could hardly have been more wrong.

8

The Lessons of Ukraine

'Every day, every metre is given by blood . . . The war is started by career soldiers, and finished by teachers, engineers, accountants.'

**Ukrainian Chief of the General Staff
Valerii Zaluzhnyi, May 2023**[1]

Within days of the anniversary of 9/11 in September 2021, those in America's military intelligence who watched Russia closely came to Chairman of the Joint Chiefs General Mark Milley with satellite footage of Russian tanks returning to the border with Ukraine. Soon, those images were accompanied by a worrying assessment: this no longer looked like an exercise or posturing, but a genuine preparation to overrun the country.

Over the weeks that followed, that consensus deepened within the US government. At the COP 26 Climate Change Conference in Glasgow at the start of November 2021, US officials took Ukraine's president to one side to tell him his country was about to be invaded. US figures in that meeting recall Zelenskyy taking the news stoically, and sitting extremely still.[2] At the time, that impressed his US counterparts. In reality, it appears the Ukrainian leader did not necessarily believe what he was being told – but if he did, he did not wish to show it. 'Everyone saw the risks differently,' Zelenskyy told the BBC after the invasion, adding that he had been called directly by French President Macron and German Chancellor Scholz. 'They . . . told me: "We talked to Putin. Putin will not invade." '[3]

Not until the very morning of the invasion would he send his own family out of Kyiv. 'It's hard to be ready,' Zelenskyy's political chief of staff Andriy Yermak later said. 'We have only ever seen such things in the movies, read about them in books.'[4]

The Ukrainians were not the only ones being briefed by the US administration on the growing threat. As in almost every major confrontation since the Cuban Missile Crisis, US intelligence briefers were not just visiting ambassadors in Washington but flying to foreign capitals, as well as addressing the North Atlantic Council in NATO's Brussels headquarters. Their message was blunt and clear: this invasion is coming, the Kremlin has more than enough forces to succeed, and the government in Kyiv does not stand a chance.

Among major European nations, only the British appeared to take that warning seriously – perhaps because the US was sharing its most sensitive material with them as well as the other members of the 'five eyes' intelligence partnership. Aside from the UK, according to US officials, only the Baltic states saw the seriousness of the situation – they had been warning something like this would eventually come almost since the moment of their independence.

To explain their scepticism, French and German officials pointed to flawed US intelligence on weapons of mass destruction in the run-up to the 2003 Iraq invasion. According to European officials after the event, their assessment was also based on simple military calculations: Ukraine was the second largest country in Europe after Russia itself, and the forces Putin was gathering were simply not enough to overrun it. But those in charge in Kyiv now also had another worry – every time the US issued a new warning of invasion, it hit Ukraine's currency and stock markets as investors fled. 'We had to strike a balance between realistically assessing the risks and preparing the country for the worst . . . and keeping the country running economically and financially,' Foreign Minister Dmytro Kuleba remembered.[5]

By the first weeks of 2022 the US, Britain and even the publicly sceptical European powers were preparing to close down their embassies in Kyiv and get their people out of the country. In snowy training areas, the last US personnel from the Florida National Guard and Britain's Operation ORBITAL took their Ukrainian counterparts through how to use incoming deliveries of Javelin and NLAW anti-tank weapons against Russian armour.[6] But they were not staying to fight. Even as the weapons were unloaded, Western soldiers and officials shredded, burnt and smashed the sensitive documents and equipment in their Kyiv embassies, transporting the remainder to airports in black SUVs to be flown out of the country on the same aircraft bringing in arms.[7]

For some who had served in both Ukraine and Afghanistan, two such withdrawals in quick succession was almost too much to bear. As the last ambassadors and their security details pulled back to western Ukraine or into Poland, there were tearful farewells – and often an appalling sense of guilt.

The Kremlin appeared happy to wait until the last Western troops were gone. Russian Defence Minister Sergei Shoigu had questioned British counterpart Ben Wallace by telephone on why UK special forces were still in Ukraine, and how long they might remain. 'There will be no British troops in Ukraine if there is to be a conflict there,' British Armed Forces Minister James Heappey told the BBC in the second week of February, warning that Russia had enough forces in position to launch a massive attack 'at no notice'.[8] Shortly afterwards, the Pentagon announced the last US military personnel in Ukraine were also pulling out. 'American citizens should not expect that the US military is going to rescue them in Ukraine at the last minute,' a senior State Department official warned.[9]

That message carried with it a not-so-subtle subtext: if the US was not willing to come into Ukraine to rescue its own people, it certainly would not be using military force to protect Ukraine itself. Ambassador to London Vadym Prystaiko spoke for many in his country. 'The airlines are cancelling flights, money has been withdrawn by investors, Ukrainians feel they've been abandoned,' he told US channel NBC.[10] It wasn't just the Ukrainians who felt that way. Even those nations such as the Baltic states and Poland that had made it into NATO feared that it might be just a matter of time before they were left to face something similar.

In Ukraine itself, an uneasy calm prevailed in the last days before the invasion. In a handful of interviews, Zelenskyy appears to have suggested that there was a deliberate decision by his government to talk down – or at least not talk up – the looming threat. 'Let people discuss in the future whether it was right or not,' the Ukrainian leader later told the *Washington Post*, noting that if more people had fled earlier the country would have become impossible to defend. 'We discussed this every day at the National Security and Defence Council . . . I have the feeling that the [Russians] wanted to prepare us for a soft surrender of the country. And that's scary.'

Nor, he diplomatically suggested, was he entirely confident that those urging him to flee genuinely had Ukraine's best interests at heart. 'I'm sure someone was really worried about what would happen to me and my family,' he said. 'But someone probably wanted to just end things faster. Generally, our inner sense was right: if we sow chaos among people before the invasion, the Russians will devour us.'[11]

Ukraine's initial survival would come down to leadership, willpower and the willingness of experienced combat veterans and ordinary people to fight for the survival of their nation. In the longer run, it would also come down to innovation, technology and industry. Ultimately, the machinations of great powers would leave the government in Kyiv scrambling for ways to maintain agency and independence. The lessons for other nations would take a while to learn – but what happened in the coming hours, weeks and years would help shape the modern world and every conflict that would follow.

*

Viewed through a conventional prism of military history, Volodymyr Zelenskyy was an unlikely candidate to be the most impactful wartime leader of the early 21ˢᵗ century. His closest military link was an uncle who fought for the Red Army during World War Two – while many Ukrainians had agonised over which side to fight for, his Jewish heritage had left very little choice. Decades later, in the chaos that followed Ukraine's unexpected independence in 1991, the country's future president had grown up largely speaking Russian, abandoning early ambitions to become a lawyer to instead work as a stand-up comic in the tough clubs of both Russia and Ukraine. By the time Putin annexed Crimea and fighting began in eastern Ukraine in 2014, Zelenskyy was running a successful TV company delivering content for both nations – but, as with many others, the conflict pushed him towards his Ukrainian identity and he shut down his partnerships in Moscow.

The next year, 2015, saw the launch of the sitcom *Servant of the People* that would radically change Zelenskyy's destiny. It was quite deliberately disrespectful towards the Ukrainian, Russian and wider global power structures. Zelenskyy played an absent-minded high school teacher, Vasily Goloborodko, whose students record him ranting angrily at the political elite. When they start a political campaign behind his back and submit his candidacy for president, his character finds himself unexpectedly the victor.

One scene in the opening episode showed better than any other how many Ukrainians viewed their national politics since independence: a group of oligarchs discussed which of them 'owned' the newly elected president, or whether he belonged to Putin. The punchline revealed their growing sense of panic as each denied knowledge – 'I thought he was yours' – and they realised he was under none of their control.[12] By the end of 2018, posters advertising the show were doubling as election promotional material as Zelenskyy ran for real power, with a party also called 'Servant of the People'. Ukraine's April

2019 election saw him elected president with almost three-quarters of the vote in the second round.[13]

Living up to all the hype, however, proved another matter. By the end of 2021, Zelenskyy's popularity was flagging, and his relationship with Ukraine's military establishment was also far from perfect. That included Ukraine's mercurial top military commander General Valerii Zaluzhnyi, whose rows with similarly blunt-talking US Chairman of the Joint Chiefs Mark Milley would soon be legendary.

Some of those missteps might not have been out of place in *Servant of the People*. In September 2020, at a high-profile visit by Zelenskyy to US exercise RAPID TRIDENT, a Javelin missile that was supposed to have been demonstrated simply failed to fire. It was a very public embarrassment and Zaluzhnyi – already struggling with relations with the president – worried that he might be fired.[14] Soon, military failure was no longer very funny.

According to later interviews, General Zaluzhnyi was one of those who believed the US warnings of a coming Russian invasion – at least enough to order some Ukrainian personnel into an intense training cycle through January and February 2022. But the fact Zelenskyy didn't agree made preparations harder.[15] It also left the president and his family vulnerable in the opening hours of the invasion – at one stage, a Russian fighter jet making a deliberately low pass across the capital came so close to the fleeing party that Zelenskyy's wife Olena said she could feel its sonic boom 'inside her rib cage'.[16]

The president himself spent much of the first hours of the invasion on the phone to foreign leaders. The first was British Prime Minister Boris Johnson, enthusiastically pulling himself from bed in the small hours of the morning to channel his best Churchillian rhetoric – Johnson had written a biography of the wartime leader – to encourage Ukrainian resistance. 'Yes, Boris, we will fight,' Zelenskyy told him. Soon after that he was speaking to Macron in Paris to urge him to call Putin and encourage him to stop. The Americans still wanted Zelenskyy to flee the capital, to the mounting annoyance of the Ukrainian president as well as those around him.

By mid-morning, those leading Ukraine had realised that while foreign support might be vital in the longer term, no one outside the nation was prepared to do anything substantive to affect the battlefield in the crucial opening phase. The coming hours would be particularly important: Russian attack helicopters were already landing troops just outside the capital.

Zelenskyy had been warned personally by CIA Director William Burns that the airport at Hostomel, north-west of Kyiv, was likely to be a major focus of the Russian attempt to claim the capital, but he had been sceptical. Now told that it had been taken, he realised it could not be allowed to remain in Russian hands. 'He gave the harshest possible orders,' Zelenskyy's aide and Ukrainian politician Mykhailo Podolyak recalled later. 'Show no mercy. Use all available weapons to wipe out every Russian thing that's there.' At the airstrip, Russian commandos were preparing for the arrival of giant military cargo planes from bases in western Russia. 'They land ten of those planes,' Minister of Internal Affairs Denys Monastyrsky warned, 'and all of a sudden we'd have 5,000 Russian troops marching through the streets of Kyiv.'

Oleksiy Danilov, secretary of Ukraine's National Security and Defence Council, was one of those who had listened to US warnings. But he also believed the French and German governments were right in their assessment that the Kremlin was biting off more than it could chew, that there were simply not enough Russian troops to control Ukraine's entire territory, nearly twice the size of Germany. If Zelenskyy and his government could endure the initial onslaught, Danilov believed his country would survive.[17] Providing that happened, he believed there was much his country could teach others. 'I am more than sure that in 10, 15, 20 years there will be a big war in the world,' Danilov predicted a few months into the war. 'The opening days are absolutely decisive.'

If the Ukrainians lost, many now believed it could be the permanent end of centuries of intermittent nationhood, most likely accompanied by mass deportations – the government in Kyiv had already noted one pre-invasion article by Russian Defence Minister Sergei Shoigu suggesting the Kremlin might create a 'new city' in Siberia of several million people.[18] Others suggested Putin might resettle Ukrainians in Russia's Pacific Far East to use them as a counterbalance against mounting Chinese migration across the nearby border.[19]

Either way, the example of Russia's campaign in Chechnya in the 1990s and 2000s suggested that once Ukraine was crushed, the Kremlin would do everything to ensure the next generation were loyal fighters for Russia in whatever war might follow – including for future conquests in Eastern Europe. As one Ukrainian speaker warned counterparts at a conference three years later: 'If Russia wins, they will use our sons to kill yours in 25 years' time.'[20]

Communicating Ukraine's message abroad would be important – but getting it out at home would be even more crucial in the early stages. One of the things Ukraine had got most right, Danilov believed, was ensuring the government retained robust communication structures through which the president in particular could speak – given how much of the top team was comprised of hardcore TV professionals perhaps that was not surprising.[21] 'You have to follow certain rules if you want someone on the other side of the screen to keep watching you, to remain sympathetic,' Ukrainian Foreign Minister Dmytro Kuleba told *Time* journalist Simon Shuster later. 'You have to be winning, because people love winners. From time to time, you have to impress them with something big and unexpected, because no one can follow routine. Third, you need a clear character associated with the story to be visible to them all the time, and that's President Zelenskyy in our case. And last of all, you need a good story to tell. It's the story of a small nation kicking the ass of a larger nation that invaded it. It's bad guys attacking good guys, and good guys winning. That's what people love.'[22]

But on the military front, preparedness was hugely mixed – and it would take fast movement and ad hoc co-ordination between Ukraine's regular military, its elite special forces and newly enlisted volunteers to save the capital itself.

Commanders of one of the conventional army units most vital to the defence of Kyiv, Ukraine's 72nd Mechanised Brigade, had begun conducting reconnaissance north-west of the capital from December 2021, picking out points over the Irpin River that Russian troops would need to cross to take the city. But despite the unit's combat engineers having identified those bridges, there appears to have been no immediate plan to destroy them and deny access to the enemy until the start of the invasion. In a potential attack against Taiwan or the Baltics, such an oversight might prove fatal – but the brigade had been blooded in the Donbass, so were much more experienced than any of Taiwan's troops or even wider Western forces.

Some were more prepared than others. In the first weeks of 2022, the 72nd Brigade received ammunition and began preparing weaponry and vehicles. 'Somewhere at the top, they already understood that something would happen,' one soldier later recalled. More junior officers and mid-ranking officers, including the lieutenant colonels leading battalions and below, still suggested it might be a false alarm. 'I didn't believe in [a] full-scale invasion,' another soldier said. 'I thought it was a game, or something – maybe they [the Russians] would . . . just cross the border and go back, to scare people, and that would be it.'[23]

In fact, the US had already briefed Ukrainian commanders on the likely Russian axes of advance. One would thrust up from Crimea into southern Ukraine around Kherson and push west towards the Mykolaiv docks – birthplace of what was now China's aircraft carrier – then through to Odessa to occupy Ukraine's whole coastline and threaten neighbouring Moldova. Others would push on from the east towards Kharkiv and the

Donbass, with a particular intent to seize Mariupol and a 'land bridge' from Russia proper to Crimea.

But when it came to Ukraine's outright survival, the most dangerous elements of the Russian force were the heavily armoured if slow-moving columns pushing down from Belarus, past, and on some occasions through, the abandoned radioactive zone around Chernobyl and down towards the capital. Meanwhile, the battle still raged at the airport in Hostomel. As the scale of the danger became clear, the president gave permission for staff to get their families to safety[24] – but along the roads that crossed the Ukrainian frontier, border guards were already refusing permission for men to leave the country. Thousands were fleeing anyway, finding routes through forests, their cars left abandoned by the roadside.

Others were volunteering for the fight, co-ordinating in WhatsApp groups as they made arrangements for their families and told partners they felt they could better protect their loved ones by heading to the front. The result was chaos at recruitment offices in the capital – there was little chance of proper medical checks, nor any other vetting.

As soon as they could be collected and loaded onto buses, some were sent directly to the 72nd Brigade headquarters at Bila Tserkva, where buildings still smouldered from strikes in the first hours of the invasion. It was now a mobilisation centre, with new recruits given a helmet, flak jacket, rifle and rounds of ammunition – and sometimes not all of the above.

Barely 36 hours later, on the afternoon of January 25, some of those newly recruited troops faced the first attempt by Russian forces to cross the Irpin River. Locals helped them dig trenches with a tractor and spades, and provided intelligence on advancing troops over handheld radios. 'We did not cook food,' one soldier later recalled. 'We did not spend time and energy on it. We only fought.' Lying in positions under fire for days at a time, they could not have survived without deliveries of food and blankets from the local population, several soldiers said.

Everything depended on slowing down the Russians – and it would take innovation. In his bunker on the outskirts of Kyiv, commander of Ukraine's ground forces Colonel General Oleksandr Syrskyi was examining his maps when his aides introduced a businessman and engineer with a plan to save the capital. 'Andriy' – who told UK-based researchers a year later he did not wish to be identified – had spent the previous day examining the villages, rivers, bridges and floodplains outside the capital. He recommended blowing a small hole in a single dam. By 3.30 p.m. that Friday afternoon, a combat engineer was placing the charges exactly where 'Andriy' had suggested – and 31 billion gallons of water was set to inundate the nearby landscape.[25]

The Russians were now in trouble – particularly the force pushing down from Belarus, which in addition to having its route now blocked by the flooded Irpin River was also being worn down by repeated attacks from Ukrainian special forces, locally raised fighters and Turkish-built attack drones. At the airport, too, the Ukrainians were starting to win – particularly after Russian commanders made the critical decision to hold back the transport planes and paratroopers from launching their planned full-scale assault.

The simple truth was that neither the Russians nor the Ukrainians had been properly prepared for the battle for Kyiv, but the Ukrainians were fighting on home turf and so had learned faster. The survival of the capital, however, just opened the door to the next phase of the war – one in which international support, goodwill and ultimately raw industrial commitment would turn out to be key. In that, Ukraine's military – and particularly its elite units and intelligence – would be hugely helped by the relationships they had built up with the spies and special forces of the United States and Britain.

*

As the dust settled from Ukraine's February 2014 'Maidan' revolution that had swept out pro-Kremlin President Viktor

Yanukovych, Ukraine's new leadership realised they might shortly find themselves at war with Russia. With Crimea swiftly lost and Ukraine's army soon suffering repeated defeats at the hands of Russian-backed separatists in the eastern Donbass region, those leading its military intelligence believed that only good relations with the West – and specifically US intelligence – might turn things around.

In Washington, however, there was little appetite for such relations. American spies believed Ukraine's intelligence services were too exposed to Russian influence, not to mention allowing parts of the country's east – particularly the university town of Kharkiv – to act as a jumping-off point for Islamic State fighters to enter Europe.[26] To win over the CIA and other parts of the US 'interagency' system, Ukrainians would need to demonstrate that they had comprehensively cleaned their house – and also that they were too invaluable a potential partner to be readily ignored. Under the direction of new military intelligence chief Valeriy Kondratiuk, that is exactly what they did.

In 2015, Kondratiuk met the CIA deputy station chief in Kyiv and handed over a stack of top-secret files that Ukrainians had stolen off the Russians. Among the first were designs for Russia's latest submarines and other details of its Northern Fleet. Soon, 'backpack-loads' of documents were being handed over to the Americans, much more than US spies had asked for. 'We understood that we needed to create the conditions of trust,' Kondratiuk told the *New York Times*.

The dynamic was not always easy – particularly after Ukrainian intelligence and special forces began conducting occasional lethal operations inside Russian territory from 2016. That led to tighter rules of engagement from the Obama administration forbidding intelligence sharing with Ukrainian operations that might take Russian lives. The exchange of information, however, continued to intensify – with Britain's Secret Intelligence Service, often known as MI6, also joining in. Soon, that relationship had also been expanded to include special forces as well as the cyber operators of agencies such as GCHQ.

By the end of the decade, Putin was complaining to European diplomats that Ukraine was under the control of the CIA and MI6 – but, in reality, it was Ukraine that was pushing for an exchange of information and support at an ever faster pace.[27] From late 2021, dozens if not hundreds of personnel from the US National Security Agency and military US Cyber Command had also descended on Ukraine in their largest ever 'hunt forward' operation, identifying vulnerabilities, patching systems and removing hostile malware. That last-ditch effort, many believe, helped keep Ukraine's national infrastructure from collapsing in the face of Russian hacking efforts. But, like other foreigners, the Americans withdrew in February 2022.[28]

The first hours after the invasion showed the Ukrainian state somewhat patchy in its loyalty. While its military intelligence service had almost entirely purged its ranks from 2014 to bring in a new generation who loathed the Kremlin, civilian intelligence services still contained plenty of individuals with Russian loyalty who attempted to switch sides within hours of the invasion. In Ukraine's southern city of Kherson, defecting Ukrainian officials would hand the entire city to advancing Russian forces who themselves would only be forced out later in the year. Some commanders may have even sat on their hands until it was clear the Zelenskyy government would survive the opening hours and days, only then committing to their country's defence. Others were already chafing at the bit for orders.[29]

Not all were prepared to wait. Throughout the first days of the invasion, groups of elite Ukrainian special operators crashed around the capital in their vehicles in high-speed convoys, snapping wing mirrors off nearby parked cars. 'There are definitely untold stories,' one security expert told me, describing Ukrainian special forces as effectively 'self-tasking' in the first few days, commanders responding to tip-offs or demands, some likely from US and British contacts.[30]

As it became clear Ukraine's government and capital would survive, those cross-border relationships kicked further into action. According to the *New York Times*, the United Kingdom was the first major country to begin operating small detachments of troops again within Ukraine, providing advice, weaponry and supporting what soon became lethal operations. In April, heavily armed British special forces commandos in civilian clothes escorted two senior Ukrainian generals out of the capital and across the Polish border in a convoy of black SUVs, heading straight to the US Army's European headquarters in Wiesbaden in Germany.

There, in what had previously been a music auditorium but was now a makeshift headquarters and operations room, the Ukrainians were brought to meet Chris Donahue, the already legendary US special operations officer who had led the 82nd Airborne and been the last soldier to step onto the plane out of Kabul. Now leading America's 18th Corps, he had also been assigned to lead the US support to Ukraine. ' "I will never lie to you. If you lie to me, we're done," ' General Mykhaylo Zabrodskyi, one of the two Ukrainian generals recalled Donahue telling him at their first encounter. 'I feel exactly the same way,' the Ukrainian replied.

Since the dawn of time, military campaigns had been shaped by the competing egos, insights and agendas – not to mention the highly personal dislikes, hatreds and divisions – of senior commanders and politicians. Ukraine would prove no different.[31]

*

With the rest of the world watching – including both China and Taiwan – the stakes were the highest seen in any shooting war since at least Korea in the early 1950s. But once the initial fight for survival had concluded, there were few easy choices.

The first schism occurred while the fight for Kyiv was still in process, as Ukraine's military chief Valerii Zaluzhnyi – beloved by the British and many of his own fighters, rather less so by some Americans – felt he was being patronised by General Milley, chairman of the US joint chiefs. It took a concerted effort by Zelenskyy to get them talking once again.

In the opening stages of the fight, Zaluzhnyi had told reporters he had made many of the major battlefield decisions, nervous of sharing too much with the presidency for fear that it might leak, but he was still working to retain Zelenskyy's trust. 'My aim was not to drag him into it,' the general said. 'What I hate more than anything else in the army is when someone shifts part of their responsibility onto their superiors.' While the Americans were still talking of evacuations and a government in exile, the military chief and president were broadly agreed on the bigger picture. 'We could not allow the capture of Kyiv,' Zaluzhnyi said. 'And on all the other vectors, we had to spill their blood, even if it meant losing territory.'[32]

The realisation dawned on Western nations that Ukraine would survive – and potentially even win if Russia kept up the poor military performance that had seen its soldiers slaughtered. That, in turn, brought both tougher decisions and unintended outcomes. According to one account from a senior US officer, the first major Ukrainian naval victory of the war – the sinking of Black Sea Fleet flagship the *Moskva* – occurred largely by accident when US and Ukrainian officers were on a call together and the ship appeared suddenly on the US radar screens. As one official involved in the exchange described it to the *New York Times*: 'The Americans go: "Oh, that's the *Moskva*!" The Ukrainians go: "Oh my God. Thanks a lot. Bye." '[33]

In December 1989, the *Moskva* had accommodated Gorbachev as he met Reagan in Malta for a summit proclaimed at the time as ending the Cold War. Now, the American tip-off was all the Ukrainians needed to hit the cruiser with two Neptune missiles, leaving her ablaze and sinking. The loss of life remains unclear to this day, but despite the initial scrupulous silence of the Biden administration on whether US intelligence had helped, within weeks it was being reported in US media that it had.[34] At each stage of further action, some would worry that they might cross the line with Russia to perhaps catastrophic escalation.

Soon, however, the US personnel at Wiesbaden were working with some 20 Ukrainians now also located at the base. The rules of engagement banned handing information directly to the Ukraine team, so the US devised a form of words in which identified Russian forces were described as 'points of interest'. 'If you ever get asked the question: "Did you pass a target to the Ukrainians?" you can legitimately not be lying when you say: "No," ' said one US official. But by the middle of 2022, US 'points of interest' had helped the Ukrainians strike major Russian headquarters in the occupied Kherson region – killing several senior commanders – as well as more warships of Russia's Black Sea Fleet headquartered in Sevastopol.[35]

By then, most of the large defence technology firms like Palantir were on the ground, increasing Ukraine's capability to crunch large amounts of data to make such judgements.[36] Delivery of US HIMARS drastically increased the tempo at which such strikes could be made, further growing Russian losses.

Ukraine made considerable advances through the summer of 2022, preparing to thrust south to retake Kherson – where a string of killings and attacks on Ukrainian 'collaborators' had made clear the way the tide was turning.[37] The fall of Kherson at the end of August opened the door to a thrust across the Dnipro River to cut Crimea off again from Russia's 'land bridge' – in the words of US General Donahue, striking at Crimea's 'neck'. In the run up to that offensive, Russia's frontlines began to collapse faster than expected.

'Go, go, go, you have them on the ropes,' Donahue told Ukraine's Ground Commander Oleksandr Syrsky. According to the *New York Times*, at this point the Ukrainians wavered – and so did some in Washington. Since the Cold War began, the US and Kremlin high command had wargamed the use of tactical atomic weapons in the event a key frontline collapsed. Now, US intercepts of Russian military conversations suggested that outcome was being genuinely considered. While there was a fair chance those conversations were intended to be heard, others thought them genuine – with some in Washington seeing the risk of nuclear war as high as 50 per cent. Biden, recalling his student memories of the Cuban Missile Crisis almost exactly half a century earlier, was particularly concerned.

Whatever the reality, the Ukraine offensive faltered, while the Russians entrenched themselves with the support of mercenaries from the infamous Wagner Group. From the end of 2022, Donahue was rotated back to concentrate on the 18th Airborne Corps – and those who replaced him were more cautious. The focus shifted to the ultimately unsuccessful Ukrainian offensives of 2023, and then 2024. Rows continued between individuals, nations and institutions; the Ukrainians complained the US was too slow to deliver long-range arms, while US officials told reporters political infighting had undermined otherwise solid plans. In time, Zelenskyy also fired top general Zaluzhnyi – now seen as a potential rival for the presidency – and reassigned him to London as ambassador, while elections scheduled for 2024 were postponed as impractical given the still-unending conflict.[38]

Next, the US set up a new military command to handle long-term Ukraine support. Pentagon officials publicly vowed that Washington would stand by Ukraine 'for as long as it takes'.[39] It was, of course, a largely hollow promise: America's support would only last as long as its leaders instructed that it should. The longer the war went on, the more dependent Ukraine became on its outside backers – and the less it was the master of its destiny.

In the first three years of the conflict, the US alone would provide more than half a billion rounds of small arms and grenades, 10,000 Javelin anti-tank missiles, 3,000 Stinger anti-aircraft rockets, 272 artillery pieces, 76 tanks, 40 HIMARS units, 20 Mi-17 helicopters and three Patriot air-defence batteries, as well as training for F-16 pilots using aircraft donated by the Netherlands and Denmark.[40] The Europeans had provided more besides, including several hundred German-made Leopard 1 and 2 main battle tanks – and in the case of more committed nations, more covert support.[41] 'Britain's role in Ukraine is deeper than we fully acknowledge or publicise,' wrote Josh Glancy in the *Sunday Times* following a trip there, noting the 'near reverence' with which a prime ministerial delegation was being treated. 'But Zelenskyy knows all about it. As does Putin.'[42]

Then, of course, there was the new technology, including drones and missiles punching ever deeper into Russia – as well as making it harder for tanks and personnel to survive and conduct attacks on the frontline. For all that, though, Ukraine's demographics remained among its greatest weaknesses. The tough years just before and after independence had seen a further collapse in Ukraine's already falling birth rate, and it simply did not have the traditional spare numbers of young men every nation in history has used throughout their major wars. In an effort to protect those that did exist, Ukraine's lower age of conscription was set at 27 after the invasion, then reduced in 2024 to 25.

It was a decision that fundamentally baffled the military commanders of the US and Britain. Top US officer in Europe Chris Cavoli told Ukrainian commanders to 'get your 18-year-olds into the game'. By the third year of the war, many of those arriving at the front were in their fourth or fifth decade of life, and often not surviving much longer.[43] Cavoli's suggestion was not one that went down well within Ukraine itself, where pro-Russian propagandists had long labelled the strategy of the West as 'fighting to the last Ukrainian'.

Certainly, multiple nations in central and Eastern Europe believed that as soon as fighting halted, the Kremlin would rearm to take their countries too. But that did not seem to worry Trump, who wanted a peace agreement as soon as possible and was working towards that goal before even before he entered office.

The Ukrainian frontline was now unlike anything seen in modern times: enough so that what Western experts sometimes saw as key lessons from other recent wars could instead prove deadly errors. Few anecdotes showed that so brutally as Ukraine's huge number of combat amputations: some 100,000 in the first three years of war. According to a review by a senior Ukrainian surgeon, as many as 75 per cent were a consequence of unnecessarily applied tourniquets left on limbs too long. The reason for that appeared as simple as it was appalling: Western combat medicine taught soldiers to apply them frequently to stem bleeding on the assumption that casualties would then be reassessed by a major medical centre often within 60 minutes. That training had then been applied to Ukraine's troops and frontline first responders, but in an environment of drones, artillery fire and limited medical facilities they were instead left on for hours and sometimes days.

By late 2024, a NATO medical team visiting Ukraine was warning that urgent action must be taken to give more sensible advice – and also ensure Western forces did not make the same mistake in a major conflict in which they too might struggle to evacuate their wounded.[44]

Many complaints within Ukraine's own military blamed its wider repeated failures on a 'Soviet-style' structure and ethos that made it hard to acknowledge errors and frequently sacrificed large numbers of personnel to hold untenable ground or recapture lost positions.[45] In reality, many of the anecdotes would have been familiar to anyone who had served within any modern Western militaries. One Ukrainian defence source told me that the largest obstacle was the presence of mid-ranking Ukrainian majors and colonels with little or no recent frontline experience, often in positions where the only primary power they could exert was to veto activity, block promotions and stop things from happening.[46]

Others reported similar toxic structures on the frontline itself. 'If a brigade commander says that he thinks the [higher] commander's order is a wrong order, the commander replaces him with someone who will say; "Roger that, I will do it,"' said career army officer Anatolii Kozel, himself removed from a battalion commander's position in 2023 after complaining of inadequate training and equipment to a Western journalist. Providing frontline commanders did not rock the boat, he said, few higher up the command chain would complain about unnecessary losses.[47]

Even as late as autumn 2024, some of Ukraine's outside backers remained robustly optimistic. 'A Ukrainian victory will show the world the good guys can and will win,' former UK Prime Minister Boris Johnson told an event in Kyiv that September. 'It will have an effect on stability, and send a message of hope around the world.'[48] Within Ukraine, however, a rather more bitter narrative was taking hold. As frontline Ukrainian soldier Hanna Vasyk told the same event: 'The answer to the common question: "When will the Third World War begin?" is, in my opinion, that it has already started.'[49]

*

By the start of 2025, the growing assumption in Washington, Europe and Ukraine was that the new administration would indeed find a way to halt the fighting, even if opinions varied widely over whether that was a good idea.

Trump entered office having pledged to end the conflict within 24 hours – but by May 2025 his frustration at having failed to do so was becoming ever more apparent. That 24-hours pledge, he told reporters, had been 'sarcastic', not to be taken literally. The brief pause in weapons, supplies and intelligence support following his disastrous February meeting with Zelenskyy had not been repeated – but there were also no signs of the Pentagon considering new supplies of weapons once those already earmarked and paid for under the previous Biden administration were exhausted.

Judging by the president's social media posts, he believed Ukraine should give up its lost territory – and perhaps even a little more – to the Kremlin. 'Nobody is asking Zelenskyy to recognise Crimea as Russian territory but, if he wants Crimea, why didn't they fight for it 11 years ago when it was handed over to Russia without a shot being fired?' Trump wrote in a social media post that April. 'The situation for Ukraine is dire – he can have peace, or he can fight for another three years before losing the whole country.'[50]

'I think Trump finds Zelenskyy annoying,' one European diplomat in Washington told me – although the funeral of Pope Francis at the end of April 2025 gave the two leaders the chance to have an almost private conversation in the iconic surroundings of St Peter's Basilica. A few days later, they both signed the mineral deal postponed from February – but it still conferred no security guarantees, and the US president seemed rather more interested in post-ceasefire business with the Kremlin. 'Russia wants to do large-scale trade with the United States when this catastrophic "bloodbath" is over, and I agree,' Trump wrote after a May call with Putin. 'There is tremendous opportunity for Russia to create massive amounts of jobs and wealth. Its potential is UNLIMITED.'[51]

At some points, particularly after the US president described Zelenskyy as a 'dictator without elections', it looked as though his administration envisaged treating Ukraine like a defeated country, potentially making it pay reparations for US military support. For US officials who had devoted years to keeping Ukraine free, this approach was hard to bear. 'The policy since the beginning of the Trump administration has been to put pressure on the victim, Ukraine, rather than the aggressor, Russia,' wrote US ambassador to Kyiv Bridget Brink after her angry resignation. 'Peace at any price is not peace at all – it is appeasement.'

Some Ukrainians, in contrast, believed Trump was pushing for what would be a 'good enough outcome' for their country:

leaving it free and sovereign, if partially occupied.[52] But it still wasn't bringing peace – even after the US administration made it clear it would block NATO membership for Ukraine.[53] As the Kremlin kept up missile strikes on Ukraine, including some of the heaviest of the whole conflict so far, even the president's patience looked like it might be wearing thin. 'I've always had a very good relationship with Vladimir Putin . . . but something has happened to him. He has gone absolutely CRAZY!' wrote Trump in late May after multiple strikes on the Ukrainian capital. 'Missiles and drones are being shot into cities in Ukraine for no reason whatsoever . . . needlessly killing a lot of people.'[54] Speaking from the Kremlin, Putin's spokesman Dmitry Peskov said the comments were 'connected to an emotional overload of everyone involved'.[55]

It seemed unlikely Peskov intended that comment to refer to his own boss's mental health. In Washington, however, some US officials had been raising the question since the summer of 2020, when the Russian leader had released his long rambling article on Ukraine, apparently written during his time isolating from the Covid-19 pandemic. Speculation on Putin's mental condition was also linked to his growing age – he was going to to turn 70 in 2022 – and his desire to ensure his place in history as one of the greatest Kremlin leaders.[56]

As the fighting dragged on through summer 2025, expectations earlier in the year that a deal might come were replaced by talk of yet more losses. Ukrainian officials said they believed the Russians were losing perhaps as many as twice the number of Ukrainians killed and injured – but given the respective size of those two nations, and their respective cultures, perhaps that did not matter. Speaking to the *Guardian*, frontline Ukrainian officer Alex Budilov described Russian attacks beginning with a tank so covered in metal sheeting to protect it from drone attack it was referred to as a 'barn', followed by motorcycle-borne assault troops and finally just human waves of infantry. It showed Russian commanders willing to take colossal losses 'for the fleeting appearance of success'. 'It's a very Russian idea that you are part of something bigger . . . you sacrifice your life to do something for history,' he said, 'It's a totalitarian mind virus.'[57]

It was a historical reputation openly embraced by those closest to the Kremlin. 'No one can suffer like the Russians,' Russian Defence Minister Sergei Shoigu had told British counterpart Ben Wallace in a meeting shortly before the full-scale invasion, warning that his nation would keep fighting regardless of sanctions or other setbacks.[58] It came with the clear threat of violent domestic coercion – weeks into the war, Putin had described opponents of the 'special military operation' as 'scum and traitors' who lived 'metaphorically' in the West but would be spat out 'like a gnat'.[59]

Among the Russian population, opinion pollsters referred to those who embraced the Kremlin wartime narrative most fully as 'turbo-patriots' – and they made up roughly 20 per cent of the population, more or less the same proportion as those who quietly opposed the conflict and were willing to reveal that they wished the Putin regime was not in office. The majority, however, expressed broadly apathetic views, a safety-conscious school of thought some described as 'learned indifference'.[60]

Meanwhile in China – another nation with a legacy of objectifying state-inflicted suffering – another leader was also ageing, eyeing up his legacy and believed to be considering his own risky military campaign, this time against Taiwan. Xi and Putin had their own complex relationship, but one thing at least was becoming clear: the Russian leader was not a man who found it easy backing down. And neither, judging by his history, was his Chinese counterpart.

9

'Better Than Allies' – Inside the 'Axis of Upheaval'

'In the face of changes in the world of our times and history, China will work with Russia . . . and play a leading role in injecting stability into a world of challenge and disorder.'

Xi Jinping meeting Vladimir Putin, Samarkand, Uzbekistan, September 2022[1]

By the time a young Xi Jinping was pulled onto the stage to be denounced – it was the mid-1960s and he was likely 16 or less – he had been imprisoned, interrogated and probably also beaten. He was tall for his age, in part the consequence of good nutrition and healthy living in his early years, thanks largely to his family's status as early Communist party activists who had then risen fast.

But during China's 'Cultural Revolution' such family associations could be dangerous. Xi's father Xi Zhongxun had been a leading political commissar in the PLA as it had fought the Japanese occupation and then the Nationalists in China's civil war, becoming one of the best-known senior party officials in the early 1950s. But several of his close political contacts had then become the victims of Mao's harsh internal purges, followed by himself. One of his daughters – Xi's sister – was said to have been selected for particular attention, driven by psychological torture to kill herself in custody. Now, it was the teenage Xi himself being paraded, forced to wear the cone-shaped metal hats Mao Zedong's Red Guards used to humiliate their prisoners. According to family legend, Xi's own mother – forced to disown her husband following his arrest and transportation to a prison camp – not only watched her son Xi's degradation, but also joined the shouts of 'Down with Xi Jinping'.

Xi himself rarely talked publicly of what had happened, aside from an interview with Chinese journalists in 2000 as he established himself as a rising leader. Some of the details of his public denunciation – including his mother's presence – come from a single family source years after the event. By Xi's own account, he was questioned by Red Guards who threatened him repeatedly with death. 'We can execute you 100 times,' they told him.

Xi's father's fall from grace had seen the teenager rebranded as a 'gangster child' – but his stubborn streak had got him into trouble before, he noted, and it did so again as he told the guards they could only kill him once – prompting them to tell him he had just five more minutes before he would be shot.

That did not transpire. Instead, he was taken back to a cell and made to read the works of Mao, then allowed to go into exile in the countryside in Shaanxi province where his family had roots and where his now-imprisoned father was still viewed with affection. There, the young Xi was put to work digging ditches as he began to carve out the start of his own political career, reading newspaper articles to villagers and leading discussions.[2]

Years later, those who met or even just observed Xi as he got older would often comment on the effect they believed his youthful years of hardship had. Lee Kuan Yew, founder of Singapore, would even describe him as one of the 'Nelson Mandela class of persons', someone who had endured 'trials and tribulations' to emerge with 'iron in his soul'.[3] But rather than follow the Mandela path, Xi would use that 'iron' to make himself China's most powerful leader since Mao, determined to make that nation the strongest it had ever been.

As Xi's family was politically rehabilitated, he was put firmly back on a path to power, first as a civilian official working alongside those at the very top of the defence ministry in Beijing. It was a huge shift for a young man who had only recently been digging ditches and sometimes living in a cave. Xi's biographer Michael Sheridan describes the abrupt return of China's future leader to power and status as a 'formative experience', cementing a firm lifelong belief that the growth of Chinese power required both strategy and commitment – with unity between the party and PLA critical to delivering stability and influence.

Prior to his fall from grace, Xi's father had been one of the most important quartermasters in Mao's army. Now, Xi himself was often wearing uniform as part of his role at the defence ministry, developing not just what would become his future powerbase but also a long-term respect for China's military culture and bureaucracy.[4]

Xi already had one military ally from his youth: up-and-coming army officer Zhang Youxia, another 'second-generation red' roughly three years older than Xi and also from a Shaanxi family. Xi's father and Zhang's had served together in the Chinese Civil War, the older Zhang as a general commanding troops and the older Xi as his political commissar. Both fathers had been 'purged' during the Cultural Revolution, and the two younger men had grown up together, described by Xi's family as sometimes like brothers.

Zhang would enjoy a successful parallel career to Xi, including combat service as a company commander during China's brief and unsuccessful war with Vietnam in 1979.[5] Meanwhile, working for China's Defence Minister Geng Biao gave Xi himself a front-row seat to the diplomatic rapprochement between the United States and China initiated by Richard Nixon and Henry Kissinger throughout the 1970s. It also would have given him plenty of exposure to older officials who believed China had been poorly treated by the Soviet Union during the early Cold War decades. According to Xi's biographer Sheridan, the walls of the offices the future Chinese leader worked in contained maps showing territory Russia had seized from

Beijing in previous wars, while Defence Minister Geng later told his US counterparts those running the PRC had concluded the Kremlin wished to keep the Chinese nation permanently subservient to Russia.

While his family came from inland, Xi would carve out much of his own political career on China's coastline closest to Taiwan, including serving as mayor of Xiamen – the city that quite literally looked down on the Taiwanese-occupied Kinmen archipelago – and then governor of Fujian province. Both of those roles brought him into contact with Taiwanese businesses – and he must have noted the development of multi-party democracy on the island with significant concern. They also allowed him to maintain close links with the growing Chinese military.

In 2017, five years after taking power, the Chinese leader shored up his military power base by appointing his boyhood friend now General Zhang Youxia to the top position in the PLA. As senior deputy chairman of the Central Military Commission – a body chaired by Xi as president – Zhang now outranked both China's defence minister and the Chinese counterpart of the chairman of the US joint chiefs of staff.[6] When it came to deciding whether or not to invade Taiwan, what these two men quietly thought, believed and talked about between themselves was likely more important than any other factor.

Xi's biographer Sheridan said the Chinese leader and those around him likely remained more cautious than many believed when it came to launching a full-scale assault, suggesting they were more likely to put their efforts into ongoing subversion and intimidation. 'Every sensible thinker in Beijing knows that a war could be disastrous . . . and China has many other options,' he told me. But if those at the top of the PRC believed they had the option of a swift victory, he warned that they might move fast to take advantage. Certainly, there seemed little chance of Xi giving up his Taiwan rhetoric, which presented Taiwan 'reunification' as critical to China's own 'rejuvenation'.[7]

As a young Xi had been learning to survive in the chaos of 1960s China, another young man born just over a year before him had been building his own survival story and future power base on the streets of the Soviet Union's second city Leningrad. By the early 2020s, that city was once again St Petersburg – and Xi and Vladimir Putin were starting to work much more closely together to reshape the world.

*

The opening of the 2022 Beijing Winter Olympics was a very different event to those of the summer games 14 years earlier. Whereas 60 national leaders had attended the former, this time it was down to 22, including Putin. US President Joe Biden and the leaders of Europe were notable by their absence, engaged in a 'diplomatic boycott', the result of Beijing's treatment of ethnic minority Uighurs, its crackdown in Hong Kong and other rights abuses. 'If you look back at . . . 2008, they [China] were willing to show the world that they speak the same language, that they were part of some idea,' said Chinese artist Ai Weiwei, the designer of the 'Bird's Nest' stadium now living in exile in Portugal. 'But . . . now, the Chinese Communist Party is in a very different position. The whole tone has changed.'[8]

Xi – who in 2008 had been the vice premier responsible for delivering the games – had had a decade to entrench his position since assuming the presidency in 2012. China's economy was three times the size it had been in 2008. But as the athletes gathered at the end of January, there was one feature in common between this and the earlier summer games: as the world awaited the opening ceremony, Russia was on the brink of war in Europe.

In 2008, the war had been with Georgia, and Russian troops and planes had been moving against that nation just as the opening ceremony began. This time, the run-up to the February opening ceremony was dominated by reports of the massing of Russian tanks and personnel on the borders of Ukraine, with repeated warnings from the US and Britain that Putin was planning to invade. How much knowledge Chinese officials and Xi had of those plans would remain secret for years – but the rumour in diplomatic circles was that Beijing had made it clear that this time around any Russian military action must wait until the games were over.

If that annoyed the Russians, they gave no indication.[9] As early as 2019, Xi had told Russian media, 'President Putin is the foreign colleague that I have interacted with the most extensively – he is my best friend and I greatly treasure our friendship.'[10] Now, as Russia dismissed US talk of a coming invasion of Ukraine, Xi announced what he and Putin called a 'no limits' partnership just before the opening ceremony.

In fact, there was still plenty of distrust: one leaked undated Russian intelligence document from the early 2020s, likely just before the invasion, referred to China as an 'enemy'. The document – from the foreign-facing Federal Security Service once run by Putin himself and known as the FSB – described a 'tense and dynamically developing' intelligence battle between spies in Moscow and Beijing. It was a reminder of the complex and sometimes violent internal politics integral to both states. 'You have the political leadership, and all these guys are for rapprochement with China,' said Andrei Soldatov, an expert on Russian spy craft now living in exile. '[But] you have the intelligence and security services, and they are very suspicious.'[11]

Such suspicions were often justified. Multiple Western analysts would later suggest Putin had not been entirely truthful with Xi, giving the Chinese the impression he planned a much smaller operation rather than a full-scale attempt to seize the entire country. Some detected a cooling of relations following the invasion, a series of Chinese moves to remind the Kremlin that the goodwill of Beijing was neither absolute nor to be taken for granted. A year after the invasion, in February 2023, China's government demanded mapmakers in the country relabel at least eight locations in the Far East and Pacific Russia with Chinese names held under the Qing dynasty more than a century earlier. It was, some suggested, a not-so-subtle reminder of just which nation was more powerful in the modern era – and that China could yet invade Russia itself if it wished.[12]

For now, however, both remained committed to their partnership. At the G20 summit in Bali in November 2022, Xi and Biden expressed common ground in their opposition to the use of nuclear weapons in Ukraine, Chinese and US officials later said – but Beijing could not be persuaded to be more critical than that, and was still holding back from calling Russia's attack against Ukraine 'an invasion'.[13] As Xi prepared to visit Putin in March 2023, he appeared to double down on the relationship and express his determination to grow it further.

Almost certainly on government encouragement, Chinese firms had cut back their relations with Russia in the first months of 2022. But by the end of that year, trade was significantly rebounding – and by early 2023 there were growing signs Beijing was throwing itself much more deliberately behind the Russian war effort. The Chinese leader arrived in Russia only three days after the International Criminal Court issued a warrant against Putin for war crimes in Ukraine. 'That Xi, the leader of the second most powerful country in the world, is ready to visit Moscow during the war with Ukraine is hugely symbolic,' said Russian analyst Alexander Gabuev at the Carnegie Institute, noting that Russia's diplomatic isolation elsewhere in the world significantly increased its dependence on Beijing. China accounted for more than 40 per cent of Russia's total imports, according to official data, and Beijing was also able to import much cheaper oil and gas from Russia that sanctions stopped from going to the West.[14] Xi's March 2023 visit saw him announce a 'new era' in relations, as well as a televised pre-departure conversation. 'Right now there are changes the likes of which we haven't seen for 100 years – and we are the ones driving these changes together,' Xi told Putin as they said goodbye for the cameras. 'I agree,' said Putin. 'Take care please, dear friend,' said Xi, shaking his hand for an extra moment.[15]

In reality, the war was already putting Putin's position under pressure. Barely three months later, rogue Russian contractors from the Wagner Group, under their chief Yevgeny Prigozhin, briefly marched on Moscow before standing down. For China, and Xi in particular, a successful coup against Putin would have been disastrous – not least because it would have dramatically ramped up speculation that the same might happen in Beijing. 'China is agnostic about where the frontlines in Ukraine are,' said Gabuev at Carnegie. 'What they care about is that Putin doesn't lose this war so that the regime collapses and a pro-Western government is installed in Russia.'

But that balance of overlapping interests – together with their overlapping stories, personal and national ambitions and fears – did seem to have fuelled a genuine connection, suggested Gaubev: 'They are just six months apart in age; their fathers both fought in World War Two. Both have daughters – and they are increasingly like an emperor and a czar, equally obsessed with (the risk of pro-Western pro-democratic) "colour" revolutions.'[16]

*

Immediately following the February 2022 Ukraine invasion, some Western nations had hoped Beijing could be persuaded to abandon Putin altogether – but those hopes faded swiftly. As then NATO Secretary General Jens Stoltenberg put it: 'They don't share our values, freedom, democracy. And that's also the reason why they try to deny sovereign, democratic nations the right to choose their own future.'[17] According to US think tank the Center for Strategic and International Studies, by mid-2024 there had been more than 100 joint Russian–Chinese military drills, increasing in both frequency and size over the preceding decade – and with the majority conducted from

2017.[18] During 2024 alone, multiple Russian and Chinese warplanes conducted joint patrols towards the US border in Alaska, while China's Coast Guard announced that for the first time it would work directly with Russia in the Arctic. According to Ukrainian officials, up to 60 per cent of components in Russian weapons being used in the conflict came from Chinese firms,[19] while Russian oil boosted China's strategic energy reserves.

Whether the relationship was close enough to actively co-ordinate on any future offensives against Taiwan, the Baltic states, Ukraine or anybody else was not the sort of thing outsiders could readily tell. Despite the increase in training together, few Russia- or China-watchers believed those forces had anything like the interoperability the US had built up over decades with its NATO allies and others such as Japan or even the Philippines. Still, by acting together, anyone could see that a co-ordinated Russia–China axis could better overstretch the US in a global confrontation – clearly both leaders and nations were wedded to campaigns to dominate what they saw as historic empires.

Talk of 'CRINKs' as a sweeping term for China, Russia, Iran and North Korea and a new 'Axis of Upheaval' showed many in the West believed in an even broader growing threat. Iran and North Korea were very much the junior partners, but they offered other avenues to needle the United States and overstretch its resources – as well as, for Russia, a source of supplies and even personnel. In the Middle East, US commanders believed both Moscow and Beijing now fed information and weapons components to the Houthi militants in Yemen. Russia was providing even more support for North Korea, including advice on nuclear weapons and submarines, in return for North Korean troops fighting against Ukraine. In the event of China attacking Taiwan, some US commanders and analysts believed it was almost inevitable North Korea would launch its own parallel attack against the South. They also suspected the opposite was true, and that any attack launched from North Korea might be seen by Beijing as the best moment to attack Taiwan while the world was distracted.

All the individual dynamics within those relationships – Russia with North Korea, Iran with China, and every other pairing – had its own complex character and history. The most important, though, remained between Moscow and Beijing, and specifically between Xi and Putin.

In the US, Trump and Vance had talked of how their formative environments had taught them never to show weakness and to respond aggressively to any form of disrespect. For Vance that had been the poverty-stricken schoolyards of Appalachia, while for Trump it had been the cut-throat, low-budget real-estate markets of New York in which his father worked. Trump had looked to escape by embracing a much more luxury real-estate dynamic.

No one should doubt the genuine toughness of those environments. But Putin, Xi and almost all of those in their immediate power structures had been raised in conditions where it could sometimes be fatal to show weakness, and where an almost psychotic commitment to their objective was vital to survive.

*

Xi had been shaped by the Cultural Revolution's hardship and brutality, while Putin's first years were overshadowed by the war that had finished seven years before his birth. The Leningrad of Putin's youth was still recovering from an almost three-year siege by Nazi forces from 1941 that killed an estimated 800,000 or more civilians and perhaps at least as many combat troops.[20] According to Putin's own account, both of his parents were heavily traumatised by what they had seen and done, particularly by the death of his eldest brother during the siege (while many accounts attribute this death to starvation, Putin himself – who was not born until 1952 – says he was told the cause was most likely diphtheria).

Like Xi's family but from very different social standing, Putin's family had some experience of authoritarian state brutality – his grandfather had worked as a chef at one of Stalin's dachas during the purges of the 1920s and 1930s. 'Few people who spent much time around Stalin came through unscathed, but my grandfather was one of them,' Putin later told three Russian reporters who wrote a short biography, *First Person*, published shortly after he took the presidency in 2000. He also talked of the war service of his father, who volunteered first on submarines and then for behind-the-lines missions, some involving sabotage.

The stories Putin's father told clearly shaped his son's view of warfare. At one point, his father's entire detachment was betrayed to the Germans by Estonian collaborators, and only four of the 28-strong group made it home alive. Immediately afterwards, his father was sent to hold a tiny strip of land on the Neva River – the last patch of Soviet soil on the far bank – that the Germans were determined to capture but never did despite enormous losses; a heroic resistance that was nevertheless later judged an unnecessary waste. 'There are always a lot of mistakes made in war – that's inevitable,' said Putin in 2000. 'But when you are fighting, if you keep thinking that everyone around you is always making mistakes, you'll never win. You have to take a pragmatic attitude and you have to keep thinking of victory.'[21]

Just as important were the tough life lessons Putin learned in the square block in which he shared an apartment with his parents. He said he did not remember exactly why or when he first got beaten up by an adult man – but he remembered that he had insulted someone 'for no good reason so he immediately beat me up and I deserved it'. That taught him several lessons: both to be respectful, but also that he needed to be 'tough' and 'ready to instantly respond to an offence or insult'.[22]

In his early interviews after becoming president, Putin several times referenced his judo instructor as a particular key influence – but never gave his name. Researchers into Russian organised crime suggest this may have been semi-legendary figure Leonid Usvyatsov or 'Leo the Sportsman', born in 1936, who was locally renowned for combining coaching youth judo with a Mafia career.[23] Whatever the truth, Putin's mentors nudged him towards the KGB. Then, from 1989, Communist East Germany, where he was based before the Eastern Bloc unravelled, simply ceased to be.

By the time 'Leo the Sportsman' was gunned down in 1994 – his gravestone later read 'Mafia until I die' – much of the Soviet-era world in which Putin had built his identity as a KGB lieutenant colonel had collapsed entirely. To what extent any organised crime connections helped re-establish Putin, first in St Petersburg and then in national Russian politics, remains predictably obscure. At some stage he was apparently desperate enough for money to moonlight as a taxi driver, something he was only willing to admit in early 2022 in a documentary on the unravelling of the Soviet Union that came out days before his invasion of Ukraine. 'Honestly, it's not very pleasant to speak about,' he told the documentary, in which he also described the collapse of the Soviet Union as a 'tragedy'.[24]

With hindsight, it may not have been surprising that the Russian leader appeared to see the invasion of Ukraine, in part, as a step to recover from that 'tragedy': from the start, Putin believed some of that loss could be regained by well-directed violence. As he climbed the greasy pole of post-Soviet Kremlin politics under Boris Yeltsin, Russia's military was losing a war to Chechen separatists. As Putin moved from head of the FSB security service to prime minister and then president between 1998 and the start of the millennium, he oversaw a brutal military crackdown that destroyed much of the regional capital of Grozny and killed tens of thousands, maybe more. In interviews at the time, Putin presented the campaign – which he described crudely as pursuing Chechen militants to their outhouses – as an 'answer back' for their offences against the

Russian state. In another, he described the Chechen rebels as a 'kid' who he had no doubt 'was going to get his head kicked in'.[25]

By the 2020s, both Putin and Xi had a whole ideological and historical underpinning to their plans to restore what they claimed were their nations' rightful lands – particularly Xi, whose *Xi Jinping Thought* of economic and state policy was required reading for Communist Party officials, PLA officers and other personnel. Having both abolished term limits, they were absolute monarchs in all but name – but without clear heirs. In the short term, Xi's anti-corruption purges and the trend for any of Putin's rivals to end up dead or exiled kept their places secure – but that could not last for ever. In some ways, conflicts helped entrench that power – but losing such a war might not be politically survivable.

For a West attempting to deter a Chinese Taiwan invasion or a further Russian land grab into Eastern Europe, that represented leverage – in the most grossly simple terms, neither leader was going to take such action unless they believed they would win. The exception to that calculus, however, might come if they believed that they were losing power, and that launching a conflict was the best way of clinging on.

Another scenario – and it became more likely every year as the two leaders got older – was that at least some of the quietly ambitious officials and commanders around them were already scheming their own rise to power and might use a war to get there. For some, including frontline commanders, that might offer opportunity that might not otherwise exist – a very different incentive when it came to taking risks.

How any future Russian or Chinese leaders might approach the relationship between their nations was anybody's guess. Within Russia, there had long been mutterings of the dangers of becoming a 'Chinese colony', and as the Ukrainian war progressed these started to get louder.

Putin needed more firepower and muscle than Xi was willing to provide, and he was prepared to step into China's own 'sphere of influence' to strike a deal to get it.

*

Few countries in history had spent so many decades preparing for potential war as North Korea, and Putin was determined to harness some of the results. In September 2023, roughly a month before Putin's next visit to Beijing, the massive armoured train of Kim Jong Un crossed into Russia to take him to the Russian leader.[26] Already running down Russia's enormous arsenal of artillery shells, Putin was pulling out all the stops to persuade the government in Pyongyang to provide supplies and deepen a relationship that would eventually see North Korean troops thrown into battle during 2024.[27]

Russia's links with North Korea went back to World War Two – but for most of that time, Pyongyang's principal backer had been China, and successive governments in Beijing had got used to telling members of the Kim dynasty what they could and could not do. As late as 2023, China was estimated to be responsible for as much as 98 per cent of North Korean trade, and its 1963 mutual defence deal with Pyongyang was the only formal military alliance committing the PRC to war if its neighbour was attacked.[28] Putin now moved to match the latter with Russia's own mutual defence agreement, signed in Pyongyang by him in June 2024 and formally written into Russian law a few months later.[29] By then, thousands of North Korean troops were already fighting in support of Russia's invasion of Ukraine, although the deal with Kim appeared to limit their use to fighting within Russian territory to rebut Zelenskyy's invasion of the Kursk region and not Ukraine itself.

By the start of 2025, Ukraine's government estimated that roughly a third of the 11,000 or so North Korean troops sent to Russia had been killed in combat – but only a very small handful had been captured. According to Ukrainian troops, North Korean fighters were much more likely than their Russian counterparts to attempt to blow themselves up or commit suicide rather than be taken. 'Self-detonation and suicides, that's the reality of North Korea,' said 'Kim', a 32-year-old former North Korean soldier who had defected to the South. 'The soldiers who left home to fight there have been brainwashed and are truly ready to sacrifice themselves.'[30]

US officials suspected North Korea's wishlist from Moscow in return included missile, atomic warhead and submarine technology, all critical to building up Pyongyang's nuclear arsenal and giving it the ability to strike the US mainland. As of the end of 2024, US commanders believed the North had both the rockets and the warheads, but had not yet been able to put them together.[31] The North Korean threat to its southern neighbour remained high – and Pyongyang hoped to find some benefit in the post-coup political confusion in South Korea. That, of course, delivered yet another drag on US and allied forces, all to the advantage of Moscow and Beijing.

*

The same was true of ongoing tensions with the last member of the so-called 'CRINKs' or 'Axis of Upheaval': Iran. For much of the current century, the government in Tehran had been quietly but heavily dependent on Chinese purchases of oil, often sending shipments through unorthodox routes to evade Western sanctions. Russia was equally important as the primary supplier of weapons to Iran, with the Tehran government returning the favour by arming Russia in Ukraine.

The Kremlin also had its own long-running relationship with Hamas, inviting some of its leadership back to Moscow shortly after the October 7 assault in 2023.[32] It was a crude but simple move that allowed Putin to demonstrate a degree of support for the Palestinians, as well as to again highlight America's growing military overstretch. That was also true of the fight of Yemen's Iran-backed Houthi rebels, who were soon getting their own support from both Moscow and Beijing.

According to the *Wall Street Journal*, US intelligence officials believed the Kremlin was supplying targeting information directly to the militants, as well as selling anti-ship missiles to Iran that might well then find their way to Yemen.[33] As in Ukraine, Chinese components were at the heart of almost every self-assembled system in the Middle East, while both government and private-sector intelligence analysts noted that Russian and Chinese ships – with some exceptions presumed hit accidentally – tended not to be attacked.[34]

By the middle of the 2020s, both Russia and China were also steering their direct diplomatic support to Iran on the nuclear issue; a dramatic change from a decade earlier in which they had – albeit quite reluctantly – joined the US in pressuring Tehran to do a deal with the Obama administration to give up atomic processing. In March 2025, senior Chinese and Russian officials met with Iranian Deputy Foreign Minister Kazem Gharibabadi in Beijing for discussions on the renewed US pressure on Tehran from Trump to give up nuclear enrichment. The result was a formal Russian–Chinese statement demanding that dialogue should only resume based on 'mutual respect', that all sanctions should be lifted and that Iran's right to enrich uranium and use nuclear energy peacefully should be 'fully' respected.[35]

Within the same month, Chinese and Russian warships joined their Iranian counterparts for several days of joint naval drills at the very entrance to the Gulf, conducting exercises that included strike operations against supposedly enemy vessels. With the US ramping up its own forces in the region to increase pressure on both Iran and Yemen, it was an unashamed reminder that those three nations could – potentially at least – act together militarily if they wished.[36] Russian and Chinese warships were also increasingly turning up at other points around the world, including the Caribbean. Beijing now had its first acknowledged overseas naval station and surrounding base at Djibouti, as well as civilian ports around the world, while Russia had its Mediterranean naval base at Tartarus in Syria – until it was ousted by the fall of Bashar al-Assad and his government in December 2024.

That ability to distract globally would be useful in a major war. The question was whether either Xi or Putin might be approaching the point where they would risk such a conflict. What was apparent was that both Russia and China were militarising their societies and radicalising their commanders in a way that suggested they were prioritising confrontation and perhaps eventually combat.

Such behaviour had, of course, become standard in both Iran and North Korea, where confrontation with the West had long been a way of life. For Russia and China to act as if expecting war, though, brought a wholly different scale of threat. At the very least, it suggested that those in power in Moscow and Beijing expected the kind of multi-year or even multi-decade confrontation faced by Tehran and Pyongyang, and believed they could survive that best together.

*

By the start of 2025, the Russian economy was not just on a war footing, it was becoming increasingly dependent on the conflict in Ukraine. By most estimates, military spending now made up to 10 per cent of the Russian economy, with tanks, armoured vehicles and ammunition driving the manufacturing sector to keep growing. But even consumer spending in other areas was heavily Ukraine-driven, fuelled by salaries and bonuses to military personnel and even casualty payouts to their families when soldiers died. 'Over time, Russia's ability to maintain and develop a dynamic non-military economy is being cannibalised,' warned former UK ambassador to Moscow Sir Laurie Bristow. 'If they ever come to unwinding the war economy, there won't be the civilian economy left to take up the slack.'

The conflict was already delivering a significant cost to ordinary Russians, with double-digit inflation and interest rates. Energy exports – significantly discounted due to Western sanctions – kept up economic growth, but if the war ended economists warned that these too were likely to collapse, unless military spending was maintained even after fighting stopped in Ukraine. Bill Browder – once the largest foreign investor in Russia then thrown out in the 2000s before his lawyer and friend Sergei Magnitsky was arrested and died in custody – warned that Putin's approach to conflict was 'straight out of Machiavelli': 'If you're worried about people being angry with you, you create an enemy and start a war.'[37]

In China, the CCP appeared to be taking steps that would help it to do the same if needed. From the moment he took power in 2012, Xi moved to pack the Central Military Commission – the key military decision-making body that was part of the Chinese Communist Party and chaired by the president himself – with those who shared his aims and kept their distance from the West.[38] Before long, greater ideological training was part of the PLA curriculum, and political officers were again becoming much more powerful. China's entire popular culture was also being quietly shaped to be more nationalist and militaristic.

As the protagonist of the 2015 film *Wolf Warrior* slaughtered his way through foreign bad guys, including US mercenaries, to save a range of hostages, the tagline read: 'Whoever attacks China will be killed no matter how far away.' Soon, the phrase 'wolf warrior' was being used to describe a new generation of assertive Chinese diplomats[39] – while a host of other films and series venerated jet pilots, soldiers and those building and commanding the first aircraft carriers in the People's Liberation Army Navy. Other messaging was subtler. China's many manufacturers of plastic building toys akin to Lego bricks, for instance, had switched their focus from rip-offs of Western models such as Harry Potter to deliberately accurate models of

Chinese aircraft carriers and missiles. Such models were intended to be built by foreigners as well as the Chinese – their instructions were entirely pictorial, with no text at all.[40]

Then there was the crackdown on corruption, first largely focused on the civilian regional leadership and commercial sector but swiftly extended to the PLA. There was little doubt Xi believed there was genuine malfeasance within parts of the military, and he was particularly infuriated when that delayed or complicated the building of the military juggernaut he wanted. But it was also a powerful lever of control. US officials became accustomed to their counterparts being stripped of office, including two defence ministers. It was a reminder of just how opaque and centralised the Chinese military structure could often be, as well as how insular and nationalistic it was now becoming.

In 2013, Xi's first year in power, I had interviewed PLA Major General Chao Liu, the first Chinese officer to command a UN peacekeeping mission overseas. From his Cyprus headquarters he led a mission dominated by British and Argentinian troops, with multiple other nationalities. Approximately the same age as his new president Xi, the general was urbane, friendly and spoke surprisingly frankly – although he did insist on recording the interview too. He talked of his own family suffering and challenges during the Cultural Revolution, his military father's advice to join the PLA to gain an education and permanent income, his year at the London School of Economics, and the experience of working in a largely British headquarters with a Chinese military background. 'People in uniform are similar but the system is quite different,' Liu told me. 'What I've learned in this [UN] mission is that every decision is based on discussion. In China, it is quite different . . . You just make a decision and you don't expect to discuss it.'[41]

By the mid-2020s, such interaction would have been all but impossible – certainly, it was hard to imagine the modern PLA sending such a senior general to be surrounded by foreigners with only a single PLA driver.[42] The PLA continued to support United Nations operations, and if anything its defence engagement with other nations increased – but only on terms with which the current rulers in Beijing felt themselves entirely comfortable.

In November 2023, three weeks after Putin visited Xi in China, the Chinese leader sent his old friend General Zhang to the Kremlin to talk directly with Putin and senior Russian military commanders. According to Russian state TV, the Chinese military chief had come 'to further strengthen military technical co-operation'. Putin told Russian television that increasing Russia–China co-operation was a 'serious factor stabilising the global situation', although stressed it stopped short of a true 'military alliance'.[43]

Chinese and Russian overlapping messaging went back at least to the start of the Covid-19 pandemic in 2020, with Russian and Chinese media outlets sometimes amplifying each other, particularly in areas of the 'global south' including Southeast Asia and Latin America.[44] By 2025, intelligence sources also reported Chinese officers deployed close behind Russian frontlines with Ukraine, operating with the direct agreement of both Moscow and Beijing to learn lessons from that war. There were also Chinese mercenaries – some captured by Ukraine – with one source estimating the total number at as many as 200. According to US security officials, they were not believed to have direct government links,[45] although the mere fact adverts for Russian contractors seeking fighters in Ukraine continued to circulate on Chinese social media suggested a degree of official acquiescence – and perhaps also a growing interest in gauging the popular response to recruitment for an actual shooting war.

One video, viewed hundreds of thousands of times across multiple platforms, looked like a mainstream Russian military advert with Chinese subtitles overlaid. It showed young men leaving their day jobs to fight and asked viewers: 'Do you want to show strength here? Is this the path that you long for? You are a tough man, be like them!' Others highlighted the pay and sign-on bonuses, the latter sometimes as high as over $20,000. Another video unambiguously targeted at Chinese recruits featured a female Russian social media influencer outlining the pay and benefits.

Others claimed their motivation was more complicated. One former Chinese soldier who flew to Russia on a tourist visa in 2023 to join up told a Chinese journalist he did so in part to gain real experience of combat – adding that he also wanted to show people at home what the 'brutal' reality of war was like. 'I realised I might die here one day, so I have decided to share some real experiences, since China's people haven't been through a war in a long time,' he said, adding that he hoped China would 'refrain from starting or joining wars'.[46] In fact, how ready China really was for conflict – and how willing its people might be for the accompanying sacrifices – was becoming one of the more important questions in the world. According to a study by the US Army War College in late 2024, the PLA was massively reforming its reservist recruiting bases in a way that would allow it to train much larger numbers of recruits in the event of a protracted conflict.[47]

Visiting a Chinese strategic missile brigade in October 2024, Xi addressed dozens of PLA rocket troops clad in camouflage in front of a hangar full of nuclear-capable rockets. His words – instructing an intensification of training and combat preparedness – were greeted with furious but not particularly spontaneous applause. According to state television, the visit was followed by an 'important speech' to senior military leaders that instructed tighter discipline within the military. It also included repeated warnings to crack down on corruption, as well as the need to 'raise awareness' of potential wars and crises.[48]

Watching the video, it was impossible to avoid noticing the contrast between the slightly portly leader and his much younger officers – and, as in Russia, that would only get more obvious and potentially destabilising as the years progressed.

Younger commanders were clearly coming through. In March 2025, at a public gathering in Beijing to mark the 20th anniversary of the Taiwan anti-secession law, head of China's Eastern Theatre Command General Lin Xiangyang – reportedly aged 60 years of age, so easily with time for further ambition – announced his forces were ready to deliver 'complete reunification' if so ordered. That, he said, included enough new technology to hold off 'external forces': code for the PLA's rapidly rising missile stockpile to keep US warships back.[49]

But both Putin and Xi appeared keen to hang onto their ageing military chiefs: Russian Chief of the General Staff General Valery Gerasimov, who turned 70 years of age in 2025, while Zhang was 75. There were plenty of voices in Russia who blamed Gerasimov – famously credited with inventing Russia's new forms of 'hybrid warfare' – for the failures in Ukraine. But he had another attribute that he clearly offered Putin: no one viewed him as a potential president, in part because he was so advanced in years.

Mark Cozad, a former US Air Force intelligence officer and RAND Corporation researcher who is one of the few to be an expert on both the Russian and Chinese militaries, described the focus on 'political reliability' as one of the overlapping features. But there were also many differences.[50] According to a RAND study based on Chinese military writings and social media commentary, Beijing's new generation of military thinkers believed that Russia's military establishment had overstated their ability to use hybrid methods – a combination of nuclear and conventional military threats along with sabotage, subversion and disinformation – to isolate Ukraine and stop it fighting. The results for Russia, the Chinese believed, had been catastrophic – and they believed China must not overstate its ability to deter the US from intervening in any future war.

That meant being prepared to fight hard and keep on fighting.

The PLA's National Defence University Joint Operations Academy staff, training China's very top commanders, warned its students that 'almost all military leaders hope to achieve "winning without fighting", but most of them will fail'. Instead, they recommended the PLA 'must be mentally prepared for a tough battle with casualties'. Chinese researchers were also critical of what they viewed as poor Russian command, control and communications as well as use of intelligence and space – they were particularly envious of the Starlink satellite communication system launched by Elon Musk and SpaceX for its ability to provide critical data at key times.

The RAND researchers noted two more general observations they found particularly disturbing. The first was that Chinese military and strategic thinkers examining Ukraine put almost no effort at all into looking at how conflict might have been avoided; instead they focused purely on what lessons they could draw to win a future war. Secondly, aside from some broad comments that Russia's nuclear arsenal had helped the Kremlin deter the West from intervening more directly in Ukraine, there was little published discussion of atomic weapons.[51] Just because those options were not being talked about in public, though, did not mean they were not being considered behind closed doors. Ever since it had acquired its first atomic weapons in the 1960s, China had followed a rather different path to most other nuclear-armed nations, maintaining a relatively small number of mobile road-launched rockets. These had been designed to ensure that any state that attacked China with atomic weapons would know it risked losing several cities in return – but kept Beijing's arsenal much smaller than those of the United States or Russia. Successive governments in Beijing had pursued a 'no first use' policy when it came to atomic weapons, the only nuclear-armed nation aside from India to maintain that approach into the 2020s. Looking at events in Ukraine, however, some Western and Chinese analysts believed that position might be about to shift, with Xi prepared to follow Putin in threatening a nuclear response if the US and allies intervened in a PLA attempt to overrun Taiwan.[52]

Even if that did not happen, those who watched China's comments on nuclear policy particularly closely suspected it was on the brink of adopting the same 'launch on warning' tactics already used by the US and Russia for Beijing's growing atomic arsenal. That meant that in the event of multiple missiles heading for targets in mainland China, China might fire back first with a widespread and devastating atomic strike even before the incoming weapons touched the ground. It was a strategy that would dramatically increase the risks of unintended Armageddon – particularly in an environment in which widespread conventional missile strikes were also set to be a feature of any conflict. Once a missile was fired, no one could truly tell what warheads it was carrying until they detonated – by which time it might be too late to respond.[53]

In other nations too, those conversations had reached a scale unseen in the current century – and while the resulting rising danger of an exchange of nuclear arms brought back plenty of Cold War memories and fears, the 'balance of terror' of the 2020s was already much more complicated.

10

The Engines of Armageddon

*'The modern conception of war to which in my lifetime we
have become accustomed is now completely out of date . . . The
answer to an atomic bomb on London is an atomic
bomb on another great city.'*

**Memorandum by British Prime Minister
Clement Attlee, August 28, 1945**[1]

In mid-March 2025, Prime Minister Keir Starmer and Defence
Minister John Healey boarded the British ballistic missile
submarine *Vanguard* somewhere in the waters off western
Scotland. The reportedly 204-day patrol was one of the longest
ever conducted by any 'bomber' submarine – a measure of how
stretched Britain's ageing vessels had become. Descending into
the control room, they received a 'hot' debrief on the time at sea
then were pictured on the upper deck with crew members
relishing their first true fresh air in more than half a year. With
the audio track deliberately scrubbed from video released to the
British media, it was impossible to hear their conversation – or to
know whether those involved mentioned Starmer's instructions
to its captain that it carried in its safe.[2] Almost certainly, no one
but the Prime Minister knew what he had written. According to
briefings since the first UK ballistic missile submarine patrol in
1969, each commander has held detailed instructions in the
event of losing contact with the Royal Navy headquarters at
Northwood. The exact steps remain a secret – but it has long

been said they include listening for civilian broadcasts from the BBC. If the Radio Four *Today* programme is off the air and Britain's military and government are also incommunicado, the captain will open the 'safe within a safe' to extract the 'letter of last resort'.

Writing those letters is one of the first duties of a new British leader upon taking office: the moment, in the words of Whitehall historian Lord Peter Hennessy, that they discover 'what being Prime Minister is all about'. To help them, the new arrival is swiftly briefed by Britain's defence chiefs and senior civil servants who outline scenarios, target sets and detail the devastation British submarines could unleash. They offer several potential orders for the submarine commander: including transferring his vessel to the command of the US or Australia, if those countries or their leaders still exist; or telling the captain to use their own initiative. The incoming prime minister also has the option to order a limited or massive nuclear strike against the likely source of an attack – in the case of Britain, by the mid-2020s that was once again the Russian Federation.

No one but Starmer knew what he had written after his election victory in July 2024 – the letter had sat locked up and unopened throughout HMS *Vanguard*'s nine months at sea – and, providing the moment never arrived, it would be destroyed unread when he left office. Previous prime ministers had talked of the heavy psychological burden of even just considering the options.[3] As he headed back to London after his official visit to the *Vanguard*, the *New York Times* reporter who had accompanied him noted that the PM seemed a little distant, 'Twenty-four hours, 365 days, year after year after year, for 55 years,' mused Starmer, referring to the more than half a century in which British missile submarines had kept up their 'continuous at-sea deterrent': 'It has kept the peace for a very long time.'

The truth, though, was that there was a growing consensus that nuclear-armed submarines alone were not enough to keep the country safe. Both Russia and China were now clearly preparing to be able to fight conventional wars in their immediate neighbourhood – but while that implied nuclear weapons might no longer be enough to prevent conflict, they might well still be key to the development of any major conflict, particularly how it ended.

Alongside that disquieting reality, threats to the British nuclear submarine force were also clearly growing. Undersea sensors, suspected to be Russian-built, were being found by the Royal Navy, or just drifting ashore. At the top of the Ministry of Defence, there was now a fast-growing belief that Britain, the only nation to depend entirely on missile-carrying subs for its nuclear deterrent, must 'diversify' at speed. Some suggested it might not even be much more than a decade until breakthroughs in technology – particularly ultrafast 'quantum' computing – allowed the detection of submerged submarines from space even in deep ocean, negating their deterrent value.

The Starmer government had already given the order to push ahead with the next class of *Dreadnought* ballistic submarines, the first already taking shape in the giant sheds of the British Aerospace plant at Barrow-in-Furness, on England's north-west coast – supposedly ready to enter service in the 2030s. Now, Starmer's government was also secretly considering a switch from purchasing the vertical take-off F-35B Joint Strike Fighters that could fly from Britain's carriers to buying a dozen runway-launched F-35As already flown by the US and other allied air forces. Not only were they cheaper, but they were specifically designed to carry US-made tactical atomic bombs, smaller and less destructive than the 'strategic' or 'city-killer' weapons carried on the submarines.[4] If Russia unleashed its smaller 'tactical' nuclear weapons carried by its planes or missiles, that would offer the UK a way to respond in kind. For the RAF to use those US bombs in war or crisis would likely require the agreement of Trump or any future US president. But if that deal broke down, Britain had built its own air-dropped atomic bombs before, during the first Cold War, and perhaps it could again.

Dropping such weapons had been a terrifying business even by the standards of 20th-century atomic war plans – as former Cold War Tornado fast jet pilot Air Marshall Greg Bagwell described it, the aircraft dropping the weapon was likely to be barely four miles distant when it detonated.

'No one ever had to do it so we never found out what happened,' he said. 'But of course the reason you have them is because the other side has and you need to deter them.'[5] During the first Cold War, this had been known as Mutually Assured Destruction (MAD) – and in the modern era too, it appeared to be generating its own sometimes idiosyncratic forms of madness.

For Britain – which had spent billions keeping up a 'continuous at-sea deterrent' during an era where the threat was almost negligible – that meant that now atomic war was plausible again, the ageing submarines needed to be kept operating at almost any cost. This meant submariners coming ashore complaining that food supplies had almost been exhausted – with crew members told to move as little as possible within their bunks to conserve vital calories – as well as multiple reports of declining mental health.[6] In perhaps the most excruciating incident, the commander of one ballistic missile submarine was said to have deliberately filmed imagery of himself having sex with a more junior sailor – before then sharing that footage with another young crewmember, all while the submarine was still at sea. The admirals and senior officials who also ended up having to scrutinise the footage were predictably appalled, and fired him very quickly.[7] A host of other incidents on UK submarines at sea – both ballistic missile-carriers and smaller nuclear attack subs – included sexual harassment and assault of both male and female personnel, prompting official apologies and the removal of senior figures and awards.[8]

For those in Washington making broader US nuclear policy, much bigger issues were now in focus. When US war planners had gamed what to do if the first Cold War went 'hot', they had imagined one massive nuclear exchange between themselves and the Soviet Union. Now with China building up its arsenal to the same level as Russia – perhaps fighting the US together, but perhaps also separately – the US now had to prepare for something hugely more complex that included managing a potential mass-nuclear exchange with one large enemy nation while retaining sufficient atomic weapons to be ready to deter – and if necessary fight – another similar conflict in the future. Alternatively, they might need to be ready for a 'protracted nuclear exchange': one with periodic nuclear exchanges over weeks or years.[9]

What was clearer still was that the UK – and arguably the US as well – had thought too little of atomic arms since the Berlin Wall came down. The Kremlin and Beijing, meanwhile, had taken both extremely seriously – and their past two decades of effort now looked like bearing fruit.

*

Amid the fjords and closed 'military cities' outside Murmansk, Putin's Russia spent the first quarter of the new century preparing for climate change and the return of the threat of nuclear war. By 2024, the Kremlin had eight atomic icebreakers escorting shipping through the melting Arctic,[10] while its air and naval facilities around Murmansk had been thoroughly rebuilt, secured behind miles of barbed-wire fencing around rehabilitated runways, docks, new nuclear-warhead storage bunkers and test ranges for the next generation of missiles.

The end of the Cold War had left Russia's atomic arsenal something of a joke. 'I can tell you this, when we are loading rockets into our submarines, somebody always drops one,' one former Soviet submariner told the *New York Times* in 2000 just after Putin came to power, while almost 100 ageing submarines – many with nuclear fuel still aboard – rotted in nearby inlets.[11]

Some elements of Russia's nuclear deterrent force were still relics of the Cold War – although now often with deadly, much more modern twists. The oldest bomber in the modern Russian fleet, the Tupolev-95 'Bear' first flew in 1952, like its US counterpart the B-52. Unlike the B-52, however, it was propeller driven, albeit with sweptback wings like a more modern jet. Similar to the more recent Tupolev-160 'Blackjack' supersonic jet and heavy bomber, the 'Bears' carried long-range cruise missiles, either conventional or nuclear. Plenty had already been in action striking targets in Ukraine, launching their weapons from the relative safety of Russian airspace.

Newer weaponry was deliberately designed to threaten the United States. In 2018, Russia test-fired its newest, largest intercontinental missile, the Sarmat – also nicknamed the 'Satan-2' – rumoured to be capable of orbiting the world and so hitting a target from any direction to evade counter-missile defences – including those that might one day make up the 'Golden Dome'.[12] By the early 2020s, the Kremlin had also revamped its Cold War-era force of more traditional ballistic missile submarines, launching its new 'Borei' class.

The Russian Navy was still a far cry from its Cold War peak, when it was able to field enough cutting-edge nuclear submarines to threaten to cut NATO's North Atlantic supply lines from the US to Europe just as German U-boats had tried to do in two world wars. But, like its predecessor, it was prepared to push its submarines and crews to their very limits – even when that brought occasional disasters. The fleet had barely recovered its reputation from the disaster of the *Kursk* in 2000, with the loss of 118 lives, when fire broke out onboard Russia's most secret submarine, the *Losharik*, off the Norwegian coast in 2019.

According to Western intelligence experts, *Losharik* – the name meant 'Shark' – was unlike any other known submarine in military service: nuclear powered and capable of diving to enormous (if classified) depths, as many as ten times of those reached by mainstream military subs. Her suspected purpose included interfering with the undersea cables that connected

North America to Europe. That required an innovative design: while the outer hull looked like that of most military submarines, the inner hull was a series of hardened metal spheres connected by hatches barely large enough to crawl through. When a fire broke out in July 2019, it killed 14 of her 19 crew.

Exactly what happened was unclear, but nearby Russian fishermen deep inside the Arctic Circle said they saw a giant submarine – likely not the *Losharik* but a larger former ballistic missile carrier acting as a mothership that could carry the small submarine attached to her – abruptly break the surface, the crew bursting onto her decks and shouting loudly. The combination of secrecy, imagery and dramatic stakes bought immediate comparisons to Cold War submarine films such as *The Hunt for Red October* – as well as a reminder that the highly secretive jostling between Russian, US, British and other European submarines under the Arctic, Pacific and Atlantic had very much restarted.[13]

The loss of the submarine was a clear embarrassment to the Kremlin – but its naval commanders now moved fast to reassert themselves. At the end of October 2019, Norwegian intelligence reported ten-plus submarines – eight atomic powered – mounting the Russian Navy's largest show of force since the end of the Cold War. Several of the smaller vessels held back to secure waters near Russia's Arctic coastline, the so-called 'bastions' in which Russian missile submarines often hid, or moved towards maritime trade points where they could menace allied shipping. Others, including several ballistic missile submarines, headed for the North Atlantic, where they would be able to threaten US cities with short-notice strikes. Norwegian intelligence sources told local media that this was not an exercise in the traditional sense, but a deliberate military piece of posturing. 'The goal is to show that Russia can reach the US,' they said.[14]

It was a point Putin had made directly to Trump a year earlier by showing him a video in which a Russian hypersonic missile plunged towards a landmass similar to Florida – something Trump's Russia adviser Fiona Hill believed implied a direct threat to his precious Mar-a-Lago estate. 'That got Trump's attention,' she later said. 'Trump was like: "Why did he do that? Real countries don't have to do that."'

Putin, of course, had no intention of Russia being treated like any other nation. In 2018, Russia's economy was valued at around $1.7 trillion, roughly comparable to New York State, or Italy – but neither of them had the ability to blow up the US, or indeed the world. Hill believed that what she saw as Trump's excessive 'deference' to the Russian leader was in part a consequence of his being 'terrified' of the risk of nuclear exchange – and that the Russian leader was adept at using that to his advantage.[15]

She was likely right – but that dynamic was scarcely unique to Trump. Russia's nuclear arsenal had been a key factor in the Obama-era decision not to intervene when Putin annexed Crimea in 2014 and then backed Russian-speaking insurgents seizing parts of eastern Ukraine – and it had been an overwhelming driver of Biden administration policy throughout the much larger 2022 invasion. General Mark Milley, then chairman of the joint chiefs, had no time for Trump: he later told *Washington Post* journalist Bob Woodward he believed he was a 'fascist to the core' and the 'most dangerous person to this country'.[16] But he had no problem telling Politico that throughout the invasion, his personal priority had been avoiding catastrophic escalation.[17]

It was a lever the Kremlin pulled relentlessly. At the start of the invasion, Putin's rhetoric had implied his government could use atomic weapons against any country that tried to intervene, ordering Russia's nuclear forces to a 'combat alert'.[18] That autumn of 2022, as Ukrainian forces pushed forward, the Russians had again talked of nuclear release, while US intelligence intercepted conversations suggesting the use of tactical weapons was being genuinely considered if Russia's front collapsed. It all helped deter the US and other nations from doing 'too much' to support the Ukrainians – including supplying long-range conventional strike missiles such as the US ATACMS, finally delivered just after the November 2024 US election as the defeated Biden administration prepared to hand over to Trump.

The ATACMS was a conventional-only weapons system, as the Kremlin was aware. Their response, however, was a direct attack against Ukraine with Russia's new 'Oreshnik' intermediate-range ballistic missile, capable of carrying multiple warheads on independent re-entry vehicles. It was a rocket sufficiently powerful that it would trigger US early warning systems designed to alert of nuclear attack – and Russian officials ensured their US counterparts were aware in advance that it was about to be launched.

The 'Oreshnik' was not particularly effective with a conventional warhead – indeed, given that it had been designed for a nuclear strike it had no need to be as accurate as other modern weapons systems. Much of the damage to the Ukrainian city of Dnipro appeared to be to largely abandoned garages and other outbuildings. Still, the video footage of the warheads plunging through the clouds from space – the first time multiple independent warheads on a ballistic missile had been used in anger – delivered the striking imagery that the Kremlin wanted. As always with Russian nuclear posturing, the point was to be noticed – and leave the other side afraid.[19] As Chair of the NATO Military Committee and former Dutch defence chief Admiral Robert Bauer put it very bluntly: 'I am absolutely sure if the Russians did not have nuclear weapons, we would have been in Ukraine, kicking them out.'[20]

In reality, some of the Kremlin's new 'wonder weapons' were showing problems. An attempt to test-fire the giant land-based Sarmat in September 2024 from a test range near Murmansk ended in failure, the rocket falling back to the Earth and leaving a 60-metre circle of scorched earth around the launch site. It was the second failure in the previous two years[21] but, as always, it was swiftly followed by a newly claimed success.

Early that October, Putin told an event in the Black Sea city of Sochi that Russia had successfully tested its latest cruise missile, the 'Burevestnik' (NATO codename 'Skyfall'), said to have a nuclear-power engine intended to give it a range of more than 10,000 miles. Exactly what that test involved was clearly known only to the Russians and Western governments that tracked the missiles with radar and satellites – but it was certainly nothing like that range. Still, its overarching message was clear: Russia wanted its enemies to know that even the most sophisticated ballistic-missile defences could be penetrated, overwhelmed or simply outflanked by other weaponry.[22]

That also appeared to be the purpose of Russia's new submarine the *Belgorod*. The *Belgorod* was a true Cold War throwback, a modified 'Oscar'-class missile submarine whose construction had begun in 1992 but then been delayed by every crisis in modern Russian history, including the Covid-19 pandemic, finally entering service in July 2022 a few months after the invasion of Ukraine.[23]

As well as acting as a mothership for 'special-mission' submarines like *Losharik*, the *Belgorod* was designed to carry 'Poseidon', a weapon described by Russian media as a true 'Doomsday device'. This giant torpedo, supposedly atomic powered, could be launched from a submarine to race hundreds of miles or more under the ocean to trigger a giant nuclear explosion and radioactive tsunami designed to obliterate coastal cities and aircraft-carrier battle groups. According to arms control group the Bulletin of Atomic Scientists, Russia wanted around 30 'Poseidons', able to strike the United States even if the US stepped up its missile defences on a massive scale. First announced in 2016, some reports suggested it could be in service as soon as 2027.[24]

The 'Poseidon' was namechecked by the Kremlin in a February 2024 speech by Putin in which he warned any new 'invader' of Russia would face absolute destruction.[25] And yet, when Ukrainian forces launched an offensive into Russian territory near Kursk a few months later, the Kremlin was much quieter when it came to atomic warnings. That did not, however, mean the threat had gone away.

Ukraine pointed to another danger. In Europe and the Pacific, the confrontations over places like Ukraine, Taiwan and the Baltic states were driving a rapid build-up of long-range conventional cruise and ballistic missiles likely to be fired in huge numbers in the first days of any conflict. Increasingly, some of those same systems – the Russian Iskander, for example – were also capable of carrying atomic warheads. By the end of the Biden administration the US was also looking at putting nuclear warheads back on its Tomahawk cruise missiles, almost certainly one reason China had become so publicly infuriated over the (so far conventional) Typhon rocket deployment in the northern Philippines.

France – the only European nation with its own air-launched atomic-armed cruise missile – was also now showing off that capability. Shortly after Russia announced the further deployment of nuclear-tipped Iskanders to Belarus in May 2025, France conducted the latest test-firing of its ASMPA-R long-range cruise missile with an inactivated warhead.[26]

In the first Cold War, the deployment of medium-range high-speed atomic weapons to Turkey and Cuba had brought the world to the brink of Armageddon in 1962. It happened again in the early 1980s with the deployment into Europe of the Soviet SS-20 and the US Cruise and Pershing missiles, whose ability to strike each other's capitals in minutes had unsettled both sides so much that they had signed the 1987 Intermediate-Range Nuclear Forces agreement to scrap such weaponry entirely (this was the agreement the young Trump had hoped in vain to negotiate with Gorbachev). By 2018, however, Russia's much-publicised work on nuclear cruise missiles had prompted the US under Trump himself to quit that treaty and start work on its own weapons.[27]

As late as 2016, the Obama administration had been talking of global nuclear disarmament. But within two years, US officials were warning they might respond with nuclear force for a particularly devastating cyber attack – for example, one that blew up a nuclear power plant[28] while the Pentagon was restocking America's own atomic arsenal.[29] By then, in US war colleges and military academies, an effort was restarting to bring a new generation of commanders up to speed with this risk – and its opening scenarios were terrifying.

What was even more alarming was that by the middle of the 2020s, those wargame scenarios were beginning to look extremely prescient.

*

By 2018 – the second year of Trump's first term – the increasingly aggressive rhetoric and missile launches pursued by North Korea had dramatically increased nervousness that the US mainland might one day face at least a limited atomic strike. At Fort Greely in Alaska, several dozen long-range inter-ceptor missiles were now on standby around the clock, ready to blast spacewards at multi-supersonic speeds. Those oper-ating the interceptors described their mission as 'trying to hit a bullet with a bullet' – by the time the 'kill vehicle' approached the target warhead, its speed was approaching 15,000 miles per hour.

It was hoped that US interceptors could destroy a small handful of incoming missiles – the most North Korea was believed capable of mustering. The Pentagon described it as a 'no fail mission' – in other words, a single atomic warhead striking the US mainland was such a horrific concept it could simply not be allowed to happen.[30]

In a much larger conflict, though – one with Moscow, Beijing or both – the handful of US interceptors could be overwhelmed or outflanked by much larger volleys of Chinese or Russian missiles. No one, for now, believed either nation would begin a war with such a strike. But a broader conflict could escalate that way with apocalyptic consequences.

Already, the mid-ranking officers studying at US Marine Corps War College in Quantico, Virginia, were confronting the appalling choices they and their commanders might face in such a war. In just two days that simulated several weeks of conflict, the 2018 course found themselves coming to the brink of worldwide nuclear exchange.

In the scenario devised by their professor, James Lacey, the War College students – men and women who might soon be commanding battalions or warships – faced a worldwide conflict set in 2026 in which an economically struggling China attacked Taiwan just as a Kremlin that had already conquered Ukraine and the Baltic states launched a new offensive into Poland. As they did so, North Korea went on the offensive against the South, and the US found itself inevitably stretched beyond its strategic limits.

Most of the participants had joined the US military after the end of the Cold War, and it swiftly became apparent the scale of casualties from such a major conflict outstripped anything in their experience or lifetime. As the camouflage-wearing players moved counters around maps on tables – the 'battles' were fought out on a commercially produced physical wargame set – the calculated casualties on all sides outstripped 150,000 in the first week of fighting. Russia's invasion of Poland saw 60,000 allied casualties in a single day. 'As there was not enough American combat power to fight and win three simultaneous major conflicts, hard strategic choices were unavoidable,' Lacey wrote.

Ultimately – as in the real-world conflict in Ukraine – no side had the level of combat forces they truly needed to prevail. First, North Korean use of chemical weapons pushed US commanders towards nuclear release. Then, US military leaders in Europe also requested atomic weapons after one of their overstretched divisions was encircled and faced annihilation. 'Every time a theatre commander suffered a setback, they requested authority to employ nuclear weapons,' Lacey wrote.[31]

The fact that it was the American-led side moving first to nuclear release might have been a surprise to those who had become used to the massive US military superiority of the 'war on terror'. But it broadly tracked with wider discussions already taking place within the US national security establishment. It also broadly matched the expected reality throughout most of the first Cold War, in which numerically inferior NATO forces in Europe expected to have to fall back on tactical nuclear weapons to hold back a Soviet advance.

By the middle of the 2020s, a wholescale re-equipping of America's ageing atomic arsenal was now starting in earnest, with Sentinel missiles replacing the ageing 'Minutemen' in their midwest silos, *Columbia*-class submarines replacing the Cold War-era *Ohio*-class, and the new stealth B-21 'Raider' replacing the previous generation B-2 stealth bomber. Some ageing systems were still expected to be in use well into the mid-century, including some B-52 bombers approaching a century in age. Almost all of those replacement programmes, however, faced potential and sometimes dramatic delays. Frequently to blame were the challenges of finding the industrial capacity to physically build them – particularly the *Columbia*-class ballistic submarines that were supposed to deliver America's most survivable deterrent. The US just didn't have enough welders or nuclear engineers, and that meant submarines, bombers and missiles were coming off production lines much slower than US commanders now believed was necessary.

That alone worried some, while others warned another top priority should be building a much more sophisticated command, control and analysis system to make nuclear decisions, an upgrade on the one that had existed since the first Cold War. The need to potentially make lightning-fast decisions was accompanied by a major disagreement between experts on whether artificial intelligence in such an environment was a blessing or a curse.[32]

'Most of the nuclear-armed states are upping their rhetoric about . . . nuclear weapons, and some are even issuing explicit or implicit threats about using them,' warned nuclear policy researcher Matt Korda at the Stockholm International Peace Research Institute (SIPRI) in early 2025. His colleague and boss SIPRI director Dan Smith warned that with 'communication channels between nuclear-armed rivals closed or barely functioning, the risk of miscalculation, misunderstanding or accident are unacceptably high'.[33]

As of the middle of the 2020s, almost 90 per cent of nuclear warheads in the world remained American and Russian – 88 per cent according to nuclear watchdog the Federation of American Scientists. The Kremlin had the largest arsenal: just over 1,700 deployed atomic warheads, another almost 2,700 in reserve and 1,200 'retired' awaiting their disposal. The US had slightly smaller numbers: more than 1,600 rockets deployed, 1,900 in reserve and 1,300 awaiting their disposal. Britain and France had less than 300 each; India and Pakistan roughly 170 apiece; while the secretive arsenals of Israel and North Korea were estimated at 90 and 50 devices respectively. By far the fastest growing, though, was that of China – which had more history of taking serious atomic risks than any other nation, even North Korea.[34]

*

In the first Cold War, the Kremlin's refusal to share nuclear technology with Beijing had been a major factor in the Sino-Soviet split. According to former Soviet leader Nikita Khrushchev, at some point in the mid-1950s – either before or during the first crises of the Taiwan Strait from 1955, in which the US threatened a nuclear response if Beijing attacked Taiwan or its offshore island – the Kremlin had a device ready to be sent directly to Beijing. Then, for reasons he did not explain in detail, those running the Soviet Union changed their minds. 'We didn't want to give them the idea that we were their obedient slaves and would give them whatever they wanted,' Khrushchev wrote of the USSR's relationship with Mao's Beijing. The Chinese, however, were determined – Chen Yi, a former army marshal who became foreign minister in 1958, argued that a nuclear weapon was necessary 'even if we had to pawn our pants'. In fact, the situation was even worse than that – China was in the midst of its Cultural Revolution famine, so the investment in atomic arms almost certainly came at the cost of many lives.

The USSR did provide some basic support with missiles – but, according to Chinese officials, it was extremely limited and again intended to keep Beijing in a subservient position. Even after China detonated its first atomic bomb in 1964, there were widely expressed international doubts over whether it could mount a warhead on a rocket. This was, after all, something only the US and Russians had so far worked out how to do – the French were still struggling, while the British had given up the fight and bought into US rocket programmes.

By mid-1966, however, the Chinese believed they had a working model – and they were prepared to take more risks than any other nation before or since to demonstrate it worked. In October 1965, China fired a nuclear-tipped ballistic missile more than 500 miles to the Lop Nor nuclear test range, overflying populated areas to get it there. 'It was a somewhat risky assignment,' Marshal Nie Rongzhen wrote in his autobiography, published in 1985 and serialised in a Chinese state publication. 'If by any chance the nuclear warhead exploded prematurely, fell after it was launched or went beyond the designated target area, the consequences would be too ghastly to contemplate.'[35]

According to the Nuclear Weapons Education Project at the Massachusetts Institute for Technology (MIT), that test – later revealed to have been conducted with a Dong-Feng 2 rocket and a 12-kiloton atomic warhead – remains the only occasion on which a nuclear-armed ballistic missile has flown above a populated area.[36] The Chinese government announced the result a few days later; having previously only claimed its first three atomic detonations as 'nuclear explosions', Beijing was now prepared to say that it possessed 'atomic weapons'.[37]

From then, Chinese engineers worked on ever larger Dong-Feng rockets, prioritising first variants that could strike the immediate neighbourhood – including US bases in Taiwan and the Philippines – and then slightly further to reach Moscow and the US Pacific territory of Guam. With the development of the Dong-Feng 5 in the early 1980s, they could strike the continental United States – and by keeping those missiles mounted on highly mobile trucks they believed they could keep them survivable enough to deter either the US or Russia from launching atomic strikes on them. By the end of the 20th century, China was the only nation to have publicly pledged never to launch a first strike against an enemy.[38]

By the aftermath of the third Taiwan Strait crisis of 1996, however – in which Beijing had fired several ballistic missiles into the waters around Taiwan – US strategists were starting to suspect China had another aim in mind: using the implied threat of atomic war to limit outside involvement in a regional offensive such as one against Taiwan. One US military strategist termed that approach 'winning the limited war' – although the Pentagon publicly briefed that the PLA currently lacked the capability for any such campaign.[39]

By the 2020s, though, that was changing fast – and as a rising global power that viewed itself as equal to the United States and Russia, Xi's PRC believed it needed one of the largest global arsenals. The more than 300 missile silos in northern and western China came to be increasingly stocked with weapons; China's half-dozen ballistic-missile submarines were conducting their own undersea deterrence patrols; and its conventional and atomic long-range rocket stocks also kept on growing.[40] Despite reports of multiple arrests of senior officials within China's rocket forces for corruption, and suspicions that some of those silos might have been improperly or poorly built, US analysts believed the programme was still moving forward.[41] Perhaps most dangerously of all for the United States, China was also now working on its own long-range strategic stealth bomber, the H-20, considered by the US Strategic Command to possess a reported range of 5,000 miles and the ability to threaten the US mainland.[42]

That growth of arms was fast closing the gap with Washington and Moscow. As of January 2024, China was estimated to have 500 atomic warheads, the world's third-largest atomic arsenal – and to have increased that by almost 100 in the preceding 12 months. With some of those warheads reported to be fitted to their missiles during peacetime, there were predictions China intended to match the much larger deployed arsenals of Russia and the United States.[43]

The Pentagon backed up those warnings, suggesting their national arsenals might be roughly matched by 2033.[44] Close observers of Washington noticed that those who favoured complete nuclear disarmament were leaving the Biden administration's nuclear policy and arms control teams, to be replaced by much tougher-minded strategists. 'That tells you that they are looking at the classified information as well, and it has them really worried,' one national security academic told me.[45]

That raised an obvious next concern: whether any form of arms control agreements might be possible in the coming era, or whether we would simply witness a free-for-all race for nuclear supremacy last seen in the early Cold War years.

Ever since the late Cold War, US and Russian warheads stocks had been constrained by a series of strategic arms reduction treaties known as 'START'. The last of those – timetabled to expire in February 2026 – was not believed by anyone likely to be extended or replaced particularly soon. 'We must prepare for a world where constraints on nuclear weapons arsenals disappear entirely,' outgoing Assistant Secretary of Defense Vipin Narang told a nuclear policy conference in summer 2024. The years following the end of the Cold War, he said, now looked like just an 'intermission' between two eras of nuclear confrontation. Narang predicted the world was entering 'nothing short of a new nuclear age – multiple revisionist nuclear challengers, each rapidly modernising and expanding their nuclear arsenals and openly threatening to employ nuclear weapons to achieve their aims'.[46]

In his first term in office, Trump had pulled the US out of the 2015 Obama-era Iran nuclear deal, the 1987 Intermediate Nuclear Forces Treaty and the 1992 'Open Skies' agreement under which Russian and US government aircraft could scrutinise each other's territory for unacknowledged nuclear activity. In the run-up to his 2024 election victory and January 2025 inauguration, however, the topic of renewed atomic arms control came up several times – and Trump raised it again at World Economic Forum in Davos three days after taking office. 'Tremendous amounts of money are being spent on nuclear, and the destructive capability is something that we don't even want to talk about today because we don't want to hear it,' he said, in response to a question on US–China relations. 'So we want to see if we can denuclearise, and I think that's very possible.'[47]

According to his first-term adviser on Russia, Fiona Hill, Trump's 'obsession' with disarmament of the 1980s had never gone away – he would often reference the searing apocalyptic imagery of several major 1980s TV shows that imagined atomic war. 'He believes that he personally is the answer,' she said, joking that what the US president really wanted was a 'Super Trump Arms Reduction Treaty' that covered all types of nuclear weapons and brought their numbers down.[48] 'There is quite a weird optimism within the nuclear community about Trump,' Francesca Giovannini, head of the Project for Managing the Atom at Harvard

University, told Politico in spring 2025. 'There is an idea that he has a political space that no other president before him had to make a good deal with Russia, China and Iran.' Citing personal conversations with Chinese officials, she said some Chinese contacts had suggested Beijing favoured Trump over Harris in the 2024 election because 'he seems to have more political space to compromise'.

Against that, though, was a very different dynamic that worried atomic specialists: the risk that the growing abandonment of US allies might send a host of other nations from South Korea to Saudi Arabia and Poland scurrying to build their own atomic weapons.[49]

In a speech to the Lowy Institute in Australia, Rose Gottemoeller, Obama's Under Secretary for Arms Control and International Security – scarcely a Trump supporter – suggested the sort of deal she thought that Trump might get. The first stage – potentially negotiable as part of a peace deal on Ukraine – might be for Trump and Putin to agree that even once the New START treaty expired neither would push beyond its limit of 1,550 deployed warheads or 700 delivery vehicles. The next would be to get China to agree to cap its nuclear arsenal at exactly that same limit, part of a grand bargain that she suggested would establish those three nations as the world's pre-eminent 'nuclear triumvirate'.[50]

It wasn't hard to imagine what objections more hawkish Republicans might raise to such a scheme – particularly if it had been promoted by the Democrats – given that it would leave Russia and China outgunning the US two-to-one on warhead numbers. If America engaged in a major nuclear exchange on those terms with one potential enemy, it would be hugely vulnerable to the other in its aftermath. In theory, America's nuclear allies – Britain and France, together with any other nations that might embrace atomic arms – could make up the difference, but that would involve enormous proliferation, something no previous US administration would ever have endorsed.

Whether warhead numbers themselves really made a difference was another question – a simple count, after all, did not necessarily distinguish between a low-yield tactical nuclear warhead of very limited destructive power or a 'Poseidon'-type device that might devastate an entire continental seaboard if exploded underwater. Nor was it entirely clear whether Russia and China should truly be treated as allies of each other or potential foes – or, perhaps more accurately, both. It was noteworthy, after all, that the supposedly 'Poseidon'-carrying *Belgorod* was slated to be assigned to the Pacific fleet,[51] from which she could threaten both US and Chinese coastlines if so needed.

Nor was it clear how any of these approaches would interact with Trump's other 'big idea' to reduce atomic risk to the United States: the 'Golden Dome' defence shield, a potentially colossal increase of the existing US interceptor fleet backed up by space sensors and likely also lasers.

Without doubt, mid-2020s technology was considerably more advanced than when Reagan had suggested the broadly similar 'Star Wars' Strategic Defense Initiative concept in 1983, worrying the Russians as well as America's European allies – but protecting an entire continent from perhaps hundreds of approaching warheads was still an enormous challenge.

'We think they will struggle to get the technology to work,' one European diplomat in Washington told me, noting a return to 1980s concerns that a US unable to defend itself from Russian missile strikes might then give up defending European nations.

Even a single nuclear detonation anywhere in the world, however, could still have devastating consequences, including catastrophic unintended escalation.

*

Wargaming how escalation might progress after the first atomic blasts was very far from easy. In her 2024 bestseller *Nuclear War*, journalist Annie Jacobsen traced a hypothetical but catastrophic atomic escalation taking place in hours, triggered by a North

Korean atomic strike against the United States which led to Russia and China responding with a catastrophic nuclear exchange after wrongly concluding the US response was aimed at them. In such a situation, commanders said they would try to be proportionate. 'If somebody launches a nuclear weapon against us, we will launch one back,' Jacobsen quoted former US Strategic Command Chief John E. Hyten, describing an 'escalation ladder' in which, 'They launch two, we launch two.' But the opportunity for error was enormous. Given the time taken for a ballistic missile to fly, a US president might only have minutes to decide whether to launch America's own weapons before a city like Washington was destroyed, events escalating terrifyingly fast beyond the point of no return. That was the scenario Jacobsen followed in her book: the entire world laid waste by arsenals within hours of that first atomic detonation.[52]

Some believed that, in reality, escalation might instead come over several days. In former British General Sir John Hackett's 1978 fictitious history *The Third World War*, set in the early 1980s, he imagined Soviet leaders launching a single nuclear strike against the English city of Birmingham, seeking a ceasefire with NATO and to consolidate territorial gains in Europe. Instead of buckling, the US and UK responded with two single Trident rockets – one each from a US and British submarine – that annihilated the Soviet city Minsk, in the real world now the capital of Belarus.

In the book, the shock produced by that action prompts the fall of the Soviet Union and the ending of hostilities – but it makes clear other much worse outcomes were also very plausible.[53] In a more modern scenario devised by former NATO Deputy Supreme Allied Commander British General Richard Shirreff, a future version of Putin, who had successfully seized the Baltic states, was imagined threatening an atomic strike as European forces advanced to push him back. In Shirreff's scenario – written for the UK's *Daily Mail* – those threats produced a surprise atomic strike against the

Russian city of Volgograd by a post-war Ukraine with a secret atomic programme – again leading to the fall of the present Kremlin regime.

Only a handful of years earlier, the idea that increased proliferation of nuclear weapons might help stabilise the world would have been truly radical. But by the mid-2020s, it was quietly becoming if not widespread, then at least discussed within places such as the new US administration – although it was difficult to gauge how many officials really favoured Poland, Germany and South Korea building their own atomic bombs. Working out what the Trump administration truly thought was made much harder by the fact that many jobs within the Pentagon still remained unfilled as the year progressed – while the officials that were in place were already being worked to their limits. 'I've heard it's a pure ghost town,' Matt Costlow, who had worked for the Pentagon's Office for Nuclear and Missile Defense Policy in the first Trump administration, said in April 2025. 'There's just no one there. The staff that is there is spread so thin it is causing this paralysis.' The most likely reality, he said, was that the new appointees had a range of views – and were predictably shy of sharing them until they knew where the president himself came down. Within those countries now tempted to acquire atomic weapons, some suggested the most telling thing was not the handful of voices coming out in favour, but the increasing lack of those voicing disagreement.

That was particularly true in South Korea, where no senior politician had mentioned atomic weapons since the embattled President Yoon – originator of the unsuccessful coup – had been forced from office shortly after the Trump inauguration. But politicians from the more liberal Democratic Party of Korea – which had traditionally opposed developing atomic arms – had also gone abruptly silent on the topic. At the very least, politicians there talked of 'nuclear latency', meaning a situation where the country did not acquire atomic weapons but maintained sufficient stores of equipment and components to build them almost overnight.

That was also increasingly the likely situation in Japan and Germany, the two defeated powers of World War Two, for whom acquiring such weapons would once have been unthinkable domestically and unacceptable to neighbours. 'The nuclear debate is still taboo in Japanese society, but since the Russian invasion of Ukraine there has been a total wake-up call . . . about what kind of additional military power to possess,' said Junjiro Shida, a national security expert at Meio University in Okinawa. Brad Roberts, Director of the Center for Global Security Research at Lawrence Livermore National Laboratory, said he expected multiple nations and small groups of states, perhaps even the Nordics, to begin clandestine nuclear activities in the coming years.[54]

Already in existence were the improbable-sounding NATO 'nuclear sharing' arrangements first proposed under John F. Kennedy in which dozens of US nuclear bombs were held at NATO bases in Belgium, the Netherlands, Germany, Italy and Turkey, ready to be transferred to the air forces of those countries in the event of widespread atomic war. The fact that Dutch, Belgian, Italian, Turkish and German pilots trained throughout that earlier confrontation to drop US atomic bombs was something some already struggled to believe – the fact that this arrangement and its associated training continued throughout the modern era was much less widely understood. Still, after the events of Russia's full-scale Ukraine invasion, there were plenty of those glad that it had indeed endured – and the annual NATO STEADFAST NOON drills in 2023 and 2024 were the most realistic yet.

According to a NATO video, the STEADFAST NOON scenario imagined an unnamed but nuclear-armed aggressor overrunning parts of Europe – and dozens of NATO aircraft conducting realistic dropping of freefall atomic bombs in order to push them back. As well as the dropping of the weapons themselves, officials said the exercise included multiple elements drawn from recent events in Ukraine and beyond, including electronic warfare surveillance and the use of small enemy attack drones that might threaten aircraft, particularly when they were on the ground.

According to official briefings, the 2024 iteration, largely based in Belgium, involved some 60 aircraft from 13 nations and roughly 2,000 personnel. Whereas previous STEADFAST NOONs had primarily used ageing aircraft such as the F-16 or Tornado, whose nuclear role was a holdover from the Cold War days, the 2024 exercise utilised the F-35A, with Dutch aircrews the first outside the United States certified to use the fifth-generation stealth fighter to conduct atomic strikes with US weapons.

None of those exercises, US and NATO officials went out of their way to stress, involved live atomic weapons – those remained firmly under lock and key.[55] The US had been particularly sensitive to such things after a series of atomic mishaps, most recently in 2007 when several nuclear-armed cruise missiles were accidentally loaded onto a B-52 strategic bomber at Minot Air Force Base in North Dakota and travelled halfway across the country before anybody noticed. That incident – which US Air Force personnel were instructed 'NOT' to call the 'Minot Incident' in a training package that was inevitably leaked – ultimately prompted the resignation of the head of the US Air Force and several other senior leaders. Multiple senior officials were also disciplined over another incident in 2006 in which identified 'nuclear weapons components' were shipped to Taiwan, also by mistake.[56]

The US military of the 2020s believed it had moved on from such errors, as did its Western allies. 'It would send entirely the wrong message if we were to cancel this long-planned exercise because of war in Ukraine,' then NATO Secretary General Jens Stoltenberg told reporters in 2022, as pro-Kremlin pundits claimed the drills might trigger widespread atomic war.[57]

By the mid-2020s, voices in several nations – including South Korea, Japan and Poland – were saying that they should be allowed to join in US 'nuclear sharing' programme. Whether that would be enough to make them feel safe, however, was another question: particularly as the era of Trump and Vance brought its own challenges.[58]

The closest US relationship was, of course, with Britain – from the 1960s the two nations shared a US-held stock of first Polaris and then of Trident missiles, 'lent' to the UK to be used on Britain's submarines. Some questioned whether that made the UK nuclear deterrent 'independent'. Even France, which made so much of its deterrent being 'French from end to end' was widely believed to have needed US support to get its warheads and missiles to work properly together, and a highly classified relationship continued into the current century. 'The Americans have their own relationship with the French, and they don't tell us what they share,' one former British official in Washington told me in the early 2010s.[59]

The truth was that almost every major US ally now looked excessively dependent on American support, whether to underpin their own atomic weapons programme, or as a US ally relying on its atomic weapons to provide what was known euphemistically as 'extended deterrence': the explicit, formally agreed but rarely spoken pledge that the US would respond with atomic force if a closely allied country was attacked with nuclear arms. That protection was judged particularly vital for US allies geographically nearest to Russia, China, Iran or North Korea – but whether the US would be willing or able to offer such support in the 2030s and beyond looked suddenly more doubtful.

Even more than South Korea, Poland was now the most prominent nation to explicitly suggest it might develop its own atomic arms, but those discussions were also taking place behind closed doors in plenty of other nations.

That included Iran, whose claims of having abandoned its clandestine nuclear programme in 2003 were widely disbelieved, and which had spent the decades since in often fraught negotiations over what atomic activity it should be allowed as part of peaceful nuclear development. In fact, the US and its allies – particularly Israel – had little doubt that Iran had retained its interest in atomic weapons, and by 2025 might be in a position to manufacture them within a matter of just weeks if it so chose.

Throughout that time, Israel's on-and-off Prime Minister Benjamin Netanyahu had threatened war to stop that happening – but partly through concerted US and European diplomatic efforts, and partly through the threat of what Iran itself might do if hit, that had been avoided.

After the Hamas attacks of October 2023, however, Israel took a very different approach to warfare than it had pursued before – one that would reveal even more about how the world was changing.

11

The Middle East on the Brink

*'The Middle East . . . has become a proverbial Hotel
California; the United States can check out any
time it likes, but it can never leave.'*

**Major Brennan Deveraux, US Army War College
Strategic Studies Institute, April 2024[1]**

In February 2024, the head of Hezbollah in Lebanon, Hassan
Nasrallah, gave his followers a simple message: he wanted them
to avoid using mobile phones in order to escape surveillance by
Israeli spies, adding: 'Put it in an iron box and lock it.'[2] Nasrallah's
paranoia was understandable – aged 62, he was one of the
most experienced practitioners of the shadow war between
Israel and its enemies across the region, particularly those
groups long backed by Iran. Having briefly attended a religious
seminary in that nation shortly after the 1979 revolution,
Nasrallah was as committed to its ideals as any Iranian – and
likely more than most – and viewed it as a model for other Shiite
groups to follow. That made him an enthusiastic collaborator
with the Islamic Revolutionary Guard Corps (IRGC) headquartered in Tehran – and from around 2012, it also made him
and his Hezbollah fighters key figures in Syria's civil war.

Most importantly, at least when it came to regional geopolitics
and his paymasters in Tehran, Nasrallah and his fighters from
Hezbollah had enough firepower overlooking Israel –
particularly short- and medium-range rockets often hidden in

civilian settlements – to cause enormous damage if they wished. It was one of the few constraints that held Israel back from taking more direct military action on Iran – and although Nasrallah and his commanders did not yet know it, it was a constraint Israel was determined to remove.

They would use technology to do so. Even in times of relative peace, the struggle for the Middle East could be a bloody one – particularly for those on the receiving end of US or Israeli intelligence attention. Both nations were masters at tracking electronic devices, emails and telephone connections; data which could be used for targeted assassinations involving drones or airstrikes. Such information could be gathered over decades, fed into databases, analysed with software from firms like Palantir, and used to generate organisational charts and 'target packs'. In the aftermath of the Hamas attacks from Gaza in October 2023, Prime Minister Benjamin Netanyahu widened strikes to southern Lebanon from which Hezbollah rockets periodically slammed into Israeli towns and cities. The gloves were coming off further, and Nasrallah was right to be concerned.

The first solution pursued by Hezbollah was to use walkie-talkie radios to limit interception. By the early 2020s, they were using electronic pagers, again believed to be less vulnerable to interception than conventional mobile phones. There was, however, a fatal problem with this strategy: it had been penetrated by the Israelis from the very start. By 2024, many of the walkie-talkie radios and pagers being used by Hezbollah in both Lebanon and Syria had not been made in Taiwan as the Islamist group believed, but within Israel by manufacturers linked to a secretive military unit known as 'Unit 8200', usually described as a counterpart to the US National Security Agency or Britain's GCHQ. From roughly 2022, this included the use of a company in Hungary with a licence to build pagers from the original Taiwanese design, secreting small amounts of plastic explosive into each battery area to quite literally put a bomb in the pocket of hundreds of Hezbollah fighters.

By summer 2024, some in Hezbollah's security directorate were getting suspicious of the pagers, and were preparing to send them to Iran for testing. It was a fateful decision – one that would unleash an Israeli military campaign that would change the Middle East for ever.

Within the Israeli security state, only a handful of individuals were aware of the explosives hidden in the pagers. Faced with their discovery, Netanyahu ordered their immediate detonation. On September 17, all of the pagers within Lebanon and Syria exploded simultaneously, followed by a second round of blasts the following day targeting the walkie-talkies often being used to co-ordinate the victims' funerals. In total, Lebanon's ministry of health put the death toll at 30, including at least two children, while the number of injured was said to have run to several thousand. Almost all appear to have been members of Hezbollah or associated partners. Iran's ambassador to Lebanon was among the injured, later telling reporters that the pager in his office for emergency communication during power blackouts had also exploded.[3]

It was a strike unlike any other in military history, leaving Hezbollah stunned and dislocated – but having fired its perhaps once-in-a-lifetime secret weapon, Netanyahu's government was determined to take maximum advantage. The war in Gaza had generated enormous international outrage, which perversely lowered the political cost of any further action. Domestically, his government was facing growing challenges – not least because the Gaza war appeared to be going nowhere – and so a gamble on dramatically degrading Israel's greatest foes had its own political logic. In the days after the pager explosions, Israel launched a massive air offensive and smaller ground incursions into southern Lebanon, targeting leadership facilities and hidden missiles aimed at northern Israel.

Until the very end, Hezbollah's leader Nasrallah – who had been too paranoid to carry a pager himself – does not appear to have believed Israel would come after him as part of its much larger offensive aimed at taking out the majority of Hezbollah's missiles. His body was recovered several days after a devastating Israeli strike on his concealed bunker complex – he was said to have suffocated in the ruins, reportedly found alongside the body of an Iranian general.[4]

It was a sign of things to come. Within weeks, Israel's Netanyahu would issue secret orders to his military to prepare for a campaign designed not just to destroy the Iranian nuclear programme – something his government had long hoped to do – but also perhaps to bring down the Iranian regime in its entirety. It was a plan that would also take the United States back to the edge of another Middle Eastern war just as it hoped to extract itself finally from that region.

*

As the pieces moved into place for perhaps the most serious confrontation in the Middle East in living memory, a secretive US base in the Qatari desert would again co-ordinate the action. Al Udeid was the regional headquarters of the US Central Command covering the Middle East, supporting and supported by a larger US-based HQ in Tampa, Florida. It also housed the US-led Coalition Air Operations Center (CAOC), which co-ordinated all US air activity nearby.

The CAOC traced its heritage to a collection of tents set up beside a Riyadh runway in the aftermath of Saddam Hussein's 1990 invasion of Kuwait, and it had grown wildly from there. The US-led military response back then to first dissuade Iraq from attacking Saudi Arabia and then to evict its army from Kuwait marked the start of a much more active military posture in the Middle East that would prove almost impossible to quit. Enforcing the no-fly zones and UN resolutions on Iraq in time turned into counterterrorism missions following 9/11, supercharged still further by the invasion of Iraq in 2003. Throughout the long Iraqi and Afghan campaigns, the CAOC was essential in co-ordinating military air activity, including vital airstrikes to support beleaguered or encircled troops.

Until 2013, the fact that the base was located in Qatar at all was kept from the public eye, with visiting journalists forced to sign a nondisclosure agreement stating that they would only reveal that it was 'somewhere in Southwest Asia'. By then, as well as co-ordinating America's twin war zones in the region, it was also tracking the skies above Syria, where Russia was already beginning to play a much more active role.[5]

From 2014, as Islamic State militants suddenly seized control of huge swathes of both Iraq and Syria, that role became more important still – particularly as Russian forces began to intervene directly in the Syria conflict from 2015 onwards, sometimes coming into close proximity with US personnel. When US airstrikes were launched in Syria against suspected Russian Wagner Group mercenaries threatening US special forces and their Syrian allies in 2018, they were co-ordinated directly from the CAOC. According to later accounts, that engagement – rumoured to have left as many as several hundred Russian mercenaries dead – was particularly brutal. The air operations centre in Qatar had its own liaison function with the Russian military, designed to reduce the risk of accidental conflict, but the Russians on the other end of the line absolutely denied that the tanks and troops firing on US forces near a refinery in central Syria had any Russian connection. Those listening in on transmissions from the ground, however, could clearly hear Russian being spoken.

By 2018, Russian support for Assad's government in Syria was at an all-time high – it would be cut back considerably after the full-scale invasion of Ukraine in 2022. With several hundred Russian-speaking and Syrian forces advancing with tanks and armoured vehicles, officials spoke repeatedly to their Russian military counterparts, who again denied any knowledge of the force. 'The Russian high command in Syria assured us it was not their people,' Defense Secretary Jim Mattis told senators later in the year. He said he then directed 'for the force . . . to be annihilated'. Commanders in Qatar sent in jets, drones and attack helicopters, which wiped out the column.[6]

It was, with hindsight, a sign of the approach that both the first and second Trump administration would take when it came to military action: the issuing of a warning, then the use of much more overwhelming force than might have been agreed by the Obama or Biden administration. But it was also seen as a warning of the risk of having small detachments of US troops deployed in risky areas.

'We told the Russians we were going to kill them and we killed them,' is how one former intelligence official described it to me. Exactly what was going on behind the scenes on the Russian side remains a matter for debate. With hindsight, it may well have been an early sign of the bad blood between the mainstream Russian military and the Wagner contractors under Putin's former catering manager Yevgeny Prigozhin. Divisions between the Wagner Group and mainstream Kremlin powerbrokers eventually grew to the point that the mercenaries attempted to march on Moscow in mid-2023, followed by their rapid dismemberment as an effective organisation and the death of Prigozhin in a plane crash.

But it was also a reminder of the fast-rising international stakes, coming just as fighting between Iran's proxies in Yemen and the Saudi and Emirati governments was again breaking out. By September 2019, long-range drone-missile strikes fired from Yemen were inflicting considerable damage on Saudi Arabian oil facilities.[7] Throughout the 2020s, developments became more complex still – and following the Hamas attack on Israel of October 2023, also much more interconnected in sometimes violent ways.

While the air planners and controllers at the CAOC were kept busy co-ordinating activities across the Middle East – including, from early 2024, the US strikes on Yemen – US Central Command was also looking at the bigger picture, what one US think tank referred to as a 'cacophony of influence' that took in the rising influence of China and the dramatically increased clout of the Gulf states, who themselves, with their own complex international relations, were already reshaping the region's geopolitics.

In 2020, the last year of the first Trump administration, the United Arab Emirates and Bahrain had signed the US-brokered 'Abraham Accords' to normalise relations with Israel, an effort the Biden team had continued throughout their first three years in office. By late 2023, Saudi Arabia too had looked ready to sign – indeed, one popular theory was that the Hamas attack on Israel that October was in part deliberately designed to block that process. If that was the case, it was partially successful – Israel's campaign in Gaza removed any prospect that Riyadh might sign anything so high profile in the immediate term. But even without formal diplomatic agreement, US officials working in the region noted that Israel was starting to reorientate its attention from diplomacy with the US and European countries to step up its own informal relations in the Gulf. Behind closed doors, there were plenty of suspicions that Israel and some of the Gulf states were likely happy to discuss their shared distrust of Iran, and perhaps even occasionally their shared priority and plans.

Simultaneously, though, all three major Gulf states – Saudi Arabia, the United Arab Emirates and Qatar – were building their own relationships with China and maintaining those with Russia. In the case of the UAE, that included the alleged partial construction of a military port. After US officials raised complaints with the Emirati government in 2021, work on that facility – near the main container port in Abu Dhabi – was said to have stopped, only to have restarted in 2023.[8]

When I visited the Gulf in 2023 and 2025, no one would talk on the record about what was truly happening there – but Western security sources flagged a growing Chinese business and industrial presence as well as increased trade. Both the UAE and Saudi were also unapologetic over their ongoing relationships with Russia – although at the Dubai Airshow in 2023, the US and Russian delegations were put at opposite ends of the runway to minimise diplomatic awkwardness.

US planners talked of countering Chinese influence across the region as one of their top priorities – but the truth was the messy overlapping relations of the Gulf region also offered opportunity for backchannel diplomacy and sometimes serious negotiations. Qatar having multiple relationships with militant groups was vital to any talks with groups such as the Taliban and Hamas, while Saudi Arabia hosted US talks with Russia on Ukraine. Oman – by far the friendliest Gulf nation with Tehran – had hosted both public and secret talks going back at least as far as the Obama era. 'Nothing in the Middle East is monolithic,' Hayat Alvi, Middle East expert and outgoing Associate Professor of National Security Studies at the US Naval War College, reminded me in early 2025. Despite their often hefty experience of operations in the region, she noted that few of her military students truly had the 'deep understanding' to connect the pieces.

Few areas saw as much disagreement as how to handle Iran, where some US and Israeli hawks had been calling for military intervention and regime change since at least 2003, while others pushed for restraint even as Iran built up its military capabilities and international negotiators pushed for clarity on its atomic programme. By the end of the 2010s, US commanders were preparing for conflict with a degree of realism that had not been seen before. That included a drill in early 2019 in which control of all US-led air operations in the Middle East was transferred to Shaw Air Force Base in South Carolina for 24 hours, demonstrating the ability to keep operations going even if CAOC in Al Udeid was damaged or destroyed.[9]

For the head of US Central Command General Michael 'Erik' Kurilla and his team, the aftermath of the October 2023 attacks felt like 'an earthquake', ushering in the most intense period of US military activity in the region for several years. He described it as an era of both threat and opportunity, with Iran and its proxies working harder than ever to grab what they saw as a 'once-in-a-lifetime opportunity' to reshape the region, and militant groups, particularly Islamic State, also ready to take advantage of any openings they saw.

Kurilla was a frequent visitor to both Israel and the Oval Office – and, as his testimony to the Senate Armed Services Committee in June 2025 made clear, he shared much of the Israeli assessment that this was a moment of critical vulnerability for Tehran that the US should also take advantage of, describing a 'strategic window of opportunity to secure its interests in the Central Region; protect the homeland, secure our economic prosperity, ensure freedom of navigation and prevent a nuclear armed Iran'.[10]

Exactly what that meant in detail he did not say – but in Washington there were plenty of voices who argued that by showing strength in the Middle East, the US (in general) and Trump administration (in particular) could re-establish broader deterrence in a way that would grab the attention of Russia as well as China. For others, it was an unnecessary distraction. Either way, throughout 2024 and the first months of 2025, it had not been the US but Israel driving most of the developments.

The first signal that Israel was looking to up its game against Tehran and its allies came in April 2024, when an airstrike against Iran's consulate in the Syrian capital Damascus killed a number of senior Iranian officers and prompted Iran's first-ever strike against Israel itself.

With hindsight, that may have been exactly Israel's plan. The mass Iranian strike – comprising more than 200 drones, cruise and ballistic missiles – proved largely ineffective: most incoming weaponry was shot down by US, Israeli, British, French and Jordanian warplanes, or Israel's own 'Iron Dome' defences, in a massive operation masterminded by the CAOC in Qatar.[11] Israel's military retaliation a week later appeared to be deliberately light: a drone strike against air defence facilities near Tehran's nuclear site at Isfahan. But the message was clear: Israel had the political will as well as the technical ability to hit Iran, and that included Tehran's atomic weapons programme too.[12] Israel again showed its ability to strike inside Iran with the assassination of Hamas leader Ismail Haniyeh at the end of July with a bomb hidden in what both the militants and Iranian authorities clearly believed was a highly secure safe house in Tehran. Israel's secret services had conducted killings in Iran before, but the audacity showed their rapidly growing confidence.[13]

At the start of October, Iran struck again at Israel, a retaliation for both the Haniyeh killing and losses of Iranian personnel in Lebanon. This time it did not bother using the drones that had proved so vulnerable to interception back in April, but instead a salvo of some 200 ballistic missiles, killing one Israeli and one Palestinian. While Israel's defences again proved reasonably effective, multiple missiles still got through to strike airbases and other targets, although a news blackout ensured most of the damage remained largely unreported.[14]

This Iranian attack inadvertently provided justification for the largest Israeli strike so far, one designed to both show the reach of the Israeli military but also open the door for further action. Those strikes, in November 2024, were closely watched around the world, not least for the performance of Israel's US-built F-35s against Iran's Russian-supplied S-400 air defences. The results were seen as particularly heartening by the Europeans, who were relying on the same aircraft to take the fight to Russian soil in the event Putin ever sent his troops into NATO states. According to Britain's defence chief Admiral Radakin, the Israeli strikes used more than 100 aircraft but less then 100 munitions, with no aircraft in the first wave needing to get closer than 100 miles to the target. Through using the fifth-generation F-35 combined with what he called 'exquisite targeting and extraordinary intelligence', Radakin said the raid had destroyed almost all Iranian air defences and their ability to produce ballistic missiles for at least a year. It was, he said, a compelling example of using the latest technology and planning to deliver a 'disproportionate advantage'.[15]

It was also a compelling example of how each of the major confrontations in the world, from the Middle East to Ukraine and Taiwan, were becoming increasingly interlinked and overlapping, often rewriting the rules of international relations and sometimes even warfare as they did so – not to mention bringing with them the risk of unintended consequences, dragging other regions and powers into a fast-rising conflict.

Throughout 2024, both Israel and Iran had been relatively careful in their escalation, sometimes waiting weeks between retaliatory strikes – in the case of Israel, giving the government in Tehran advance warning of the targets. Meanwhile, Israel continued to pursue its campaign in Gaza, with its relentless volume of strikes guided by technology supposed to deliver pinpoint accuracy. In fact, it appeared to be delivering even more death and human suffering.

*

Israel's high-tech surveillance systems had failed to alert the authorities to the Hamas attacks of October 2023, but they'd still gathered enormous amounts of data on Gaza and its estimated 2.3 million population residents: more data, in fact, than any human analysts could cope with. As the Israeli counteroffensive started in the days after the October assault, Israel's military intelligence turned to some of the most sophisticated AI systems ever used to tell it where to strike to best wipe out Hamas, its fighters, weapons stockpiles and often deeply buried leadership and headquarters.

According to reporting by Israeli media outlets +972 and Local Call – later corroborated by multiple other major media organisations – the two most important AI systems were known as 'Gospel' and 'Lavender'. That their existence was revealed so relatively quickly – Gospel by December 2023, Lavender a few months later – speaks to just how disturbed some Israeli military personnel in the operation rapidly became over the way in which AI targeting had changed the way that Israel fought.

Gospel and Lavender used overlapping datasets, but generated different targets: Gospel marked buildings and structures that the software believed Hamas operated from, while the even more controversial Lavender tracked suspected Hamas members to their home address. That effectively put them on a 'kill list', with Israeli forces almost invariably striking those targets at night when suspects were most likely to be at home, alongside family members.

As is relatively normal practice with other militaries, including the US and UK, Israel had struck the homes of top military commanders and suspected terrorist leaders, knowing that this would result in collateral deaths. But in Israeli campaigns, the intelligence teams had only enough resources to prioritise the most senior leaders – building up a 'target pack' that included assessments of likely civilian casualties. Those packs were then passed to senior Israeli officials, who decided if the target was important enough to justify those additional 'collateral' casualties. All of that took time and effort, which limited the number of targets that could then be hit.

Such decisions, Israeli military sources acknowledged, were often already judged to be 'brutal'. But in the aftermath of the October 2023 attack, two things changed almost overnight. The first was that the Netanyahu government took the decision to authorise strikes on any members of the thousands-strong Hamas military wing, not just leaders, simultaneously approving 15 to 20 civilian casualties for every militant eliminated. That number could be lifted to 100 casualties or more for senior Hamas leaders such as battalion or brigade commanders, Israeli military sources told the journalists. The second was that the number of strikes authorised was dramatically increased – indeed, in the early days and weeks of the offensive, the IDF was conducting as many hits as it could with available weaponry and aircraft.

Those decisions alone would have dramatically increased both the bloodshed and destruction, but the number of strikes would still have been limited by the number of targets generated by human intelligence analysts. That process, however, was now handed to Lavender and its automated systems, which took all the available information on most of the two million-plus Gazans in the strip and allocated them a numerical value that described how likely they were to be a Hamas militant. The top of that list alone yielded more than 30,000 potential targets – Israel's military began striking them immediately, often hitting hundreds of targets in the small hours of every morning.

Israeli officials maintained that they were waging one of the most accurate campaigns in military history – and that was, in some ways, technically correct. But the sheer volume of attacks – and the fact that even the Israelis themselves believed an indication from Lavender was at best only 90 per cent accurate – inherently led to high numbers of civilian deaths. Alongside Lavender, another system – known colloquially and darkly as 'Daddy's Home' – tracked individual militants, usually by their phones, to alert the Israelis once they were likely in their place of residence, leaving little doubt that nearby families of the supposed militants would be killed too.[16]

Subsequent United Nations data suggested that was exactly what was happening: more than half of the 11,000 reported fatalities in the first five weeks of the Israeli campaign – more than 6,000 people – came from just 825 families. More than 300 families suffered ten or more deaths apiece.[17] Israel's defenders had some justification in claiming the strikes were not entirely indiscriminate – but the death, suffering and devastation that came with them exceeded anything that would have been seen as proportionate in any previous conflict of the current century.

From the start, the offensive saw widespread strikes on hospitals – often used by Hamas to store weapons – as well as the deaths of more than 100 UN staff and 200 health workers in the opening weeks alone. Soon, almost all hospitals and the last functioning flour mill in Gaza were out of action, with more than 100,000 buildings destroyed, including more than 40,000 homes, and another quarter of a million reported damaged. Aid shipments into Gaza were also being heavily controlled, with food shortages already rising fast.[18]

Without doubt, the shock of the October 7 attack was a major factor in the scale of the response. One Israeli military source told +972 there was '. . . hysteria in the professional ranks. They had no idea how to react at all. The only thing they knew to do was to start bombing like madmen to try and dismantle Hamas capabilities.' Another source described the atmosphere as 'painful and vindictive'. In one case, the IDF blew up four buildings in a single strike because they believed a high-value target was in one of them. 'No one thought about what to do afterwards, when the war is over, or how we live with Gaza,' said yet another. 'We were told: now we have to fuck up Hamas, no matter what the cost. Whatever you can, you bomb.'

The capabilities provided by AI were also shaping the response more than most initially appreciated. 'Once you go automatic, target generation goes crazy,' said one Israeli source. Within days it was clear that some of the targets generated by both Lavender and Gospel were incorrect – errors included using Hamas payroll data that inadvertently identified health and civil defence workers as members of the militants, as well as relying too heavily on mobile phone numbers often passed to other family members. But as one Israeli servicemember put it, every time one name was identified as being incorrect and taken off the list, there were another 37,000 names behind it.

So many targets were being generated that Israel did not have enough precision laser-guided bombs to hit them – so more junior militants were allocated less accurate 'dumb bombs' that often inflicted even greater damage on the area with more accompanying casualties.[19] As often in a democracy at war, there were multiple paradoxes in play. The BBC documented one incident in which Israeli intelligence repeatedly phoned one individual in Gaza to get him to co-ordinate the evacuation of his entire apartment complex – believed to be home to a Hamas armaments supply store – before it was bombed to smithereens. Such an action doubtless saved several hundreds of lives – but those Gazans were then left homeless in an increasingly devastated landscape.[20]

With journalists barred from the Gaza Strip aside from the Palestinian media workers already trapped there when the war began, getting to the bottom of what had really happened in any individual strike fast became extremely difficult – sometimes impossible when fighting was particularly fierce.

The bigger picture was also unclear. Even Israel's more supportive Western partners were asking what its exit strategy might be. Within the wider region, there was a growing body of opinion – not just on the 'Arab street', but also among foreign ministries – that the suffering being inflicted on the Palestinians was itself the strategy, and the Netanyahu government wanted the entire population of Gaza to leave the territory, ideally forever.[21]

Among Israel's Western allies – and even to an extent within Israel itself – the idea that this campaign might be intended to drive out the civilian Gaza population initially struggled to gain traction. Few doubted that Israel's security state was genuine in its determination to wipe out Hamas, and it was already apparent that there was not that much concern for who might get hurt along the way. Evicting more than two million people, though, was a very different matter: outright 'ethnic cleansing', in the humanitarian language of the 1990s.

The idea first appeared in the Israeli press at the start of 2024, with reports that former British Prime Minister Tony Blair had agreed to spearhead talks on the 'voluntary resettlement' of Gaza's population with nearby Arab states. It was swiftly denied by both Blair and the foundation he led, but it was now in the public eye – and that might well have been deliberate.[22]

From the end of 2024, the idea resurfaced with a vengeance, as part of Trump's plan to transform Gaza into a 'Mediterranean Riviera' of hotels and casinos, with the population apparently moved to what he called a 'good fresh, beautiful piece of land'. At a February 2025 press conference with Netanyahu, one of Trump's first after taking office, the new US president even suggested the US might take ownership of Gaza while the Gulf states handled the relocation and rebuilding.[23]

In fact, the Gulf states were opposed to this idea – as were Egypt and Jordan, who had spent decades making it clear to successive Israeli governments that they might go to war to prevent the mass expulsion of Palestinians onto their territory. Now it had been raised, however, the Netanyahu government was explicitly pushing the mass expulsion option. By mid-2025, amid widespread international frustration, the Israeli leader was describing the Trump Gaza proposal – which he called 'revolutionary' and 'brilliant' – as the precondition for the end of Israeli action.[24]

Israel's military occasionally escorted foreign journalists into the Gaza Strip in an effort to show just how precise some of its strikes truly were, and to push back against reporting that suggested the strikes were indiscriminate. As they showed reporters through the shattered remnants of a tunnel system beneath a hospital in which the latest Hamas leader had been killed, one officer told a *Telegraph* reporter it had been a remarkable achievement to be able to destroy the tunnel system without wiping out the health facility.

The truth, though, was that the hospital was still damaged – and, more to the point, it was effectively the only working hospital left amid the widespread devastation. Hunger was also now increasing fast, with Gaza's residents risking their lives to visit feeding stations run by a US-run contractor.[25] There were multiple reports of the long queues and surrounding areas being struck by Israeli fire, often killing dozens, while images of hungry children and talk of deaths from malnutrition dramatically ramped up wider foreign anger.

Given the scale of destruction, it was perhaps surprising that the official death toll from the Hamas-run Gaza Ministry of Health was as low as 55,000. Also still trapped amid that suffering were an estimated 20 remaining Israeli hostages, plus the bodies of roughly another 30. Domestically and internationally, the Gaza conflict was becoming a mounting political challenge for Netanyahu and his government.[26] In Europe and the Middle East, long-running sympathy for the Palestinians and antipathy towards Israel was now steadily increasing – and bringing with it mounting enthusiasm for recognising the twin Palestinian enclaves of Gaza and the West Bank as a separate state.

Even in the US, widespread sympathy for Israel following the October 2023 attacks was gradually being replaced with public disquiet. Initially, almost exactly 50 per cent of Americans had backed the Israeli response, with 45 per cent opposed – but by mid-2025, only 32 per cent of those polled still declared support for Israeli military action. Among Democratic voters, opposition was considerably higher – making it increasingly challenging for more centrist figures eyeing up a 2028 presidential run to find common ground between those who still supported Israel and those beginning to use words like 'genocide'.[27]

It would become even harder as Netanyahu's government firmed up its official position to include removing much of Gaza's population. But as spring turned to summer in 2025, US intelligence officials tracking the movement of munitions and air exercises within Israel were among the first to conclude that something else was coming, and Israel might be in the final preparations for a much larger assault against Iran, one aimed not just at its atomic programme but at toppling the Tehran regime itself.[28]

*

Ever since the Israeli state came into existence, its intelligence and security apparatus had been engaged in secret wars with a series of foes believed to be plotting the complete destruction of the nation. For those who had only just escaped the Holocaust, nothing was more important than destroying these schemes early – and that meant a willingness to use tactics that might have given other nations second thoughts.

The first of these campaigns, recently declassified, saw Israeli spies conducting bombings, kidnappings and sometimes hiring hitmen to stop former Nazi-era rocket scientists from working for Egyptian leader Gamal Abdel Nasser in the early 1960s.[29] Other Israeli foes included Syria and Iraq, whose 'Osirak' nuclear reactor was destroyed in an Israeli airstrike in June 1981.[30] All of those, however, paled in comparison to the scale of the campaign waged by the Israeli state in the current century to slow Iran's development of atomic weapons.

It was a campaign sometimes waged in direct co-ordination with the United States – including, reportedly, the Stuxnet computer worm first detected by IT security specialists in 2010. According to a remarkably frank briefing to the *New York Times* – once again the standard recourse of a US administration choosing to spread news – that computer worm had been created by US and Israeli experts under the previous Bush administration to tear apart Iranian atomic centrifuges.[31] Operating independently to the US, Israel was by that point assassinating multiple Iranian atomic scientists – while a series of explosions within Iran in 2012 were also rumoured to have killed multiple Iranian military personnel. That was followed by an unusually high degree of apparent Iranian retaliation, including attacks on Israeli diplomats in Thailand and Georgia, as well as tourists in Bulgaria. Many of these were rumoured to have been carried out by either Hezbollah or the 'Quds Force' of the Islamic Revolutionary Guard – but getting to the bottom of what was really going on was all but impossible.

What was clear, a decade into the new century, was that this was not a confrontation limited to Israel and Iran. In 2011, US officials reported they had foiled an Iranian plot to kill the Saudi ambassador to Washington[32] – while the 2010s saw a steady escalation of cyber attacks and drone strikes as Saudi Arabia and the United Arab Emirates engaged in their own proxy war in Yemen with Iran-backed Houthi forces.

Following the 2003 invasion of Iraq, successive US administrations had tried to downplay the scale of their proxy fight with Tehran, including the multiple attacks on US troops by Iranian-backed Iraqi Shiite militia. The rise of Islamic State from 2014 briefly put that force on the same side as the US, supporting a joint campaign that ranged across Iraq and Syria. By the end of the Trump administration in 2020, though, those militia were back periodically assaulting US outposts during times of heightened tension.

Trump's decision in January 2020 to order a drone-strike assassination of Islamic Revolutionary Guard Corps Quds Force commander Major General Quassem Soleimani was intended to assert that the US would no longer allow Iranian-backed militia to attack its outposts and kill its personnel. The new Trump administration's Operation ROUGH RIDER, launched against the Houthis barely a month into the new administration in March 2025, was designed to send a similar message, even if its initial stages were overshadowed by the leaking of the Signal conversations about them between senior administration members.

Like Israel, the US military was in possession of cutting-edge analysis software from Palantir and other providers that meant it had many more identified targets than it could hit – but US Central Command was trying to drop as many bombs as it could manage. This wasn't just about degrading the Houthis and their ability to hit ships passing through the Red Sea – it was also about demonstrating to other potential foes, most notably Iran and China, that the new Trump administration would not pull its punches.

The problem, as the Biden administration had found with the deployment of the *Eisenhower* battle group a year earlier, was

that consumption of ammunition and missiles on that scale –
$200 million worth in the first three weeks – diminished US
weapons stocks much faster than they could be replaced.[33] An
estimate at the start of May ramped up that figure to
approximately $1 billion consumed in the first month alone,
bolstered by the loss of several MQ-9 Reaper drones and two
F/A-18 fighter jets inadvertently dropped off the side of the
aircraft carrier *Harry S. Truman* as she turned rapidly to avoid
fast-falling Houthi missiles.

At the start of May, the White House abruptly instructed
Central Command to 'pause' offensive operations, effectively
claiming victory after the Houthis agreed they would no longer
target US ships. 'We hit them very hard and they had a great
ability to withstand punishment,' the US president said
immediately afterwards. 'You could say there was a lot of
bravery there . . . They gave us their word that they would not
be shooting at ships any more, and we honour that.'[34]

There was some scepticism over whether that deal was likely
to last – indeed, attacks continued against non-US shipping,
particularly vessels linked to Israel. But there was an almost
audible sigh of relief from US military logistics planners as the
Yemen strikes came to an end after more than 50 days, particularly
from those responsible for finding enough weaponry to support a
major Pacific conflict. Trump and his top team were keen to have
a few negotiating successes chalked up early, to show strong
willpower and strengthen their hand for whatever happened next.

In reality, these were only likely to be partial wins – but their
aim was to shape much larger events. Even before he had
entered office, Trump had dispatched Middle East envoy Steve
Witkoff to use a barely concealed threat of enormous US
firepower to get most of the remaining hostages held by Hamas
freed. Success in the Gulf with the Houthis – and making it
clear the new Trump administration was prepared to drop
many more bombs than its predecessor might have – was all
part of building that larger narrative of success and credibility.

So far the largest economic play of Trump's presidency yet was his imposition of tariffs on almost every country in the world at the start of April, the so-called 'Liberation Day' that antagonised America's enemies and allies alike and sent global stock markets reeling for several weeks. In some ways, it was the same negotiation tactic used with the Houthis: a fearsome display to 'shock and awe', followed by a deal. The question was whether that approach – dismissively referred to by opponents as 'TACO' for 'Trump always chickens out' – would be used with Iran, and whether it would work.

In 2018, Trump had pulled the US out of the deal struck three years earlier by the Obama administration, Russian, Chinese, European and Iranian officials that had theoretically seen Tehran rule out atomic weaponry while allowing for the enrichment of uranium for peaceful use. Supporters of that agreement – officially known as the Joint Comprehensive Plan of Action (JCPOA) – always maintained that it offered the best and most lasting hope for peace. Critics – including Trump and Netanyahu – claimed Iran was always going to try to push ahead towards atomic weaponry. In early 2020, shortly after the killing of Major General Soleimani, Iran announced it would no longer consider itself bound by any of the enrichment limits of the JCPOA, likely bringing an atomic weapon closer to completion.[35]

The process of negotiations and inspections that had brought the JCPOA into existence meant a lot was known about Iran's atomic programme and its two main enrichment facilities in bunkers at Natanz and Fordo, the latter at least 80 metres deep and surrounded by air defences. In the 2010s, both the US and Israel worked on weaponry to penetrate to that depth, but the only weapon believed large enough was the GBU-57A/B Massive Ordnance Penetrator, a 30,000-pound 'bunker-busting bomb'. Each was believed to be able to penetrate up to 60 metres deep, and one could be dropped after another to reach deeper buried targets. Initially, that was larger than any non-cargo aircraft was designed to carry – US Air Force officials said they had found a way to carry it on the B-2 stealth bomber and had dropped it in tests.[36]

Israel, in contrast, had neither a non-nuclear weapon that big nor a non-cargo plane to carry it. But by spring 2025 it was deeply advanced in its own covert planning for an attack within Iran – and, as with its penetration of Hezbollah the previous autumn, this was an operation that would have to be launched sooner rather than later.

*

As Israeli officials reminded journalists, a massive conventional bomb was not the only way to neutralise a bunker. That looked like a not-so-subtle reference to Israel's own atomic arsenal – but it was also a reminder of its other military capabilities.

At the start of September 2024, shortly before triggering the pager attack on Hezbollah in Lebanon, Israeli helicopter-borne commandos had conducted an audacious raid several hundred miles into Syria where they had seized an entire under-defended bunker complex used by the Iranians to store and manufacture missiles for shipment to Lebanon. The speed with which the successful operation was publicised suggested that they wanted to both impress their US allies and make their enemies nervous – but it was also a stark demonstration that the Assad regime in Syria was struggling to secure even the most sensitive facilities on its soil.[37]

That Assad's reign unravelled less than three months later still came as a shock, even to those who had long pointed out that Russia's war in Ukraine had forced it to withdraw much of its support from its ally in Damascus. To what extent the Israelis were involved in the rapid advance of Hayat Tahrir al-Sham's rebel movement towards the capital is difficult to say. By and large, the rebels owed their victory to support from Turkey, and relations between Israel and Ankara had been severely soured by events in Gaza. Nevertheless, as Syria's new president, former

Al Qaeda fighter Ahmed al-Sharaa, entrenched his power, he made it clear Iranian proxies, and particularly Hezbollah, were no longer welcome.[38]

This was a profound game-changer, particularly when it came to Israel's ability to act against Tehran – and it was a sign of just how self-defeating the Hamas attack on Israel in October 2023 had inadvertently proved for the Iran-led 'axis of resistance' that included Hezbollah, the Houthis and Hamas itself. From being able to threaten Israel from Gaza, Lebanon and Syria, Hezbollah and Hamas were now all but destroyed, and Israel retained the capability to take out new leaders as they arose.

If Netanyahu's later claims that detailed planning for the attack against Iran began in November 2024 are accurate – and there seems no significant reason to doubt them – then it is likely Trump's victory that month in the US election may have been the final factor. For all the isolationist tendencies of some of the MAGA base, Trump and many of his backers had long supported Israel, and criticised Obama and the Democrats for being too soft when it came to stopping an Iranian atomic bomb. As he would soon acknowledge publicly, US CENTCOM chief General Kurilla too believed this was a rare if not unique chance to inflict damage on Iran to reduce it as a threat, and he was likely making that case in private directly to the president.

According to Netanyahu, the strike was ready to be launched in April 2025 – but was not carried out for 'various reasons', likely largely down to Trump, who gave the Iranian regime a 60-day deadline to give up enrichment or face the consequences.[39] It was a warning conveyed directly to Iranian supreme leader Ayatollah Ali Khamenei by Saudi Arabian Defence Minister Prince Khalid bin Salman – son of the Saudi king – on April 17, Gulf and Iranian sources told my Reuters colleagues in the region a few weeks later. The prince had been Saudi ambassador to Washington during Trump's first term, and the sources said he'd made it clear to the Iranians their time was running out to avoid an Israeli strike that might well end up being backed by the United States.[40]

Less than two years earlier, Chinese officials had brokered a rapprochement between Iran and Saudi Arabia that allowed both to move on from the proxy wars that they had waged for years. At the time, Chinese Foreign Minister Wang Yi had pledged Beijing would start a 'wave of reconciliation' across the region and had specifically promised heightened Chinese support for Tehran both diplomatically and financially.[41]

In March 2025, less than a month before the Iran–Saudi meeting, Russian and Chinese warships had conducted high-profile drills with their Iranian counterparts in the Gulf of Oman in a striking show of solidarity.[42] From April, though, those forces appeared gone – few doubted that Saudi and likely other Middle East officials had appraised Beijing of Israel's impending attack on Iran, and, for then at least, neither the PRC nor the Kremlin wanted to be around. If America wanted to launch itself into another Middle East intervention, Russia and China would likely let it happen.

What was happening in the Middle East was just part of a much bigger picture. When it came to hearts, minds and money, both Moscow and Beijing believed that they might now have the advantage in the 'global south'. But, as with the Middle East, those dynamics were far from 'monolithic'. Indeed, as the US and Israel considered their options against Iran at the start of May 2024, one of China's longest-running Asian partners – Pakistan – was on the brink of war with another nation – India – that counted both the US and Russia among its closest friends.

Meanwhile, Trump's wider campaign of tariffs to redress what he viewed as a global trading balance that was 'unfair' when it came to US interests were starting to have diplomatic as well as economic consequences. So were his efforts to engage on issues of war and peace with Moscow and Beijing, with the 'global south' caught firmly in the middle.

12

The Battles for the Global South

*'You can have no enemies and be irrelevant. If you are
relevant, some problems will accompany that.'*

**Indian Foreign Minister Subrahmanyam
Jaishankar, 2025**[1]

In the small hours of May 7, 2025, multiple jets of the Indian
Air Force approached Pakistani airspace, grimly aware that
they were running the gauntlet of recently provided Chinese-
built defences. This was the largest conventional military
strike any nuclear power had launched into the territory of
another nuclear-armed nation in recent history, most likely
ever, and the Indians were operating under much more
restrictive rules of engagement than their pilots might have
wanted. That included not entering Pakistani territory – they
would fire their missiles from Indian airspace across the
mountainous border.

Barely six months earlier, a much larger force of Israeli jets
had shown what was possible with their strike inside Iran, using
long-range weapons and the US-made F-35s to destroy Tehran's
Russian-manufactured air defences. The Indians, however, were
using much older French Rafale and Mirage jets – and even if
the Pakistani air defences locked onto them with radar, the
Indians were ordered to hold their fire until actually fired on.
With Chinese-manufactured J-10 interceptors fast scrambling
to meet them, that left the Indians at a marked disadvantage

when the first missiles started flying – and it would cost them several aircraft.

It was, analysts from London think tank the Royal United Services Institute wrote a few days later, an example of what they call 'restraint under fire', intended to ensure 'managed escalation' – and almost certainly much more tightly controlled than would have been the case if either nation had not held atomic arms.[2]

As the larger, more powerful state, India appeared incentivised to talk down the scale of the fight – but the Pakistani side reported up to 125 jets battling for over an hour, firing missiles at each other from distances sometimes as great as 100 miles. Those ranges allowed the entire battle to take place without aircraft on either side leaving their own airspace, thus reducing the risk of pilots being shot down in enemy territory. The Pakistanis claimed they had disrupted the Indian attack significantly, forcing the attacking jets to make several runs against their targets – and giving the Pakistani defenders more time to warn civilians in the area.[3]

Still, Pakistani officials said dozens had been killed, and vowed retaliation. Within hours, Pakistani forces were shelling Indian border areas in Kashmir, with more civilians dead. By the morning of May 7, global headlines were dominated by talk of South Asia's atomic power being on the brink of Armageddon, and the difficulties of finding 'off-ramps' to avoid escalation. What had already occurred was a much larger military exchange than anything seen in the region before, including the 2019 Indian strike into Pakistan following another militant attack.[4] The main Pakistani counterstrike began the following evening, long-range conventional missiles targeting several Indian military facilities, predominantly airbases.

In Ukraine, it had become routine for both the Kremlin and Kyiv to conduct dozens if not hundreds of drone strikes against each other every day, sometimes deep within each other's territory. By May 9, it looked as though India and Pakistan were also moving in that direction, each blaming the other for over-responding in the tit-for-tat attacks. India had unleashed several hundred drones to strike Pakistani bases and radar installations in several major cities. As with Russia and Ukraine, those drone strikes were highly targeted. Like Israel with its attacks on Iran in December 2024, India was deliberately hitting Pakistani air defences in a way that would open the door to allow a larger Indian strike – perhaps even one that might target Pakistan's atomic weapons.

In many respects this was still a smaller conflict than the 1999 war the two had fought over the disputed line of control near Kargil in the Himalayas, which had lasted months and included more plentiful shelling as well as occasional actual fighting face-to-face. But that war – which occurred shortly after both India and Pakistan had conducted their first explicit atomic tests – had remained limited to a less-than-125-mile stretch of front, with no deeper strikes into each other's territory. The last time the two nations had done something like this was 1971, before either had atomic weapons.

Now, though, India in particular was working to redraw those rules, explicitly intending to conduct strikes and other military operations in a way that would remain short of atomic escalation. Its military leadership would later talk of a co-ordinated military 'escalation control mechanism' – essentially, a system of targets, goals, meetings and approval processes – designed to prevent things from getting out of hand. 'I think there's a lot of space before that nuclear threshold is crossed, a lot of signalling before that,' India's Chief of Defence Staff General Anil Chauhan told a Reuters colleague a few weeks later.

Chauhan paid an unusual compliment to his Pakistani military counterpart, saying that both sides had shown 'a lot of rationality in their thoughts as well as actions', and that he expected that would also apply to any nuclear decisions. The result of what fast became known as the 'four-day war' – and the fact further escalation had not taken place – meant 'a modern space for conventional operations . . . has been created, and this will be the new norm', he suggested.[5]

In Washington, more South Asian atomic brinkmanship was the last thing that was wanted, particularly given all the other crises that were also underway. At the height of the confrontation, Vice President JD Vance had suggested that, while the administration wanted de-escalation, 'We are not going to get involved in the middle of a war that is fundamentally none of our business.'[6] In fact, both Trump and Secretary of State Marco Rubio were already being pulled into the conflict, talking with leaders on both sides and later taking some credit for both sides standing down.

Such engagement brought diplomatic risks – officially, both nations on the brink of war denied they wanted outside intervention. India, as a country ruled for many years by a foreign power, did not want 'too much foreign influence on [its] decision-making', Foreign Minister Subrahmanyam Jaishankar had warned earlier in the year. During the first Cold War, New Delhi had made much of its 'nonalignment', partnering with both the West and the Soviet Union but working to avoid overly taking sides. It was trying something similar now: buying plenty of military stores from Russia while also stepping up US security engagement. But Jaishankar warned those relations should not be mistaken for subservience, or even neutrality: India was too great a power for that.[7]

Alongside China, India was now without question one of the great powers of the world, simultaneously wooed by almost all the others – even Beijing, which had fought its own brief but bloody battles near their disputed Himalayan border as recently as 2020. But even the smaller nations of the so-called 'global south' were fast discovering their relevance.

As they had learned in the aftermath of Russia's full-scale invasion of Ukraine – and again during Trump's blitz on trade negotiations – the fragility of their economies could also leave them more vulnerable than most to major shocks, even on the far side of the world. The initial 2022 Ukraine invasion saw significant food price spikes in many nations – while by 2025, discounted Russian oil smuggled out through 'shadow fleet' unregistered tankers was critical to keeping down inflation. China, India and Turkey were some of the largest direct buyers of such Russian energy, but frequently resold it, its relative cheapness helping keep wider global oil prices down.

All of that would come into play as the Trump administration worked to move forward with its trade negotiations and pushing Putin towards a peace deal on Ukraine, including imposing sanctions on India and China to punish them for buying Russian oil. Coming almost together as they did, those actions would bring with them unintended consequences, annoying many in the so-called 'global south' and pushing them diplomatically closer to Beijing.

*

According to a review by the Carnegie Endowment for International Peace, the phrase 'global south' was first used by left-wing US academic Carl Oglesby in 1969, and then again by former West German Chancellor Willy Brandt in a 1980 report to refer to countries south of the 'Brandt Line'. This was a line running round the world with Europe and the US to the north and developing countries to the south, with wild distortions necessary to take into account Australia and New Zealand.

As the Carnegie review team noted dryly, the first problem with the phrase 'global south' was that substantial numbers of the designated countries – and, if one counted India, China, Pakistan and Mexico as members, the majority of the global population – were actually part of the northern hemisphere. Within the group – by some counts more than 130 nations – there was also huge variety. Some countries, including much of Latin America and southern Africa, were broadly at peace albeit with enormous social problems and some of the highest global crime rates.

Others, such as Sudan, the Democratic Republic of the Congo (DRC) and Myanmar – previously known as Burma – were perennial war zones, or mired in crushing poverty. Meanwhile, even if you discounted the phenomenally wealthy Gulf states – who in Brandt's day would still have been broadly seen as mostly 'third world', with the exception of Kuwait and Saudi Arabia – average earnings in 'global south' nations now ranged from highs of above $30,000 a year to less than a tenth of that for the poorest nations.

Navigating the different narratives and histories – and the often shifting approach to geopolitics that they produced – was now vital for any nation, individual or organisation operating at a global level. Samir Puri, a former British diplomat who spent the start of the 2020s teaching international relations in Singapore, noted the striking variety of ways in which he had seen a modern Indonesian politician approach the world within a single speech. It was, he said, an increasingly representative example of the awkward path that many nations walked. 'He started by referring to Indonesia as a "victim of colonialism", referring to the Dutch era,' said Puri. 'He then quoted Nelson Mandela, saying "your enemy is not necessarily our enemy", implying that they were not going to join America in an anti-China bloc. Then he praised America and praised China one after the other. I say that because it's one of these clear examples of a big country that is not going to be biddable one side of the fence or other.'[8]

That did not mean, of course, that the great powers would not try.

*

In October 2024, with the US election imminent, Vladimir Putin hosted delegates from more than 20 nations for the largest ever 'BRICS' summit in Kazan in southern Russia. With the

Biden administration and its allies still determined to isolate Russia economically and diplomatically, it was a savage reminder to the West that much of the world was now charting a very different course.[9]

When he created the 'BRIC' acronym for Brazil, Russia, India and China in a research paper in November 2001, the new head of the Goldman Sachs economics team Jim O'Neill was looking for a 'big idea' to define the coming decade. The idea occurred to him, he later said, as he witnessed the 9/11 attacks, reflecting on the globalisation that had allowed the hijackers to bring mayhem to New York and Washington. The biggest winners of that process, he said, would be the world's emerging economies – particularly the four BRIC nations – and the moment had now come for investors to take those markets much more seriously. At the time, those four nations made up 8 per cent of the world economy – but within a decade it was 20.[10] Initially, the BRIC nations themselves did little to engage directly with the concept – but the aftermath of the global financial crisis, in 2009, saw Russia host the first BRIC summit, with South Africa invited at the second summit in Brazil the following year to join what then became the BRICS.

The third summit, in 2011, was the first to be held in China – hosted on Hainan Island on the edge of the South China Sea, a reminder that Beijing saw a very direct link between its growing global clout and more regional ambitions.[11] Its 2024 summit in Russia saw its membership doubled to ten nations: Egypt, Ethiopia, Iran, Saudi Arabia and the United Arab Emirates, with Indonesia joining in 2025.[12]

For the Kremlin, membership of the BRICS provided a ready shorthand for legitimacy among much larger emerging economies – and its success in persuading United Nations Secretary General António Guterres to attend the BRICS meeting in Russia in 2024 underlined that point. It also appalled the US administration and many in Europe, particularly given the arrest warrant for Putin at the ICC.[13] Still, the more one looked at the new nations admitted to the BRICS in 2024, the more apparent it became that arguably their greatest common theme was a mounting reputation for disregarding human rights.

Beijing was unlikely to have a problem with that, but within Beijing there were clearly those who believed its own enormous investment programme in emerging economies deserved a proper 'brand', as well as more resources. Launched in Kazakhstan in 2013 by Xi the year after he took power, and then made even more ambitious with further announcements in Indonesia later that same year, China's Belt and Road Initiative (BRI) was a hugely ambitious multibillion-dollar plan to reorientate the world's sea, road and rail routes primarily through enormous Chinese loans and projects.

Launching in Central Asia was itself a statement of intent, particularly given the centuries of rivalry for control of that strategic region between Moscow, Beijing and a host of other powers including India, Turkey and Iran. But the BRI agenda was aimed much wider than the 'global south' – through reconnecting pre-existing railways, it reached deep into the industrial heart of Europe, aiming to reduce travel times and increase the number of trains running from China. By the 2020s – and particularly following the Covid-19 pandemic – European nations were putting limitations on their dealings with Beijing, although nothing as serious as those imposed by the United States. In the rest of the world, however, China still found plenty of opportunities, including trading Covid vaccines for political and economic access.

Equally significant were Beijing's efforts to push 5G systems run by Chinese tech giant Huawei, whose networks US and Western officials warned were almost certainly surveilled by China's state security.[14] Under both the first Trump and Biden administrations, US officials pushed foreign regulators to label the Chinese technology 'high risk' and instead invest in more expensive solutions supplied by Finland's Nokia and Sweden's Ericsson. In Europe that battle was largely unsuccessful until Russia's full-scale invasion of Ukraine – even some of the Baltic states were initially prepared to consider Huawei until they concluded their entire networks might be handed to Russia in advance of an invasion.[15] In the developing world, Huawei's low-budget offer almost always finished the dominant player.[16]

Then there was the debt: by 2017 China was the largest lender in the world, outstripping multilateral institutions such as the International Monetary Fund and World Bank, with multiple nations now owing Beijing more than 10 per cent of their gross domestic product.[17] The 2020s pushed those numbers even higher, with those owing most as a proportion of their economy including Pakistan, Kenya, Zambia, Laos and Mongolia – and more and more of those countries were struggling to pay.[18]

For US military commanders, particularly those focused on Africa, Asia and Latin America, this increasingly looked like a battle at risk of being lost without a shot being fired. 'Beijing has gained ground by offering our partners short-term gains that leave them vulnerable to unsustainable debt, environmental degradation and informational security risks,' warned the top US commander responsible for Latin America, US Southern Command chief Admiral Alvin Holsey. 'China claims to have always been a member of the "global south", and is using BRI . . . to expand its access to rarer minerals and control of ports, space facilities and telecommunications infrastructure for a potential dual-civilian military purpose.'[19]

The Trump administration entered office intent on winning one quick victory on that front in Panama, determined to evict Hong Kong-based firm CK Hutchison from the port operations it had owned at both ends of the Panama Canal, as well as pushing back other Chinese influence and infrastructure. Perhaps unsurprisingly, Trump's opening threat to annex the US-built waterway and potentially the remainder of the country prompted fast concessions, including an initial agreement that CK Hutchison would sell up to a US consortium led by finance giant BlackRock. The US announced it had also persuaded Panama to allow US military vessels to pass through the canal without paying charges, and had a green light for a heightened presence of the US military.

Pushback, however, was almost immediate. Panamanian centre-right president José Raúl Mulino said he had told Defense Secretary Hegseth that a return to permanent US bases – included in an earlier treaty draft – would be 'unacceptable' and 'set the country on fire'.[20] The port concessions sale itself also required the approval of regulators in Hong Kong, with official Chinese pressure from the mainland making that look increasingly unlikely.

A further US embassy announcement that Huawei equipment from towers near the canal had been replaced with 'more secure' US technology kickstarted another row, with more complaints from residents over US behaviour. 'That communique from the United States embassy has no reason to comment on the decisions that concern the national government,' Mulino told reporters, adding that he was determined his nation should not be dragged into broader US–China rivalry. 'Let them fight their problems in Washington or in Beijing, but not in Panama's backyard,' he said. 'Please respect that Panama is not part of that bilateral conflict.'[21]

That refrain was becoming increasingly common from states that felt themselves trapped between great powers – particularly those that felt they had little to gain and much to lose from clearly taking sides. But while the US–China rivalry was arguably becoming the largest single force shaping 'global south' events, there were now plenty of other players.

*

As Pakistan took on India in May 2025, their Chinese-built J-10 warplanes were lionised for their initial performance in shooting down several French-built Indian jets. But as India fired back with its own unique range of French and Russian weaponry, the government in Islamabad turned to Washington rather than Beijing to calm things down. According to analysis by the Stimson Center in Washington DC, that likely included a deliberate decision to move or otherwise increase the readiness of the Pakistani nuclear arsenal towards the end of the 'four-day war', a move apparently intended to push the US to tell India to stop.[22]

The suggestion that Pakistan, outmatched by Indian missiles, used the nuclear threat to sue for peace certainly tallied with Indian media reports claiming New Delhi was prepared to continue airstrikes but was persuaded not to by US Secretary of State Rubio.[23] It would also fit with the messy overlapping interests of the 'global south' in general and South Asia in particular.

Pakistani officials, perhaps unsurprisingly, were unwilling to confirm they might have engaged in some light atomic blackmail – but, equally, were keen to remind the world that their nuclear status made them an unpredictable adversary. 'Nothing happened this time,' said Pakistani Chairman of the Joint Chiefs of Staff General Sahir Shamshad Mirza, also speaking to Reuters at the Shangri-La Dialogue in Singapore. 'But you can't rule out any strategic miscalculation at any time.'[24]

If that was intended to push other nations to reconsider arming India, it clearly did not work. No sooner had the 'four-day war' concluded than Russia, France and the United States resumed their jostling to sell India their assorted weapons systems, including fifth-generation fighters the F-35 and the Su-57. In previous years, worries over such sensitive technology leaking might have prompted both Washington and Moscow to have second thoughts on such a sale – but now such details were buried in the race to build and retain relations.

India, meanwhile, was clearly now limbering up for longer confrontation. As a teenager in 1965, a young Narendra Modi had watched wounded Indian servicemen evacuated from an earlier war with Pakistan through his home province of Gujarat, setting up stalls to serve them tea. Modi had been forbidden by his parents from joining the armed forces, but a resident of the area recalled him 'charged up and voluble on how all Pakistanis should be decimated'.[25] In 2016, two years after first being elected prime minister, Modi had suggested India should pull out of the treaties with Pakistan that controlled the flow of water through the subcontinent's major northern rivers. 'Blood and water cannot flow together,' he told officials, following a series of earlier Pakistani-linked militant attacks.[26]

In May 2025, he again used that phrase in a public speech vowing to do just that: in the aftermath of the militant attack the previous month, he had announced India was putting the 1960 Indus Waters Treaty 'into abeyance', meaning India did not believe that it was still bound by it. Signed after years of negotiations, the treaty set specific limits on how much water India could block or extract from the rivers on which Pakistan depended. Now, Indian officials were told to plan for massive dams, lakes, hydroelectric plants and earthworks.[27] Within weeks, Modi appeared to be suggesting that all water flow into Pakistan might cease – at least if terror attacks continued within India. Pakistan, for its part, said it was open to discussions – but that any interference in the water flow might be a cause for war.[28]

While the nuclear status of both players clearly affected the equation, the face-off contained many of the characteristics of other conflicts within the so-called 'global south': it involved multiple nations; it had its roots in resource competition as well as centuries of conflict; and, behind the diplomatic language, some of the themes within it could, on close examination, be interpreted as almost genocidal.

Few conflicts of the world, however, revealed more about evolving technology, geopolitics and the brutalising effects of war than the fighting that raged on and off in Libya – ironically the very nation in which Western military intervention and 'regime change' had annoyed both Russian and Chinese leaders so much from early 2011.

*

As far back as the 5th century BC, Greek historian Herodotus described Libya as divided between four distinct power centres, two of them indigenous to North Africa and two already foreign. The outsiders were the Phoenician settlers from Lebanon, around what is now the Libyan capital of Tripoli, and the Greeks who settled around the eastern city of Benghazi. The original locals were the 'Libyans' who dwelt along the northern coastline, and the ethnic African 'Ethiopians' whose territory began further south in the Sahara.[29]

It therefore would not have taken Herodotus long to work out what was going on in Libya in the summer of 2011, as the so-called 'Arab Spring' sparked first protests and then outright armed revolt. That prompted Muammar Gaddafi – a true 'Libyan' from the coastal town of Sirte – to move to crush the rebel enclaves starting with Benghazi – and to do so he had forces that included plenty of mercenaries from elsewhere in Africa. That offensive, however, was halted by NATO air and missile strikes, opening the door to several much larger confrontations.

Western leaders hoped Gaddafi's fall would allow Libya to become a stable oil-producing power on Europe's southern flank, and that the host of newly wealthy Arab states piling in to support different rebel groups were all part of that process. In fact, post-Gaddafi Libya would fall apart within a year, many foreign embassies fleeing after US ambassador Chris Stevens was killed by an angry mob and militants while visiting Benghazi.

For much of the decade that followed, US officials would not risk staying overnight on Libyan soil: US diplomat Stephanie Williams, who later led UN efforts on getting Libya back together, recalled trips in and out of Tripoli in the back of US military Osprey tiltrotor aircraft accompanied by the head of US Africa Command, 'making a lot of noise'. Other nations, however – Russia, Turkey, Greece, France, Italy, Qatar and the United Arab Emirates, to name just a few – were all staking a claim, deepening an already messy selection of military relationships, arms shipments and murky business interests.

It would turn out to be a historic turning point: UN Security Council Resolution 1973, authorising a no-fly zone over Libya, would be the last time Russia and China would endorse any kind of UN-related agreement for 'humanitarian intervention', or imply any kind of international 'right to protect' endangered civilians. 'The story of Libya since 2011 reflects the wider global dysfunction we have witnessed,' said former envoy Williams. 'It was here we first saw the rise of middle powers getting involved, as well as mercenaries . . . Fast forward to 2019 and Libya had also become the largest theatre of drone warfare in the world.'[30]

Libya's population remained small – just over seven million in 2023, spread across an area three times the size of France – but it did not take long for the country to be divided between its eastern and western centres. Dominating eastern Libya – but sometimes striking hard towards the capital Tripoli from which the UN-recognised government was still trying to rule – were rebel forces under Libyan Field Marshal Khalifa Haftar. A former mid-ranking officer from the early days of Gaddafi's rule, Haftar had spent two decades in exile living in Langley, Virginia, near to CIA headquarters – presumably at least in part to take advantage of the protection that might offer against potential Libyan assassins. In the aftermath of Gaddafi's fall, he was appointed to lead Libya's new army because the US believed he would act as a barrier against Islamists and associated groups, but he soon went rogue to lead his own quasi-independent state in eastern Libya.

By the middle of the decade, Haftar was turning to the Kremlin for support[31] – opening the door to the Wagner Group of mercenaries. From 2019, Turkey stepped up its own involvement in the conflict, bringing with it an army of new unmanned aerial vehicles that it was keen to demonstrate.

Armed Turkish and Chinese drones were also part of a complex set of arms sales sometimes linked to the Gulf states. Throughout the 2010s, the US had refused to sell weapons-carrying versions of its Predator drones to a range of Middle East governments – so several, particularly Iraq, the UAE and Saudi Arabia, purchased Chinese drones instead. Some had already been observed conducting strikes against Islamic State, while those sold to the UAE were believed to be also operating over Libya and Yemen.[32]

What was really going on was often obfuscated – something increasingly the norm in the conflicts of the 'global south'. One Canadian review of front companies, illegal arms transfers and sanctions breaches revealed at least one UK-registered company that appeared to have roots reaching back to Beijing, smuggling Chinese-made Wing Loong drones to government-backed warlords in Libya. According to the investigators, they appeared to be part of a wider web involving the sale of subsidised oil cargoes, some of which also found their way to China.[33]

According to a later report for the United Nations, the first truly autonomous drone attack in history – in other words, one in which the weapon decided what to attack and therefore kill – likely occurred in March 2020 in northern Libya, just as the world was distracted by the Covid pandemic. The report claimed that government forces had used Turkish Kargu attack drones set to an 'autonomous mode' to attack Haftar's forces as they attempted to flee. According to the report, 'The lethal autonomous weapons systems were programmed to attack without requiring data connectivity between the operator and the munition.' This may well have been the first time an automated weapon killed someone without a 'human in the loop'. Whether that was truly the case was much less obvious – the UN researchers were not able to confirm details, including whether the strikes targeted vehicles or individuals, and even whether anyone was killed.[34]

Whatever the truth in northern Libya, drones and deep secrecy and distortion would fast become the norm in other conflicts taking place far from the eyes of global media. From November 2020 onwards, drone strikes began to be reported in Ethiopia as a particularly vicious civil war erupted in its Tigray region – again, the drones were suspected to be predominantly of Turkish and Chinese provenance, and thought to be operated both by the government as well as other intervening states. In 2021 alone, that conflict displaced 5.1 million Ethiopians, while African Union mediators estimated as many as 600,000 people died in the two years of fighting, many from starvation as well as air raids.

As a 2025 report from the European Council on Foreign Relations noted, the number of airstrikes in previous conflicts in Africa and elsewhere in the developing world had always been limited by the cost of aircraft and small size of local air forces. The proliferation of drones changed that situation almost overnight. They also made governments much more confident of military victory and less willing to come to the negotiating table. 'Drones were made for war!' Ethiopian Field Marshal Birhanu Jula said in late 2023. 'We purchased them for battle, not to parade them in the media. If we find groups of extremists, we will strike them.' The Ethiopian army chief followed that by telling the reporter that his government did not target civilians – but the reported death toll strongly suggested otherwise.[35]

At one stage during the Tigray war in 2021, the rebels appeared to be on the brink of taking the Ethiopian capital Addis Ababa. US and Western diplomats pushed frantically for a ceasefire. In earlier decades they might well have succeeded. Instead, the Ethiopian government was able to acquire more drones – and, according to US diplomats, they came primarily from the US, Turkey and UAE, as well as Iran.[36]

All that helped the government defeat the rebellion – accompanied by a two-year internet outage that also restricted telephone and other communications access. Even the head of the World Health Organisation Tedros Adhanom Ghebreyesus, who came from the region, said he had been unable to reach relatives. 'I don't even know who is dead or who is alive,' he told reporters.[37]

The entire war in Tigray had been waged with almost no talk of international action or intervention. Indeed, by the middle of the decade, many conflicts that would have once prompted foreign action – whether in Somalia, DRC or South Sudan, largely under UN auspices, or the US, French and European-led anti-jihadist campaigns in the Sahel – were all either over or looked set to be scaled back almost to the point of nonexistence.

First in Mali, then Burkina Faso, Guinea and Niger, military takeovers backed by Russian mercenaries and troops removed the governments on which foreign forces had relied for their legitimacy. By the time of the full-scale invasion of Ukraine in February 2022, French troops and European trainers were being withdrawn from Mali in their entirety – a remarkable moment given the dominant French presence in the region for more than 200 years.[38]

By then, Sudan too was in chaos after another coup d'état in late 2021, largely mounted by the local paramilitary Rapid Support Forces (RSF), also linked to Wagner Group and accused of a host of killings and human rights violations going back to their origins as pro-government Janjaweed militia in Darfur at the beginning of the century. By 2023, the RSF and military leadership of Sudan were at each other's throats in part over resources, with plenty of allegations that the Wagner Group was also involved in extracting Sudan's gold.[39]

As in Tigray and Libya, getting to the bottom of what was really going on could be almost impossible – and it got more complex still after the Wagner Group and its founder Yevgeny Prigozhin mounted their own rebellion against the Kremlin in

June 2023. Over the months that followed, reports from the region indicated that the Russian government was reasserting control over the group, rebranding it as Russia's 'Africa Corps' and deploying teams of dozens, sometimes several hundred, instructors as 'regime protection packages' to pro-Moscow governments. It was a strategy that continued to pay dividends, with Niger the latest country to ask the Russians to come in while kicking out previous long-term detachments of US and European Union troops and training missions.[40]

The outbreak of fighting between the Rapid Support Forces and Sudanese army in April 2023 opened the door to another catastrophic conflict. UN estimates talked of 13 million displaced people, while US officials estimated as many as 150,000 people might have died from war-related causes in the first year of the conflict alone, including from widespread hunger and disease.[41]

At points during 2023 and 2024, different elements of the Russian government were backing different sides within Sudan, with the remnants of the Wagner Group still supporting the RSF while the Kremlin cut its own deal with the government in Khartoum. That included an agreement to open a Russian naval logistics facility at Port Sudan on the Red Sea coast, publicly confirmed by Sudanese Foreign Minister Ali Youssef Ahmed al-Sharif in February 2025.[42] With fighting ongoing in Khartoum, Port Sudan was now the de facto capital of the military-run government – and the fact the Russian military was looking at having a presence there was a substantial deal. Months earlier, the fall of the Assad regime in Syria had deprived the Kremlin of its Mediterranean naval base – but a presence in the Red Sea would give it a front-row seat to observe US operations against Yemen, as well as China's first overseas naval base in Djibouti further to the south.

Barely three months later, though, at the start of May – indeed, only a few days before the start of the 'four-day war' between India and Pakistan – the harbour facilities at Port

Sudan suffered heavy damage in a sustained drone attack. Satellite imagery showed considerable damage to fuel storage sites and the military headquarters. Sudanese military sources said the drones appeared to be Chinese manufactured, and different elements of the Sudanese military accused the United Arab Emirates of supporting the attack, suggesting it had either come from UAE military installations in nearby Puntland and Somaliland or that the drones had been flown into Sudan on Emirati military transports.

Then there was the question of whether Beijing had known that Chinese drones were being used. Analysts at US think tank the Jamestown Foundation suggested this was likely, and that Chinese officials had at least tacitly endorsed the attack to rein in Russia's naval growth in the region.[43] Whether that was true was anybody's guess – what was certain was that all involved were going to great lengths to keep matters as opaque as possible.

That was particularly the case when it came to foreign involvement, especially from the Gulf states. According to the *New York Times*, Saudi Arabia, Qatar, Turkey and Iran had all either sold arms to or paid for weaponry for the government side, while Ukraine had briefly sent a detachment of special forces to help the military government against Wagner in the first days of the war.[44]

Once again, the UAE emerged as a growing player – and a very controversial one. In the first month of the war there were almost daily Emirati cargo flights to a remote airstrip in Chad near the Sudanese border, ostensibly for humanitarian aid but also said to be providing weapons to the RSF. The UAE itself rigorously denied backing any side in the conflict or providing weapons.[45]

As violence worsened, particularly in the western region of Darfur, Sudan's government continued to claim the UAE was the primary backer of the RSF. In March 2025 they filed a complaint at the International Court of Justice accusing the

UAE of complicity in genocide. The UAE described it as a 'cynical publicity stunt' aimed at diverting attention from the 'widespread atrocities' committed by the Sudanese government itself.[46]

This, then, was the way wars increasingly evolved in the so-called 'global south': catastrophically brutal, fuelled by opaque geopolitical rivalry and with emerging technology twinned with medieval-style violence and brutality – an environment in which nations such as the three main Gulf states, or even Moscow and Beijing, might wage proxy wars against each other. Even before the collapse of humanitarian aid funding from the US and Europe, combatants were becoming increasingly effective at keeping out international aid agencies and journalists. In that respect, a conflict like the one in Sudan was like the war in Gaza – only much worse in terms of casualties, and with even less international coverage and attention.

Such wars were mercifully limited in number – aside from those in Africa, the only other international conflict raging on this scale was taking place in Myanmar. There, the military junta that ousted a democratically elected government in 2021 was being armed by both Russia and China, who again were providing drones as well as other weaponry. Moscow and Beijing were also able to block any UN resolutions criticising the Myanmar government or authorising international action. Myanmar's rebels, though, had proved remarkably adept at using drones, finding ways to order cheap material from China, including 3D printers, and using them against the military.

Rebel groups in Myanmar talked of chatting on the internet to fighters and engineers in Ukraine, Gaza and beyond for tips, and also shared videos of successful drone 'kills', often set to pumping music. In some cases, drones were said to have persuaded young conscripts at military outposts to surrender just by hovering over their positions.

That the rebels were said to be reliant on 'crowdfunding' – from, among others, the several million Myanmar citizens living outside the country's borders – spoke to both their innovative and chaotic nature, with hundreds of armed groups taking on the junta often with no clear command chain. Some groups were led by politicians, some by former soldiers, others by lawyers – and apparently at least one poet.

Whether crowdfunding alone explained the technology heading to Myanmar's rebel militia was a topic on which US journalists in particular appeared strangely reluctant to probe for further details. 'Although countries like the United States have pledged money for democracy-building and placed financial sanctions on members of the military regime . . . they have not publicly allocated money for the armed rebellion,' the *New York Times* noted diplomatically.[47]

If there was covert assistance, however, it increasingly looked like it would not be enough to significantly change the outcome of fighting in Myanmar. Spring 2025 brought not just a new US administration but a devastating earthquake, as well as intensified airstrikes, internet blackouts, and the heightened conscription of young people for work gangs and military service. It then yielded a rough ceasefire, but its imposition appeared limited.[48]

For the Myanmar military leadership, the entry of Trump and his team – with their much more transactional approach – was fast seen as an opportunity: Myanmar had several mines producing 'rare earths' and other minerals. Soon, US officials and their Myanmar counterparts were engaged in preliminary negotiations, a sign of just how abruptly priorities had changed. For those leading the US military, it was a dramatic shift from the approach favoured under Biden – but there was no choice but to make it work.

*

A few weeks before Biden's final devastating presidential debate performance in June 2024, African defence chiefs and their US and NATO counterparts met in a luxury hotel on the outskirts

of the Botswana capital Gaborone. It was the first time such a
meeting had been held on African soil, a measure of both the
ongoing distrust of the US and its military across that continent
but also recent progress. When the United States Africa
Command (AFRICOM) had first been set up in 2007, not
a single African nation had been prepared to host its headquarters or its meetings – so the fact more than 30 countries
were prepared to attend this meeting and engage was seen a
broad success.

In fact, the level of US and allied attendance at the Botswana
conference was unprecedented. US Chairman of the Joint
Chiefs General 'CQ' Brown – later to be dismissed by Trump
in the first days of his new administration – and Chair of
NATO's Military Committee Dutch Admiral Robert Bauer
were both present. But, as AFRICOM commander US
Marine General Michael Langley acknowledged as he briefed
reporters, in some respects the continent was becoming 'less
safe' as terror groups including Al Qaeda and Islamic State
expanded operations while US and European forces were now
largely evicted from West Africa following recent Russian-
backed military coups.[49]

Langley did not sugarcoat that loss – but, he argued, 'Our
way forward is to engage.'[50] The official press release noted that
both Niger and the Central African Republic – both increasingly
seen as Russian proxies – were among the nations attending the
US-led meeting in Botswana. So were representatives of
multiple countries seen as extremely close to China. They
included Zimbabwe, which one African journalist told Langley's
press conference was actively engaged in spreading anti-
American disinformation in nearby Zambia, claiming that the
Zambian government had secretly invited US forces to open a
military base and even move the headquarters of AFRICOM
to the capital Lusaka.[51] As he arrived in Botswana for the
meeting, top US military chief Brown acknowledged that
the US and its allies were in a complex battle for influence

across the continent – and that meant having as many conversations as possible.[52]

The conference host Botswana – landlocked, diamond- and resource-rich and with a population of less than 2.5 million people – received a donated $30 million C-130 Hercules transport aircraft just as the meeting concluded, described by US officials as both a reward and investment to support wider southern African peacekeeping and disaster response.[53] But there was no suggestion the deal would do anything to block the recent Chinese purchase of Botswana's Khoemacau copper mine completed only a few weeks earlier, where Chinese firm MMG said it would invest $700 million to at least double production.[54] Another major Chinese copper deal would be signed a few weeks later, this time in nearby Zambia.

The Biden administration believed it could swing at least one major African nation away from China: Angola. Later in 2024, the president would become the first US leader to visit the former Portuguese colony that had endured decades of civil war before spending much of the current century embracing Chinese investment.

While Beijing lent billions in ways that often took African nations decades to repay, the US was working on several projects in Angola, including two major solar farms and rail links reaching into landlocked mineral-rich areas of Zambia and DRC, often alongside the European Union. 'This commitment is only going to continue to grow,' USAID administrator Samantha Power told local journalists as she rode the new Benguela railway.[55]

As Biden visited Angola, administration spokesman John Kirby tried to dissuade reporters from viewing the trip solely through the prism of international rivalry. 'There is no Cold War on the continent,' he said. 'We are not asking countries to choose between us and Russia and China.' Almost in his next breath, though, he criticised the aggressive lending practices often associated with the Belt and Road Initiative. 'Too many countries have relied on spotty investment opportunities and are now wracked by debt.'[56]

What really had the US worried, many analysts believed, was that China might persuade Angola or another West African state to allow it to open a naval base on the Atlantic. Some of those worries persisted under the new Trump administration, but they were now twinned with a massive pullback from US humanitarian aid and similar intervention. When it came to Angola, it fast became uncertain whether the investment would continue.

When AFRICOM chief General Langley spoke to journalists following the next African defence chiefs conference in Nairobi in May 2025, he made it clear that, like US allies in Europe, African states were expected to do more in their own defence. 'We are having honest conversations about burden sharing,' he said. 'It's essential that all partners around the world – Africa included – take more ownership in their regional and continental security.'[57]

With the incoming Trump administration moving fast to shut down USAID and much of the US support to United Nations agencies, a whole global ecosystem of humanitarian support that had sustained the world for decades was simply collapsing overnight. For Somalia, with 25 per cent of its total budget coming from the US, that put the entire existence of an already fragile state into doubt. For the dozens of African nations where US funding made up 10 to 20 per cent of their total health budgets, it would mean the collapse of medical supplies, unpaid doctors and rising deaths.[58]

For slightly wealthier nations, it was the Trump 'Liberation Day' tariffs that posed the larger problem: at best creating disruption and lowering profits for sometimes already marginal businesses; at worst knocking them out of existence altogether. Angriest of all, perhaps, were the growing number of usually poor nations who suddenly found themselves on the US 'travel ban' list that prevented their citizens from visiting the United States at all.

The switch from the Biden-era 'global south' charm offensive to the frankly blunt dismissal of the Trump era was unquestionably brutal – and the fact that the previous administration had been so effusive with its pledges of support just made it all the worse.

Bright Simons, a policy analyst in Ghana, said governments in developing nations needed to realise that the rules of the game in Washington had changed. What that meant, he added, was that they needed to recognise that unless they could keep up with the 'hyper-transactional and low-consultation model' of the new administration, they would simply be left behind.[59]

Meanwhile, China was already moving fast to fill the gap. Visiting Vietnam – a nation several US administrations had gone to considerable lengths to court over the course of several decades – in April 2025, Xi criticised Trump's tariffs and called for the government in Hanoi and other regional nations to align more closely with Beijing to protect their economies against US-inflicted pain.[60]

The next month, the presidents of Brazil, Colombia and Chile arrived in Beijing for meetings that Brazil's President Luiz Inácio Lula da Silva said were intended to make relations with China 'indestructible'. Lula described China as a much greater advocate for 'free trade' than the US under Trump, while Colombia's President Gustavo Petro said the visit showed his nation's desire not to look 'only one way' towards the US.[61]

Still, it remained a multidimensional battlefield. In the run-up to the G20 summit in South Africa at the end of 2025, President of South Africa Cyril Ramaphosa kept up his efforts to engage with Trump despite the latter's accusations of 'white genocide' within South Africa, anxious to minimise the loss of trade and keep connections open with the White House.[62]

South Africa had already burnt many of its diplomatic bridges with Washington by referring Israeli Prime Minister Benjamin Netanyahu to the ICC over Gaza. It also maintained its own relationship with Russia, which continued to build out its media and other networks across Africa, Southeast Asia and beyond. For the Kremlin, its increasingly worldwide influence campaigns – such as a podcast entitled Global South Pole, hosted by website Sputnik Africa, and apparently aimed largely at Nigeria – were in some ways a retooling of its Cold War anti-colonial campaigns. That included fuelling discontent via social media in some of the handful of remaining European colonial possessions, including the largest French Pacific territory New Caledonia, a few hours' flying time from the coast of Australia.

For China, it was more about resources – particularly anything that might be valuable to a growing superpower in the decades and centuries to come, even if the technology to properly exploit them did not yet exist, as with many of the undersea minerals (and more) beneath the South China Sea and other waters. It was a race the US and its allies were only just beginning to aggressively engage with – along with a growing realisation that in a serious long-term industrial face-off, or even outright war, the balance of power might now be moving in the wrong direction.

That put Taiwan firmly back in the spotlight, as well as the handful of locations across Eastern and northern Europe where a major war might start.

13

The Race to Stop a War

'We have to stop admiring the problem and we
have to start executing.'

**Incoming Chairman of the Joint Chiefs of Staff
US Air Force General John Daniel Caine, Senate
confirmation hearing, April 1, 2025**[1]

From the middle of 2024, clips of a forthcoming TV series entitled *Zero Day Attack* imagining what a Chinese invasion might look like began circulating heavily on Taiwanese social media. Shot in the style of a thriller, the series outlined what many believed were the most plausible scenarios: a sudden Chinese blockade of Taiwan, with the PLA threatening invasion if the island did not surrender. In the show, many characters reacted with disbelief. 'Is there really going to be a war?' a TV presenter asked in an early scene, shortly before broadcasts were interrupted by a Chinese newsreader delivering news of 'peaceful unification with the Motherland'.

'The feeling that war is imminent is something that most people in peaceful countries find hard to relate to,' *Zero Day Attack* director Lo Ging-zim said, shortly before the show finally aired in mid-2025. 'In Taiwan, everyone thinks about it, but no one talks about it. But if we don't make that fear tangible, if we don't turn it into drama, we have a hard time getting people to start a dialogue quickly.'[2]

It was a concern shared openly by the Tawianese government – and despite ongoing questions over the country's military effectiveness, most agreed they were getting more professional. 'We must build the nation's army into a modern force that can protect Taiwan, and fight and win wars,' Defence Minister Wellington Koo – described by Japanese newspaper *Nikkei* as 'Taiwan's own Iron Duke', after the Duke of Wellington – told military cadets at a graduation ceremony. New steps included setting up a cell modelled on the Pentagon's Defense Innovation Unit and building a more 'asymmetric' military based on drones and missiles rather than the easy-to-destroy warships, landing craft and larger weaponry favoured by Koo's predecessors.[3]

How much US and other foreign support Taiwan was likely to receive in a war – particularly when it came to fighting – might depend heavily on how long the island could hold out. The new Taiwanese President Lai Ching-te and his defence minister were determined to show that the government could hold itself together in the first hours and days. Koo was described as giving top commanders much clearer direction on reform. 'This is the first time they're actually taking the job seriously,' said Taiwan analyst Kitsch Liao at the Atlantic Council. 'They feel like the situation is tense enough and are not just going through the motions.'[4]

By early 2025, Taiwan's planning was developing a degree of realism unseen in previous decades, some elements absorbing lessons from Ukraine and other conflicts and others taking advantage of the realities of the modern island and capabilities of its industry. That included plans to move troops and ammunition through the Taipei Metro and other tunnels across that megacity[5] – according to former US intelligence officer Mark Cozad at RAND, PLA discussion papers on an invasion of the island indicated that they were particularly concerned at how the underground battle might play out.[6]

The Lai government's tougher line on China and rhetoric describing Taiwan as effectively already independent – as well as its growing co-operation with the US military and access to foreign arms – was clearly angering Beijing. Japan and South Korea were rumoured to be particularly supportive, but so were several European countries – and not just those such as the Czech Republic and Lithuania that chose to publicise those links. According to the Japanese news agency Nikkei, between 2022 and 2024 the number of foreign diplomats based in Taiwan increased by roughly 25 per cent to almost 400 individuals, with the Japanese embassy growing to 40 foreign diplomats from only 25. The United Kingdom's diplomatic mission grew a similar amount, with Britain the first European country to sign a trade deal with Taiwan in 2023 and reported to also be providing technology for Taiwan's new submarines. Connections with Australia – providing Taiwan's energy requirement in the form of gas and coal – were also on the rise, while the 'American Institute in Taiwan', the de facto US embassy, had more than doubled in size from 2009 to more than 500 personnel, both American and local.[7]

In addition to that civilian presence, the number of US military trainers on the island was also sharply rising. Retired US Admiral Mark Montgomery, whose spring 2025 testimony to a Congressional panel revealed the number had reached 500 personnel, argued the number should at least double further.[8]

The presence of so many Americans – both contractors and serving military personnel – created headlines on both Taiwan and the mainland, with the Hong Kong-based *South China Morning Post* describing it as 'openly testing' Beijing's previously described 'red lines'. On Taiwan itself, one expert described it as the beginning of a shift from US 'strategic ambiguity' towards much greater clarity.[9] In fact, there were plenty of divisions within the new US administration on how to approach 'the Taiwan question'. And while some of those who believed in prioritising the Pacific favoured an increased presence of force on the island, others were already calling for the number of US personnel on the island to be cut, arguing that current levels risked being too 'provocative'.[10]

At his confirmation hearing in the US Senate, incoming Pentagon number three Elbridge Colby repeated his previously voiced concerns that the island was not doing enough in its own defence, warning that unless that changed America could not be expected to fight to defend it. 'Taiwan's fall would be a disaster for American interests,' Colby said. But he said such a loss would not be 'existential' – unlike losing a major war with China in a way that risked 'decimating' the US military. His recipe for Taiwan to save itself and become deserving of US military aid was very simple: increase Taiwan's current 3 per cent defence budget to more like 10 per cent of GDP, and prepare more seriously to fight.[11]

The new Lai government in Taipei appeared open to that plan – but it was here that the US and Taiwanese politics produced problems that might prove insurmountable. Lai and the Democratic Progressive Party had won 2024's presidential vote, but the KMT and a handful of other small opposition parties had between them a slim majority in parliament.

Despite its deepening contact with Beijing, many KMT parliamentarians still declared they were opposed to forced 'reunification' across the strait. But while the DPP claimed Taiwan as a de facto nation in its own right, the KMT stuck to its line that the island was fundamentally Chinese. To this, the KMT added a further narrative: they were the moderate voice of peace, while the DPP were putting Taiwan on a collision course with China and must be restrained – particularly through the parliamentary rejection of their plans for rising military spending.

At his Senate confirmation hearing, Colby described this potential inability to spend more on defence as 'disturbing'. For the DPP it was almost existential. By the middle of the year, they were engaged in a frantic effort to trigger by-elections in multiple KMT constituencies to take back control of parliament.

It might sound absurdly technical – and it was – but the democratic battle for the future of the island was critical to its ability to fund and build its own defence, and it would need to be continually refought throughout the years to come.

It was a situation Beijing was working to exploit. As Institute for the Study of War analysts Daniel Shats and Matthew Sperzel put it to me, there was much more to Beijing's strategy than overt military posturing. It was also pushing ahead with its 'soft power' effort, presenting the mainland as richer, more successful and furnished with better infrastructure – underlined with more aggressive messaging designed to intimidate Taiwanese residents. 'They want to create an atmosphere of claustrophobia, of inevitability,' said Shats, through everything from military drills to social media campaigns.[12]

Taiwan also looked like it might be losing leverage, along with its near monopoly of advanced microchip production. Under pressure from US and European buyers, the Taiwan Semiconductor Manufacturing Corporation (TSMC) was opening factories in Germany and Arizona, and while their initial production output was reported to be disappointing, it was almost certain to improve. At the start of March 2025, Trump met TSMC chairman C. C. Wei in the Oval Office, barely four days after his disastrous meeting with Ukraine's Zelenskyy in the same room. While this meeting went considerably better – Wei was a lot more diplomatic, announcing a further $100 million investment in the US – those watching from Taiwan were alarmed to see Trump suggest that the opening of TSMC fabrication plants in Arizona was good news in the event that 'something happens'.[13]

For a moment at the start of March, Taiwan-watchers talked of the island facing abandonment – and with it also likely invasion, or, at the very least, the eventual election of a pro-Beijing government that might just hand the island over to the mainland. Then came the unexpected leak of the Pentagon's interim strategy document for the new administration, signed

personally by Secretary of Defense Pete Hegseth within weeks
of his appointment – and making Taiwan the focal point of
America's face-off with Beijing.

'Denial of a Chinese fait accompli seizure of Taiwan – while
simultaneously defending the US homeland – is the Department's
sole pacing scenario,' it read.

For the Taiwanese, the new Pentagon guidance was the most
encouraging thing they had heard for ages. 'This memo makes
Taiwan the focus of US global defence strategy as never before,'
said William Chung at Taiwanese military-focused think tank
the Institute for National Defence and Security Research. 'We
were afraid . . . the Trump administration will ignore Taiwan
just like Ukraine and make a deal with China. From the look of
things now, that is not going to happen.'[14]

In reality, the new administration in Washington was indeed
still working on a deal – and while initial negotiations through
Trade Secretary Scott Bessent focused on trade and economics,
any agreement on that front was expected to open the door to a
direct Trump–Xi meeting much later in the year.[15] Already,
there were suggestions that this might yield a much broader
strategic bargain, one that might include the US pulling back
on direct support to Taiwan.

That intensified the urgency of getting weapons to the
island. Mid-2025 saw the delivery of the first Altius unmanned
loitering munitions from defence giant Anduril, announced by
founder Palmer Luckey on a visit in which he also revealed the
firm would open an office on Taiwan and develop AI products
with Taiwanese institutions. 'This is the kind of partnership
that matters,' Luckey told an AI event at Taiwan National
University. 'Working side-by-side, we can integrate AI,
autonomy and advanced systems at a speed that matches the
threats we face.'

Luckey revealed that both US and Taiwanese officials had
been critical about the speed with which the deal was done –
but he said his own firm had also 'taken financial risk' by

starting production early to ensure delivery could happen within six months of the contract being signed.

Luckey wasn't just advocating for Taiwan to buy weapons from his company; he was calling for Taiwan's technicians and engineers to emulate Ukraine in starting their own domestic weapons industry – and to do so fast.[16] That should not have been a surprise. In the halls of the Pentagon and INDOPACOM in Hawaii, there were already concerns that the slow pace of action on almost every other front might leave China thinking it might win a limited or even a much longer war – and in doing so, start something catastrophic.

At the same time, some were also expressing mounting nervousness over the influence of Colby. 'I'm deeply worried that [he] buys into the authoritarian worldview that . . . Putin is a dictator, and Xi is a dictator, and Trump aspires to be a dictator, so let's just let all the dictators get together and divide up the world,' said Democratic Congressman Adam Smith. 'That is a horrific policy.'

'Bridge' was definitely making a new crop of enemies, including some Republicans who viewed him as being on a one-man battle to abandon allies and do less in the world. But he also had supporters. Former Trump National Security Council official Alexander Gray described him as 'a skilled bureaucratic tactician' whom opponents complained about when they believed they were losing to him in an internal fight.[17] In reality, those public endorsements served only to confirm that there were underlying internal disagreements in the Pentagon – but meanwhile, there was also a very real worry that US and allied resources were inadequate and time was running out.

*

As he toured the region at the start of 2025, US INDOPACOM commander Admiral Samuel Paparo stressed that US forces still retained the military edge if ordered to stop a Chinese invasion of Taiwan at that current moment. But he warned that the balance was shifting swiftly against the United States. In 2024 alone, the Pentagon estimated that PLA military units had increased their activity around Taiwan by some 300 per cent, and China's industrial strength meant it could keep ramping up its forces much faster than the US had so far proved itself able to match. 'I remain confident in our deterrence posture, but the trajectory must change,' Paparo told Congressional officials, warning that the current advantage was being rapidly eroded as China built up forces. 'There are gaps in defence fuelling support points,' he said. 'Those are the locations where aircraft and warships would load fuel and distribute fuel. There are shortfalls in our tanker fleet to keep enough fuel in the case of a contingency. And there are gaps in the combat logistics force.'[18]

Some Congressional leaders voiced even more concerns. 'God forbid, if we were in a short-term conflict, it would [have to] be short-term because we don't have enough munitions to sustain a long-term fight,' warned Republican Oklahoma Representative Tom Cole, Chair of the House Appropriations Committee. Acting Chief of Naval Operations James Kilby's own warning was scarcely less subdued. 'If we go to war with China, it's going to be bloody and there's going to be casualties and it's going to take plenty of munitions,' he warned. 'So our stocks need to be full.'

In fact, those worries were growing. Testifying before the House Appropriations Committee, Kilby warned that precision-guided weapons such as the Tomahawk, the Long-Range Anti-Ship Missile and heavyweight torpedoes were all in short supply, and that the Pentagon needed other suppliers. 'They may not be able to produce the same exact specifications but they might be able to produce a missile that is effective, which is more effective than no missile,' he said.[19]

Ironically, the US's weakest areas were those that had been among its greatest strengths during World War Two, when it had mass-produced materiel such as the 'Liberty Ships', which kept the Allies supplied, as well as smaller landing vessels critical to the Pacific war. The US had few such equivalents in the mid-2020s, and, critically, no ability to build them in a hurry. The question was whether other options could be found – and to what extent unmanned systems could be rushed into service.

Once again, Anduril was pushing hard to take the lead – albeit with a growing range of other smaller firms following behind – as well as racing to build drones. At the start of 2025, Anduril announced 'Arsenal-1', its new 'hyperscale' mass production facility on the outskirts of Columbus, Ohio. The first weaponry was due to come off its production lines by July 2026, conveniently located just next to Rickenbacker airport with its two runways capable of handling military cargo planes to take its products directly into action. Further production facilities making unmanned submarines and other weaponry were already spinning up in Rhode Island, Georgia and California.[20]

The scale of broader effort was growing every month. Beijing was already believed to be building more missiles than the US and wider allied industry could match, and, unlike those supplying Ukraine, it was not consuming them in action. If a major new Pacific conflict arose, the US military believed Beijing might well commence by unleashing as many long-range missiles as it could. Their objective would be simple: first exhaust or overwhelm the US air defences, then destroy as much US military capability as possible, particularly aircraft on the ground and warships, and persuade Washington to hold other heavy forces – its bombers, fast jets and carriers – much further from the war zone, where they could not intervene.

Modern US commanders believed the trick to avoiding that fate involved spreading forces out, a concept the US Air Force called 'agile combat employment'. That meant deploying often small detachments of aircraft to multiple newly reconditioned bases around the potential conflict zone with stores and fuel. At best, that would make those forces more likely to survive and at worst, make the Chinese use up more missiles to hit them.

The race was on to prepare for those strikes – then counter them immediately. It was a test America and its partners had failed catastrophically in December 1941 when, despite years of war preparations, aircraft and ships parked nose to tail in Pearl Harbor were destroyed in minutes, followed by the rapid collapse of US and other forces in the Philippines, Malaya, Sumatra and Singapore.

As US Defense Secretary Hegseth landed on Guam in March 2025 – becoming the first senior Trump administration official to visit the Pacific region – US military engineers were clearing seven decades' worth of vegetation from disused World War Two airfields to prepare them for another conflict. Hegseth told US personnel that they were 'living in history', calling them the 'tip of the spear' of forces in the Western Pacific facing China. That confrontation, he suggested, was already delivering stark lessons for the Pentagon.

'We're going to learn a lot [from the air defence systems on Guam] and apply them to defences on the continental United States,' Hegseth told reporters and civic officials, adding that the US would respond to an attack on Guam as it would for any other strike on US territory. Guam Governor Lou Leon Guerrero welcomed Hegseth's comments, but expressed concern that its small hospital of less than 30 beds would likely be quickly overwhelmed.[21]

Also likely to face alarming odds would be the small detachments of US soldiers and marines increasingly deployed across the region, often manning highly mobile missile batteries such as the newly introduced Navy–Marine Expeditionary Ship Interdiction System (NMESIS). The first of these deployed into the northern Philippines overlooking Luzon Strait during the spring 2025 US–Philippines BALIKATAN military drills, closer to mainland China than US cruise missiles had ever been before.[22]

Although it was not publicly acknowledged at the time, the US-led military activity in the Philippines in early 2025 was by far more directly connected to Taiwan than anything before. That included inviting Taiwanese officials to visit drills being conducted with Japanese and Filipino troops, a tacit acknowledgement that building the capability of those forces to fight effectively together was a significant part of US plans to keep Beijing deterred.[23] The US Army had also stepped up its game across the Pacific: deploying and defending a range of medium- and long-range weapons, as well as supplying the necessary troops to protect the Korean peninsula or any other significant landmass. As head of the US Army in the Pacific General Ronald Clark told a think tank event in Washington DC, China had committed huge resources to targeting US warships and airfields – but much less to counter mobile land-based weaponry and sensors that could be rapidly moved and readily concealed. Pre-positioning of supplies and munitions was already underway, he said, including in Japan and northern Australia. New weaponry included hypersonic weapons, autonomous systems and drones that could be readily shipped, he added, but equally important were the relationships between regional US commanders, as well as those with local partners. 'Having been in the region for nine years it's never been as good as it is now,' Clark said. 'It is too late [when conflict starts] to start asking: "Do I trust you?" It has to happen now.'[24]

US military facilities in Hawaii, and even on the mainland, were also bracing for new dangers. In mid-2025, US Air Force Brigadier General Doug Wickert told civic leaders near Edwards Air Force Base in California that if China attacked Taiwan in the coming years, they should be prepared for their immediate region to suffer massive disruption from the start. That included, he suggested, being prepared for Chinese cyber attacks that took down the electrical grid, perhaps for weeks or months.[25]

As he passed through Pearl Harbor on his way to Guam, Hegseth described his mission in terms of 'rebuilding deterrence from the ground up'. But, after Ukraine, deterrence in the 2020s meant also being prepared to fight a much longer war – and the fact that America's defence industrial base was simply not prepared was nowhere more evident than in the realm of shipbuilding, where most estimates put total Chinese capacity, both civilian and military, at an astounding 200 times that of the US. In a serious fight for the Pacific, that difference might guarantee a victory – but some of China's dominance could also be offset by the still-vast shipyards of Japan and South Korea.

Trump's first few weeks in office had left US–Japan relations reeling. Prime Minister Shigeru Ishiba had been the first major foreign visitor to the White House in January – but, frankly, that had been so early in the administration it offered little insight. The Japanese had been appalled by the Trump administration's early moves on both Ukraine and Europe, as well as the trade war rhetoric – and the visit from Hegseth at the end of his Asia–Pacific trip was intended to set the relationship back on track. So was a follow-on trip from US Navy Secretary John Phelan to both Japan and South Korea, touring the shipyards of both and meeting with their largest shipbuilding firms to talk about collaboration with the Pentagon.[26]

This effort wasn't new – the Biden administration had been engaging with shipyards as far away as India to talk about their possible use to support the US in a major war, preventing damaged US vessels from having to limp all the way back to the US Western Seaboard for repairs. Japan itself – grimly aware that its own cities and dockyards were well within range of many Chinese weapons – was even experimenting with repairing its own vessels in Sri Lanka.

Many of these dilemmas and debates would have been familiar to those who had fought America's first Pacific war from 1941 to 1945 – but, as in that conflict, consideration also needed to be given to the hugely fast advances in technology.

On that front, Trump's unorthodox, unexpected pick as Chairman of the Joint Chiefs would have something to say.

*

When Trump announced the appointment of Lieutenant General John Daniel Caine as America's new top military officer – as he fired previous Chairman 'CQ' Brown, Chief of Naval Operations Lisa Franchetti and several other officers – few outside the largely closed world of intelligence and special operations knew his name at all. The first references that came up were from Trump's own speeches, and they were enough to alarm anybody about the political independence of the military.

Trump, visiting Iraq as president in 2018, had first met Caine during the fight against Islamic State, with the US Air Force officer introducing himself by his nickname 'Raising' and immediately pledging that he could defeat the militants in a week. According to Trump, the same trip saw Caine don a 'MAGA' hat and tell the president, 'I'd kill for you, sir.' Even before he was appointed chairman, Caine denied the story, and the veracity of the other elements was also unconfirmed. But the president was clearly enamoured, describing Caine as a 'real general, not a television general'.[27]

Caine was without doubt an unorthodox pick as chairman of the joint chiefs: technically, the Goldwater–Nichols Act of 1986 required any candidate to have previously served as either the head of one of the US armed services, as a regional combatant commander or in other senior roles. This could be waived, however, if Congress chose to do so. The Republican majority meant Trump had the votes – but in fact, Caine's nomination would gain bipartisan support. In part that was down to the remainder of his background – which was extremely unusual for a general.

Caine had qualified in the US Air Force ROTC programme at Virginia Military Institute, a 'private military college' that was not formally part of the military in the same way as West

Point, Annapolis or their US Air Force counterpart at Colorado Springs. Instead of then transferring into full-time military service, he joined an Air National Guard unit in Syracuse, New York, training, effectively, as a part-time fighter pilot alongside civilian roles. Such careers were not rare, but they rarely led to the most senior appointments. Caine explained his choice: with the military cuts of the early 1990s, he feared that any role as a full-time Air Force pilot might swiftly be abolished, leaving him trapped behind a much less interesting desk. By September 11, 2001, however, he must have forged both a solid reputation and a hankering for responsibility, as he had been posted as head of weapons and tactics for the regular 121st Fighter Squadron tasked with defending Washington DC, from Andrews Air Force Base.

As news broke that the Twin Towers had been hit, Caine called the US Secret Service to ask what was needed to defend the White House and wider government, only to be told that they did not know and would get back to him. By the time they phoned back, the Pentagon had also just been hit and Vice President Dick Cheney could be heard in the background ordering fighters to shoot down any aircraft that approached. Handed a faxed set of rules of engagement authorising him to do just that, Caine spent more than seven hours airborne that day, turning away several aircraft from the now-protected airspace.

That appeared to be almost his last role in the 'war on terror' he was allowed to talk about in detail, his career passing through special operations and culminating in appointment as the CIA's Associate Director of Military Affairs. Despite the 'associate' in the title, that made him the CIA director's primary military adviser and liaison, dealing directly with the Pentagon[28] as well as service chiefs and combatant commanders such as Chris Cavoli and Samuel Paparo. It also made him the principal interlocutor with the Joint Staff at the Pentagon – the team that drove the US military machine – including, presumably, whichever bits the CIA needed to 'borrow'.

In his written confirmation testimony, Caine described the Pentagon Joint Staff as the 'most professional in the world'.[29] At the annual Special Operations Forces Week – 'SOF Week' – conference in Tampa, Florida for his first speech after taking office at the start of May, he acknowledged that they were even more 'his tribe', working often on classified missions to 'create dilemmas' in the minds of potential adversaries such as the PLA.

Since 9/11, America's special operators had quietly built a global network of relations with multiple other nations – almost 70 were represented at 'SOF Week' in Tampa. Those relations, he said, would be key in future fights, but they also needed to be integrated seamlessly with more mainstream military forces and the private sector. 'We have to find every ounce of combat capability, every ounce of cognitive effect . . . given some of the things we are facing out there,' he said, his 15 minutes on the floor earning a standing ovation from a very friendly crowd.[30]

Such a background in special operations was not unusual at the top of Western militaries – but alongside those roles, Caine had also spent several years out of uniform as a businessman, investor and entrepreneur, at one point trying to sell to the US military. That, he said, gave him insight into private-sector challenges, as well as how the Pentagon could become 'a better buyer'. 'We've got to be properly armed,' he told his second major public event at an AI trade fair, claiming that the fast-moving world of technology start-ups was equally his 'tribe'. 'Our adversaries are working together, sharing technologies and intelligence at unprecedented levels, decreasing the time required to field advanced technology,' he said, also warning that the US and its allies needed to get technology to commanders while they were still at the peacetime planning stage – and 'not at the point of crisis or conflict'.[31]

That meant a profound sea-change in the speed at which major weapons programmes were developed. 'During

World War Two and the early Cold War ... technology ... went from concept to combat in under five years,' he told the House Armed Services Committee. 'Today it takes 16 years to develop a basic ground vehicle and more than 20 years for a fighter jet.'

Fixing that would need to be done alongside the new suddenly announced priorities including Trump favourites the 'Golden Dome' defence shield and F-47 fighter.[32] The president had demanded that both should be in service by the end of his term in 2029 – but behind closed doors, few in the defence sector believed that would be possible.

In fact, the US defence industrial complex was now already struggling with a new problem that threatened to fast become a crisis – a growing shortage of critical minerals and components exported from China. From April 2025, in response to Trump's initial round of tariffs, China had begun requiring licences for exports of specific rare earths including a range of substances vital for high-tech magnets and other projects – and while it reduced those restrictions as part of a preliminary deal that June, it maintained its embargo on sales to firms serving the Pentagon. With China responsible for two-thirds of rare earth mining and an even higher proportion of refining, the result was hugely reduced supplies and dramatically rising prices. One company complained it was being offered samarium – vital for magnets that could operate at high temperatures in jet engines – at 60 times the price of the beginning of the year. Another said it had almost exhausted its stocks of germanium, used in infrared vision equipment and for hardening bullets and projectiles. Other firms reported they were now facing Chinese demands for exact details of the defence projects they were working on as a prerequisite to gain an export licence for materials – all slowing down or threatening to halt production.

Once again, it was a case of a threat that had been clear for years – at least since the Chinese boycott on rare earth exports to Japan in 2010 – that had simply been ignored. By mid-2025, the Trump administration had taken a stake in one major US rare earth mining firm and another in Canada, providing a much-needed infusion of investment. But that would take years to show results.[33]

Meanwhile, Ukraine was showing how fast technology was moving – and how incredibly vulnerable mainstream militaries, including their atomic weapons platforms, had suddenly become.

*

Ukraine's Operation SPIDER'S WEB had been 18 months in the planning, officials disclosed afterwards, co-ordinated by the Security Service of Ukraine that was also the brains behind some of their more audacious strikes in the Black Sea. SPIDER'S WEB, however, was both considerably bolder and even more strategic in its effect, designed to strike multiple airbases deep in Russia from which the Kremlin's bombers flew to launch missiles against Ukraine – but which the Russian military believed were too far away for Ukraine to strike.

Already, Ukraine was building ever longer-range drones to fix that problem – but against a country as vast as Russia, even that approach could quickly reach its limits. SPIDER'S WEB would use smaller weapons – 117 'first-person view' quadcopters of the type normally employed much closer to the frontline. These were smuggled into Russian territory – and then hidden inside the roots of prefabricated wooden huts that could be carried by trucks. An image later shared by Ukrainian authorities showed around 20 drones concealed in every unit.

This was exactly the concept of 'containerised' drones General Clark had been talking about in the Pacific – but with the added twist of being concealed before penetration deep into hostile territory. The trucks had been driven in some cases more than 2,000 miles across the Russian Federation to within striking range of at least five major Russian airbases. The resulting attacks came simultaneously on the first day of June, just before Russian and Ukrainian negotiators were due to meet for scheduled talks in Istanbul.[34] 'The Russians looked pretty sheepish at the talks,' a security expert told me shortly afterwards, speaking from Kyiv. 'They almost certainly assumed that they were safe from a major attack before the talks because the Ukrainians would not want to upset Trump. Everyone here is pretty chipper – but also wary of what happens next.'[35]

Details continued to drip out in the days that followed. According to a Ukrainian source speaking to Reuters, for most of the attack the drones were piloted remotely via the Russian cell-phone system – although Ukraine's intelligence services said artificial intelligence had also been used in the face of Russian jamming. According to Russian news site Baza, quoting security and military sources, the drivers of the trucks – hired through a transport firm that appeared to have been set up by the Ukrainians – were unaware of anything unusual until the drones began to launch themselves from their vehicles. The Ukrainians claimed that more than 40 Russian aircraft had been hit, half of them destroyed, although US sources said they believed the true number was lower. Video and satellite imagery left no doubt that multiple Russian planes – many of them clearly the ageing but still iconic Tupolev-95 long-range atomic bombers with their propeller-driven engines – had been left in flames. The mainstay of the Russian bomber force, capable of carrying huge numbers of missiles, Tu-95s had not been built in decades, making them almost impossible to replace.[36]

As well as reducing the aircraft available to attack Ukraine, the raid also cut the number of aircraft potentially available to launch nuclear weapons in any atomic war. Trump's Ukraine envoy Keith Kellogg told Fox News that this inherently made the Kremlin's response much harder to predict. 'When you attack an opponent's part of their national survival system . . . their nuclear triad . . . you don't know what the other side is going to do . . . I think that's what we're trying to avoid.'[37]

Speaking a few days later, though, he suggested the strike could become a 'forcing function for peace' by making the war too costly for Russia.[38]

Some suggested that the change of tone might indicate that Trump himself had been impressed with the strike's audacity – although the president warned that the Russians would seek revenge.[39] Across the world, and within the Pentagon, military leaders were worrying how vulnerable they might be to similar attacks. 'I should have thought every base commander on the planet is worried this morning,' said a security expert in Kyiv, noting just how impossible it was to search every truck, container or outbuilding within striking range of key bases, ports and airfields.[40] Another expert said it showed the limitations of local jamming systems: 'The problem is they overheat.' Even 'kinetic' systems such as anti-drone machine guns could suffer similar problems, as could laser systems such as Israel's 'Iron Beam'.[41]

Within days, NATO chief Mark Rutte was warning in a London speech that the alliance needed to increase spending on air and missile defence by at least 400 per cent. To achieve that, and everything else that was now necessary, he said he expected alliance nations to put themselves on a 'wartime footing'.[42] But even in the most vulnerable states on the edge of Russian territory, there was widespread scepticism that would happen.

*

At the start of May 2025, the new US ambassador to NATO Matthew Whitaker appeared to confirm what had been rumoured ever since Trump's re-election: that the US intended to cut back its troops stationed in Europe, although he said discussions were unlikely to start until after the NATO summit in mid-June. 'President Trump just said ... this is going to happen and it's going to happen now,' he told a conference in Estonia. 'This is going to be orderly, but we are not going to have any more patience for foot-dragging in this situation ... We just need to work through the practical consequences.'

The Baltic states were particularly nervous they might lose the small detachments on their soil, including a HIMARS battery in Estonia and a force of Apache attack helicopters temporarily in Latvia. US officials were similarly upfront about their intent to push every NATO member to spend at least 5 per cent of their gross domestic product on defence, more than twice what most of them spent at present.[43]

Behind closed doors, most European diplomats acknowledged that getting the majority of nations to anywhere close to 5 per cent – with the exception of Poland and the Baltics, by far the most exposed countries – on pure military power was unlikely in the extreme. As defence ministers met in Brussels, NATO chief Rutte pushed something of a compromise: at the summit, nations would agree to an immediate goal of 3.5 per cent – which was not quite the same as spending it – plus another 1.5 per cent in infrastructure and defence-related activities. The latter definition was deliberately broad, including building roads and railways that might help in time of war but would not have previously counted towards defence-spending goals. Those targets were also set a long way in the future: 2032, a date so distant some nations judged it useless.

'We don't have time for seven years,' said Estonia's Defence Minister Hanno Pevkur.[44] His own country's strategy for survival, he had told a conference a few weeks earlier, was to follow the example of Ukraine and embrace drones and other tech to turn itself into a 'fly that can paralyse an elephant'. But while some drones were taking part in Estonia's HEDGEHOG spring drills, together with British, French and other NATO troops, officials noted that those exercises and most alliance war plans remained heavily dependent on traditional equipment such as tanks – as well as US support.[45]

In Russian-speaking Narva, where Estonia was now planning to open its patrol base, residents with Russian passports appeared more confident than ever that the town should be part of Russia. 'Russia is magnificent,' one of them told a French TV crew. Estonia's border guard commanders overlooking the river said they had no contact with their Russian counterparts on the other side, but provocations were constant. Those ranged from the removal of buoys that marked the limits of Russian and Estonian territory, to the jamming of radio and GPS signals, as well as concerts every May to mark the end of World War Two broadcast on enormous screens so that Russian speakers could watch them from the Estonian side.[46]

According to Estonian General Vahur Karus, existing NATO forces in Estonia were expressing enthusiasm to be posted at the new base. 'They're actually very eager to operate in places like Narva,' he said. 'There's a kind of exotic appeal.'[47] That was almost certainly a reference to the British, still leading the roughly thousand-strong Enhanced Forward Presence battle group roughly two hours from the border – and apparently champing at the bit to be much closer. If the Kremlin ever did move against that outpost – or, indeed, it was attacked by local rioters or insurgents – they could well be among the first in harm's way. That British-led NATO detachment would likely find itself in the midst of a country in total chaos, attempting to evacuate its entire civilian population. 'If anyone thinks the war won't start from Narva, they are mistaken,' Estonia's most senior military officer Major General Andrus Merilo told a Polish journalist – adding that as soon as the attack was launched, Estonia would begin destroying its own civilian infrastructure to slow the Russian advance. 'We must be ready for the city's infrastructure, including roads, to be made impassable for enemy forces . . . When Russia goes to war, its goal is always territorial conquest.' Estonia must also be prepared to be cut off from the rest of Europe if Russian troops attacked Latvia and Lithuania, he said, perhaps leaving air and sea links across to Finland as the only way to get the population out.[48]

That pointed to a larger issue. In the three years from 2022, with the Biden administration dramatically stepping up its presence in Europe, European members of NATO had been largely content to let the US dominate continental war planning from within NATO structures. By the middle of 2025 that confidence had gone – and individual nations as well as small 'minilateral' groups were making their own separate decisions on how they might defend themselves. It was a significant rebalancing of how the alliance had worked during every previous era of confrontation going back to 1949, when NATO's first Supreme Commander Eisenhower had brought everyone together. Now, in contrast, those countries closest to the threat – the Nordics, Baltics, Poland and even other small and medium-sized nations like the Netherlands – were working out what they might do in the first days of a war, particularly if the US failed to join.

In particular, that meant dramatically ramping up capabilities such as long-range missiles to strike deep into Russia, sometimes launched from warplanes but often fired from trucks. It also meant forward nations, such as Finland, working out what weaponry might be based on NATO territory to threaten Russia's precious nuclear, naval and air facilities around Murmansk. The degree to which this would change how a confrontation might turn out was hard to overstate: the NATO model of the Cold War, in which the top US commander in Europe would tightly control any weaponry striking Soviet territory, could at worst be replaced by half a dozen loosely coordinated nations determined to start raining destruction – albeit conventional rather than atomic – into Russia in the first hours of any conflict.[49]

The British themselves still talked an optimistic game. British Army chief General Sir 'Roly' Walker told a conference in June 2025 that new technology was already increasing the effectiveness of his formations by roughly 30 per cent in training, with one experimental brigade able to hit targets ten times further away with ten times more force. The addition of new drones and long-range strike capabilities under what the UK called Project Asgard, Walker promised, would take the approximate 1,000 troops of the British force within Estonia 'from a strategic trip-wire to an invasion-stopping capability'. 'A better-trained force will often defeat a bigger and better-equipped one,' he said, comparing the UK detachment in the Baltic states and its much larger potential Russian foe to David and Goliath.[50]

Lieutenant General Chris Donahue, now commanding US land forces in Europe – who would lead NATO ground forces in the event of any war – cautioned against suggestions that drones could remove the need for significant allied troop numbers. 'You still have to do the basics really well,' he said. 'You still need manoeuvre brigades to hold terrain and that's not going to change at any point in our lifetime.' But he also talked of the importance of 'the network': the ability to pass data across drones, headquarters, aircraft and frontline combat units including those of assorted allied states. Deployed properly, he said, it should be possible to use that arsenal so that actual human troops did not come into direct contact with the enemy 'until you're really deep into that fight'.

As commander of first the 82nd Airborne Division and then the US 18th Airborne Corps, Donahue had been at the forefront of AI and other technology – and now he painted a bold vision of what that would mean in Europe. 'We have exponential growth on things,' he told podcast and website War on the Rocks in mid-2025. 'I'm not going to go into it in detail but it's not good for our adversaries.' The key challenge now was scaling up production of those systems to build that 'magazine depth' – and there he described the industrial capability of NATO's 32 member nations as a huge inbuilt advantage, one that if exploited properly could go a long way to redressing US and allied weaponry supply problems, not just when it came to Europe but also the Pacific.[51]

That, however, relied on the relationship between the US and its allies staying functional – and not all believed that could now be counted on. After their initial panic following the US suspension of intelligence-sharing with Ukraine in early 2025, most US and Asian allies had gradually recommitted themselves to purchasing US weapons as a way to maintain a good relationship with Washington. But they also increasingly now wanted other options and networks as well, including stronger relations with non-US suppliers. Poland was buying yet more tanks from South Korea,[52] while Australia – perhaps in expectation of being disappointed by the US on AUKUS – was buying frigates from Japan. In the words of Defence Industry Minister Pat Conroy, Australia wanted the ships as fast as possible given its 'challenging strategic circumstances' and the fact that Japan's shipyards were already building exactly the same class meant the first vessels could be delivered as soon as 2029. In order to avoid the traditional cost overruns due to endless reworking of specifications, he said the government had explicitly instructed that any changes that alter the original order required ministerial approval.[53]

Meanwhile, international confrontation was expanding ever further above the atmosphere into the dark reaches of space. Whether or not a true world war was on the cards, the struggle already underway for resources, territory and influence was spreading beyond the Earth – and it was being shaped by fast-shifting geopolitics, technology, personalities, egos, money and international rivalry.

14

Space and the Battle for the Future

'The Chinese have very deliberately plotted a course . . . to demonstrate that China is the dominant power in space. Their intent is to catch up and surpass the United States by 2030.'

Former NASA executive Daniel L. Dumbacher's testimony to US House of Representatives Space and Aeronautics Subcommittee, February 2025[1]

Some 250 miles above the Earth, two tiny figures clung to the outside of the Chinese space station *Tiangong* as it spun around the planet at almost 5,000 miles a second. The older of the astronauts, 48-year-old Colonel Cai Xuzhe, would later recall this moment for Chinese state television, describing the rich blue of the planet – and the even brighter red of Communist China's flag on the white skin of the spacecraft.[2] It was December 2024, less than a week before Christmas, and, as the world awaited the arrival of the second Trump administration, the PRC was looking for another victory to assert dominance over the United States.

Mission commander Cai had all the attributes of a modern Chinese hero, at least according to state media, including a working-class family who had been dedicated Communist Party volunteers since before the civil war. Cai himself had been obsessed by aeroplanes when growing up, joining the People's Liberation Army Air Force as soon as he left school and reportedly volunteering to fly in remote corners of mainland

China known for their harsh weather conditions. Now, particularly when he passed above his home province of Hebei, he would look down on Earth as a living embodiment of China's dream to expand its power beyond the planet. 'I treat every spaceflight as my first,' he once told the *People's Daily*, apparently referring both to his ongoing sense of wonder and the dangers of space.[3]

If space was dangerous, *spacewalking* was even more so, even though no nation had yet to lose an astronaut while doing so, most previous fatal mishaps having taken place within the Earth's atmosphere, either while ascending or descending. Cai was floating outside the capsule, alongside 34-year-old fellow fighter pilot Lieutenant Colonel Song Lingdong. The only astronaut remaining inside was 34-year-old Wang Haoue, China's third woman in space. She had been a senior civilian rocket engineer researcher at China's largest space contractor before being recruited by the PLA Astronaut Corps, in which she was now a lieutenant colonel. If anything went wrong outside the station, Wang – floating by her console in zero gravity – would have to work with mission control to find a solution to get her colleagues back alive.[4]

But if everything went according to plan, their spacewalk lasting more than eight hours and 56 minutes would beat the record set by two Americans in 2001. 'While admiring the wondrous views of space, we also had a deep feeling of the weight and greatness of the manned space endeavour,' said Song on re-entering the station. The statement appeared to have been deliberately crafted to respect their US and Soviet predecessors – although US journalists would strike a somewhat different tone. 'Chinese spacewalk apparently breaks a record (barely)', proclaimed the *New York Times*.[5]

Oh well, the Americans could mock. As far back as the 1990s, even as the US had worked with Yeltsin's Russia on plans for what would become the International Space Station, both nations had looked to bar the Chinese from the project – officially because Beijing's programme remained under PLA control, but also to stop them stealing secrets.[6] But Beijing would have the last laugh: with Russian–Western relations wrecked by the invasion of Ukraine, the ISS programme would now shut down by 2030 at the latest. Then, what might yet be the first, last and only truly international station to orbit the Earth would be crashed into the region of the South Pacific known as the 'pole of inaccessibility': the farthest point from land.[7]

Crippled by sanctions, the Russian space programme was a fragment of its former self – and the Chinese could likely pick what remaining pieces of it they wanted as part of a future joint Moon base. The Europeans who had also partnered on the ISS might or might not continue to work with NASA; the new Trump administration ushered in a particularly wild and unpredictable phase for US-led activity in space. Certainly, no one else was likely to be in a position to have a manned space platform in orbit throughout the early 2030s, and it was a position the People's Republic was determined to exploit, build from and defend.

The PRC's space programme was nothing if not ambitious – its aim was to finally outstrip the US as the largest player in space, and hold that dominance for ever. Becoming the leader in manned space travel was part of that agenda – but, as with almost every other sphere of this activity in the 2020s, so were drones, other unmanned systems and the artificial intelligence that would guide them. In 2021, China became the first nation to successfully land an exploratory rover probe near the south pole of the Moon, regarded as the most promising location for a long-term outpost. Beijing wanted to get its first astronauts landing on the surface by 2030, and it intended to use robots to build a base capable of periodically hosting humans by 2035.[8] According to a drip feed of announcements, work was already underway involving 3D printed bricks that could be mass produced from materials already on the lunar surface. That system was scheduled to be landed on the Moon in 2028 to start production before China's astronauts landed.[9]

That included plans to identify and mine deposits of helium-3, rarely found on Earth but believed to be a potentially potent source of future clean energy through fusion. China was just one of many players working to find deposits and develop its techniques[10] but it appeared to be gradually moving ahead of others, including the US. Some suggested success might lead not just to Beijing getting the edge in space, but also its being able to generate much more power on Earth to support enhanced artificial intelligence and future quantum computing.[11]

By 2038, China's space agency hoped to be building a robot base on Mars, again following up with human astronauts – the Chinese phrase was '*Taikonauts*', from the Chinese word for 'Cosmos' – and then establishing a lasting human presence. Alongside that was an almost equally ambitious timetable for sending ever more sophisticated probes to other planets in the solar system – and perhaps one day beyond. By the end of the 2020s, China's Academy of Sciences intended to launch a long-range telescope known as 'Earth 2.0' or 'ET' to observe around two million of the closest stars and search for a planet with a habitable temperature and atmosphere. It was, European space scientists noted, likely to be at least a decade in advance of equivalent NASA projects still being designed and, in most cases, not yet funded.[12]

China's scientific literature suggested an ambition to support decades' worth of expansion into space – developing, for example, a battery designed to draw chemicals from the Martian atmosphere to generate power without the need to bring energy from Earth.[13] Some of that activity was already taking place aboard the *Tiangong* station; more than 200 scientific projects were undertaken in its first three years of operation, which included tests of microchips and new synthetic materials, as well as the impact of prolonged spells in space on multiple organisms.[14]

As early as 2013 – when China became the first nation since the 1970s to land a new probe on the Moon – PRC scientists had talked of it as a potentially 'beautiful' source of resources to support further exploration into space.[15] Now it looked as though they might well beat the United States to get astronauts back to the lunar surface. The depth of China's programme, former NASA executive Daniel Dumbacher warned a Congressional panel in early 2025, meant that they were now comprehensively 'out-planning and outpacing' the United States. The next race to the Moon, he warned, was less about being 'first' – and much more about 'continuous presence, values and technical leadership'. China, he warned, was determined to become the dominant power through building its infrastructure first. 'China does what it says it's going to do, plus or minus a year,' he said, while describing US plans to get human astronauts back to the Moon by 2030 as 'very suspect' and already as having missed most of their key milestones.[16]

Beijing was also increasingly publicly committed to defending that position, including through cutting-edge robotics and threats of the use of force. As 2025 began, Chinese media reported the space station crew were using an AI-enabled robot known as 'Xiao Hang' – or 'Little Space' – to conduct maintenance and experiments,[17] but that was only the beginning. Five months later came the first serious suggestion that the *Tiangong* would be fitted to carry what sounded like its own weaponised armed drones. Described as for 'self-protection', the robots would grab hold of any approaching object to push it away. 'In such cases, we first try to assess their intent,' senior scientist Sun Zhibin from the National Space Science Centre said. 'Then we choose how to respond – whether by dodging, adjusting our orbit or releasing a small robot to try to grab the object.'

Chinese officials presented that decision as a natural and apparently reluctant response to the foreign spacecraft that had approached *Tiangong* ever since it was built in orbit, some of which they said had come close enough to endanger the station and its crew. Several of those craft, the Chinese clearly believed, came from the US military. The very first to approach the station, however, had been Starlink satellites owned by SpaceX, whose mercurial founder Elon Musk was already changing the rules for how humanity worked in space.[18]

*

The space race had, of course, always been driven by conflict, geopolitics and personal ambition. The first human object to enter space was a Nazi German V2 rocket largely built by slave labour and launched from the Baltic coast on June 20, 1944 by rocket pioneer Wernher von Braun barely a week after the D-Day invasion sealed the fate of Hitler's Reich. That rocket, fired directly upwards, was estimated to have reached roughly 100 miles above the Earth, well above the 62-mile 'Kármán Line' that would come to define the limits of space where the atmosphere thins to almost nothing.[19]

Less than two months later, the V2s began falling on London; the start of a campaign that continued until the very end of World War Two and killed several thousand people in Britain and the recently liberated parts of Western Europe. Even more – as many as 20,000 by some estimates – died as slave labourers working on the V2 rockets in horrific conditions, first at Peenemünde and then in deep concrete bunkers within Germany, as the Allies advanced towards Berlin.[20] Von Braun surrendered to the Americans in the last phase of the war, while Soviet troops took Nazi scientists into custody and both victorious nations seized as many of the German rockets as they could.

In fact, the first years of the Cold War would shape the space race well into the current century. The US ran its own rocket programme throughout the war, with a handful of guided missiles entering service by the end of the fighting – and one of its leading lights, by 1945 a colonel in the US Army service, was Chinese-born physicist and engineer Qian Xuesen. He had been fleeing China's civil war when he arrived in the US on a scholarship in the mid-1920s, his family connections placing him firmly on the side of Chiang Kai-shek rather than Mao's Communists.

Qian – who helped found the Jet Propulsion Laboratory in Pasadena, California, that went on to develop almost all of US spaceflight – was one of the first US personnel to debrief von Braun after his surrender. But while the former Nazi scientist would become the leading driver behind America's military rocketry and then NASA and the space programme, Qian found himself frozen out of US government circles after Mao's victory on the Chinese mainland led to the growing belief that all Chinese were Communists. His position became even grimmer after the outbreak of the Korean War in 1951, leading to his deportation back to China in 1955.

Whether he was truly a spy while in US service is impossible to say – although, like many of the top scientists of his day, he may well have attended some Communist meetings and perhaps even joined the US Communist Party. Even if his loyalties were firmly with the Eastern Bloc, those who knew his work felt returning him to China was a grave mistake: former Navy Secretary Dan Kimball described it as 'the stupidest thing this country ever did . . . He was no more Communist than I was'.

Whatever the truth of his loyalties, Qian appears to have gone straight to work for the PRC as soon as he arrived. By the time of his death in 2009 at the age of 99, Chinese official media credited him as the father of Beijing's atomic weapons, rocketry and space programmes. By then, Beijing had put its own first astronaut in space (in 2003) and was starting to use its vast resources and high economic growth to challenge US dominance in space.[21]

But that was not the only way in which the ghosts of the past would shape the space race of the 2020s and beyond. As von Braun began his own personal propaganda campaign to encourage space exploration in the early 1950s, he wrote a range of popular science and science-fiction pieces designed to fan enthusiasm. One of them, *The Mars Project*, imagined a future colony on the planet in the 1980s overseen by a brilliant administrator known as 'the Elon'. According to Errol Musk, father of the future space entrepreneur, that name in that book had been one of the inspirations for naming his son – although Elon was also a family name.[22] Both Musks have been often unreliable narrators, but by the 2020s the younger Musk had turned that detail into part of his own personal legend – and it fuelled his conviction that it was his destiny to take mankind to Mars, whatever that might take.

*

Even by his own accounts, Errol Musk was not an easy father. Elon's decision to emigrate to the US in 1989 as soon as he turned 18 appears to have been, in part, a move to get away from him – but at least one biography suggests he was also keen to avoid conscription into the apartheid military, which continued for white South Africans until 1993.[23]

By the late 1990s, Musk was a rising name in the fast-growing world of electronic commerce, becoming CEO of PayPal before being ousted in a 2000 boardroom coup masterminded in part by future right-wing billionaire Peter Thiel. Thiel went on to found defence data giant Palantir and bankroll a generation of politicians including Trump and JD Vance. But Musk was able to retain good relations with both Thiel and other PayPal investors, opening the door to future ventures.[24]

Shortly after leaving PayPal, Musk was (according to his own story) browsing the NASA website looking for its plans to go to Mars and was shocked to find that it did not appear to have any. 'I have always wanted to do something in space,' he said to a friend. 'I'm going to colonise Mars,' he told a group of PayPal former colleagues a few weeks later. 'My mission in life is to make mankind a multi-planetary civilisation.' 'Dude, you're bananas,' one of his ex-colleagues told him.[25]

Those who worked with him say Musk started with the idea of space colonisation and then worked backwards to make a space and rocket business. It was not an easy journey – in 2008, both SpaceX and Tesla, the electric car company he ran in tandem, almost unravelled into bankruptcy. But by the end of the 2000s SpaceX had a working rocket – the *Falcon 9* – capable of delivering payloads into orbit, including for NASA and the Pentagon, and was in discussions to deliver a manned rocket.[26]

What Musk realised faster than many others was that the microelectronics revolution would make satellites much smaller. That, in turn, created a huge opportunity for whoever could build the smaller rockets that could launch them, ones much cheaper than the larger Cold War-era boosters other firms relied on, often launched from Russia. By the end of 2010s SpaceX was also operating the largest rockets in service, now becoming even more central for the operations of NASA and the Pentagon as well as private sector clients, and galloping far ahead of other billionaire rivals also keen to make their mark in space.

It was still a bumpy ride. In 2018, Musk launched a red Tesla Roadster sports car from the top of a SpaceX rocket he said was intended to hurl towards Mars, complete with a dummy driver and the David Bowie tracks 'Life on Mars' and 'Space Oddity' continuously on loop. But while the vehicle escaped Earth's gravity, it missed the red planet by a substantial margin to fall into an orbit around the Sun.[27]

It was a reminder of how much more challenging Musk's Mars ambitions were compared to all he'd achieved so far. By 2019, some major investors were also becoming alarmed by his outspoken and apparently often unfiltered use of social media – at one point revealing sensitive corporate data potentially in breach of US market regulations. One investor described him on Twitter as acting 'like a child'.[28]

By then, however, the first Starlink satellites were being unloaded into orbit from SpaceX's Falcon rockets. Three years later, Musk would purchase Twitter and rename it 'X'. It was a move that would bring him firmly into the political arena, with all its controversy and distractions.[29]

By the time Russia invaded Ukraine in February 2022, Musk was estimated to be worth more than $400 billion and was already a household name. As Putin's troops advanced towards Kyiv, Musk's new Starlink satellites became critical on the battlefield. Within weeks of the invasion, with Russia targeting communications with bombs, missiles and cyber attacks, white oval and rectangular Starlink receivers became ubiquitous across the wartorn nation. Speaking to a Politico podcast a few weeks later, journalist Christopher Miller described how troops would often dig a shallow trench several inches deep to protect them from shrapnel and bullets while still being able to receive information from the low-orbit satellites above.

Those satellite connections were then used for everything from Zoom conversations with commanders to plotting the positions of enemy troop and vehicle concentrations – as well as private conversations with family and playing computer games to stave off boredom (this was still early in the war, when neither side had yet refined their capabilities to track electronic emissions and destroy their source, a development that would spur yet more abrupt changes in technology but make it harder to use Starlink in frontline positions).

Even before the conflict, Miller said, technology-focused Ukrainians had developed something of a Musk obsession – Teslas were more common in Kyiv than most other European cities – and this was only deepened by the war. 'There's something Ukrainians like about Elon Musk,' Miller said in 2022. 'They like the fact that there is this controversial billionaire helping them.'[30] 'The huge number of lives that Starlink has saved can be measured in the thousands,' said Ukraine Minister of Digital Transformation Mykhailo Fedorov in 2023, telling journalists that Ukrainian artillery units could use it to get target information 20 times faster than at the beginning of the conflict. That, of course, meant that Starlink was also helping kill Russians.

Problems emerged most significantly from October 2022 – the same point that the US and several European governments began to worry that Russia might go nuclear. Musk ordered the service to be shut down in regions of government-held Ukraine on the borders of Crimea, cutting a key communications system just as the government in Kyiv was preparing to attack. This was not how contractors and service providers were expected to behave in a military campaign – but Musk was no ordinary businessman, SpaceX no ordinary business and Starlink in 2022 was approaching a monopoly.

Nowhere was more worried than Taiwan, with military posturing by China increasing almost every month and a growing number of its undersea communication cables were being cut. In the event of a blockade, the government in Taipei would be desperate to keep communications open – and Starlink no longer looked like a reliable provider.

The biggest problem was Musk himself, and his other business interests – it had not escaped the notice of Taiwanese officials that roughly half of Musk's Tesla cars were built in mainland China. Even before the Ukraine war, Taiwan had been looking for another option: in June 2023, Taiwan's Minister of Digital Affairs was in meetings with British-based OneWeb, a rival firm to Starlink that had gone bankrupt but had been bailed out by the British government.[31]

Britain's own historic efforts in space had been relatively limited: post-war governments refused to pay for a fantastically mad scheme to put an astronaut in the nose of an enlarged German V2 rocket to become the first person in space almost a decade before the US and Soviet Union attempted such a thing.[32] But by the 2020s, space was no longer an arena that could simply be ignored – and it was one in which losing that connectivity could cost not just a single conflict but the survival of a nation and welfare of its economy.

*

The Ukraine conflict made Musk more controversial – but it also entrenched his dominance, not least because Western sanctions meant rival operators could no longer use Russia's space agency to launch their platforms. By 2023, the 4,500 satellites supporting Starlink made up an astounding 50 per cent of all the 7,000-plus working satellites in orbit. Even OneWeb, the second largest and second fastest-growing operator – with some 700 low Earth orbiting satellites by the end of 2023 – paid SpaceX to launch some of its rockets after its Russian launch plans unravelled.

Traditional communications satellites often sit in geosynchronous orbit some 22,000 miles above the planet. The Low Earth Orbit (LEO) satellites by Starlink and OneWeb are usually stationed less than 400 miles above the Earth and move at high speed, each able to cover a relatively small patch of ground beneath – but a constellation of several hundred, and certainly several thousand, can deliver global coverage.

As former RAF officer turned OneWeb executive Chris Moore explained to me in 2023, each satellite was the size of a washing machine – and they were travelling at more than 16,000 miles per hour: 'It is difficult to jam because it's moving so quickly, and you have multiple satellites in view at any one time.' But he acknowledged that making the business itself work was something of a 'rollercoaster', with the firm merging with French operator Eutelsat – also government-backed – not long after its UK government bailout.[33]

The Ukraine conflict marked the start of an era of dramatically increased confrontation and conflict in both near and far Earth orbit, much of it initially classified and only gradually leaking into the public sphere. Ever since the Soviet satellite *Sputnik* first circled the world in 1957, major powers had used them to observe their rivals, detect changes in defence posture and deliver early warnings. By the 1980s, both the US and Soviet Union had satellite systems at the heart of their early warning systems, while in the post-Cold War world the US had enjoyed decades of dominance in which its spy satellites were unmatched. That, however, was starting to change fast by the early 2020s.

By 2021, Chinese surveillance satellites were described as hoovering up geographical and resource data – for instance, far out at sea and in disputed maritime zones, locations where undersea mining might one day be possible with drones.[34] The new and more powerful platform *Yaogan-41*, sitting in geostationary orbit more than 20,000 miles above the Earth, was able to see huge areas, including Taiwan and the South China Sea, with obvious military implications. 'Paired with AI algorithms and sufficient computational resources, capabilities afforded by *Yaogan-41* will make it more difficult for the United States and its allies to hide vessels larger than an automobile in the Indian and Pacific oceans, other than submarines,' wrote the Centre for Strategic and International Studies.[35]

In the event of a major war, taking out or blinding *Yaogan-41* might well be a top US priority: the US, Russia and China had previously demonstrated the ability to strike and destroy objects in orbit, always criticising each other when they did so. The side effects of debris from such strikes was hugely unpredictable, hence the new focus on grappling with and breaking satellites. But the ability to strike objects in orbit was getting closer all the time, and the planning for it ever more intense. In May 2025, private sector analysts Slingshot Aerospace said a Russian 'space object' – dubbed *Cosmos-2588* – was likely deliberately 'chasing' a US government satellite and might have the ability to destroy it.[36]

Two months earlier, the US Space Force reported five Chinese 'objects' practising what General Michael Guetlein called 'dogfighting in space . . . manoeuvring in about around each other in synchronicity and in control'. Guetlein described efforts by potential hostile nations to shadow US satellites as a 'cat-and-mouse game', adding that they were also conducting cyber attacks on US space infrastructure such as satellites and ground stations on an almost daily basis.[37]

The US had its own 'unmanned spaceplane', the still largely secret X-37B, which had touched down in Vandenberg Space Force Base in California at the start of March 2025 after more than 434 days in orbit on a classified mission. The US Space Force revealed it had conducted a breakthrough series of 'aerobreaking' manoeuvres in which it used atmospheric friction to change course in orbit. Space Force described the performance as proof that the US could continue to 'push the boundaries of novel space operations' in a 'safe and responsible manner'.[38]

US officials found much to criticise in Beijing's approach to space. In 2007, China had used a missile to destroy one of its own cold weather satellites in orbit, creating more than 3,000 trackable pieces of debris that still posed a risk to satellites and the International Space Station almost two decades later. Those serving in US military space operations at the time described it as a 'pivot point', the first moment in which leaders and planners truly began to think of space as a potential future battlefield.[39] Others argued the US had itself been quietly militarising space since at least the 1980s, when it had shot down one of its own satellites with a specialist high-altitude missile launched from an F-15 fighter.[40]

The resulting orbital debris, however, was now a growing worry. When Russia conducted its own anti-satellite weapon test in November 2021, just as it assembled troops on Ukraine's border for the forthcoming invasion,[41] US officials judged the time had come for Washington to announce a moratorium on anti-satellite weapon testing, hoping other states would do the same. 'Simply put, these tests are too dangerous and we will not conduct them,' said Vice President Kamala Harris as she announced the ban in April 2022.[42]

US officials remained worried by a Russian satellite launched shortly after the Ukraine conflict began – *Cosmos-2553* – suspected to be a radar radiation sensor satellite for a future space-based atomic weapon that could blind and destroy other satellites. By spring 2025, private firms tracking objects in space noted that

Cosmos-2553 had suffered some form of catastrophic failure. It was spinning wildly and was apparently no longer under the control of its Russian operators.[43]

Clearly, activity in space was evolving very fast. One thing that was not progressing nearly as well as planned, however, was America's civilian manned space programme under NASA.

*

In May 2024, the three men and one woman who were scheduled to become the first humans to leave low Earth orbit in the 52 years since the last Moon landing in 1972 climbed into the *Artemis* capsule to simulate their mission. 'The training team did a great job,' said Canadian astronaut Jeremy Hansen, set to be the first non-American to go beyond low Earth orbit. 'We didn't simulate launch – but once we got orbit, we simulated getting things out, making sure the water system [was] working, setting up the toilet . . . going through that whole choreography, all the way until we set up our sleeping bags and then go to bed.'[44]

The NASA *Artemis II* mission was not intended to land on the lunar surface itself, just to travel the roughly quarter-million miles to the Moon, fly around it and return to Earth. In 2022, *Artemis I* had made the trip unmanned, testing the new NASA Space Launch System booster – the largest rocket ever made, bigger even than the *Saturn V* of the 1960s or Musk's *Falcon Heavy* that had been the previous largest rocket of the current century. Even more important was the *Orion* capsule that would protect the crew – and that was where the problems started. According to NASA officials late in 2024, the heat shield on the *Orion* capsule did not function as well as hoped – and if the astronauts could not return to Earth safely from their trip, then they could not be launched at all.[45]

By the middle of 2025, the launch of *Artemis II* was scheduled for spring 2026, with *Artemis III* supposed to land astronauts on the Moon's surface itself in 2027. But there remained hefty

scepticism over whether those dates were achievable, particularly the latter. The 21st century had not been kind to NASA
when it came to human spaceflight. In February 2003, the space
shuttle *Columbia* had disintegrated over the southern United
States as it returned to Earth. That doomed the shuttle programme, with its last mission taking place in 2011 – and from
that point on the US was forced to rely on Russian rockets to get
its personnel to and from the International Space Station. It was
an embarrassment the Kremlin was happy to exploit: 'You go
to space because we take you,' Russia's ambassador to Washington told an event I attended in the city in 2013.

The Space Launch System and *Orion* capsule were NASA's
attempts to change that: to be built by the government itself,
with NASA also intending to use the new Starliner from Boeing
and the Dragon from SpaceX to support further human
spaceflight. As of mid-2025, none were really working – and,
most damaging of all, the issues with Starliner occurred just
after the craft had deposited two US astronauts on the
International Space Station. Not until Musk's Dragon – which
had flown its own first manned mission into orbit in 2019 – was
ready to retrieve the pair of astronauts in March 2025 could
they be returned to Earth; what should have been a week-long
mission instead lasted for nine months.[46]

The nine months those two astronauts – Butch Wilmore and
Suni Williams – were trapped in orbit saw Musk become hugely
more political, first appearing on a podcast with Trump and
then comprehensively endorsing him as the election neared.
From July 2024, Musk became a campaign mainstay – the
hugely impressive imagery of his SpaceX gantry catching a
reusable Starship booster as it returned to Earth was an easy
addition to Trump's messaging that Musk understood how
business worked and how it could be used to do amazing things.
Trump entered the White House promising to get to both the
Moon and Mars, while Musk appeared an almost permanent
White House resident.

The question was whether that relationship would last – and how playing politics might gel with Musk's desire to push further into space. The initial signs were mixed: SpaceX's new Starship booster appeared to be advancing well in 2024. But early 2025 saw repeated setbacks, including multiple explosions destroying several boosters.[47]

To minimise the distance, Musk hoped to launch a Starship towards Mars when the planets next aligned at the end of 2026, with the rocket arriving in 2027. The only passenger, he said, would be an Optimus humanoid robot, one of the latest products built by Tesla. Musk hoped to send further rockets in every launch window – roughly every two years – including humans as soon as possible. That Mars programme had no relationship with NASA – it was Musk pushing out into space on his own.[48]

But the Starship booster was also scheduled to take the crew of *Artemis III* to the Moon as soon as 2027 – in part in acknowledgement of the problems with the NASA-built Space Launch System used on the first two Artemis missions. Each Starship failure pushed that mission back, knocking the entire US space programme off its schedule. Essentially, SpaceX had thrust forward so fast that it was becoming a single point of failure for US activity in space, both civilian and military – and this would become more of a problem as relations between Musk and Trump broke down.

China, meanwhile, kept on pushing ahead. When journalists from Spain's *El País* newspaper visited China's Jiuquan launch facility in the Gobi desert in April 2025, they found crowds of visitors from as far away as Shanghai waving flags and singing patriotic anthems. One huge billboard showed an image of President Xi, tellingly in military uniform, encouraging the public to 'explore the vast universe' and 'build a powerful space country'. The comparison with the mercurial progress of Musk and the US space programme was obvious – a spokesman for China's space agency told reporters preparations for a moon landing by 2030 were 'proceeding satisfactorily'.

Unauthorised briefings on that progress were ruthlessly discouraged. 'Leaking secrets leads to imprisonment; protecting secrets brings happiness; selling secrets leads to execution,' read another enormous sign, together with a telephone number to report acts of espionage.[49] That, of course, was likely even more true when it came to Beijing's military activities in space.

In time, China's International Lunar Research Station wrapped in other partners: in May 2025, Russia and China signed a deal to provide a nuclear reactor for the station by 2036.[50] Unlike the joint Russian–US deal that administered the International Space Station, this would still be a Chinese-run station, with Beijing calling the shots. Other international partners include Senegal, United Arab Emirates, Serbia, Switzerland, Indonesia, Pakistan, Panama and South Africa,[51] all part of Beijing's long-term strategy to embrace the 'global south' and other 'neutral' nations.

That looked like a response to NASA's Artemis programme, which included more than 50 international partnerships built around a manned return to the Moon and progression onto Mars.[52] But as NASA administrator Bill Nelson warned as he left office at the end of 2024, the Artemis programme itself was in growing trouble and the small 'Gateway' space station designed to sit near the Moon was on the brink of cancellation. 'We must have a shared sense of urgency among all these partners,' he said. 'It is vital for us to land on the south pole so we do not cede portions of the lunar south pole to the Chinese.'[53]

The US and China were not the only players – but they were the most important. In August 2023, India landed its own robot probe near the lunar south pole, the first nation to do so – and a reminder that it too saw expansion into space as key to both national prestige and future resources.[54] As NASA struggled for sufficient funding, the private sector space race, however, was still powering ahead in low Earth orbit – as was its military counterpart.

Worldwide, the total mass launched into space more than doubled from 2022 to 2024 – and without Musk the US might well have been outdone by China. In 2024, however, SpaceX was responsible for 134 successful launches – more than half the global total – with state-owned China Aerospace and Science Corporation the second largest worldwide with 47 launches.[55]

Each Chinese launch, like those of Russia, was closely scrutinised by America's new space warriors – or 'guardians', as they were known officially. In the event of a fight in space, part of their job would be to attempt to safeguard the critical global positioning and communications satellites on which much of the Earthbound economy depended, from financial markets to the supply chain for food and other essential products. The more contested and congested space becomes, the harder that will be.

Throughout the first months of 2025, US military comments on space shifted noticeably to a much more hawkish stance. For years, senior US military leaders had talked of the importance of space to all nations, and of their hopes that it would remain an area of international co-operation. Now they were talking of potential war, and the need for preparedness and deterrence. 'There has never been a war in space and we don't want a war to start in space or extend into space,' US Space Command chief General Stephen Whiting told a conference in Colorado in April 2025. 'But we must apply our best thinking to be ready.'[56] Addressing a Chicago think tank a few weeks later, Whiting got even more specific, saying Xi's order to his military to be ready to attack Taiwan by 2027 delivered 'urgency' to his command. 'What we are doing every day is planning so that we are ready to conduct operations in space if there is a conflict.'[57]

The fact that the US had both a 'Space Force' and 'Space Command' was a cause for confusion, as was the fact that General Whiting was part of the first – although not its chief; that was another general – while leading the latter. As he was forced to explain incessantly, the situation was neither as contradictory nor as complex as it immediately looked.

The US Space Force, its creation ordered by Trump in 2019, was the newest of the armed services, the first to be created since the US Air Force had been cut out of the US Army in 1947. That had been relatively late to create an independent air force – but it was still less than 30 years after Britain's RAF had become the first such service in the world (officers in the British Army and Royal Navy spent the decade leading up to the RAF's 2018 centenary suggesting that it should not take that for granted, repeatedly referring to it as 'the Hundred Year Experiment'). By the 2020s, the fact that many navies and armies might soon be operating more – if smaller – flying drones than their nation's air forces was raising awkward questions.

The underlying purpose of US Space Force was to provide personnel and necessary equipment, including space drones, satellites and military space platforms like the X-37B. It was also its responsibility to get craft into orbit, contracting firms like SpaceX for the satellite-launch capacity that was becoming increasingly sought after.

US Space Command (SPACECOM), meanwhile, was a 'combatant command' that drew its personnel from across the US forces – although many came from Space Force. Like most of the other US combatant commands, including AFRICOM, EUCOM and INDOPACOM, that meant its 'area of responsibility' was bounded geographically. As its commander General Whiting put it, SPACECOM's responsibilities began at 'the Kármán Line' and then ran out 'to infinity'.

Like other combatant chiefs – and particularly Samuel Paparo in the Pacific – Whiting and a significant proportion of his staff spent much of their time preparing war plans for how America and its allies would fight in his designated region. Also like them, he was in constant contact with allies and partners, running never-ending training intended not simply as preparation for war but, in some cases, to be noticed by potential foes.

It also meant working relentlessly with companies, large and small, to provide the capability to operate in space and fight if need be. Space Command chief General Whiting noted that it was US private companies that were driving space innovation, with much of the activity in low orbit. That, indeed, was one of the NASA justifications for abandoning the International Space Station – the idea of low orbit becoming 'privatised'. Several billionaires had their own space companies now, from Amazon founder Jeff Bezos with 'Blue Origin' to Britain's Richard Branson with 'Virgin Galactic'.

In reality all of those were small compared to SpaceX – but, as with NASA, the US military was keen to move on from dependency on that firm and its unpredictable billionaire boss.

'We can't rely on one company to always be there for us,' said Colonel Douglas Pentecost, director of enterprise at Space Systems Command, responsible for getting US military satellites including 'super secret' instruments into orbit. 'That's basically taking us back to the 1980s, when we were relying on the space shuttle. And then when the space shuttle had its unfortunate accident, we had no way into space for several years.' In an effort to reduce their dependence, the US created a partnership of Lockheed Martin and Boeing, known as the 'Launch Alliance', as well as smaller firms, to get military payloads into orbit, hoping to diversify its options.[58]

In reality, in comparison to the twin-track – but still very tightly managed – civilian and military approach to space that had taken America to the Moon and helped it to Cold War victory, America's space industry landscape of the 2020s came to resemble more a battlefield between multiple feuding empires. Jared Isaacman, Trump's first pick for NASA administrator in his second term, was seen by many as the most likely to be able to handle that. Instead, his nomination would mark the start of even greater chaos.

Aged 42 when nominated, Isaacman had left school at 16 but then got rich – like Musk – working in the growing online payment sector at the beginning of the century, moving into aviation and then space. By the early 2020s he had become the first non-government-trained astronaut to lead missions in orbit aboard SpaceX-built Dragon rockets.

In his confirmation hearing at the Senate, Isaacman described NASA as 'the most accomplished space agency in the world', but warned that most of its projects were over budget and behind schedule. 'I know it is not lost on any members of this committee that we have geopolitical rivals moving at impressive speeds,' he said. 'If confirmed, I will work alongside and recruit the most talented minds in this nation so that we can concentrate our resources towards achieving the near impossible – the objectives that no other agency, company or institution is capable of achieving.'[59]

What that meant was getting the Artemis programme – or a version of it – to the Moon, and making it part of Trump and Musk's pledge to go to Mars. It would have to happen on the back of a pared-back budget and staffing roster – among the administration's most recent decisions had been the abolition of the NASA 'chief scientist' position. Still, despite that, Isaacman enjoyed broad cross-party support in Congress as well as the wider space, aviation and engineering sectors.

Until June 2025, that promised good things in space for the US. Then, despite an initial Senate committee confirmation, Trump withdrew Isaacman's nomination, citing a review of 'prior associations'. That appeared to be a reference to Isaacman's donations to the Democratic Party as recently as the previous year, apparently enough to fail an 'America First' purity test.[60]

That was unsettling enough, even before Musk rapidly delivered a second blow to US space credibility. On the back of the poor performance of Musk's Starship launcher in the first months of the year which suggested his ambition to get the first unmanned Starship all the way to Mars – a six-month journey[61] – by 2026 might be fast unravelling, deteriorating relations with the president produced a torrent of social media posts attacking Trump's budget, accusing him of being featured in the files of deceased sex offender Jeffrey Epstein – plus a threat to begin disassembling the SpaceX Dragon human spaceflight rocket.[62]

Musk swiftly withdrew almost all of the above – but the Dragon threat was no small thing. Plenty of contracts and the entire US human space programme – including the astronauts stuck on the ISS – depended on that rocket. As with Starlink in Ukraine, Musk was inadvertently bringing into question his entire credibility as a provider of space services. And he was doing so at the exact point when Trump's firing of Isaacman left the space programme rudderless. 'This is not how space policy should be made nor in my experience has been made,' warned former NASA Deputy Administrator Lori Garver. 'All of this brings into question everything about our current space programme and agenda.'[63]

Events were about to become more dramatic still. Speaking in the Oval Office, the president unexpectedly announced that Chairman of the Joint Chiefs of Staff General Dan Caine was 'going to pick somebody' as the new head of NASA and that subsequently somebody else 'will be checking them out'. Given that NASA was not part of the military, this was very unusual – and prompted speculation that the military wanted a greater say in US space policy. A day later, a White House official told Military.com that Caine would be making sure candidates matched 'America First' values and Trump's 'vision' for getting humanity to Mars. For many, this was even more disturbing.[64]

A much more successful test of Musk's Starship rocket in summer 2025 was seen to put the firm back into contention for the race to the Moon and Mars – although some of the reputational damage to SpaceX seemed more permanent.[65]

Meanwhile, however, China's space programme was also breaking new ground. In particular, China's activities around its Moon mission – and specifically its operations in 'cislunar space', the area of space in which gravity from the Moon and Earth can hold satellites in place – offered an opportunity to threaten US surveillance satellites from above, potentially without any warning. 'Most satellites are looking down, so they won't see what is above or behind them,' warned space policy expert Namrata Goswami.[66] In April 2025, China's space scientists announced their first satellite constellation in cislunar space, with at least three satellites providing connectivity for China's activities on the Moon – and whatever else they might be doing. Getting them into stable positions had proved a considerable challenge, they said – but they had succeeded.[67] That had particular potential implications for the proposed US 'Golden Dome', expected to be heavily dependent on space sensors.

In October 1957, the Soviet Union's launch of *Sputnik* had shocked Americans with a new sense of vulnerability, not least because another nation could do something theirs could not. Now the entire world was dependent on satellites, and any fighting in space could cause untold disruption. In any major conflict, the dark reaches of cislunar orbit might prove just as important as the Taiwan Strait or the Narva River. In the summer of 2025, however, there was simply just too much going on for obscure satellites to seize headlines. By the middle of the year, the US was firmly distracted by the Middle East, while Elon Musk was talking of starting his own political party – and both of those developments looked like they might be good news for Beijing.

15

'A Very Dangerous Decade'

'An obsession with tactical cleverness, coupled with a lack of strategic wisdom, may be the most dangerous form of folly.'

**Colonel Wang Xiangsui, former People's
Liberation Army officer, 2025**[1]

In the early hours of June 13, 2025, Israel took the targeting techniques it had honed in Gaza – identifying key figures and their homes using advanced technology and data crunching, then striking in the small hours of the morning – and unleashed a flurry of attack drones and missiles against the top figures in the Iranian military and atomic programme. As they did so, Israeli aircraft took advantage of the damage done to Iranian air defences in the strikes the previous year to hit remaining air defences, weapons factories and nuclear enrichment sites.

It was a surprise attack designed not just to disrupt the Iranian military machine, but also to demonstrate Israeli reach and undermine the legitimacy of the Islamic Republic. In its opening days, Israeli hackers also briefly seized control of Iranian television to broadcast a call for popular revolution – although Israeli Prime Minister Benjamin Netanyahu made it clear Israel's priority was to destroy Tehran's nuclear programme and the missiles that might carry it.

Launched only 12 days after Ukraine's Operation SPIDER'S WEB had hit Russia's bomber fleet, Israel's RISING LION operation similarly used drones, AI and espionage to strike at the heart of a well-defended police state and militarised regime. In the words of one Israeli security official, the operation relied on 'groundbreaking thinking, both planning and surgical operation of advanced technologies, special forces and agencies operating in the heart of Iran while evading the eyes of local intelligence'. According to Israeli security officials, they had even persuaded some Iranian firms to manufacture the drones without any idea who they were working for. Other drones, or their components, were smuggled in by land, sea and even inside suitcases.[2] The results were both precise and devastating: almost a complete decapitation strike on the Iranian military and Revolutionary Guard. Mohammad Bagheri, Chief of Staff of the Iranian Armed Forces, and its most senior military officer, was killed with his wife and daughter. So was Revolutionary Guard chief Hossein Salami and more than a dozen atomic scientists.[3] In total, Israel claimed to have killed more than ten Iranian senior military leaders – although at least one later appeared alive – once what would become known as the 'twelve-day war' concluded.[4]

For decades, military commanders and thriller writers had fantasised about such highly accurate targeting on this scale – but it had rarely been possible, as shown by the failed attempts to kill Saddam Hussein during the 2003 Iraq invasion. This time, though, there was little disbelief when both Netanyahu and Trump both warned they knew where Iranian Supreme Leader Ali Khamenei was hiding. The US president claimed it was only his restraining hand on the US and Israeli militaries that was keeping the Iranian alive.[5]

For years, security analysts had warned that any Israeli strike against Iran might trigger region-wide conflagration. As well as the drones and rockets now being fired nightly at Israel, Iran had spent years building up its coastal missile batteries and fleets of fast-attack boats – long believed to be part of a deliberate strategy to close off access to the Strait of Hormuz and block the export of Gulf oil and gas in a major conflict. Then there were the Houthis in Yemen, damaged but not destroyed by US airstrikes – not to mention Iran's long-established capabilities to mount attacks on foreign targets overseas.

Once Israel's strikes were underway, however – and particularly given the almost complete destruction of Iranian proxies in Gaza, Lebanon and Syria – Tehran's actual options looked considerably narrower. Going on the offensive against international shipping would almost certainly pull the US into the conflict much more deeply, potentially prompting the destruction of the remaining military and security forces keeping the Iranian leadership in place.

For almost two weeks, Israel and Iran kept up their nightly exchange of drones and missiles, while the world waited to see what Trump might do. In Moscow and Beijing, meanwhile, those preparing China and Russia for future wars appeared to scent both opportunity and danger.

*

For all the enthusiasm for the innovation shown by Israel and Ukraine, Western militaries were grimly aware of their own vulnerability to sudden drone attack. In the US, China's data breaches of both the US government and telecoms databases meant they likely had plenty of addresses of individuals to target on the first stage of any war, not to mention other geo-located points including aircraft hangars, research hubs, ports and power stations.

The mid-2020s had already seen US air bases at home and abroad struggling with apparent incursions by unidentified drone swarms, while US Central Command had worked hard to increase counter-drone defences following a strike against the US patrol base on the Syria–Jordan border in January 2024 that killed three US personnel and injured almost 50. Speaking at his Senate confirmation hearing in June 2025, new CENTCOM chief Admiral Brad Cooper – previously deputy commander in the region – said US drone defences were now 'leaps and

bounds' ahead of where they had been then. 'The nature and
character of warfare is changing before our very eyes,' he said,
warning that both Russia and China were also working hard to
get new technology not just to Iran but also some of Tehran's
'proxies', particularly the Houthis.[6]

US Air Force Chief of Staff General David Allvin described
the SPIDER'S WEB strikes as a 'wake-up moment' for
militaries around the world. 'This shows us that seemingly
impenetrable locations are maybe not [impenetrable],' he said.
'We need to pay more attention to that.' That included ensuring
US bases had better countermeasures, even within the US
itself, he said – but it also meant integrating offensive drones to
'create dilemmas for our adversaries'. US military academic
Benjamin Jensen – director of the 'Futures Lab' at Washington
think tank the Centre for Strategic and International Studies,
and lecturer at the US Marine Corps War College – compared
the new style of drone assault deep inside hostile territory to the
'ungentlemanly warriors' pioneered by Britain's Special
Operations Executive and early special forces. But he warned
they could also render it much harder to manage escalation in a
confrontation – one that might involve atomic weapons.[7]

There was also the even larger question, of how much the US
should spend on defending its own homeland capabilities versus
its ability to act and strike. 'It really comes down to finding the
resources to meet all of our priorities,' said US Air Force chief
Allvin. 'Because if all we are doing is playing defence, and we
can't shoot back, then that's not a good use of our money.'[8]

This was the debate raging within China too. 'Such attacks
could easily be carried out by secret services or through special
military operations,' said Chinese aviation analyst and former
air force officer Fu Qianshao shortly after SPIDER'S WEB,
warning that there would need to be an increased effort to
guard against infiltration, whether by humans or drones.[9]

Others, however, argued that China's industrial strength
and mass-surveillance systems should give it a hefty inbuilt

advantage if it came to such a fight. Ever since 2013, all trucks in China had been required to register with the BeiDou navigation system which allowed them to be tracked, noted former PLA colonel turned author Wang Xiangsui. He argued that China's widespread surveillance programs should reduce the risk of infiltration, while the PLA should concentrate on doing as much damage as possible to Taiwan with airstrikes and missiles in the first days of any war.

But the most important lesson, he suggested, was that a nation like China or Russia must demonstrate the willpower to keep going with a conflict even in the face of an act of 'strategic cleverness' like SPIDER'S WEB. Only by doing so could they ensure eventual victory.[10]

China's military clearly had its own distracting issues, not least the ongoing removal of multiple generals and defence officials for alleged corruption, with the PLA's top political officer, supposedly the ideological guide for others, among the latest victims.[11]

One report from RAND in early 2025 suggested US and other Western analysts had overestimated Beijing's appetite for conflict. Others drew the opposite conclusions. Andrew Erickson, a leading Chinese security expert at the US Naval War College, noted that many of the recent removals appeared to be focused on increasing combat capability, warning that Xi was if anything doubling down on his emphasis on the importance of the PLA's readiness to fight.[12]

Certainly, with US forces distracted in the Middle East, the PLA Navy quickly seized the opportunity for a very public show of strength. When the US carriers *Vinson* and *Nimitz* left their normal positions in the Pacific for the Middle East in case of heightened conflict with Iran, China's first two carriers pushed deeper than they ever had before into the Western Pacific. The originally Ukraine-built *Liaoning* and her Chinese-built but largely identical sister ship *Shandong* were conducting wargames west of the Mariana Islands, simulating strikes against each other as well as defending themselves against air raids and long-range missiles.

The PLA Navy was not just drawing regional attention to the lack of US naval strength: it was reinforcing the narrative that the balance of power in the region had shifted for good – and that one day Beijing would dominate the entire Pacific west of the Midway Islands, or even as far as Hawaii.

Already, China's third carrier, the *Fujian* – much larger than the first two and a genuine counterpart to the large US carrier force – was conducting sea trials. An unnamed fourth nuclear-powered carrier was under construction and looked set to be even larger than the new USS *Ford*, making her the largest in the world. Within a decade, the PLA might field half a dozen carriers across the region if it wished – likely more than the US might be able to deploy there.[13]

Despite all the rhetoric from the Trump administration about fixing US shipbuilding – including setting up a special team within the White House – an independent review showed all but one of 59 major naval building projects were missing both schedule and budget targets. It was, administration officials warned, a sign that money alone was not enough to bring new submarines and warships into service.[14] Trump's new pick to head the US Navy, Admiral Darryl Caudle, had headed up US Fleet Forces Command since 2021, trying to fix that problem. Now he suggested US military shipyards should learn from cruise ship companies that turn around vessels within days or weeks in contrast to the naval norm of months or years.[15]

With the *Nimitz* headed for decommissioning and the second *Ford*-class carrier *Kennedy* behind schedule and not expected to enter service until 2027 at the earliest, America's 11-carrier fleet would be down to ten vessels for at least a year.[16] Ongoing submarine-building issues now also looked like they might have worsening strategic implications: reducing the number of new *Columbia*-class ballistic missile submarines available to carry America's nuclear deterrent, and leaving the US with insufficient

Virginia-class attack submarines to meet its own needs while also delivering submarines to Australia under the AUKUS deal.

That deal – already under Pentagon review at the apparent suggestion of Elbridge Colby – now looked ever more in question.[17] The fewer ships and submarines available, the more the US would need to fall back on drones and missiles – and it would have to hope that there were enough.

*

According to the highest Western calculations, Russian fatalities in Ukraine by the middle of 2025 likely topped 250,000 – by some estimates five times all Russian wartime losses since 1945.[18] Russia had now followed Ukraine in making the latest demographic numbers secret – but Putin was still not giving up. As a report from the Carnegie Endowment for International Peace described it, '. . . that gamble is not irrational from his point of view . . . A tired Ukraine, a divided West and a restrained United States suggest that time is on his side. He is gambling that prolonging the war will deliver more than settling it now.'[19]

The best way to force an end to fighting, some of Ukraine's supporters argued, was ensuring the Kyiv government was so well armed that Russia could not advance – so pursuing the war would become 'strategically pointless'.[20] On that front, rising use of drones had created a zone several miles either side of the frontline too dangerous for significant numbers of forces to move by foot or vehicle. Even electronic jamming was of only limited utility: in 2024 the Russians had pioneered using thin fibre-optic cables to control some of their hunter-killer drones. Cutting the cables – either with gunfire, another drone or even just because they became entangled in trees – could sometimes kill the drones, but plenty still got through, snaking through the trees and trenches to drop upon their targets.

As it had been throughout the war, the pace of innovation was relentless: Ukrainian troops told reporters they were now operating drones on fibre-optic cables as long as 20 miles in length, with Russian drone cables believed to be already twice that length. As well as the ubiquitous flying drones above the battlefield, crablike unmanned ground vehicles were also entering the fight, used for everything from moving supplies to kamikaze strikes. Unlike the Russians, Ukrainian commanders told reporters they could not afford to throw away soldiers 'like cans of meat'. The use of drones meant fewer soldiers were needed to hold ground; one commander said he believed Ukraine was 'well on the way' to an army of machines.[21] On occasion, Russian troops were said to have surrendered to Ukrainian drones without a single Ukrainian soldier being present – although such incidents were the exception rather than the rule.[22]

Having produced as many as a million short-range tactical drones in 2024, Ukraine now believed it would at least double that for 2025. But Ukrainian intelligence warned Russia might be producing considerably more, helped by increasing volumes of components shipped from China.[23] Russia was also able to avoid Ukraine's shortage of soldiers, largely because it was paying volunteers high and ever-growing salaries.[24] While Ukraine's drones were slowing the Russian advance, it continued very slowly. Having held roughly a third of the provinces of Donetsk and Luhansk in 2022, the Kremlin had more than doubled that by 2025, although British military intelligence assessed it might take the Kremlin until 2029 until they controlled both regions completely.[25]

For all the Trump-pushed talk of peace, some suspected most European governments would rather see fighting continue within Ukraine, worried that any pause would see tens of thousands of Russian troops returning to bases on the borders of eastern NATO states – potentially the beginning of a countdown to a much larger conflict. Beijing too appeared content – perhaps even keen – for the fighting to keep going. Meeting EU officials, Chinese Foreign Minister Wang Yi was said to have told European counterpart and former Estonian Prime Minister Kaja Kallas that the PRC was worried that the end of conflict in Ukraine would leave the US with more weaponry, resources and focus to turn to the Pacific.[26]

Not everyone, however, was so confident that the West could keep up with Moscow and Beijing, let alone manage to maintain dominance. US Army drone trials in Alaska showed the significant shortfalls of both training and equipment. 'We aren't giving the American war fighter what they need to survive warfare today,' said Trent Emeneker, project manager of the 'Autonomy Portfolio' at the Pentagon's Defense Innovation Unit. 'What we are trying to do is fix that.'[27] Trials of unmanned surface vessels conducted by the US Navy produced more bad news after two vessels were filmed colliding and another autonomously driven speedboat appeared to change speed spontaneously, throwing its captain overboard. Some of those issues appeared to be AI glitches while others were blamed on personnel and process. 'You have got a system that is used to building big things, taking years to make a decision and now suddenly you are asking them to move fast,' said autonomous weapons expert and Atlantic Council fellow T. X. Hammes.[28]

All of this, for now, pushed yet more money into the new 'defence tech' firms, as well as more traditional defence manufacturers and others including 'big tech' companies now moving further into defence-related work. According to one survey, investment in defence companies within Europe had already grown 30 per cent in the two years to the end of 2024, now accounting for 10 per cent of all venture capital funding on the continent.[29]

Such rapid growth, however, did not come without some strains. German tech firm Helsing also faced a string of negative headlines over supposedly overpriced and not always effective drones, said to be seven times more expensive but not notably more capable than those already being mass produced within Ukraine itself.[30]

Even US 'miltech' pioneer Palantir risked becoming a victim of its own success. By mid-2025, its status as a firm combining both the wider defence and AI booms saw its shares soar to the point that the firm was valued at $430 billion, more than 100 times its annual earnings – leading it to be described by the *Economist* as 'the most overpriced company in history'.[31] That was followed by a significant pullback in its share price, as well as mounting nervousness that there might not be enough contracts available for the growing number of new companies hoping to get rich.

As RAND Europe deputy director James Black pointed out, the growing defence tech arms race was likely to bring losers as well as winners – but that was if anything fuelling bigger bets. That included fast rising interest in the emerging 'quantum computing' sector, predicted to deliver exponentially more computing power and leading to governments and companies trying to get their hands on all kinds of encrypted data in the hope that new, more powerful computers would allow them to crack its codes and read it in the future.

'There is a belief in some quarters that that there could be a huge advantage in being the first to get there,' he told me. 'But in reality sometimes it's better to be second, you get to see where the first has made mistakes and so invest much smarter. Times of geopolitical tension have always pushed technology forward.'[32]

Among those selling defence technology in Europe, some quietly noted that Poland appeared to have rather less money than might be expected given its overall military spending. It wasn't hard to guess where that money might be going, several sources suggested, speculating that they might be working on a clandestine atomic programme in case all else went wrong.[33]

*

Amid wildly varying predictions over whether its Pentagon posture review would withdraw troops from multiple locations around the world or go the other way and step up forces, the Trump administration was keen to keep up pressure on even its closest allies to step up in their own backyards. When UK officials visited the Pentagon in mid-2025 to brief US officials on the upcoming visit of the HMS *Prince of Wales* carrier battle group to Asia, Elbridge Colby – fast exchanging his reputation for civility with one of excessive bluntness – shocked them by asking directly if it was too late to cancel the deployment and bring the vessels back to Europe.

The British team were said to be taken aback – with multiple diplomatic visits planned, the cruise could not really be cancelled.[34] This wasn't the first time senior US officials had suggested European nations should focus on their own backyard first before sending forces to Asia – but that message had not necessarily got through.[35] On a practical level, the US military was offering plenty of support, including escort by US air defence destroyers through Suez Canal and Red Sea waters, where the Houthis were still just about sticking to their deal not to launch attacks on allied shipping. But alongside the freezing out of the UK and other 'Five Eyes' allies from US intelligence on peace talks on Ukraine, it raised further questions over that relationship in future.[36]

Across Europe, there remained widespread worry that if they were forced to fight without US support, the forces available might prove totally inadequate. An unclassified wargame held in a basement in London in spring 2025 by Sky News and Tortoise Media – new publishers of the world's oldest Sunday newspaper the *Observer* – had put to the test what that meant for Britain. Pulling together a team of former senior government ministers, military commanders and other experts, it imagined a situation in which Islamist militants from within Russia attacked Russian military bases near Murmansk – which the Kremlin then blamed on the UK to justify attacking it with conventional cruise and ballistic missiles. Even with clear warning, the UK's meagre air defences were only able to protect two locations at once: the ballistic-missile submarine base at Faslane in Scotland, and its key airfields in East Anglia. By the end of the first exchanges, Britain had lost at least one aircraft carrier as well as a destroyer – both struck while tied up in harbour – the Ministry of Defence main building in Whitehall, GCHQ signals intelligence agency in Cheltenham and seven RAF jets destroyed on the ground at damaged air bases.

In return, Royal Navy submarines sank a Russian submarine and a destroyer – but the country was in chaos, even though UK casualties in the scenario were relatively light, with up to 100 people dead, including civilians killed in strikes on central London as well as Heathrow Airport. The Kremlin's next step was to use a midget submarine to cut key gas pipelines to Britain, crashing the power grid. Soon, the Prime Minister was attempting to browbeat a reluctant United States and NATO into joining in the fight and restocking the UK's empty weapons stores. 'Unless our allies give us their stuff [meaning weapons], it's over within a week,' said former general Richard Barrons, playing the UK defence chief.

The most telling point came when former Defence Minister Ben Wallace – playing the part of the prime minister – asked his military advisers to offer him his own 'strategic dilemmas' with which to threaten Russia, employing existing UK forces to constrain the Kremlin's options. Almost every conventional military suggestion suffered from the same underlying problem: it lacked at least one crucial item or capability vital for success.

According to experts and former officers advising on the wargame, Britain's stealth F-35B jets lacked any long-range missiles to hit heavily defended land or sea targets safely, while the older Eurofighters which did have missiles could be detected at much greater range and would therefore likely also be shot down. When Wallace wanted to send the elite 16 Air Assault Brigade to the Norwegian–Russian border for a potential move against Murmansk, he was told they lacked air defences, transport and armoured vehicles (unless Norway would provide them) and would likely be obliterated. Most ludicrous of all was the suggestion of using the one surviving aircraft carrier to land lightly armed Royal Marines and special forces on the Russian coast – likely another suicide mission. 'It's what we've got,' said one of the naval experts, laughing at the mess. By the end, the team were left considering either conducting a unilateral nuclear strike on Russia with Britain's Trident missiles – which Russia had already made it clear would trigger the UK's total annihilation – or some other long-term vengeance by more secret means.[37]

Admittedly, when the UK did operate with allies it was still capable of delivering effect: one NATO exercise in mid-summer 2025 saw British paratroopers dropping onto the Swedish island of Gotland to link up with Swedish conscripts and reservists and then secure a runway for US and British transport planes to bring in missile launchers that could dominate the nearby Baltic.[38] Later in the summer, British Poseidon submarine-anti-aircraft joined US and Norwegian counterparts in a real-life hunt for a Russian *Kilo*-class diesel submarine believed to be shadowing the *Ford* carrier battle group in the North Atlantic.

But for a country that at 2024 prices had spent more than £500 billion on defence over the preceding decade (more than $650 billion), it was not a great display.[39] Equally striking was that while almost all of the Sky News wargame participants now said more needed to be spent, none of those who had spent much of the previous era at the top of government appeared willing to take responsibility for the current situation. 'I couldn't keep listening to it – I just got too angry,' one former defence insider told me – although others told me they welcomed the popular podcast as highlighting the need for much more money.[40]

The UK Strategic Defence Review, published on the second day of June, was supposed to deliver fixes: or as Prime Minister Keir Starmer put it, to shift the nation to 'a wartime footing'. In his introduction, Starmer pledged to oversee 'the biggest shift in mindset in my lifetime: to put security and defence front and centre – to make it the fundamental organising principle of government'. But that change would require yet more money, even beyond the pledge already made to Trump to spend 2.5 per cent of GDP by 2027 and 3 per cent by 2034. Defence Minister John Healey also told Parliament he did not expect an immediate fix to declining personnel numbers. 'We have still got more people leaving than joining,' he said.

The Strategic Defence Review's 62 recommendations ranged from the genuinely revolutionary to the minuscule, while many noticed that it contained the word 'innovation' on almost every page. Genuinely major reform included following smaller European forces in empowering Britain's chief of defence staff to dictate policy direct to the individual service chiefs, ending decades – centuries for the navy and army – in which each had been run as largely separate fiefdoms.

Other recommendations would require a huge amount of effort: not least taking the British Army's two underequipped and undermanned divisions – the majority of its fighting force – and turning them into a larger corps-sized unit that could be used effectively by NATO from the start of any conflict. Pulling that together, at least, meant that process could be led by a single ambitious corps commander, a lieutenant general who, if they were successful, might well find themselves as defence chief in due course. Other measures, such as growing the school-based military cadet force numbers by 30 per cent by 2030, would require multiple volunteers, including teachers, not to mention teenagers themselves. Over time, the review wanted 250,000 teenagers to be going through some form of cadet programme. That was roughly double the present numbers[41] – and for the first time the cadet programme was being explicitly linked to preparedness for conflict.

How 13-year-olds and their parents might react to that – or even who was to lead that conversation nationally or locally – was simply not described. Beyond the building of six new weapons factories to redress the shortage of munitions, there was little in the way of detail on a National Defence Preparedness Act to make the country much more broadly ready for a conflict than the Wargame podcast had just shown. For all the talk of drones, there was still a hefty focus on more traditional 'big buy' items, particularly ships and planes: anti-submarine frigates, air-defence destroyers, nuclear-capable F-35A jets and atomic submarines. By the middle of the 2030s, a new 'boat' – either a *Dreadnought*-class ballistic missile carrier or an AUKUS attack submarine to hunt enemy subs and ships – was scheduled to leave the giant Barrow-in-Furness manufacturing sheds every 18 months.[42]

For all the talk of potential war as soon as the late 2020s, Britain now appeared to be betting on something slightly different: a heightened period of tension lasting into the 2030s and beyond, one in which a retooled UK defence sector could increase British resilience and sell weaponry abroad.

But no matter how hard you tried to square the circle, it all came back to money, resources and political will. There was rarely enough of any – less than a year after winning a landslide victory, Keir Starmer had already faced one backbench rebellion over spending cuts while opinion polls suggested the British, French and German governments might all lose their next elections, potentially to be replaced by right-wing populists with varying degrees of support from both the Kremlin and those behind Trump's wider MAGA movement.

As alliance nations prepared for their annual summit in The Hague, Bruno Kahl, head of Germany's Federal Intelligence Service, told a podcast that the Berlin government believed Russia had concluded the alliance would not survive a serious challenge, and were preparing to test that theory. 'We are quite certain, and we have intelligence showing it, that Ukraine is only a step on the journey ... That doesn't mean we expect tank armies to roll westwards. But we see that NATO's collective defence promise is to be tested.'[43]

At the meeting itself, NATO Secretary General Rutte painted Europe's confrontation with the Kremlin as part of a much wider global face-off, going further than any of his predecessors in suggesting the most likely trigger for a Russian attack on Eastern Europe might be a Chinese invasion of Taiwan and a deliberate plan by the Kremlin and Beijing to overstretch the West.[44] But while previous major NATO summits had been attended by Japanese, South Korean and Australian leaders, this time none showed (New Zealand, always a sporadic attendee, did attend, with new Prime Minister Christopher Luxon using the opportunity to meet with European officials as well as Ukraine's President Zelenskyy).[45]

For Australia's Prime Minister Anthony Albanese, the no-show appeared to be in part political: after his meeting with Trump was cancelled when the US president left the G7 meeting in Canada early a few weeks previously, Albanese suggested another meeting – but it seemed far from certain it would happen, and he was mocked at home for 'stalking Trump'.[46] When it came to Japan and South Korea, both nations were already angered by Trump's tariffs and trade-war rhetoric, and neither had any intention of being pushed into signing up for NATO's new headline 5 per cent defence spending target that the US president now wanted.[47]

How many nations would truly reach that level was another question – Spain had already said it wouldn't, prioritising social spending over weaponry. In the run-up to the meeting, there was plenty of nervousness among European officials that the US president might not even show. In fact, he would dominate the summit, arriving just days after US airstrikes on the Iranian atomic programme brought an end to the immediate conflict between Israel and Iran.

*

Conducted by seven B-2 stealth bombers flying all the way from Whiteman Air Force Base in Missouri to Iran on the night of

June 22, Operation MIDNIGHT HAMMER was not just intended to devastate Iran's atomic programme, or even just to showcase the unique capabilities of the US military. As incoming Central Command chief Admiral Brad Cooper put it a few days later, it was intended to show the US had the willpower to strike if necessary – and would be prepared to do so again in future.[48]

That message was intended for audiences well beyond Iran – indeed, at the press conference the morning after, General Dan Caine noted pointedly that Pentagon analysts had assessed the best ways of destroying bunkers elsewhere in the world: a not-so-subtle warning to those in Moscow and Beijing.[49] 'American deterrence is back,' Defense Secretary Hegseth told the same event. 'When this president speaks, the world should listen – and the US military, we can back it up.'[50]

Whether or not the timing was intentional, it had the effect of ensuring that the NATO summit that commenced on June 24 began dominated by talk about the strikes.

Initially, many believed the tentative ceasefire would not hold.[51] 'They had a big fight, like two kids in a schoolyard,' Trump said of Iran and Israel a few days later at a joint press conference with Rutte. 'Let them fight for two or three minutes, then it's easier to stop them.' 'Daddy sometimes needs to use strong language,' interjected the NATO secretary general, an implicit reference to Trump that the US president clearly loved. 'I think he did it affectionately,' Trump told reporters.[52]

No one else would quite match that tone – but Trump could hardly have asked for a more ego-stroking series of events. In his first term, the US president had been mocked by other alliance leaders – Canadian PM Justin Trudeau had been caught doing just that in front of his French and British counterparts at the 2019 NATO London summit.[53] Now, instead of being talked of as if he were a child, Trump was being lionised as a strong and decisive leader, even as a parent.

That did not do enough to stop a headline-grabbing media row as multiple outlets seized on the president's immediate post-strike claim that the Iranian nuclear programme had been 'obliterated' – particularly after a leaked initial assessment from the US Defense Intelligence Agency (DIA) suggested the damage was less severe. From the Pentagon press room, Secretary Hegseth even singled out his former colleagues at Fox News as among 'the worst' in a furious briefing, accusing them of jumping on incomplete leaks of inaccurate information.[54] When Hegseth then fired DIA chief Lieutenant General Jeffrey Kruse barely three months later – one of a string of dismissals of senior military leaders – there was plenty of speculation it was some form of revenge.[55]

In the short term, the government in Tehran seemed keen to avoid significant further escalation, warning US officials in advance of what looked like a deliberately limited retaliatory strike on US forces. By the time the 19 Iranian ballistic missiles blasted across the Gulf, only 40 US personnel remained at Al Udeid from a normal presence of 10,000. They were the air-defence team for the base, normally stationed in Korea and led by a 28-year-old captain. He and his young crew were taking no chances: along with the Qatari air-defence team, in minutes they fired the largest number of Patriot anti-aircraft missiles ever launched in just one engagement (others would later put the number of missiles fired at 30).

But in a world of limited resources, such actions would have consequences. The total US stockpile of Patriots was only a quarter of that required by war plans, particularly for the Pacific – and continued expenditure in the Middle East and Ukraine look set to prevent it from recovering.[56] For the 'restrainers', who believed America's military was already dangerously overstretched, the speed with which the US had found itself drawn back into conflict in the Middle East was alarming. Much of Trump's MAGA base – including many veterans of the Iraqi and Afghan wars – had voted for him in part because he promised to avoid such steps. In the immediate aftermath of the US strikes, however, there were plenty of predictions that the US was heading back into its 'forever wars'.

It was a narrative the administration was keen to push back on. 'What I call the "Trump doctrine" is quite simple,' the vice president told a fundraising dinner in Ohio days after the bombing. 'Number one: you articulate a clear American interest ... in this case, that Iran can't have a nuclear weapon. Number two: you try to aggressively diplomatically solve that problem. Number three: when you can't solve it diplomatically, you use overwhelming military power to solve it, and then you get the hell out of there before it becomes a protracted conflict.'[57]

Perhaps predictably, hopes that the strikes would draw a neat line under US Middle East intervention would unravel within weeks, as the Houthis resumed attacks on Red Sea shipping and Iranian officials talked tough on resuming nuclear enrichment.

If that development was predictable, Trump himself was working hard to be much less so. As far back as the 1980s, Trump had described unpredictability as being at the heart of his 'Art of the Deal' mentality. Now, if there was a 'Trump doctrine' that trait was clearly a key element: laying down red lines, using the threat of force – or other punishments such as tariffs or sanctions – to assert power and dominance while simultaneously offering an off ramp or deal. Fundamentally, however, almost everything seemed to be viewed through the prism of power and his need to remain the focus of attention, praise and loyalty. In one televised meeting of his cabinet, that extended to asking which senior officials backed his suggestion of putting more gold leaf on the White House ceiling.[58]

Rather than a large network of well-connected individuals forming policy and bringing it to the president for approval, the system was to gauge the opinion of the president and then to match it as fast as possible. 'I've never been in a town or a political system that is so dominated by one individual,' observed then British ambassador to Washington Peter Mandelson. 'Usually, you are entering an ecosystem rather than the world of one personality . . . He is a phenomenon.'[59] That was further compounded by increasing talk of 'chaos' in the Pentagon and the gutting of the State Department – final job losses were estimated at around 3,000 – as well as scaling back of the National Security Council.[60]

Accompanying that was an increasingly apparent switch from more traditional US negotiating practice to what might be best described as 'deal-making', often led by Trump-friendly business figures rather than those with traditional diplomatic backgrounds. 'Trump gave every indication right from the beginning he was going to be purely transactional, said Ebenezer Obadare, senior fellow at the Council on Foreign Relations. 'He has thrown out the old playbook. He is not going through normal . . . channels.'

Throughout the first months of 2025, business contacts and hostage negotiators working on behalf of the Trump administration carved out simultaneous mineral deals and a peace agreement in eastern Democratic Republic of Congo, working to secure the release of three Americans on death row in that country and halting fighting between Congolese forces and Rwanda-backed militia.[61] The details of exactly what the deal involved and how it had been made were extremely murky, but it got Trump a Congolese nomination for the Nobel Peace Prize and looked set to give the US access to minerals including gold, cobalt, copper, lithium and tantalum.[62] That deal was followed quickly by suggestions the president should try something similar in Sudan.[63] By autumn 2025, the US president was repeatedly describing himself as having ended 'seven' major conflicts in his first term as well as the opening months of his second administration, the White House releasing a list that included the India–Pakistan 'four-day war', the long-running conflict between Armenia and Azerbaijan and a border spat between Cambodia and Thailand.[64]

Gaza and Ukraine, however, were proving much tougher to fix. In Gaza, the conflict was now shaped by the increasingly naked Israeli strategy to make life so difficult and dangerous for Palestinian residents that they would choose to leave, opening the door for Israeli settlements and a radical rebuilding programme based on Trump's idea of a 'Mediterranean Riviera'. What that looked like in reality for now was a sea of destroyed buildings, with worsening hunger driving Gazans to often lethally dangerous humanitarian feeding centres run by US contractors often in the midst of combat zones.[65]

Trump's tacit backing of most Israeli actions – as well as his handling of Iran – had won him another Nobel Peace Prize nomination from Israeli Prime Minister Netanyahu, now himself the subject of an International Criminal Court arrest warrant over his actions in Gaza.[66] But the president's high-profile desire to win a Nobel Prize made it even harder to gauge the answer to the most important question of the age: what would a Trump or successor administration do if China attacked Taiwan, or Russia launched an offensive into Eastern Europe?

In 2024, before his re-election, Trump claimed he had directly warned Putin during his first term: 'If you go into Ukraine, I'm going to bomb the shit out of Moscow . . . I have no choice.' He said that Putin's response was one of disbelief. 'He said, "No way." And I said, "Way," ' said Trump, in an audio recording published in mid-2025. He said he'd made a similar threat to Xi: 'He thought I was crazy,' Trump told his fellow diners, adding that the warning was successful even if Trump and Putin only believed him '5 or 10 per cent'.

Some suspected those conversations had never really happened. John Bolton, Trump's former national security advisor, said he was confident no such conversations had taken place before he left government in 2019.[67] Even if they had occurred more or less as Trump recalled, there was no telling whether or not Putin or Xi had taken those warnings seriously, nor how they saw that against the backdrop of recent events – particularly following the US initial inaction and later actions on Ukraine.

Even harder to model was the likely reaction of future presidents, even relatively known candidates such as Vance or Rubio. What was clear was that perceived weakness would likely be tested by both Moscow and Beijing.

As troops from the US, Japan, South Korea, Britain and half a dozen other nations came together for TALISMAN SABRE, the largest ever exercise to take place in northern Australia, relatively junior officials in Australia and Japan were approached by US counterparts. Much to their surprise, they found themselves pushed hard to commit to the defence of Taiwan in the event of an invasion despite the US remaining 'strategically ambiguous' on what it would do itself. The result was what one official described as a 'collective raising of eyebrows' – and a polite refusal. Japan – already refusing to spend more on defence – was not going to make any more binding commitments ahead of its elections, while Australian officials said any such decision would be down to a future government. As Asia expert Zack Cooper put it, 'It is very difficult to get allies to provide specifics about what they would do in a Taiwan conflict when they don't know either the scenario and context or America's own response.'[68]

Speaking at the Shangri-La Dialogue in Singapore earlier in the year, Defense Secretary Hegseth had repeated the call made by Democratic predecessor Lloyd Austin for European nations to prioritise their own continent's defence before getting too involved in Asia.[69] But nervousness over long-term US commitment meant that multiple Pacific nations were now the keenest they had ever been to engage with European forces and defence firms.

The arrival of British carrier HMS *Prince of Wales* at TALISMAN SABRE carrying its roughly two dozen F-35Bs arguably made relatively little genuine difference to Australia's defences: Australia now operated 72 of the more-capable F-35As, with their much greater range and weapons capabilities.[70] But with AUKUS now in doubt, Australian media coverage made it clear just how much of a confidence boost it was to have the UK sending warships the region.

UK task force commander Commodore James Blackmore described their presence as a sign of 'capability and credibility'[71] – even though the Royal Navy reportedly lacked enough working nuclear attack submarines to send one to accompany his vessels.[72] With Japan next on the schedule, he told Sky News Australia he did not yet know what route the UK government would tell his ships to take through the South China Sea – or perhaps even the Taiwan Strait, something the Australian reporter suggested would 'infuriate Beijing'.[73]

In fact, whether to even risk sending a single frigate through the Taiwan Strait was now supposedly the subject of a row in Whitehall, with the Foreign Office said to be opposed to even that.[74] EU states had their own awkward balance to strike with China, although summer 2025 saw a strengthening of EU–Japan relations[75] and talk of a defence deal with Australia.[76] The other big news in Asia was unexpectedly deteriorating US–India relations, fuelled in part by Prime Minister Modi's refusal to credit Trump and his administration for halting the brief conflict with Pakistan as well as the imposition of US sanctions over ongoing purchases of Russian oil. Given that the US was not taking similar action against European nations that continued to buy oil from Russia further intensified anger in New Delhi – and which together with separately worsening US–Brazilian relations risked pushing those two powerful BRICS closer to both Moscow and Beijing.[77]

Against a backdrop of ever more polarising domestic US politics, America's position on Russia and Ukraine continued its own never-ending shifts, some of them quite radical. For months Trump had engaged in repeated conversations with his Russian counterpart, almost always characterising them as 'nice' and supposedly productive – only for Russia to then fire increasing numbers of missiles and drones against Ukraine's cities as soon as the calls were over. It was making Trump look weak – the First Lady, he told reporters, kept reminding him how many strikes Putin had subsequently launched against Ukraine following his calls.

This did not appear to be the only source of tension. In June 2025, Hegseth and Colby halted multiple deliveries to Ukraine, including Patriot, HIMARS and artillery shells, arguing that doing so was vital to conserve and rebuild US weapons stocks. But the suspension was lifted on the orders of the White House, with several sources telling reporters the president felt he had not been properly consulted. The Pentagon disputed that, saying that the information had been passed across.[78]

Within a week, NATO chief Rutte was in the White House to seal a hastily pulled together deal in which European nations would purchase US Patriot systems to send them to Ukraine. That would relieve some of the immediate pressure on Ukraine itself – and the European nations involved could include the money when it came to their NATO spending targets – but it might deepen the strains on the US supply system. Rutte described the announcement as 'very big' and proof of Europe 'stepping up'.[79] As he did so, French President Macron – who only days earlier had signed a landmark deal with Britain to commit both their nuclear weapons to the defence of Europe if the US failed to do the same – announced further French rearmament. 'To be free in this world you have to be feared,' he told an audience on Bastille Day. 'To be feared you have to be powerful.'[80]

Not all nations were looking to be feared – for some it was enough to just look ready. In the Netherlands, that included a deal to refit commuter railway carriages as mobile hospitals for use in time of war, with airline KLM set to temporarily release former military pilots for further combat training.[81] With the

Dutch ports already central to supplying Ukraine with foreign arms, even more importantly for the defence of Europe in a major conflict the Dutch military was also acquiring railway wagons, trucks and qualified personnel to ensure supplies could keep moving even if under attack.[82]

Norway and the Netherlands were both deploying their F-35s into Poland under NATO command to protect supply lines to Ukraine – another tacit acknowledgement that if that war kept escalating it might spill beyond its borders.[83] In Sweden, officials said they were looking at extending the upper age at which military officers could be recalled to service – to as high as 70 – increasing significantly the pool of those with experience who could be used to train others.[84] Denmark was holding its own drills in Greenland, diplomatically glossing over the question of whether they were looking to deter seizure by the United States as much as by the Kremlin.[85]

Others were openly hedging their bets, not least the nations of Southeast Asia under mounting pressure from Beijing over the disputed waters of the South China Sea.[86] For the US, the fact that nations such as Vietnam and Malaysia continued to find ways to reassert their territorial claims was something of a victory – a reminder that even largely neutral nations lacked any enthusiasm for a truly hegemonic China.[87] A former US commander in the region had once described Beijing as its own worst enemy in that regard, and he was likely right.[88]

On Taiwan itself, preparations continued, as did the air of unreality. So did the political battles between the Democratic Progressive Party and Kuomintang that might determine Taiwan's fate as much as any war. Summer 2025 saw the largest, longest military drills in the island's history – ten days involving new US-manufactured M1 tanks and HIMARS missile launchers, as well as ordinary Taiwanese civilians moving into shelters for the first time in recent history.[89]

After all the brief excitement over apparent Pentagon support earlier in the year, Taiwan was now once again facing talk of potential US abandonment: Defence Minister Wellington Koo found a scheduled meeting at the Pentagon abruptly cancelled,[90] while President Lai was denied permission to land in New York on a proposed trip to visit the handful of Central America nations that still recognised the ROC. The latter was reportedly a decision made by Trump himself, a deliberate move to avoid antagonising China in the run-up to a hoped-for meeting with Xi Jinping and perhaps even a trade deal later in the year.[91]

One prominent Chinese academic suggested time was running out; Professor Zhang Weiwei of Fudan University, an institution with strong ties to the Chinese Communist Party and to Xi himself, joked with students that Taiwan would already have been 'liberated' by the next elections in 2028. 'Everything is ready,' he told them, without giving further details.[92]

There were signs Trump believed this was another conflict he had stopped, or at least postponed. On his way to meet Vladimir Putin at the start of August, the president told journalists on Air Force One that Xi Jinping had promised him China would not invade Taiwan during the current presidential term. Once again, the details of that conversation remained extremely sketchy – but even if that pledge was genuine and kept, it merely nudged the problem into the next presidential administration after 2029 or the one that followed.[93] 'I think we are looking at an extremely dangerous decade,' one former Pentagon war planner told me, although they suggested China's ageing population might eventually begin to reduce the danger from the mid-2030s onward.[94]

At his Alaska summit with Trump on the eightieth anniversary of the Japanese surrender in August 1945, the Russian leader was treated to a red-carpet reception, a ride in the 'Beast' – the armoured US presidential limousine – and a show of force including an overflight from a B-2 bomber escorted by F-35s. But it was China's giant parade almost a month later that offered the greatest spectacle, with huge lines of military equipment paraded through Beijing and Putin and North Korean leader Kim appearing as the guests of honour.

The last time Russian, Chinese and North Korean leaders had showcased such commitment to each other, Mao and Stalin had signed off North Korea's 1950 invasion of the South – a move that had almost sparked a global conflagration. Alongside Xi and the other leaders on the podium now sat China's senior military commander General Zhang, watching the president he had grown up with as a teenager after the Cultural Revolution declare that 'the Chinese people are a people that are not afraid of violence'. While Xi also committed his nation to 'peaceful development' and did not mention Taiwan by name, the rows of weaponry conveyed their own deliberate warning.[95] But Xi and Putin did not appear to be in a hurry themselves – an open microphone at their meeting in Beijing had caught them discussing the prospects of using organ transplants and other medical breakthroughs to live to 150 years of age or more.[96]

A few days earlier, Chinese officials had publicly rejected the suggestion they might sign a nuclear arms control agreement with the US and Russia,[97] apparently putting an end to talk of the global atomic treaty a younger Trump had dreamt of taking credit for since the days of Gorbachev and Reagan. Amid gossip in Washington over the US president's own health, Trump expressed his frustration about how difficult it was proving to do a peace deal on Ukraine. 'Sometimes you never know with war,' he told reporters in the Oval Office. 'War is complex and dangerous – what a mess, what a bloody mess.'[98]

It would keep on getting messier.

Afterword: A Still-Unravelling World?

Shortly before midnight on September 9, 2025, well over a dozen Russian-made 'Shaheed'-type drones crossed the border from Belarus on a course that would take them deep into Polish airspace. In the early hours of September 10, Polish F-16 and Netherlands F-35 jets deployed as part of NATO's air policing mission went into action to bring them down.

It was the first time in 76 years of NATO history that aircraft under its command had fired in defence of a member nation's airspace – and that fact alone guaranteed international attention. That was ramped up further as Poland's government demanded a meeting of the North Atlantic Council under Article Four of the alliance treaty. That was short of the Article Five declaration of a full-scale 'armed attack' that might commit allies to a similar 'military response', but still a rare and significant step.

NATO had a new Supreme Allied Commander: US Air Force General Alexus Grynkewich, a former F-16 pilot who had most recently served as director of operations for the Joint Staff in the Pentagon, who now had the challenging role of keeping alliance disagreements under wraps.[1] Poland's government warned it was the closest that nation had been to outright conflict since 1945,[2] while others made similar suggestions. 'On a scale of one to ten, where one means lasting peace and ten means war, we are approaching eight,' said Czech army chief Karel Rehka. 'The way we feel only a small sense of urgency in the Czech Republic simply does not correspond to the intelligence reports we are receiving.'[3]

Speaking in Lithuania shortly afterwards, Grynkewich described the initial operation to shoot down the drones in Poland as a sign of NATO's systems working. But he also announced the immediate launch of a new, dialled-up mission known as 'EASTERN SENTRY', in some ways an aerial counterpart to the 'BALTIC SENTRY' mission NATO had launched in 2024 after the severing of undersea cables in that region.

BALTIC SENTRY, Grynkewich told reporters, had achieved its aim: not a single Baltic undersea cable had been cut in 2025.[4] But EASTERN SENTRY would be much more swiftly tested.[5] September 19 brought the most egregious provocation yet: three Russian MiG-31 jets entering Estonia's airspace for 13 minutes as they transited along the coast towards Kaliningrad, escorted closely for much of that period by Italian F-35 jets on NATO air policing duties. Shooting down drones was one thing, manned Russian aircraft something very different – prompting unusually public discussions over the right Western course of action.

Structures set up at the end of World War Two to deliver lasting peace were now fraying at the edges. 'NATO is not working as it should,' said Danish national security academic Sten Rynning. At the root of the problem, he said, was ongoing worries about the US commitment.[6] Those worries were now being compounded by the continued delays in publishing the Pentagon's long-promised force posture review.

The announcement that the Pentagon was pulling hundreds of senior US military commanders together at the US Marine base in Quantico raised hopes that more clarity was coming on US military strategy. Instead, those travelling to Virginia from around the world found themselves lectured once again by newly rebranded 'Secretary of War' Pete Hegseth on raising fitness and appearance standards, and banishing 'woke' ideas – and were subjected to an explicit call for those who disliked the new regime to quit. The speech from Trump that followed was among his most meandering, including repeated mentions of using the military more against 'domestic enemies'.

Hegseth described renaming the Pentagon the 'Department of War' as a means not just to restore its 'warrior ethos', but also to avoid the 'mission creep' the Department of Defense had often suffered since its creation in 1947. But it was Trump's suggestion of deploying yet more US troops domestically and using US cities as 'training grounds' that really grabbed the headlines.[7]

Clearly, hostile dictatorships were not the only ones tearing up the post-war rulebook. With its new offensive in Gaza pushing up the likely death toll there to over 60,000, Israel delivered a further shock with a missile strike into the Qatari capital Doha to destroy a Hamas office. Even more than Israel's actions within Gaza itself, it openly irritated both Washington and the Arab Gulf. 'The president was very displeased,' said one White House official.[8]

Ironically, the strike within Qatar did more than any other single event to reinvigorate negotiations. The US was working with Gulf states to push a plan that rejected the mass eviction of Gaza residents in favour of a multinational rebuilding programme. It envisaged an inevitably Trump-chaired 'board of peace', also expected to include former British PM Tony Blair and participants from other Arab states, largely cutting the Palestinians firmly out of the process. Still, the new round of talks was enough to stop the fighting and persuade a weakened Hamas to release its few remaining hostages.[9]

Even if the deal could hold, the rebuilding and post-war stabilisation of Gaza would look very different to the reconstruction efforts of recent decades. The United Nations and wider humanitarian system were a shadow of their former selves; the rules for engagement under which any foreign troops might operate desperately unclear.

It was not enough to secure Trump the Nobel Peace Prize that he craved, for 2025 at least. Elsewhere in the world, the US itself was now acting with much less restraint, sinking several Venezuelan boats in international waters, accusing them of drug smuggling but destroying them and killing their crews without providing any evidence. Challenged on social media that the attack might have been a war crime, Vice President JD Vance responded that he didn't 'give a shit' what critics called it.[10] Speculation was now growing fast that the administration hoped to mount some kind of 'regime change' operation against Venezuelan President Nicolás Maduro, as well as perhaps further action in the region.

'We are about to get into some kind of fight in Venezuela, Mexico, Haiti or all three,' one Washington contact told me in autumn 2025, warning that such a confrontation might well feed back into broader global tensions. 'The war we get might not look anything like the war that we expect to have.'[11] Elsewhere, Pakistan was accused of an airstrike in Kabul, all part of an escalating face-off with Afghanistan that appeared linked to its contest with India.[12]

The appearance of unidentified small drones at airports in Denmark, Norway and beyond felt like another deliberate effort to exploit and deepen a global sense of unpredictability and chaos. It all highlighted the still-chronic shortage of air defence systems as well as almost every other kind of weapon. As arms manufacturers descended on the Excel conference centre in east London's Docklands, the companies that aroused most interest were those that could rapidly scale up manufacturing of relatively cheap munitions and other systems.

'Speed and scale of manufacture is what governments are looking for,' said Mal Crease, founder and chief executive of UK maritime drone manufacturer Kraken Technology Group, now striking deals with shipyards in both Europe and beyond to build unmanned attack boats and midget submarines. Britain's Ministry of Defence pre-contract notice for its new 'Nightfall' medium-range ballistic missile – capable of flying 500 kilometres with a 300-kilogram explosive warhead – called for a prototype to be flying within months, with mass production by the end of 2026.[13]

For all that, those within multiple governments complained progress was still too agonisingly slow and inefficient. But as Danish Prime Minister Mette Frederiksen warned, military capabilities themselves were only part of tackling the problem – what was really needed was political commitment. 'We need to be very open about [the fact] that it is probably only the beginning,' she told the *Financial Times*. 'The idea is to divide us.'[14]

Kremlin efforts to undermine democracies in Europe and beyond still delivered mixed results: October 2025 saw another election victory in Moldova for its pro-European government despite widely reported Kremlin-backed interference, including paying dissident Moldovans to bribe others for their votes.[15] But Czech elections barely a week later brought down a pro-NATO, anti-Putin government that had put itself at the forefront of sending weapons to Ukraine. As another government fell, there were growing signs that France might well be under the control of the right-wing 'National Rally' of Marine Le Pen as soon as the end of 2026. Others suggested Germany's Alternative for Deutschland might take power in Germany at almost exactly the point its increased defence spending gave it Europe's largest army. Some in Europe worried that was exactly what more right-wing factions in Washington were now directly working towards.[16]

At the very least, suspected interference was no longer limited to Putin's Russia. Research by advocacy group Global Witness in several European nations showed both Elon Musk-owned X and Chinese-owned social media platform TikTok routinely 'over-promoting' right-wing parties such as Germany's AFD.[17] The latter was another sign of growing Russia–China overlap and mutual coordination, which according to another report from the Royal United Services Institute now also extended to collaboration between their airborne forces to help the PLA learn the lessons of Ukraine.[18]

On Taiwan itself, the ruling DPP had largely failed in efforts to trigger the by-elections necessary to dislodge the Kuomintang from parliament. Taiwan's leader was now quietly cutting back on what had been his ever more explicit argument that the island was already 'de facto' independent. Opinion polls showed Taiwan's population broadly supportive of increased defence spending and arms purchases. The government was again talking of military spending at 5 per cent of GDP – but it was still not clear that the island's politics would really let that happen.

As well as buying foreign weapons, Taiwan was ramping up its own defence industry, taking advantage of the island's high-tech focus. The government announced it would create its own 'T-dome' domestic air defence system modelled on Israel's 'Iron Dome',[19] as well as working with Anduril on a home-built cruise missile.[20] Pressure from Beijing remained predictably relentless. NATO might have been successful in deterring Baltic cables from being cut, but the undersea connections to Taiwan continued to be severed.[21]

China's ever-growing fleet remained increasingly assertive across the wider region, its third aircraft carrier *Fujian* pushing out to sea towards islands disputed with Japan.[22] Beijing now claimed the disputed Scarborough Shoal as a Chinese 'nature reserve', while a water cannon attack on a nearby Philippines patrol vessel from a Chinese Coast Guard ship saw a sailor badly cut by flying glass.[23]

South Korea was hosting the Asia-Pacific Economic Cooperation (APEC) at the end of October, long suggested as a potential venue for the first meeting of the new administration between the US and Chinese leaders. When Trump and Xi spoke in mid-September, the conversation was largely limited to the future of TikTok. With the social media platform now central to Republican outreach to a younger generation, Trump had dropped his calls to ban it, but he was still pushing for its US operations to be handed over to American ownership and supervision. Even on that front, there appeared to be little real progress.[24] What looked like an initial deal on rare earth exports was also now unravelling, prompting new Trump tariffs on China.[25]

How the world's two pre-eminent superpowers tackled their rivalry and relations was now the largest question in the world. In Europe, former Danish naval chief Nils Wang told me he believed that unless there was a major US–China war, tensions with Russia would continue to fluctuate just short of outright conflict. 'But if America and China fight, we [the Europeans and the Russians] will then all fight each other.' Others suggested Beijing's military threats were a distraction from the true danger to the West: a China now pulling ahead industrially in multiple sectors including AI, energy and electric vehicles, in a way that might soon become impossible to match.[26]

In almost every Western nation there were divisions on how to tackle China. With NASA's *Artemis* mission now due to fly around the moon in early 2026 and China's robots and potential drone base not that far behind, the battle for the future of the world now stretching well beyond the parameters of the earth. Predictions over China's future were also widely different: 2025 would be the fourth successive year in which its population shrank. According to some estimates, the first half of the 2020s saw a closure of a quarter of Chinese kindergartens, some literally being rebuilt as older care facilities to match the ageing population.[27] Some believed that might make the nation much more mellow: foreign musical instrument manufacturers reported sales of guitars and saxophones to the growing number of retirees, while once reliable piano sales to hyper-ambitious parents for their children were now in permanent decline.[28] Others worried an ageing China, now home to more than half the world's industrial robots,[29] might prove even more resource-hungry – and perhaps also over-confident that it could dominate in a new era of often unmanned warfare.[30]

In Washington, Biden's former Beijing ambassador Nicholas Burns noted that it had taken well over a year for that administration to come up with a solid China policy, and it might take at least as long again for the Trump team and those that followed.[31] Within the Pentagon, Chairman of the Joint Chiefs Dan Caine was said to be engaged in a pitched if subtle action to maintain a Pacific military focus to keep Beijing deterred, rather than pulling still more forces into homeland defence and supporting US immigration deportation efforts.[32]

The announced withdrawal of up to a thousand US troops from Romania was seen by many in both Europe and Washington as a sign of things to come. But secret internal fights of perhaps even greater importance were now clearly taking place within China's PLA. By the time China's Central Military Commission met in autumn 2025, it was clear Xi had purged at least nine of his most senior generals, with more removed elsewhere in the command chain, ostensibly for corruption. Those who watched China closely told me that this appeared to include multiple figures in China's Eastern Military District: the officers likely to have been most involved with planning for Taiwan. Some suggested this might be because they were becoming overly aggressive and keen to attack, while others cautioned the opposite was also just as plausible.[33]

As Trump met Xi in South Korea on the sidelines of a wider Asia-Pacific summit, there were yet more fears in Taiwan that the US might be on the brink of abandoning the island. Opinion polls showed the population opposed as ever to 'unification' under mainland rule, and resoundingly supportive of new high-tech defence solutions, including the new 'T-dome' air defences. But they also suggested a growing sector of the population were questioning the wisdom of fighting if there was a chance the US might pull back on its support. Perhaps as a result, officials in both Japan and the nearby Philippines began to talk up the prospect of military involvement in Taiwan should Beijing invade – although whether they would do so if the US held back its forces remained somewhat in doubt.

Concerns that 2027 would be the most likely year for a Chinese attack appeared to be quietly shrinking. Instead, the focus was shifting to the political battles of 2028: another election in Taiwan, as well as in the US. A fourth consecutive win for Taiwan's ruling DPP might antagonise Beijing still further, while despite its change in leadership, KMT appeared increasingly divided over its own approach to China.[34]

Some other battles, it seemed, were also being won – at least for now. The AUKUS submarine deal was said to be now likely to go ahead despite its troubled history.[35] The INDOPACOM US military planners were already well into their work on further drills with allies through 2026 and 2027: another 'RIMPAC' naval drill across the vast waters between Hawaii and Japan, another 'COBRA GOLD' in Thailand, another 'BALIKATAN' with the Philippines.

Their counterparts at US European Command and in NATO were doing the same, with another set of 'STEADFAST' and related drills all now already scheduled to the decade end. When a US Army HIMARS unit pulled out of Estonia in the autumn to rebase into Lithuania there was considerable relief when it was replaced with a detachment of 14 US tanks, even if the fact they were still painted in desert colours suggested some hedging bets over where the next war might truly come. They and the nearby NATO force might be outnumbered by Russian opponents if Putin crossed the border, but they were a sign that, at least in the short term, the democracies remained just about united.

'The winter will be harsh, not just for your soldiers, but for your tanks as well,' Estonian defence minister Hanno Pevkur told incoming US troops, suggesting they might 'enjoy' the local tradition of jumping into icy lakes. 'I'm not sure we are ready to jump into an ice hole just yet, but we're working on it,' replied unit commander Lieutenant Colonel Andrew Jenkins, pledging his normally Texas-based soldiers would not run from any fight. 'We are aware that it is going to be cold.'[36]

The forests around the NATO base at Tapa would soon again be laden down with snow. Few truly believed a major global war would come that winter, or even the spring that followed – but it might be more likely in the following year, and the year after that.

Still, like that first Cold War, if luck and common sense could hold, it might yet be postponed and deterred indefinitely. Achieving that might require the efforts of millions of individuals over decades. But for now, at least, there was everything to play for.

Endnotes

Introduction and Acknowledgements

1 ' "The Chinese military is the largest and most modern it's ever been," Edwards AFB Commander Warns', The Aviationist, January 12, 2025
2 Interview with the author
3 Interview with the author
4 Interview with the author
5 Interview with the author
6 Interview with the author
7 'Ukraine war: Biden says nuclear risk highest since 1962 Cuban Missile Crisis', BBC News, October 7, 2022
8 'JPMorgan's Dimon: "the most dangerous time in the world has seen in decades" ', Politico, October 13, 2023
9 'Reproductive behavior at the end of the world: The effect of the Cuban Missile Crisis on US fertility', SSRN, November 14, 2012
10 'Panic buying takes hold in Delhi', The Times, May 10, 2025
11 'There will be no "short, sharp" war. A fight between the US and China would likely go on for years', Atlantic Council, March 19, 2024
12 'Commission on the National Defense Strategy', RAND, July 2024
13 'Facing Coming Storms: Talking International Defence', Spotify (and other podcast platforms) from January 2025, produced by Urban Podcasts
14 Interviews with the author
15 Interviews with the author
16 'UK will be at war by next election, says ex-Army Lib Dem MP – and will need conscription', Big Issue, February 8, 2025
17 'Pearl Harbor redux? CC draws parallels, urges preparedness', Edwards Air Force Base website, May 7, 2025
18 Oxford Essential Quotations, sixth edition, published 2018, online entry for Vegetius
19 'The return of the "War Department" is more than nostalgia. It's a message', New York Times, September 5, 2025

20 'Finnish conscripts and the meaning of sisu', NATO Multimedia, February 6, 2025
21 Interview with the author
22 ' "Forging the weapon": The origins of SHAPE', NATO website, February 11, 2021

1. Not this August – But Maybe Next

1 'Notes on the next war', *Esquire*, September 1, 1935
2 Speech also available on YouTube in Swedish
3 Speech by the Prime Minister, January 8, 2024, Swedish government website
4 'Crown Princess Victoria begins officer training together with the Officers' Programme', Swedish Defence University website, August 26, 2024
5 Speech by the Minister for Civil Defence, January 7, 2024, Swedish government website
6 'Joint Press Conference for NATO Chiefs of Defence meeting', NATO headquarters, January 18, 2024, posted on YouTube
7 'Sweden's call for population to prepare for war sparks panic and criticism', France 24, January 18, 2024
8 'Joint Press Conference for NATO Chiefs of Defence meeting', NATO headquarters, January 18, 2024, posted on YouTube
9 ' "Lights are flashing red" over global instability, says David Cameron', *Guardian*, January 14, 2024
10 ' "We have moved from a post-war to a pre-war world": Defence Secretary Grant Shapps issues chilling warning to NATO allies not meeting 2 per cent defence-spending target they are playing "Russian roulette" with West's security', *Daily Mail*, April 4, 2024
11 'Head of MI6 says "I've never seen the world in a more dangerous state" as he warns Russia would not stop if it wins in Ukraine', Sky News, November 29, 2024
12 'To prevent war, NATO must spend more', NATO website, December 12, 2024
13 'Inside the UK's top secret spy base for war', Sky News, February 8, 2024
14 'Inside the world's biggest intelligence base', *The Times*, February 8, 2024
15 'Russia regains upper hand in Ukraine', *New York Times*, January 13, 2024
16 'US general warns time running out for Ukraine without US aid', Reuters, April 10, 2024
17 'US Army ammo plant boosts artillery shell production for Ukraine', Defense News, August 28, 2024
18 'What we know about North Korea's role in the Ukraine war', *New York Times*, November 5, 2024

19 'The Second Day Summary of the 20th YES Annual Meeting – THE NECESSITY TO WIN', Yalta European Strategy, September 16, 2024

20 'Ukrainian refugees: how will the economy recover with a diminished population?', Reuters, July 7, 2023

21 'US general says Russian army has grown by 15 per cent since pre-Ukraine war', The Hill, April 11, 2024

22 Interview with the author

23 'Russia ramps up sabotage operations in Europe', Foreign Policy, June 13, 2024

24 'Defend "every inch" of NATO territory? New strategy is a work in progress', *Washington Post*, June 5, 2023

25 'Merilo: Future scenario for Estonia could be very challenging', ERR, February 10, 2024

26 'Incoming EDF chief: restricting the use of weapons donated to Ukraine a foolish move', ERR, February 23, 2024

27 Joint press conference, NATO website, January 16, 2025

28 'Patrolling Australia's vast northern expanses', Australian Government, November 28, 2024

29 'China dealt blow over the future of strategic Pacific port', Bloomberg, April 7, 2025

30 'New Defence fuel facility for Darwin', Australian Defence, November 1, 2023

31 'Japanese troops to train with Australia, US militaries in Darwin', Reuters, November 17, 2024

32 'China's missiles could reach Northern Territory, "two-thirds" of Australia, report warns', NT Independent, December 7, 2022

33 Interview with the author

34 'White paper: The Taiwan question and China's reunification in the new era', *China Daily*, October 8, 2022

35 'Mitochondrial DNA provides a link between Polynesians and indigenous Taiwanese', PLoS Biology vol. 3, July 5, 2005

36 'The indigenous Taiwanese helping prepare the country for war', Taiwan Plus News, August 25, 2023

37 Interview with the author

38 'Taiwan's military drills turn serious as China threat escalates', *Financial Times*, July 20, 2024

39 'Chinese military uses model of N. Taiwan city government building for drills', *Taiwan News*, June 4, 2020

40 Interviews with the author

41 'Kendall: in US–China "Race for Technological Superiority", AI may be the key', *Air & Space Forces Magazine*, October 29, 2024

42 'Taiwan's dominance of the chip industry makes it more important', *Economist*, March 6, 2023

43 'Military and Security Developments Involving the People's Republic of China, 2024', US Department of Defense, page X1, December 18, 2024

44 'China's astronauts are aiming to land on the Moon by 2030. They now have a new spacesuit to do it', CNN, September 30, 2024

45 'China's massive next-generation amphibious assault ship takes shape', CSIS, August 1, 2024

46 'Unpacking China's naval buildup', CSIS, June 5, 2024

47 'China is battening down for the gathering storm over Taiwan', War on the Rocks, April 17, 2024

48 Interview with the author

49 'The state of the US Navy as China builds up its naval force and threatens Taiwan', CBS News, March 19, 2023

50 'Reflecting on US defence strategy', Chatham House event, July 10, 2023

51 'Joe Biden again says US forces would defend Taiwan from Chinese attack', *Guardian*, September 19, 2022

52 Interviews with the author

53 'UK must be ready for war in three years, head of British Army warns', Sky News, July 23, 2024

54 'Military chiefs fear "nightmare" double wars against China and Russia', *The Times*, June 5, 2025

55 'Secretary of Defense Lloyd J. Austin III Holds a Press Conference Following a NATO Defense Ministers Meeting, Brussels, Belgium', US Department of Defense, October 12, 2023

56 'Troops demonstrate their ability to rapidly deploy in NATO exercise', Army MoD, February 13, 2024

57 'From the south of the alliance, Spanish forces deploy to Poland for Brilliant Jump, 2024', NATO SHAPE, February 23, 2024

58 Email exchange with the author

59 'Trump says he once told a NATO ally to pay its share or he'd "encourage" Russia to do what it wanted', Associated Press, February 11, 2024

60 'Estonian intelligence warns of potential Russian military confrontation with the West in next decade', Essa News, February 13, 2024

61 'Would Trump really leave NATO? Europe is trying not to panic', *The Times*, February 18, 2024

62 'What Europe fears', *The Atlantic*, June 3, 2024

63 'Why John Bolton is certain Trump really wants to blow up NATO', Politico, February 13, 2024

64 'Donald Trump's Taiwan remarks spark fury and concern', *Newsweek*, January 21, 2024

65 Interview with the author

66 Post by @TuckerCarlson on X, November 10, 2024

67 'Aligning global military posture with US interests', Defense Priorities, July 9, 2025

68 Interview with the author

69 'Venäjä harjoitteli hyökkäystä Suomeen ja Viroon – Näin vakava on Naton uhka-arvio', Iltalethi, December 25, 2024

70 'Why would China want a blockade on Japanese islands? Recent drill raises Taiwan spectre', *South China Morning Post*, January 2, 2025

71 'Trump says China respects him because Xi knows he is "crazy"', BBC News, October 19, 2024

72 '"I'm going to stop the wars" – Trump says, as he claims victory', *Kyiv Independent*, November 6, 2024

73 Post by @RealAlexJones on X, January 19, 2025

74 'Taiwan watches Trump undercut Ukraine, hoping it won't be next', *New York Times*, February 25, 2025

75 'Explainer: How China's rhetoric has changed during Trump 2.0', BBC Monitoring, March 18, 2025

2. 'Hellscape' in the Pacific

1 'Taiwan extends compulsory military service from 4 months to 1 year', PBS, December 27, 2022

2 Video posted to Facebook, viewed 2025, now removed

3 'Carl Vinson Carrier Strike Group arrives in the Philippines', US Navy, January 5, 2024

4 Easton, Ian, *The Chinese Invasion Threat* (2017), CreateSpace Independent Publishing Platform, Kindle location 46

5 Interview with the author

6 'Imelda Marcos's shoe collection was glimpse into a frightening reign', CNN News, May 7, 2022

7 'Locked up and re-elected: Philippines' Rodrigo Duterte wins poll from cell in The Hague', *Financial Times*, May 17, 2025

8 Reporting by assistant

9 'Taiwan enhances force posture, military recruit skills with expanded conscription', Indo-Pacific Defense Forum, May 28, 2024

10 'Taiwan's first one-year conscripts finish basic training', TaiwanPlus News, March 20, 2024

11 'Limited role for US Navy SEAL team in defense of Taiwan', VoA News, September 14, 2024

12 '"It needs to be a thousand": US has 500 military trainers on Taiwan, retired admiral says', *Stars and Stripes*, May 27, 2025

13 'US think tank report calls for removal of all 500 US military trainers in Taiwan', *Taiwan News*, July 10, 2025

14 Easton, Ian, *The Chinese Invasion Threat* (2017), CreateSpace Independent Publishing Platform, Kindle page 228

15 Interview with the author

16 '戰車不只出現在桃園 淡水人深夜直擊：有演習嗎?' [*Tanks not only appear in Taoyuan and Tamsui. Late-night live report: Are there any exercises?*] UDN News, December 10, 2024

17 Easton, Ian, *The Chinese Invasion Threat* (2017), CreateSpace Independent Publishing Platform, Kindle page 122-135

18 'M1A2 Abrams tanks arrive in Taiwan', TWZ, December 16, 2024

19 'Why do many Taiwanese resist unification with the People's Republic of China?: An overview of explanations', Air University, May 8, 2024

20 'The maps that show how China's military is squeezing Taiwan', *Guardian*, January 8, 2025

21 'Chinese cyberattacks on Taiwan government averaged 2.4 million a day in 2024, report says', Reuters, January 6, 2025

22 'China's drive to give Taiwanese visitors local IDs alarms Taipei', *Financial Times*, January 6, 2025

23 'Taiwan sees threefold surge in suspected Chinese espionage cases', CNN, January 13, 2025

24 'Recent Chinese spy cases in Taiwan: Knowns, unknowns, and implications', Global Taiwan Institute, September 4, 2024

25 'Ex-general indicted over "invasion" group', *Taipei Times*, January 23, 2025

26 'What worries me about war with China after my visit to Taiwan', *New York Times*, January 27, 2024

27 Interviews with the author

28 'Taiwan foreign minister vows to work with Trump on "democratic supply chain"', Nikkei Asia, January 7, 2025

29 'On board the BRP *Sierra Madre* in Ayungin Shoal: A journalist's first-hand account', Verafiles, September 24, 2023

30 'A game of shark and minnow', *New York Times*, October 27, 2013

31 'US Marine MQ-9A Reapers now deployed to the Philippines', USNI News, June 3, 2024

32 'How a decaying warship beached on a tiny shoal provoked China's ire', *New York Times*, November 11, 2023

33 'Filipino sailor recounts how thumb was torn off in South China Sea clash', *South China Morning Post*, June 26, 2024

34 'Philippines blames China for starved, dehydrated sailors at Sabina Shoal', *South China Morning Post*, September 17, 2024

35 'Stretched US Navy eyes risky new waters in South China Sea', Reuters, September 2, 2024

36 'Philippine envoy says South China Sea is the "real flashpoint" in Asia, not Taiwan', *South China Morning Post*, February 29, 2024

37 'USINDOPACOM Change of Command Ceremony', USNI News video, May 6, 2024

38 'US ambassador explains Biden's game-changing plan for Asia allies', *Newsweek*, April 3, 2024

39 'Philippines and partners conduct successful SINKEX in South China Sea', Naval News, May 9, 2024

40 'The US says it has successfully practiced using a low-cost bomb to sink a major surface ship. China is taking note', CNN World, July 27, 2024

41 'Top Gun in the Top End takes off over NT', *Katherine Times*, May 30, 2022

42 'Reflecting on a changing Indo-Pacific: A conversation with Admiral John Aquilino', CFR, April 17, 2024

43 'Joint exercise Cobra Gold 24 concludes furthering multinational relationships and interoperability', DVIDS, August 3, 2024

44 'US keeps missile system in Philippines as China tensions rise', Reuters, September 20, 2024

45 'US Army experiments with long-endurance drones, balloons in Philippines', Defense News, May 13, 2024

46 'Islanders on small Philippine chain worry a China–Taiwan conflict could spill over', Benar News, May 2, 2024

47 'Pentagon bets on quick production of autonomous systems to counter China', Politico, August 28, 2023

48 'Deputy Secretary of Defense Kathleen Hicks announces additional Replicator all-domain attritable autonomous capabilities', US Indo-Pacific Command, November 14, 2024

49 'Hicks underscores US innovation in unveiling strategy to counter China's military buildup', US Department of Defense, August 28, 2023

50 '"Hellscape": DOD launches massive drone swarm program to counter China', Defense One, August 28, 2023

51 'INDOPACOM boss on China: "Haven't faced a threat like this since World War II", *Air & Space Forces Magazine*, March 21, 2024

52 Briefing by Andrew's Air Force Base commander Brigadier General Doug Wickert, May 7, 2025, YouTube

53 Interview with the author

54 'Taiwan blockade's cost would be felt wider than Covid: US official', Nikkei Asia, October 7, 2023

55 'Wargaming a Chinese blockade of Taiwan', Center for Strategic and International Studies, July 31, 2025

56 'Indigenous people in Philippines's north "ready to fight"', Al Jazeera, April 9, 2024

57 'Analysts skeptical about potential of "Asian NATO"', VoA News, December 2, 2024

58 'Under Yoon, calls for South Korean nukes "normalized"', VoA News, September 9, 2024

59 'North Korean balloon dumps rubbish on South Korea's presidential compound', Al Jazeera, October 24, 2024

60 Interview with the author

3. The Return of War to Europe

1 'General: We will defend Narva just the same as Tallinn or Kuressaare', ERR News, February 7, 2024

2 Interview with the author

3 'Spotlight shifts to Estonia town if Russia tests NATO's mettle', *Financial Times*, April 11, 2014

4 'After Ukraine, US trains more special forces in Eastern Europe', Reuters, June 10, 2014

5 'Spotlight shifts to Estonia town if Russia tests NATO's mettle', *Financial Times*, April 11, 2014

6 'US sends "Ironhorse" tanks to NATO's nervous Baltic frontline' Reuters, October 1, 2014

7 'US military vehicles paraded 300 yards from the Russian border', *Washington Post*, February 24, 2015

8 Interviews with the author

9 Interviews with the author

10 'Mayor Katri Raik: I'm not leaving politics or Narva', News ERR, September 15, 2023

11 'Language tests and deportations: Latvia tightens the screws on its Russian minority', *Der Spiegel* (international edition), March 14, 2024

12 Elena Flack, *Forging the Enemy Within*, Cambridge University MA Thesis, 2024; interviews conducted 2023, pages 62–63

13 '"Make a Molotov cocktail": How Europeans are recruited through Telegram to commit sabotage, arson, and murder', OCCRP, September 26, 2024

14 'Estonian Defense Forces to build new base in Narva', ERR News, April 23, 2025

15 'Episode 10: The Baltics at the Crossroads of History', Facing Coming Storms podcast, March 31, 2025

16 'General Donahue on deterring Russia in Europe', War on the Rocks, July 3, 2025

17 'Satellite imagery analysis. What's going on in Putin's military bases behind the Estonian border and how big a threat they really pose us', *Eesti Ekspress*, November 1, 2024

18 'Military chiefs fear "nightmare" double wars against China and Russia', *The Times*, June 5, 2025

19 'The Baltics are building a defensive line against Russia. Can they do it fast enough?', *Daily Telegraph*, April 7, 2025

20 'Russia ready to launch offensive on NATO country, Poland warns', *Newsweek*, May 8, 2024

21 'Denmark to spend billions on defence, citing fears over Russian rearmament', *Guardian*, February 19, 2025

22 'Estonia calls for not making negotiations easy for Putin', Estonian World, February 16, 2025

23 'US troop numbers in Eastern Europe could continue to grow', *Military Times*, April 10, 2024

24 'Ben Wallace', The Rest Is Politics: Leading, January 6, 2025

25 'In Ukraine, new American technology won the day. Until it was overwhelmed', *New York Times*, April 25, 2024

26 'Patriot SAMbush: New details on Ukraine's destruction of a Russian A-50 in January 2024', *Defence-Express*, June 11, 2024

27 'US–Ukraine military presence in Wiesbaden', *New York Times*, March 29, 2025

28 'Rogue Russian pilot tried to shoot down RAF aircraft in 2022', BBC News, September 14, 2023

29 'West grapples with response to Russian sabotage attempts', *Financial Times*, June 4, 2024

30 Interview with the author

31 Joint press conference, NATO, January 17, 2025

32 'DOD Leaders Highlight Need for Increased NATO Defense Spending', US Department of Defense, April 8, 2025

33 'Exercise Steadfast Dart: Testing NATO's high-readiness 16 miles from Ukraine's border', BFBS Forces News, March 1, 2025

34 'In Romania, NATO is building one of its largest airbases in Europe', *Le Monde*, August 15, 2024

35 'After 2024 results voided, hard-right Romanian presidential candidate wins 1st round redo', CBC News, May 4, 2025

36 'Centrist wins Romania's tense presidential race over hard-right nationalist', NPR, May 18, 2025

37 'Whoever wins the White House faces tough choices on Ukraine', Reuters, November 1, 2024

38 'General Cavoli opening statement', Senate Armed Services Committee, April 3, 2025

39 'Baltics, Poland, Finland, Norway agree on "drone wall" to protect borders', LRT English, May 24, 2024

40 'Russia's neighbours urge NATO allies to bring back military service', BBC News, April 4, 2024

41 'First German Brigade members arrived in Lithuania', Ministry of National Defence of Lithuania, April 8, 2024

42 'Integration or separate schools? Lithuania prepares for German brigade's families', LRT English, August 24, 2024

43 'Lithuania promises "competitive" employment opportunities to German soldiers' families', LRT English, November 11, 2024

44 'Integration or separate schools? Lithuania prepares for German brigade's families', LRT English, August 24, 2024

45 'Germany surges to fourth-largest global military spender: SIPRI', Breaking Defense, April 28, 2025

46 'Canada faces pressure at NATO summit for riding on "coattails"', BBC News, July 9, 2024

47 'The Brigade Commander – Latvia (S5 E5)', Canadian Army Podcast, May 8, 2024

48 'We have no Plan B if Ukraine falls, says Estonia', BBC News, June 1, 2024

49 'Ukraine war: NATO watches Russian "Zombies" in Estonia', BBC News, May 23, 2023

50 'General Lauris Norstad interview with Eisenhower', Presidential Library, November 11, 1976

51 'Polish General warns of immediate strike on St Petersburg if Russia attacks NATO', NV.ua, October 11, 2024

52 Post by @USArmyEURAF on X, May 14, 2024

53 'Commemorations of the 80th anniversary of the Battle of Monte Cassino', TVP World, May 18, 2024

54 'East Shield', Government of Poland

55 'Poland's new East Shield plan mixes modern ISR with old-school physical barriers', Breaking Defense, May 28, 2024

56 'NATO members bordering Russia to build "drone wall"', RFE/RL, May 24, 2024

57 'Poland will not become "Russian colony again", foreign minister says', AA.com.tr, May 15, 2024

58 'Poland leads NATO on defence spend – but can it afford it?', Reuters, October 23, 2024

59 'Number of K2 MBTs in Poland increases. How many tanks do the Polish Armed Forces operate?', Defence24, March 21, 2024

60 'Europe's Conscription Challenge: Lessons from Nordic and Baltic States', Carnegie Endowment for International Peace, July 8, 2024

61 'Poland rolls out "Holidays with the Army" in a recruitment drive with Russia in mind', Associated Press, June 25, 2024

62 'Poland announces military training plan for all men', BBC News, March 7, 2025

63 Interviews with the author

4. 2024: 'The Hinges of History'

1 Interview with the author

2 'Hillary Clinton jokes about "future president"', *Washington Post*, November 30, 2012

3 Woodward, Bob, *War* (2024), Simon & Schuster, Kindle location 16

4 'Biden's foreign policy aims to "win the 21st century"', *Washington Post*, April 28, 2021

5 Interviews with the author

6 '"Turning point": Milley steps down as chair at a crucial moment for Ukraine', Politico, September 27, 2023

7 Interview with the author

8 'How DC became obsessed with a potential 2027 Chinese invasion of Taiwan', Defense News, May 7, 2024

9 'Milley makes case for rules-based order, deterrence in new era', US Department of Defense, June 30, 2023

10 'Slumping US–China trade accompanied by growing fear of war', Reuters, August 17, 2023

11 'The inside story of the secret backchannel between the US and China', *Financial Times*, August 25, 2024

12 'A godfather of Chinese nationalism has second thoughts', *New York Times*, October 27, 2022

13 'China's vanished foreign minister casts a long shadow', Politico EU, June 20, 2024

14 'Questions continue to swirl around China's "disappeared" foreign minister', VoA News, September 10, 2024

15 'Jake Sullivan: Minneapolis native among those to hatch Iranian nuclear deal', MinnPost, November 27, 2013

16 'President Joe Biden has won enough delegates to clinch the 2024 Democratic nomination', Associated Press, March 12, 2024

17 'Chair of the NATO Military Committee visits Israel', NATO News, September 28, 2023

18 'They were Israel's "eyes on the border" – but their Hamas warnings went unheard', BBC News, January 15, 2024

19 'Israel's military lays out its Oct 7 failures', *New York Times*, February 27, 2025

20 'Assessing the Gaza death toll after eighteen months of war', Washington Institute for Near East Policy, May 2025

21 'US defense secretary visits aircraft carrier, hails "lynchpin" of Middle East deterrence', Reuters, December 20, 2023

22 ' "We had mission and purpose": A chat with the CO of the USS *Eisenhower*,' Navy Times, September 17, 2024

23 Interviews with the author

24 'US shoots two missiles headed for container ship', Marine Link, December 30, 2023

25 'US and UK carry out strikes against Iran-backed Houthis in Yemen', CNN, January 12, 2024

26 ' "We had mission and purpose": A chat with the CO of the USS *Eisenhower*', Navy Times, September 17, 2024

27 'US Defense Secretary visits aircraft carrier in the Middle East, hails "lynchpin" of Middle East deterrence', Reuters, December 20, 2023

28 ' "We had mission and purpose": A chat with the CO of the USS *Eisenhower*', Navy Times, September 17, 2024

29 'The end of a strategic deployment', *New York Times*, July 16, 2024

30 'The Navy's ongoing carrier conundrum', Navy Times, June 27, 2024

31 'No US Navy aircraft carriers deployed in the Pacific', Naval News, August 25, 2024

32 'Why is the US Navy running out of Tomahawk cruise missiles?', AEI, February 13, 2024

33 'The US Navy has a missile problem in the Red Sea', *Daily Telegraph*, February 7, 2024

34 'Lockheed Martin to increase PAC-3 MSE production by 70 per cent', Shephard Media, November 15, 2024

35 'Aircraft carrier Enterprise delivery delayed by eighteen months, says navy', US Naval Institute News, March 15, 2024

36 'Report to Congress on Columbia-class ballistic missile submarine program', US Naval Institute News, February 19, 2024

37 '2021–2024 Quadrennial Supply Chain Review', Biden White House archives, December 2024

38 ' "The Decisive Decade": Remarks by Secretary of Defense Lloyd J. Austin III at the Reagan National Defense Forum', US Department of Defense, December 3, 2022

39 'Bob Woodward on *War*', CBS News, October 13, 2024

40 'We finally know the backstory of how Defense Secretary Austin got the Silver Star', Task & Purpose, January 27, 2022

41 'Congress approves waiver for Lloyd Austin to serve as SECDEF', US Naval Institute News, January 21, 2021

42 'Navy conducts first successful tests reloading missiles and rearming warships at sea', US Naval Institute News, October 15, 2024

43 'What Jake Sullivan wants the Trump administration to know about the defense industrial base', DefenseScoop, January 15, 2025

44 'Can Just-In-Time handle a new era of war?' NPR, January 30, 2024

45 'Saildrone support to Task Force 59', Saildrone website, published 2023, viewed 2025

46 'Enterprise cloud conflict could "turbocharge" AI in the Pentagon', Defense Scoop, May 3, 2023

47 'Remarks by Jake Sullivan on AI and national security', Biden White House archives, October 24, 2024

48 'Austin underscores power of partnerships at INDO-PACOM change of command', US Department of Defense, May 3, 2024

49 'US Indo-Pacific Command holds change of command ceremony', US Indo-Pacific Command, May 3, 2024

50 'A life of leadership and faith', *Hawaii Catholic Herald*, May 22, 2024

51 'A conversation with Commander of US Indo-Pacific Command Admiral Samuel Paparo', Brookings Institution, November 19, 2024

52 '"The New Convergence in the Indo-Pacific": Remarks by Secretary of Defense Lloyd J. Austin III at the 2024 Shangri-La Dialogue', US Department of Defense, June 1, 2024

53 'Defense Secretary Austin promotes new, "unique" Pacific "network of partnerships"', Breaking Defense, June 1, 2024

54 'The U.S. military plans a "Hellscape" to deter China from attacking Taiwan', *Washington Post*, June 10, 2024

55 'Xi Jinping claimed US wants China to attack Taiwan', *Financial Times*, June 15, 2024

56 'Remarks in Kyiv by Secretary of Defense Lloyd J. Austin III on Ukraine's Fight for Freedom', US Embassy in Ukraine, October 23, 2024

5. Trump Shakes the World

1 Post by @DonaldTrump on X, March 9, 2023

2 'Under the Rotunda, a historic concentration of wealth salutes Trump', *Washington Post*, updated January 20, 2025

3 'The Inaugural Address', The White House, January 20, 2025

4 'NATO Secretary General in panel discussion at Munich Security conference', YouTube, February 15, 2025

5 'US friends and foes buckle up for "America First" ', *Bangkok Post*, February 1, 2025

6 'Trump "prizes loyalty above all things": Reuters reporter on Trump's top military purge', MSNBC, February 22, 2025

7 'Donald Trump's imperial presidency is a throwback to a greedier, pernicious age', *Guardian*, March 22, 2025

8 'Vice President Vance swears in Pete Hegseth to be Secretary of Defense', The White House, January 25, 2025

9 Eisenhower, Dwight D., *The Eisenhower Diaries*, W. W. Norton & Company (1981), page 194

10 'The expanding empire of Donald Trump', *New York Times*, April 8, 1984

11 'Donald Trump, holding all the cards the tower! The team! The money! The future!', *Washington Post*, November 15, 1984

12 'Trump angled for Soviet posting in the 1980s, says Nobel Prize winner', *Hollywood Reporter*, May 26, 2017

13 'Trump gives a vague hint of candidacy', *New York Times*, September 2, 1987

14 'I was Trump's ghostwriter. A new biopic gets the most important thing right', *New York Times*, October 11, 2024

15 'The day Trump ran for president (and what people predicted)', BBC News, June 16, 2019

16 Center for a New American Security National Security Conference, June 3, 2025

17 'Inside Marco Rubio's meteoric – and precarious – rise in Trumpworld', *Washington Post*, May 14, 2025

18 'Pentagon thrown into confusion over think tank ban', Politico, July 28, 2025

19 Vance, J. D., *Hillbilly Elegy* (2016), William Collins, Kindle location 245 (Note: at the time this book was published, Vance still used a full stop between his initials representing his first names John Donald, but changed this to remove them on entering politics from 2021, making his legal first name from then 'JD'.)

20 'Trump's VP pick spells "disaster for Europe and Ukraine" ' Politico EU, July 15, 2024

21 Interviews with the author

22 'The speech that stunned Europe', Foreign Policy, February 18, 2025

23 'Trump and Zelenskyy in the Oval Office', Rev.com transcript, March 3, 2025

24 'Three weeks that changed the world: How Trump turned against Ukraine and Europe', Reuters, March 10, 2025

25 'Did Zelensky call JD Vance "b***h", "f**k" in Ukrainian? Social media users claim Ukraine president quietly muttered insult under his breath', *International Business Times*, March 3, 2025

26 Post by @kaitlancollins on X, February 28, 2025

27 'Trump and Zelenskyy in the Oval Office', Rev.com transcript, March 3, 2025

28 'Three weeks that changed the world: How Trump turned against Ukraine and Europe', Reuters, March 10, 2025

29 'The leaked Signal chat, annotated', *New York Times*, March 25, 2025

30 'Diplomat who left top secret files at bus stop poised to be UK's new NATO ambassador', *Daily Telegraph*, January 30, 2025

31 'Mike Waltz fell into an age-old trap in political history', Politico, May 18, 2025

32 '"Never heard of him": Surprise and questions greet Trump's defense secretary pick', Reuters, November 13, 2024

33 Interviews with the author

34 'Opening Remarks by Secretary of Defense Pete Hegseth at Ukraine Defense Contact Group', US Department of Defense, February 12, 2025

35 'Thunderbolt Convergence: US, NATO forces prove rapid HIMARS deployment in joint fires exercise', DVIDS (US Army), March 27, 2025

36 Hegseth, Pete, *The War on Warriors* (2024), HarperCollins, Kindle location 13

37 Ibid, Kindle location 184

38 'Hegseth, advocate for firing "woke" military leaders, picked for defense secretary', Reuters, November 13, 2024

39 'Hegseth works hard to portray himself as a man of the troops. They might not buying it', Military website, May 2, 2025

40 'War heroes and military firsts are among 26,000 images flagged for removal in Pentagon's DEI purge', Associated Press, March 7, 2025

41 'Trump to get Golden Dome options next week: defense source says', Defense One, March 27, 2025

42 'Trump open to selling allies "toned-down" version of next-gen F-47 fighter', Nikkei Asia, March 22, 2025

43 'Tokyo frets about durability of US alliance ahead of visit by Pete Hegseth', *Financial Times*, March 25, 2025

44 'Trump "angry" with Putin and threatens tariffs on Russian oil over Ukraine', Al Jazeera, March 30, 2025

45 'Senate confirms Trump's controversial pick for Pentagon policy chief', Politico, April 8, 2025

46 'War with China: Inside Taiwan's biggest ever drills', *Telegraph*: Battle Lines podcast, July 21, 2025

47 'Taiwan must get serious on defense', *Taipei Times*, May 11, 2024

48 Interviews with the author

49 'Trump turns up trade pressure on China after Beijing fails to come running', *New York Times*, March 3, 2025

50 'China says it is ready for "any type of war" with US', BBC News, March 5, 2025

51 'Explainer: How China's rhetoric has changed during Trump 2.0', BBC Monitoring, March 18, 2025

52 'US reviewing AUKUS submarine pact', BBC News, June 12, 2025

6. The Challenge for Democracies

1 MoD press 'huddle' attended by the author, Honourable Artillery Company, December 1, 2024

2 'John Healey: "Britain has a lot to learn from Ukraine's resilience"', *New Statesman*, April 4, 2024

3 Interview with the author

4 MoD press 'huddle', Honourable Artillery Company, London, December 1, 2024

5 Ibid

6 Martin, Mike, *An Intimate War: An Oral History of the Helmand Conflict 1978–2012* (2014), C. Hurst & Co., Kindle location 160–165

7 'Why recruits are quitting the Armed Forces in their droves', *Daily Telegraph*, December 24, 2024

8 'A Response to RUSI LWC24: A People Focused Perspective', Wavell Room, August 2, 2024

9 'Rise of the robots: AI to shape UK defence review', Politico EU, October 9, 2024

10 Interviews with the author

11 'Should the West have handled Ukraine differently?: Former UK Defence Secretary', The Rest is Politics podcast, January 6, 2025

12 'Chief of the Defence Chatham House Security and Defence Conference 2024 keynote speech', GOV.UK, February 27, 2024

13 'The untold story of British military chiefs' crucial role in Ukraine', *The Times*, April 11, 2025

14 'Chief of the Defence Chatham House Security and Defence Conference 2024 keynote speech', GOV.UK, February 27, 2024

15 'British innovation and Soviet-designed missiles help Ukraine take the fight to Russia', Forces News, February 12, 2025

16 'Major war could destroy UK Army in six months – minister', BBC News, December 4, 2024

17 'One fifth of armed forces not fit to fight, admits MoD', *The Times*, December 23, 2024

18 'Alistair Carns: If war erupts in Europe, I want to be ready to fight', *The Times*, November 8, 2024

19 'Alistair Carns: If war erupts in Europe, I want to be ready to fight', *The Times*, November 8, 2024

20 'Gen Z think UK is racist and would not fight for their country', *The Times*, February 10, 2025

21 'Britain doesn't want to go to war', UnHerd, June 6, 2024

22 'Australia still facing troop shortage despite 64,000 applications in 2024: Report', The Defense Post, January 9, 2025

23 'Germany: Bundeswehr ranks shrink despite recruitment drive', Deutsche Welle, February 2, 2024

24 'Europe's soldiers keep quitting, just when NATO needs them', Politico EU, March 18, 2024

25 'The future battlefield, from Europe to the Indo-Pacific', Modern War Institute podcast, May 1, 2025

26 'Ukraine's secret weapon: the £40bn tech firm that "found Bin Laden"', *The Times*, March 29, 2024

27 Interview with the author

28 Interviews with the author

29 Interview with the author

30 'Ukraine's Sea Baby drone boats shoot back now', *Forbes*, December 9, 2024

31 'Anti-drone tactics makes early Ukraine war drones obsolete', Polymer Nano Centrum Blog, November 10, 2023

32 Interviews with the author

33 Interview with the author

34 '"The business of war": Google employees protest work for the Pentagon', *New York Times*, April 4, 2018

35 Interview with the author

36 'Taiwan moves to buy 1,000 AeroVironment, Anduril attack drones', Bloomberg, October 28, 2024

37 'From court rooms to crisis lines, Chinese officials embrace DeepSeek', *New York Times*, March 18, 2025

38 'Is the PLA overestimating the potential of artificial intelligence?', National Defense University, January 27, 2025

39 'The geek who builds lethal AI weapons, with a hotline to Trump', *The Times*, February 27, 2025

40 '18th Airborne Corps' "tricky" AI journey', Signal media, August 21, 2024

41 'AI comes of age on jets and ships', Reuters, May 18, 2023

42 Post by @AlistairCarns on X, April 21, 2025

43 'Taiwanese soldiers trained to operate HIMARS in Oklahoma', *Taiwan News*, November 1, 2024

44 Ibid

45 Interview with the author

46 Interview with the author

47 'Trump's ambassador pick wants Japan to pay more for US bases', Nikkei Asia, March 14, 2025

48 'Japan on red alert as Trump rocks international alliances', Nikkei Asia, March 13, 2025

49 'Suspension of US intelligence to Ukraine reshapes global defence', Reuters, March 21, 2025

50 'Friedrich Merz was the most pro-US politician in Germany – his shift could be historic for Europe', *Guardian*, February 26, 2025

51 'Macron to EU colleagues: Stop buying American, buy European', Politico EU, March 16, 2025

52 'EU slams the door on US in colossal defense plan', Politico EU, March 19, 2025

53 Interviews with the author

54 'Plumbing woes on Navy carrier means no hot showers for 170 days', *The Times*, May 14, 2025

55 'Royal Navy Vanguard-class submarine comes home after breaking the record for the longest patrol', *Navy Lookout*, March 17, 2025

56 Interview with the author

57 '3rd EEAS Report on Foreign Information Manipulation and Interference Threats: Exposing the Architecture of FIMI Operations', European External Action Service, March, 2025

58 'The US spies who sound the alarm about election interference', *New Yorker*, October 21, 2024

59 'Former Head of MI6: Russia, China, and Trump (Sir Alex Younger)', The Rest Is Politics podcast, May 4, 2025

60 'Keir Starmer, unlikely leader of the free world', Politico EU, March 4, 2025

61 Post by @TimesRadio on X, March 19, 2025

62 Interviews with the author

63 Interview with the author

64 'Trump in talks to deploy private army to Ukraine', *Daily Telegraph*, August 30, 2025

65 'Europe must assert hard power or become a "hunted animal", France's top general warns', Politico EU, August 28, 2025

66 'Europe says it's rearming, but does it have the stomach to face Putin', *Sunday Times*, August 16, 2025

7. Countdown to Confrontation – From Churchill to Covid

1 Interview with the author

2 'Coronavirus: Half of humanity now on lockdown as 90 countries call for confinement', Euronews, April 2, 2020

3 'Captain of aircraft carrier pleads for help as virus cases increase onboard', *New York Times*, April 5, 2020

4 'Taiwan scrambles warships as PLA Navy aircraft carrier strike group passes', *South China Morning Post*, April 12, 2020

5 Gilbert, Martin, *Winston Churchill: Volume 7: Road to Victory* (1986), William Heinemann Ltd, Kindle location 575

6 Moran, Lord, *Churchill: The Struggle for Survival, 1940–1965* (1966), Houghton Mifflin Company, p. 131

7 Fenby, Jonathan, *Chiang Kai-shek: China's Generalissimo and the Nation He Lost* (2015), Simon & Schuster, Kindle location 399

8 Ibid, Kindle location 409

9 Ibid, Kindle location 402–412

10 'MOFA strongly refutes Chinese leader Xi's misrepresentation of historical facts and UNGA Resolution 2758 in signed article', Ministry of Foreign Affairs Republic of China (Taiwan), May 8, 2025

11 Wasif Khan, Sulmaan, *The Struggle for Taiwan: A History* (2024), Allen Lane, Kindle location 45–52

12 'The Taiwan Straits Crises: 1954–1955 and 1958', US Department of State, Office of the Historian

13 Wasif Khan, Sulmaan, *The Struggle for Taiwan: A History* (2024), Allen Lane, Kindle location 105

14 'For Gorbachev, Met museum and Trump Tower visits due', *New York Times*, December 1, 1988

15 'Trump's record on Russia: snubbed by Gorbachev, fooled by impostor', Buzzfeed News, September 18, 2015

16 'China's hero of democracy: Gorbachev', *New York Times*, May 14, 1989

17 'Remarks to the Supreme Soviet of the Republic of the Ukraine in Kiev, Soviet Union', George Bush Presidential Library and Museum, August 1, 1991

18 'After Soviet Union: Yeltsin curbs his vice president, moves into Gorbachev office', *New York Times*, December 28, 1991

19 'Mission impossible: how one man bought China its first aircraft carrier', *South China Morning Post*, January 18, 2015

20 'The inside story of the *Liaoning*: How Xu Zengping sealed the deal for China's first aircraft carrier', *South China Morning Post*, January 19, 2015

21 'Students in Taiwan agree to end their largest democracy rally', *New York Times*, March 23, 1990

22 'China hints at a timetable to take control of Taiwan', *New York Times*, January 31, 1996

23 'Yeltsin asks UN to help Russians in the Baltics', *New York Times*, November 8, 1992

24 'Yeltsin addresses rift with Ukraine', *New York Times*, June 23, 1992

25 'Ukraine gave up a giant nuclear arsenal 30 years ago. Today there are regrets', *New York Times*, February 5, 2022

26 'Mission impossible: how one man bought China its first aircraft carrier', *South China Morning Post*, January 18, 2015

27 'Turks keep ship going round in circles', *Washington Post*, July 21, 2001

28 'Carrier of navy's pride', *China Daily*, April 19, 2013

29 'Chinese embassy bombing: A wide net of blame', *New York Times*, April 17, 2000

30 'Analysis: Mystery of 1999 US stealth jet shootdown returns with twist', Nikkei Asia, June 3, 2021

31 Jackson, Mike, *Soldier: The Autobiography of General Sir Mike Jackson* (2007), Bantam Press, pages 272–3

32 'Singer James Blunt "prevented World War III"', BBC News, November 14, 2010

33 'British Brigadier recalls "World War Three" moment in Kosovo', Balkan Insight, June 12, 2024

34 'Top US general calls command standoff in Kosovo troubling', *New York Times*, September 11, 1999

35 'Nato shaken by confrontation with Russian bombers', *Guardian*, July 2, 1999

36 'Vietnam's rare commemoration of a deadly South China Sea battle is a quiet but direct message to Beijing', Business Insider, May 25, 2022

37 'Interview: Lt. Shane Osborn', PBS Frontline, interview conducted early autumn 2001

38 'Aircrew fly back to "very sorry" US', *Guardian*, April 12, 2001

39 'China denies Taiwan law is a war bill', *New York Times*, March 14, 2005

40 'As China showcases carrier, global naval balance shifting', Reuters, November 28, 2012

41 'Chinese carrier *Shandong* deploys nears the Philippines', USNI News, April 23, 2025

42 'Putin says US is undermining global stability', *New York Times*, February 11, 2007

43 'China resumes rare earth exports to Japan', BBC News, November 24, 2010

44 Interview with the author

45 'Government Assessment of the Syrian Government's Use of Chemical Weapons on August 21, 2013', The White House, August 30, 2013

46 'Obama forced Xi to back down over South China Sea dispute', *Financial Times*, July 11, 2016

47 'Trump's Taiwan phone call was long planned, say people who were involved', *Washington Post*, December 4, 2016

48 'Fiona Hill interview: Trump is terrified of Putin, I've seen it firsthand', *Sunday Telegraph*, May 25, 2025

49 'Trump asked Ukraine leader to look into why investigation of Biden's son ended, text of call shows', NBC News, September 25, 2019

8. *The Lessons of Ukraine*

1 'The 12 best quotes about Ukraine in 2023', *Kyiv Post*, December 23, 2023

2 '"Something was badly wrong": When Washington realised Russia was actually invading Ukraine', Politico, February 24, 2023

3 Shuster, Simon, *The Showman* (2024), William Collins, Kindle location 306

4 Ibid, Kindle location 459

5 'Road to war: US struggled to convince allies, and Zelenskyy, of risk of invasion', *Washington Post*, August 16, 2022

6 'Here's what those "bunker-defeat" rockets the US sent to Ukraine are actually capable of', TWZ, January 26, 2022

7 Interviews with the author

8 'Russia-Ukraine crisis: UK won't be able to fly people out – minister', BBC News, February 12, 2022

9 'Pentagon orders departure of US troops in Ukraine as Russia crisis escalates', CNBC, February 12, 2022

10 '"Ukrainians feel that they've been abandoned," ambassador says as crisis intensifies', CNBC, February 14, 2022

11 'Road to war: US struggled to convince allies, and Zelenskyy, of risk of invasion', *Washington Post*, August 16, 2022

12 *Servant of the People*, (S1, E1) (2015), Kvartal 95

13 'Russia warns increasing risk of "major" Ukraine offensive in coming weeks', BBC News, April 22, 2019

14 Shuster, Simon, *The Showman* (2024), William Collins, Kindle location 350

15 Ibid, Kindle location 281

16 'Ukraine's first lady Olena Zelenska takes on the trauma of war', *TIME*, July 7, 2022

17 Shuster, Simon, *The Showman* (2024), William Collins, Kindle location 306

18 'Oleksiy Danilov: Russia will collapse in our lifetime', Ukrainska Pravda, April 22, 2022

19 'Analysis: Xi–Putin honeymoon at risk as Chinese flood into Russia', Nikkei Asia, March 21, 2024

20 Interview with the author

21 'Oleksiy Danilov: Russia will collapse in our lifetime', Ukrainska Pravda, April 22, 2022

22 Shuster, Simon, *The Showman* (2024), William Collins, Kindle location 1575

23 'The Battle of Irpin River', *The British Army Review*, Spring 2024 (Issue #187), page 10

24 Shuster, Simon, *The Showman* (2024), William Collins, Kindle location 480

25 'The Battle of Irpin River', *The British Army Review*, Spring 2024 (Issue #187), pages 22–25

26 Interview with the author

27 'The spy war: How the CIA secretly helps Ukraine fight', *New York Times*, February 28, 2024

28 ' "Something was badly wrong": When Washington realized Russia was actually invading Ukraine', Politico, February 24, 2023

29 Interviews with the author

30 Interview with the author

31 'The secret history of the war in Ukraine', *New York Times*, March 29, 2025

32 Shuster, Simon, *The Showman* (2024), William Collins, Kindle pp 110–120

33 'The secret history of the war in Ukraine', *New York Times*, March 29, 2025

34 'US intelligence helped Ukraine strike Russian flagship, officials say', *New York Times*, May 5, 2022

35 'The secret history of the war in Ukraine', *New York Times*, March 29, 2025

36 Interviews with the author

37 'Collaborators and Russian-installed officials attacked since the invasion of Ukraine', *Moscow Times*, June 13, 2024

38 'US intelligence helped Ukraine strike Russian flagship, officials say', *New York Times*, May 5, 2022

39 'The Defense Department says it will support Ukraine for "as long as it takes" ', *New York Times*, November 4, 2022

40 'The secret history of the war in Ukraine', *New York Times*, March 29, 2025

41 'It took nearly two years, but large numbers of German-made Leopard 1 tanks are finally arriving in Ukraine', *Forbes*, December 26, 2024

42 'Keir Starmer on the benefits U-turn and his toughest week yet', *Sunday Times*, June 28, 2025

43 'The secret history of the war in Ukraine', *New York Times*, March 29, 2025

44 ' "Cult" of tourniquets causing thousands of unnecessary amputations and deaths in Ukraine, say surgeons', *Daily Telegraph*, August 4, 2025

45 'As Ukraine's fate hangs in the balance, "Soviet" command culture damages war effort', Kyiv Independent, March 27, 2025

46 Interview with the author

47 'As Ukraine's fate hangs in the balance, "Soviet" command culture damages war effort', Kyiv Independent, March 27, 2025

48 'First day summary of Yalta European Strategy Meeting – the necessity to win', Yalta European Strategy, September 15, 2024

49 'Second day summary of Yalta European Strategy meeting - the necessity to win', Yalta European Strategy, September 16, 2024

50 'Zelenskyy hits back at Trump's claims he is prolonging war by not ceding land to Russia', Euronews, April 23, 2025

51 'Trump and Putin want to talk business once the Ukraine war ends. Here's why it won't be easy', Associated Press, May 31, 2025

52 'Can Trump seize a win in Ukraine?', Just Security, June 5, 2025

53 'Trump's new position on the war in Ukraine: Not my problem', *New York Times*, May 20, 2025

54 'President Donald Trump says Russian leader Vladimir Putin "has gone absolutely CRAZY!"', Associated Press, May 26 2025

55 'Kremlin calls Trump "emotional" after US president says Putin is "crazy"', BBC News, May 26, 2025

56 'US intelligence weighs Putin's two years of extreme pandemic isolation as a factor in his wartime mind-set', *New York Times*, March 5, 2022

57 '"That idiot Putin wants to take it all": Russia kamikaze tactics fuel a slow advance in Ukraine', *Guardian*, July 27, 2025

58 'Defence Secretary Speech at RUSI Land Warfare Conference 2022', GOV.UK website, June 28, 2022

59 'Putin's chilling warning to Russian "traitors" and "scum" is a sign things aren't going according to plan', CNN, March 17, 2022

60 'Alternate reality: How Russian society learned to stop worrying about the war', Carnegie Endowment for International Peace, November 28, 2023

9. 'Better Than Allies' – Inside the 'Axis of Upheaval'

1 'Xi Jinping's key quotes on China–Russia ties', CGTN, May 16, 2024

2 Sheridan, Michael, *The Red Emperor: XI Jinping and His New China* (2024), Headline, Kindle pp. 48–55

3 'CO15071 | Lee Kuan Yew's China Wisdom', Nanyang Technological University, March 30, 2015

4 Interview with the author

5 'General Zhang Youxia: Xi Jinping's "sworn brother" now his deputy on China's top military body', *South China Morning Post*, October 25, 2017

6 Ibid

7 Interview with the author

8 'In Beijing, Olympic spectacle and global power games', *New York Times*, February 4, 2022

9 '"No wavering": After turning to Putin, Xi faces hard wartime choices for China', *New York Times*, March 7, 2022

10 '"He is my best friend": 10 years of strengthening ties between Putin and Xi', *Guardian*, March 21, 2023

11 'Secret Russian intelligence document shows deep suspicion of China', *New York Times*, June 7, 2025

12 'Analysis: Xi–Putin honeymoon at risk as Chinese flood into Russia', Nikkei Asia, March 21, 2024

13 'China's Xi: Nuclear wars cannot be fought in Ukraine – China foreign minister', Reuters, November 15, 2022

14 '"Good old friend": Putin offers praise for Xi ahead of first trip to Russia since Ukraine invasion", *Guardian*, March 20, 2023

15 'China's Xi tells Putin of "changes not seen for 100 years"', Al Jazeera, March 22, 2023

16 'Why Xi Jinping is still Vladimir Putin's best friend', Politico EU, March 20, 2023

17 '"Shared resentments" but Russia ties could be "awkward" for China', Al Jazeera, February 23, 2022

18 'How deep are China–Russia military ties?', ChinaPower (CSIS)

19 'China contributes 60 per cent of Russian weapons' foreign components, says Ukraine', Euractiv, September 24, 2024

20 'The siege of Leningrad (1941–1944)', *Digital Encyclopaedia of European History*, Sorbonne University website

21 Gevorkyan, Nataliya, Timakova, Natalya, and Kolesnikov, Andrei, translated by Fitzpatrick, Catherine A., *First Person: An astonishingly frank self-portrait by Russia's president Vladimir Putin* (2000), PublicAffairs, extracted in *New York Times*, May 14, 2000

22 Hill, Fiona and Gaddy, Clifford, *Mr Putin: Operative in the Kremlin* (2015), Brookings Institution Press, Kindle page 164

23 'Pure poison: Putin's links to espionage, terrorism and organised crime', Byline Times, August 27, 2020

24 'Vladimir Putin says he resorted to driving a taxi after fall of Soviet Union', *Guardian*, December 13, 2021

25 Hill, Fiona and Gaddy, Clifford, *Mr Putin: Operative in the Kremlin* (2015), Brookings Institution Press, Kindle page 168

26 'Kim Jong Un: North Korea leader enters Russia to visit Putin', BBC News, September 12, 2023

27 'Putin meets Kim, says Russia will help North Korea build satellites', Reuters, September 13, 2023

28 'The China–North Korea Relationship', Council on Foreign Relations, November 21, 2024

29 'Putin signs into law mutual defence treaty with North Korea', Reuters, November 9, 2024

30 'North Korea's suicide soldiers pose new challenge for Ukraine in war with Russia', Reuters, January 14, 2025

31 'Six takeaways from commander of US Indo-Pacific Command Admiral Samuel Paparo', Brookings, December 6, 2024

32 'Hamas visit to Moscow shows strained relations with the Kremlin', Memri, February 5, 2025

33 'Russia Provided Targeting Data for Houthi Assault on Global Shipping', *Wall Street Journal*, October 24, 2024

34 'Russia provides targeting support to Houthi attacks on commercial shipping', Foundation for Defense of Democracies, October 26, 2024

35 'China, Russia back Iran as Trump presses Tehran for nuclear talks', Reuters, March 14, 2025

36 'Iran, China and Russia launch annual joint naval drills as Trump upends Western alliances', CNN World, March 10, 2025

37 'Trump is being played by Putin – Russia will never accept a peace deal', *Sunday Telegraph*, March 2, 2025

38 'China's other transition: Military to be led by new generation', *Washington Post*, October 23, 2012

39 'The rise and fall of the Wolf Warriors', The China Story (undated)

40 'A wonky memento and a China metaphor', The Interpreter, December 10, 2024

41 'Chinese general leads troops in Cyprus as Beijing embraces UN role', Reuters, March 27, 2013

42 Ibid

43 'Putin meets senior Chinese general, hails growing military ties', *Moscow Times*, November 8, 2023

44 Interviews with the author

45 'Chinese nationals fighting for Russia in Ukraine are mercenaries – US officials', Reuters, April 11, 2025

46 '"Do you want to show strength here?": Russia's ads recruiting Chinese mercenaries', *Guardian*, April 10, 2025

47 'China's next step in modernizing the People's Liberation Army: A new reserve service system', Army War College, December 5, 2024

48 'Xi urges strategic missile troops to enhance deterrence, combat capabilities', CCTV Video News Agency, October 19, 2024

49 'Mainland China's PLA "ready to fight" for Taiwan at any time, commander warns', *South China Morning Post*, March 16, 2025

50 'Russia and China's militaries: similarities and differences (S1, E25)', Facing Coming Storms podcast, August 4, 2025

51 'China's lessons from the Russia–Ukraine war', RAND Corporation, May 22, 2025

52 'China's no first use of nuclear weapons policy: change or false alarm?', Royal United Services Institute, October 13, 2023

53 'Is China changing its nuclear launch strategy?', *Foreign Policy*, August 5, 2025

10. The Engines of Armageddon

1 Hennessy, Peter, *The Secret State: Whitehall and the Cold War* (2003), Penguin, Kindle location 45

2 'Keir Starmer welcomes submariners home after record deployment', *The Times*, March 20, 2025

3 'The mysterious instructions to Britain's Trident-armed subs in case of nuclear apocalypse', Forces News, July 5, 2024

4 'UK to purchase US jets capable of carrying nuclear weapons', *Financial Times*, June 25, 2025

5 'Nukes in the sky: The RAF goes nuclear (again)', *Forces News* YouTube channel, June 25, 2025

6 'Fears of "serious loss of life" on nuclear submarine when "supplies ran low"', *Daily Telegraph*, October 25, 2024

7 'Submarine captain sacked for making sex vid while in charge of nuclear missiles & sharing filthy clip with junior sailor', *Sun*, August 11, 2024

8 'Three submarine captains stripped of OBEs over bullying claims', *The Times*, June 24, 2025

9 Interviews with the author

10 'Here comes *Yakutia*, Russia's newest nuclear icebreaker', The Barents Observer, December 30, 2024

11 'Russia's north: Politics and nuclear junk are hot', *New York Times*, February 23, 2000

12 'Russia releases "Satan 2" missile test footage', CNN World, March 30, 2018

13 'A deep-diving sub. A deadly fire. And Russia's secret undersea agenda', *New York Times*, April 20, 2020

14 'Secret submarine operation: "The aim is to show that Russia can reach the US"' (translated headline from original Norwegian), NRK, October 29, 2019

15 'In conversation with Fiona Hill on Donald Trump's nuclear nightmares', Engelsberg Ideas, June 3, 2025

16 'Trump is "fascist to the core", Milley says in Woodward book', *Washington Post*, October 12, 2024

17 '"Something was badly wrong": When Washington realized Russia was actually invading Ukraine', Politico, February 24, 2023

18 'Deter and divide – Russia's nuclear rhetoric & escalation risks in Ukraine', CSIS, December 4, 2024

19 'Russia fired new ballistic missile at Ukraine, Putin says', Reuters, November 22, 2024

20 'NATO military chief says troops would be on ground if not for Russian nukes', *Newsweek*, November 10, 2024

21 'Russia's new Sarmat ballistic missile "blows up during test launch"', *Guardian*, September 23, 2024

22 'Putin claims Russia successfully tested a nuclear-powered missile', *New York Times*, October 5, 2023

23 'Russian Doomsday sub *Belgorod* spotted in the Arctic', USNI News, October 5, 2022

24 'One nuclear-armed Poseidon torpedo could decimate a coastal city. Russia wants 30 of them', Bulletin of the Atomic Scientists, June 14, 2023

25 'Putin warns West that sending troops to Ukraine risks "tragic" global nuclear war', PBS News, February 29, 2024

26 'France successfully conducts evaluation launch of ASMPA-R nuclear missile (with inert warhead)', The Aviationist, May 24, 2024

27 'US completes INF treaty withdrawal', Arms Control Association, September 2019

28 'Pentagon suggests countering devastating cyberattacks with nuclear arms', *New York Times*, January 16, 2018

29 'To counter Russia, US signals nuclear arms are back in a big way', *New York Times*, February 4, 2018

30 'Fort Greely stands firm in the face of North Korean threat', US Department of Defense, October 11, 2017

31 'How does the next great power conflict play out? Lessons from a wargame', War on the Rocks, April 22, 2019

32 'Updating nuclear command, control, and communication', CSIS Nuclear Network, January 3, 2025

33 'States invest in nuclear arsenals as geopolitical relations deteriorate – New SIPRI Yearbook out now', SIPRI, 12 June, 2023

34 'Status of world nuclear forces', Federation of American Scientists, March 26, 2025

35 'China's atomic weapon story told', *New York Times*, May 5, 1985

36 Ibid

37 '1966: China reports perfect test of a guided A-missile', *New York Times*, October 28, 2016

38 'Making sense of China's missile forces', NDU Press, February 5, 2019

39 'Chinese missiles: Winning the limited war', *Strategic Analysis: A Monthly Journal of the IDSA*, June, 2000

40 'Chinese nuclear weapons, 2025', Bulletin of the Atomic Scientists, March 12, 2025

41 'China's nuclear buildup is on track despite graft scandals, Pentagon says', *New York Times*, December 18, 2024

42 'Statement of General Anthony J. Cotton Commander, United States Strategic Command', Senate Armed Services Committee, March 26, 2025

43 'Role of nuclear weapons grows as geopolitical relations deteriorate – new SIPRI Yearbook out now', SIPRI, June 17, 2024

44 'New Pentagon report claims China now has over 500 operational nuclear warheads', NPR, October 19, 2023

45 Interview with the author

46 '"Nuclear Threats and the Role of Allies": Remarks by Acting Assistant Secretary of Defense for Space Policy Dr Vipin Narang at CSIS', US Department of Defense, August 1, 2024

47 'ACA welcomes Trump's acknowledgement of the "tremendous" cost and dangers of nuclear weapons and interest in "denuclearization" with Russia and China', Arms Control Association, January 24, 2025

48 'In conversation with Fiona Hill on Donald Trump's nuclear nightmares', Engelsberg Ideas, June 3, 2025

49 'Trump may be triggering the fastest nuclear weapons race since the Cold War', Politico, April 11, 2025

50 'Trump puts nuclear weapons on the agenda. The world should listen', The Interpreter, April 16, 2025

51 'Источник: ВМФ в 2021 году получит сразу три АПЛ' [*Source: The Navy will receive three nuclear submarines in 2021*], August 9, 2021

52 Jacobsen, Annie, *Nuclear War* (2024), Torva, Kindle location 47

53 Hackett, General Sir John, *The Third World War* (1978), Sidgwick & Jackson, pages 287–309

54 'Trump may be triggering the fastest nuclear weapons race since the Cold War', Politico, April 11 2025

55 'STEADFAST NOON with 13 allied airpowers over Europe', Media Magik Entertainment, October 21, 2024

56 'You can call 2007 nuke mishandling an embarrassment, but don't call it the "Minot incident"', Air Force Times, June 25, 2019

57 'Is NATO's nuclear strike exercise badly timed?', BFBS Forces News, October 21, 2022

58 Interviews with the author

59 Interview with the author

11. The Middle East on the Brink

1 'Don't forget about the Middle East,' War Room – US Army War College, April 25, 2024

2 'How Israel built a modern-day Trojan Horse: exploding pagers', *New York Times*, September 18, 2024

3 'Iran's envoy to Lebanon claims Hezbollah pager that injured him was in his office as protective measure', *Times of Israel*, April 24, 2025

4 'Behind the dismantling of Hezbollah: Decades of Israeli intelligence', *New York Times*, December 29, 2024

5 'Hagel lifts veil on major military center in Qatar', *New York Times*, December 11, 2013

6 'How a 4-hour battle between Russian mercenaries and US commandos unfolded in Syria', *New York Times*, May 24, 2018

7 'Two major Saudi oil installations hit by drone strike, and US blames Iran', *New York Times*, September 14, 2019

8 'China's basing quest in the Gulf: Pipe dream or strategic reality?', Atlantic Council, June 13, 2025

9 'Air Force just tested its big backup plan if its Air Ops center in Qatar gets attacked', TWZ, September 30, 2019

10 'Statement for the record General Michael "Erik" Kurilla', United States Central Command, June 10, 2025

11 'Iran launches "over 200 drones, ballistic and cruise missiles" towards Israel in first ever direct attack', *Independent*, April 14, 2024

12 'Attack on Iran next to nuclear site sends message: We could have done worse here – analysis', *Jerusalem Post*, April 19, 2024

13 'Bomb smuggled into Tehran guesthouse months ago killed Hamas leader', *New York Times*, August 1, 2024

14 'How effective was Iran's attack? The Israeli public doesn't have the full picture', *Times of Israel*, October 6, 2024

15 'Chief of the Defence Staff RUSI Lecture 2024', Ministry of Defence, speech by Admiral Sir Tony Radakin, December 4, 2024

16 ' "Lavender": The AI machine directing Israel's bombing spree in Gaza', +972 Magazine, April 3, 2024

17 'Hostilities in the Gaza Strip and Israel – reported impact: Day 45', United Nations Office for the Coordination of Humanitarian Affairs (OCHA), November 20, 2023

18 Ibid

19 ' "Lavender": The AI machine directing Israel's bombing spree in Gaza', +972 Magazine, April 3, 2024

20 ' "I'm calling from Israeli intelligence. We have the order to bomb. You have two hours" ', BBC News, November 8, 2023

21 Interviews with the author

22 'Tony Blair says he won't help resettle Gazans elsewhere, dismisses report as a lie', *Times of Israel*, January 2, 2024

23 'Timeline: Trump's remarks on plan to take over Gaza, displace Palestinians', Reuters, February 20, 2025

24 'Netanyahu sets implementation of Trump's Gaza relocation plan as condition for ending war', *Times of Israel*, May 22, 2025

25 'Inside Hamas leader's secret Gaza tunnel & North Korea doubles nukes', *Telegraph*: Battle Lines podcast, June 9, 2025

26 'As Israel turns its focus to Iran, the death toll mounts in Gaza – and hunger deepens', NPR, June 17, 2025

27 '32 per cent in US back Israel's military action in Gaza, a new low', Gallup polling, July 29, 2025

28 'New intelligence suggests Israel is preparing possible strike on Iranian nuclear facilities, US officials say', CNN, May 20, 2025

29 'Warning to Iran: The Mossad's ruthless pursuit of Egypt's missile scientists', Haaretz, September 23, 2022

30 'Air strike at Osirak', *Air & Space Forces Magazine*, April 2012

31 'Obama order sped up wave of cyberattacks against Iran', *New York Times*, June 1, 2012

32 'Iranian plot to kill the Saudi ambassador thwarted, US officials say', CNN, October 12, 2011

33 'US strikes in Yemen burning through munitions with limited success', *New York Times*, April 4, 2025

34 'Why Trump suddenly declared victory over the Houthi militia', *New York Times*, May 12, 2025

35 'What was in the Iran nuclear deal and why did Trump withdraw the US from it?', ABC News, June 22, 2025

36 'What to know about bunker-buster bombs unleashed on Iran's Fordo nuclear facility', AP News, June 22, 2025

37 'The Israeli raid on Syria that exposed the weakness of hardened targets', Mosaic Magazine, May 28, 2025

38 'As other Arab States condemn Israeli attacks on Iran, Syria is notably silent', *New York Times*, June 17, 2025

39 'PM: Israel couldn't wait any longer to strike Iran; IDF confirms hitting Isfahan nuclear site', *Times of Israel*, June 14, 2025

40 'Exclusive: Saudi warned Iran to reach nuclear deal with Trump or risk Israeli strike', Reuters, May 30, 2025

41 'China-brokered Saudi-Iran deal driving "wave of reconciliation", says Wang', Al Jazeera, August 21, 2023

42 'China, Iran and Russia hold joint naval drills in Mideast as tensions rise between Tehran and US', AP News, March 12, 2025

12. The Battles for the Global South

1 Interview with the author

2 'Calibrated Force: Operation Sindoor and the Future of Indian Deterrence', RUSI, May 21, 2025

3 'India launches attacks on Pakistan after Kashmir massacre', CNN, May 7, 2025

4 'Pakistan claims to have downed Indian warplanes, vows response to strikes', *Washington Post*, May 7, 2025

5 'Chief of defence staff admits to losing aircraft, "rectifying" plan to hit Pakistan deep', *Indian Express*, June 1, 2025

6 'Danger grows as India and Pakistan appear to escalate military clash', *New York Times*, May 8, 2025

7 '"Don't want too much foreign influence on our decision-making": Jaishankar on India's foreign policy', *Times of India*, February 23, 2025

8 'Westlessness: Navigating a world beyond Western rule', Facing Coming Storms podcast (S1, E16), May 25, 2025

9 'A defiant Putin closes global summit aimed at reshaping global order', NPR, October 24, 2024

10 'A decade on, rise of BRICs shaped by September 11', Reuters, September 10, 2011

11 'China cements role as top of the Brics', *Financial Times*, April 14, 2011

12 'What happened at the BRICS summit?', Reuters, October 24, 2024

13 'UN's Guterres arrives in Russia for controversial BRICS summit', Euronews, October 23, 2024

14 'Is China's Huawei a threat to US national security?', Council on Foreign Relations, February 8, 2023

15 Interview with the author

16 'How Huawei and open RAN misfires hurt Ericsson, Nokia and telcos', LightReading, September 18, 2024

17 'China's Overseas Lending', Stanford: Center on China's Economy and Institutions, 2021

18 'China is now the biggest debt collector in the developing world, report says', NPR, May 28, 2025

19 'Statement of Admiral Alvin Holsey', US Southern Command, February 13, 2025

20 'US seals Panama deal to deploy troops to canal amid Trump's takeover threats', *South China Morning Post*, April 11, 2025

21 'China condemns US "malign influence" over Panama's plan to replace Huawei towers', *South China Morning Post*, June 18, 2025

22 'Four Days in May: The India–Pakistan Crisis of 2025', Stimson, May 28, 2025

23 'View: India was ready for round II, Pakistan begged US for intervention on May 10', *Hindustan Times*, May 18, 2025

24 'Exclusive: Pakistan, India close to completing border troop reduction, senior Pakistani general says', Reuters, May 30, 2025

25 Marino, Andy, *Narendra Modi: A Political Biography* (2014), HarperCollins Publishers India, Kindle location 31

26 'Blood and water cannot flow together: PM Modi at Indus Water Treaty meeting', *Indian Express*, September 27, 2016

27 'Exclusive: India weighs plan to slash Pakistan water supply with new Indus river project', Reuters, May 16, 2025

28 'Modi says Pakistan will not get water from Indian-controlled rivers', Reuters, May 22, 2025

29 *Herodotus – Book IV*: Chapters 145–205, Vol. II of the Loeb Classical Library edition, 1921

30 'Searching for peace in post-Qaddafi Libya', Brookings, June 25, 2025

31 'Libyan general Khalifa Haftar meets Russian minister to seek help', *Guardian*, November 29, 2016

32 'Column: Chinese, local drones reflect changing Middle East', Reuters, March 7, 2019

33 'Inside China's secret plan to send weapons disguised as Covid aid to warlord', *Daily Telegraph*, December 26, 2024

34 'A military drone with a mind of its own was used in combat, UN says', NPR, June 1, 2021

35 'Deadly skies: Drone warfare in Ethiopia and the future of conflict in Africa', European Council on Foreign Relations, February 28, 2025

36 'Foreign drones tip the balance in Ethiopia's civil war', *New York Times*, December 20, 2021

37 'Feature: Six million silenced: A two-year internet outage in Ethiopia', Reuters, September 29, 2022

38 'France announces withdrawal of troops from Mali, reshaping the fight against Islamist extremists in West Africa', *Washington Post*, February 17, 2022

39 'The two generals fighting in Sudan helped Putin plunder the country's gold to fund Russia's war in Ukraine', Business Insider Africa, April 15, 2023

40 'Year after failed mutiny, Russia tightens grip on Wagner units in Africa', *New York Times*, June 25, 2024

41 'War in Sudan: How two rival generals started Africa's largest conflict', *New York Times*, March 21, 2025

42 'Russia's naval base in Port Sudan: A gateway to Africa and the Indian Ocean', Horn: International Institute for Strategic Studies, March 5, 2025

43 'Drone attacks on Port Sudan jeopardize plan for Russian Red Sea naval base', The Jamestown Foundation, May 28, 2025

44 'War in Sudan: How two rival generals started Africa's largest conflict', *New York Times*, March 21, 2025

45 'Talking peace in Sudan, the UAE secretly fuels the fight', *New York Times*, September 29, 2023

46 'Sudan accuses UAE of being complicit in genocide', *New York Times*, March 6, 2025

47 'A ragtag resistance sees the tide turning in a forgotten war', *New York Times*, April 20, 2024

48 'The four horsemen of Myanmar's "apocalypse" ', Nikkei Asia, April 19, 2025

49 'Digital Press Briefing with US Marine Corps General Michael Langley, Commander, US Africa Command', US Department of State, June 27, 2024

50 Ibid

51 Ibid

52 'US struggles with shaky relations and troop cuts in African nations as military leaders meet', AP News, June 24, 2024

53 'Remarks by Ambassador Van Vranken: Commemorating the C-130 Cargo Aircraft Grant', US Embassy in Botswana, June 28, 2024

54 'MMG to invest $700 million to double copper output at Botswana mine', Reuters, June 12, 2024

55 'USAID administrator Samantha Power promotes Lobito corridor investment in Angola', Africa News, April 27, 2024

56 'Biden arrives in Angola on his only trip as President to Sub-Saharan Africa', *New York Times*, December 2, 2024

57 'Digital Press Briefing on the African Chiefs of Defense Conference 2025 with the Commander of US Africa Command, US Marine Corps General Michael Langley', US Department of State, May 30, 2025

58 'As the US exits foreign aid, who will fill the gap?', *New York Times*, February 22, 2025

59 '"A big slap in the face": Africans jolted by Trump's new travel ban', *New York Times*, June 6, 2025

60 'China, Vietnam sign deals as Xi visits Hanoi amid US tariff tensions', Reuters, April 14, 2025

61 'Brazil's president seeks "indestructible" links with China amid Trump trade war', *Guardian*, May 12, 2025

62 'China, Vietnam sign deals as Xi visits Hanoi amid US tariff tensions', Reuters, April 14, 2025

13. The Race to Stop a War

1 'To consider the nomination of: Lieutenant General John D. Caine, USAF (Retired) to be General and Chairman of the Joint Chiefs of Staff', Senate Armed Services Committee, April 1, 2025

2 '"Firing a loud shot": Taiwan TV show *Zero Day* aims to spark debate over potential China invasion', *Guardian*, August 4, 2024

3 'Taiwan turns to own "Iron Duke" Wellington Koo to deter China', Nikkei Asia, August 6, 2024

4 'Taiwan's military drills turn serious as China threat escalates', *Financial Times*, July 20, 2024

5 'Taiwan troops train to use subway to their advantage during Chinese invasion of Taipei', TWZ, July 14, 2025

6 Interview with the author

7 'US, UK, Japan diplomatic contingents in Taiwan are bigger than ever', Nikkei Asia, May 8, 2025

8 '"It needs to be a thousand": US has 500 military trainers on Taiwan, retired admiral says', Stars and Stripes, May 27, 2025

9 'US's 500 military personnel in Taiwan an "open test" of Beijing's red lines', *South China Morning Post*, May 26, 2025

10 'US think tank calls for removal of all 500 US military trainers in Taiwan', *Taipei Times*, July 10, 2025

11 'Taiwan should spend 10% of GDP on defense, Pentagon No. 3 pick Colby says', Nikkei Asia, March 5, 2025

12 Interviews with the author

13 'TSMC buys time with $100bn US investment pledge', *Financial Times*, March 31, 2025

14 'Taiwan reassured – and surprised – by Pentagon focus on deterring China', *Washington Post*, March 31, 2025

15 'Trump says he will meet China's Xi if a trade deal is struck', Reuters, August 5, 2025

16 Anduril press release, August 5, 2025

17 'Pentagon policy chief's rogue decisions have irked US allies and the Trump administration', Politico, July 8, 2025

18 'US prepares for long war with China that might hit its bases, homeland', Reuters, May 19, 2025

19 'Navy leaders look to expand munitions options as supplies run low', *Navy Times*, May 14, 2025

20 'Andruil building Arsenal-1 hyperscale manufacturing facility in Ohio', Andruil website, January 16, 2025

21 'Secretary of Defense makes historic visit to Guam', YouTube, March 28, 2025

22 'USMC anti-ship missile deployment to highly strategic Luzon Strait is unprecedented', TWZ, April 21, 2025

23 'The Philippines is quietly working with Taiwan to counter China', *Washington Post*, July 14, 2025

24 'Strategic landpower dialogue: A conversation with General Ronald Clark', CSIS, June 27, 2025

25 'Pearl Harbor redux? CC draws parallels, urges preparedness', Edwards Air Force Base: The Center of the Aerospace Testing Universe, May 7, 2025

26 'Navy secretary pushes US-allied shipbuilding ties during stop in South Korea', Stars and Stripes, May 2, 2025

27 'What we know about Dan "Razin" Caine, Trump's pick to be the top US military officer', CNBC, February 22, 2025

28 'Senior CIA officer reflects on defending Washington, DC on 9/11', CIA website, September 11, 2023

29 'To consider the nomination of: Lieutenant General John D. Caine, USAF (Retired) to be General and Chairman of the Joint Chiefs of Staff', Senate Armed Services Committee, April 1, 2025

30 'Joint chiefs chairman Caine has an "algorithm" for US "winning"', Breaking Defense, May 8, 2025

31 'Caine calls on industry: "Focus on fighting the next war, not fighting the last war"', US Department of Defense, June 4, 2025

32 'Statement of General John Daniel Caine', House Armed Services Committee, June 12, 2025

33 'China is choking supply of critical minerals to Western defence companies', *Wall Street Journal*, August 7, 2025

34 'Ukraine claims drone attack hit 40 Russian bombers as talks set to resume in Turkey', CBS News, June 2, 2025

35 Interview with the author

36 'How Ukraine pulled off an audacious attack deep inside Russia', Reuters, June 4, 2024

37 'Trump's special envoy concerned over Ukrainian Spider's Web operation, saying "risk levels are going up"', Ukrainska Pravda, June 4, 2025

38 'Trump's envoy Kellogg says Ukrainian strike on Russian strategic bombers could become "forcing function for peace"', Ukrainska Pravda, June 6, 2025

39 'Putin will seek revenge for Ukraine drone attack, warns Trump', BBC News, June 4, 2025

40 Interview with the author

41 Interviews with the author

42 'NATO needs 400% increase in air and missile defence, Rutte will say in London', Reuters, June 9, 2025

43 'Drones, doubts as US allies look to NATO summit', Reuters, May 30, 2025

44 'Pentagon chief confident NATO will commit to Trump's defence spending target', Reuters, June 5, 2025

45 'Drones, doubts as US allies look to NATO summit', Reuters, May 30, 2025

46 'Estonian city of Narva prepares for potential Russian invasion', France24, April 7, 2025

47 'Estonian Defense Forces to build new base in Narva', News ERR, April 24, 2025

48 'Estonia could evacuate all citizens if Russia attacks, says top military man', TVP World, November 25, 2024

49 'MWI podcast: A survey of Europe's defense and security landscape', Moden War Institute, May 31, 2025

50 'Chief of the General Staff speech at RUSI Land Warfare Conference 2025', UK MoD, June 17, 2025

51 'General Donahue on deterring Russia in Europe', War on the Rocks podcast, July 3, 2025

52 'Poland doubles down on South Korean tanks with $6.5 billion deal', Defense News, August 1, 2025

53 'Australia acquiring frigates "as fast" as possible', Sky News, August 4, 2025

14. Space and the Battle for the Future

1 'Step by step: The Artemis Program and NASA's path to human exploration of the Moon, Mars, and beyond', February 26, 2025, US

House of Representatives Committee on Science, Space and Technology Space and Aeronautics Subcommittee

2 'Live: Special coverage of Shenzhou-19 crew's return to Earth', CGTN (China Global Television Network), April 30, 2025

3 'Profile: Cai Xuzhe, returning to space 22 months after his first spaceflight', Xinhua Net (Chinese State Media), October 30, 2024

4 'Chinese astronauts complete world record-breaking spacewalk at 9 hours', *South China Morning Post*, December 18, 2024

5 'Chinese spacewalk apparently breaks a record (barely)', *New York Times*, December 19, 2024

6 'Blocked by US, China finds its own way to space', *New York Times*, May 23, 2007

7 'International Space Station will plummet to a watery grave in 2031', *Guardian*, February 3, 2022

8 'The far side of the Moon was once a vast magma ocean, Chinese lunar lander confirms', Space website, March 18, 2025

9 'China to 3D-print bricks on the Moon using lunar dirt in 2028 to pave way for future base', Space website, April 10, 2025

10 'Interlune plans to gather scarce lunar helium-3 for quantum computing on Earth', Space News, January 23, 2025

11 'Retired general issues terrifying warning about China mining the Moon: "Power for the entire world"', *Daily Mail*, May 26, 2025

12 'China to launch "Earth 2.0" exoplanet observatory in 2028', Space News, August 22, 2024

13 'China scientists develop space battery that can run on Mars' atmosphere', *South China Morning Post*, October 8, 2024

14 'Space, the other battlefield between China and the United States', *El País*, May 3, 2025

15 'Why China is fixated on the Moon', BBC News, 29 November 2013

16 'Step by step: The Artemis Program and NASA's Path to Human exploration of the Moon, Mars, and beyond', US House of Representatives, Committee on Science, Space and Technology Space and Aeronautics Subcommittee, February 26, 2025

17 'Smart robot helps out astronauts on China's *Tiangong* space station', Space website, January 12, 2025

18 'China plans to arm *Tiangong* space station with self-defence bots, scientist says', *South China Morning Post*, May 29, 2025

19 'First man-made object in space: Myths & facts explained', Orbital Today, September 20, 2022

20 'The terrifying German "revenge weapons" of the Second World War', Imperial War Museum

21 'The two lives of Qian Xuesen', *New Yorker*, November 3, 2009

22 ' "The Elon": How a Nazi rocket scientist invented the world's richest man', Mind War, December 29, 2024

23 'Elon Musk left a South Africa that was rife with misinformation and white privilege', *New York Times*, May 5, 2022

24 'How Peter Thiel, "PayPal Mafia" ousted Elon Musk from CEO job – and saved SpaceX', *New York Post*, September 13, 2023

25 Isaacson, Walter, *Elon Musk* (2024), Simon & Schuster, London, Kindle loctation 91

26 'Adding rocket man to his résumé', *New York Times*, February 15, 2010

27 'SpaceX launched Elon Musk's Tesla Roadster toward Mars 5 years ago. Where is it now?', *Observer*, February 6, 2023

28 ' "It's not even smart." Elon Musk's tweets and taunts annoy some of Tesla's biggest fans', *Washington Post*, February 26, 2019

29 'Elon Musk completes $44 billion deal to own Twitter', *New York Times*, October 27, 2022

30 'How Elon Musk's Starlink changed the war in Ukraine', Politico Tech podcast, June 13, 2022

31 'Taiwanese minister to make rare Britain visit this week', Reuters, June 11, 2023

32 'How a Nazi rocket could have put a Briton in space', BBC News, August 24, 2015

33 'From Ukraine to Taiwan, satellite firms wrangle with geopolitics in space', Reuters, October 5, 2023

34 'China launches mineral survey and science outreach satellites', Space website, December 28, 2021

35 'No place to hide: A look into China's geosynchronous surveillance capabilities', CSIS, January 19, 2024

36 'Russia's new Cosmos satellite orbiting near US sat, piques ASAT fears', *Breaking Defense*, May 30, 2025

37 'China practicing on-orbit "dogfighting" tactics with space assets, Gen. Guetlein says' Defence Scoop, March 18, 2025

38 'Secretive US Space Force X-37B space plane "breaks new ground" with return to Earth after 434 days in orbit (photos)', Space website, March 7, 2025

39 'Saltzman: China's ASAT test was "pivot point" in space operations', Air and Space Forces Magazine, January 13, 2023

40 'Throwback: When a US F-15 shot down a satellite', Simple Flying, September 28, 2024

41 'Russian direct-ascent anti-satellite missile test creates significant, long-lasting space debris', US Space Command Public Affairs Office, November 15, 2021

42 'US bans anti-satellite missile tests', BBC News, April 19, 2022

43 'Russian satellite linked to nuclear weapon program appears out of control, US analysts say', Reuters, April 25, 2025

44 '*Artemis 2* astronauts simulated a day in the life on their Moon mission. Here's what they learned', Space website, May 15, 2021

45 'NASA's Orion crew capsule had heat shield issues during *Artemis 1* – an aerospace expert weighs in', Space website, December 31, 2024

46 'NASA's Suni Williams and Butch Wilmore finally return home after more than nine months in space', CNN, March 18, 2025

47 'A massive rocket explosion stirs up talk of setbacks. Are Musk's Mars ambitions farther than they seem?', CNN, June 19, 2025

48 'Musk still hoping for first starship to Mars next year', Space Policy Online, May 29, 2025

49 'Space, the other battlefield between China and the United States', *El País*, May 3, 2025

50 'China, Russia may build nuclear plant on Moon to power lunar station, official says', Reuters, April 23, 2025

51 'Senegal among new members of China's ILRS Moon base project', Space News, September 5, 2024

52 'Artemis Accords', NASA

53 'NASA Artemis Moon missions delayed until 2026 and 2027', *New York Times*, December 5, 2024

54 'India on the Moon! *Chandrayaan-3* becomes 1st probe to land near lunar south pole', Space website, August 23, 2023

55 'Space launch statistics: Commercial launches, SpaceX, and more', The Motley Fool, March 4, 2025

56 'Space Symposium 40: Whiting stressed US must prepare for conflict to ensure peace', US Space Command, April 8, 2025

57 'Securing the final frontier with General Whiting of US Space Command', Chicago Council on Global Affairs, May 23, 2025

58 'What does the US Space Force actually do?', *New York Times*, November 8, 2023

59 'Nominations hearing for Jared Isaacman to be Administrator of the National Aeronautics and Space Administration and Olivia Trusty to be a member of the Federal Communication Commission', US Senate Committee on Commerce, Science and Transformation, April 9, 2025

60 'Trump drops NASA nominee Jared Isaacman, scrapping Elon Musk's pick', *Guardian*, June 1, 2025

61 'Mars & beyond: The road to making humanity multiplanetary', SpaceX

62 'Trump and Musk trade insults as row erupts in public view', BBC News, June 6, 2025

63 'T+304: The Musk/Trump breakup, Jared Isaacman's withdrawn nomination, and Starship flight 9 (with Lori Garner)', Main Engine Cut Off (MUCO) podcast, June 7, 2025

64 'White House asked Joint Chiefs chairman for candidates to lead NASA, worrying experts', Military website, June 6, 2025

65 'SpaceX giant Starship Mars rocket nails critical tenth test flight in stunning comeback', Space website, August 27, 2025

66 'Who would win a war in space?', *Telegraph*: Battle Lines podcast, April 21, 2025

67 'China's three-satellite constellation is the first of its kind for use in the Earth-Moon region', Orbital Today, April 18, 2025

15. 'A Very Dangerous Decade'

1 'This is why Operation SPIDER'S WEB will never work for Taiwan', The China Academy, June 5, 2025

2 'Ships, trucks, and suitcases: How Israel reportedly got its attack drones into Iran', June 15, 2025, *Times of Israel*

3 'Iran holds state funeral for military leaders killed in Israel conflict', BBC News, June 28, 2025

4 'Video shows top Iranian commander alive, defying death reports', Newsweek, June 25, 2025

5 'Iran holds state funeral for military leaders killed in Israel conflict', BBC News, 28 June, 2025

6 'To consider the nominations of Vice Admiral Charles B. Cooper II, USN, to be Admiral and Commander, United States Central Command; and Lieutenant General Alexus G. Grynkewich, USAF, to be General and Commander, United States European Command and Supreme Allied Commander, Europe', Senate Armed Services Committee, June 24, 2025

7 'Ungentlemanly robots: Israel's operation RISING LION and the new way of war', CSIS, June 13, 2025

8 'Allvin calls Ukraine drone strikes a wake-up call for US air defense', Military Times, June 3, 2025

9 'How Ukraine's Operation SPIDER'S WEB attack on Russia holds important lessons for China', *South China Morning Post*, June 7, 2025

10 'This is why Operation SPIDER'S WEB will never work for Taiwan', The China Academy, June 5, 2025

11 'China ousts top general from elite military body as purge grows', Bloomberg, June 27, 2025

12 Ibid

13 'How are Chinese aircraft carriers pushing limits and testing boundaries in the Pacific?', *South China Morning Post*, July 3, 2025

14 'SECNAV Phelan on shipbuilding: "We have to get urgency into the system"', US Naval Institute News, August 1, 2025

15 'Do cruise lines have answer to US Navy maintenance problems? Trump's pick for top admiral wants to find out', Business Insider, July 29, 2025

16 'Carrier *John F. Kennedy* delivery delayed two years, fleet will drop to 10 carriers for one year', USNI news, July 7, 2025

17 'US to complete the review into AUKUS defence pact in autumn', Reuters, July 30, 2025

18 'Russia's battlefield woes in Ukraine', CSIS, June 3, 2025

19 'Ukraine's new theory of victory should be strategic neutralization', Carnegie Endowment for International Peace, June 18, 2025

20 Ibid

21 'Dispatch: Ukraine turns to machines to spare troops from drone-infested "grey zone"', *Daily Telegraph*, July 5, 2025

22 '"Surrender to the drones": Ukraine's robot-led assault stuns Russian forces', Kyiv Post, July 19, 2025

23 'China helps Russia pull ahead in drone war race with Ukraine', Politico, June 5, 2025

24 'Putin forced to send wounded back to fight and offer huge military salaries as Russia suffers a million casualties', The Conversation, June 11, 2025

25 'How much of Ukraine does Russia control?', Foreign Policy, August 18, 2025

26 'Exclusive: China tells EU it does not want to see Russia lose its war in Ukraine: sources', *South China Morning Post*, July 4, 2025

27 'Drones are key to winning wars now. The US makes hardly any', *New York Times*, July 13, 2025

28 'The US Navy is building a drone fleet to take on China. It's not going well', Reuters, August 20, 2025

29 'The funding revolution for defence tech companies', Taylor and Wessing, July 9, 2025

30 'AI defense startup Helsing draws fire for tech and tactics', Bloomberg, April 8, 2025

31 'Palantir might be the most overvalued firm of all time', *Economist*, August 12, 2025

32 Interview with the author

33 Interviews with the author

34 'Pentagon policy chief's rogue decisions have irked US allies and the Trump administration', Politico, July 8, 2025

35 'Britain "more helpful" closer to home than in Asia, says US defence chief', *Financial Times*, July 27, 2021

36 'Trump intel chief freezes out Five Eyes allies on Ukraine', Politico, August 22, 2025

37 'The Choice' (E5), The Wargame podcast, Sky News and Tortoise Media, June 23, 2025

38 'The tiny Swedish island regiment tasked with protecting Europe from Russia', *Daily Telegraph*, June 17, 2025

39 'UK defence spending', House of Commons Library, May 28, 2025

40 Interviews with the author

41 'MOD sponsored cadet forces: 1 April 2023', UK MoD, July 6, 2023

42 'SDR: UK sets goal of 12 SSN-AUKUS boats from late 2030s', Calibre Defence, June 3, 2025

43 'Russia could send "little green men" to test NATO's resolve, German intelligence boss warns', Reuters, June 9, 2025

44 'The head of NATO thinks President Trump "deserves all the praise"', *New York Times*, July 5, 2025

45 'Luxon departs NATO summit after meeting with Ukraine's Zelensky', RNZ, June 26, 2025

46 'View from The Hill: Albanese decides against pursuing Donald Trump to NATO', The Conversation, June 20, 2025

47 'Japan, South Korea abruptly pull out of NATO summit', Foundation for Defense of Democracies, June 25, 2025

48 'Confirmation hearing transcript', Senate Armed Services Committee, June 24, 2025

49 '"15 years of incredible work": The inside story of the mission to bomb Iran's nuclear sites', Air and Space Forces, June 26, 2025

50 'Hegseth says Trump's Iran strike shows American deterrence is back: "When this president speaks, the world should listen"', *New York Post*, June 22, 2025

51 'Trump lashes out at Israel and Iran: "They don't know what the f--- they're doing"', NBC News, June 24, 2025

52 'NATO chief calls Trump "Daddy"', Politico, June 25, 2025

53 'NATO summit: Trump calls Trudeau "two-faced" over video', BBC News, December 4, 2019

54 '"You've been the worst!" Pete Hegseth browbeats former Fox news colleague for her reporting on Iran strikes', *Independent*, June 26, 2025

55 'Hegseth fires head of Defense Intelligence Agency, Lt. Gen. Jeffrey Kruse', *Washington Post*, August 22, 2025

56 'US only has 25% of all Patriot missile interceptors needed for Pentagon's military plans', *Guardian*, July 8, 2025

57 'Vance outlines the "Trump Doctrine" at political dinner in Ohio', Politico, June 24, 2025

58 'In Cabinet meeting, Trump takes a golden opportunity to talk interior décor', *Washington Post*, July 8, 2025

59 'Peter Mandelson: "There's a kernel of truth in everything Trump says"', *The Times*, July 12, 2025

60 'State Department starts firing more than 1,350 workers in Trump's shake-up of diplomatic corps', Reuters, July 13, 2025

61 'How a US mission to push a Trump deal in Congo unravelled', Reuters, July 11, 2025

62 'Rwanda, Congo sign peace deal in US to end fighting, attract investment', Reuters, June 28, 2025

63 ' "Peacemaker" Trump can end Africa's biggest war, former White House advisor says', Fox News, July 12, 2025

64 'How many wars has President Trump really ended?', BBC News, August 20, 2025

65 'Israel, please let aid organisations do our jobs in Gaza', *Guardian*, June 24, 2025

66 'Netanyahu says he nominated Trump for a Nobel Peace Prize. From there, it's a secretive process', AP News, July 8, 2025

67 'Trump says he threatened to bomb Moscow if Putin invaded Ukraine', *The Times*, July 9, 2025

68 'US demands to know what allies would do in event of war over Taiwan', *Financial Times*, July 12, 2025

69 'Remarks by Secretary of Defense Pete Hegseth at the Shangri-La Dialogue in Singapore (as delivered)', US Department of Defense, May 31, 2025

70 'Final F-35A aircraft delivered', Australian Defence website, December 19, 2024

71 'Britain vows more presence in the Indo-Pacific', Sky News, July 13, 2025

72 'Fury as Royal Navy has NO attack submarines at sea to defend its surface fleet in "ridiculous shambles"', *Sun*, July 23, 2025

73 'Britain vows more presence in the Indo-Pacific', Sky News, July 13, 2025

74 'David Lammy's attempt to stop the Royal Navy transiting the Taiwan Strait is a disgrace', *Daily Telegraph*, August 21, 2025

75 'EU and Japan prepare difficult balancing act with US', Euronews, July 23, 2025

76 'Europe and Australia commit to security and defence partnership', European Council website, June 17, 2025

77 'A challenging moment for the US–India relationship', Brookings, August 13, 2025

78 'Trump administration resumes sending some weapons to Ukraine after Pentagon pause', AP News, July 10, 2025

79 'Trump agrees to send weapons to Ukraine', Politico, July 14, 2025

80 'France to quicken defense-spending boost in bid to be "feared"', *Defense News*, July 14, 2025

81 'Army in talks to use former NS trains as mobile field hospitals', Dutch News, July 14, 2025

82 'Dutch military adds railway steel to rush troops to NATO's east flank', Defense News, February 7, 2025

83 'Dutch, Norwegian F-35s to guard Ukraine supply lines in Poland', Defense News, July 7, 2025

84 'Sweden eyes extending military officers' conscription age to 70', Reuters, July 14, 2025

85 'Exclusive: Danish general says he is not losing sleep over US plans for Greenland', Reuters, June 27, 2025

86 'Southeast Asian nations look to hedge their way out of troubled waters in the South China Sea', The Conversation, June 18, 2025

87 'US commander says China has failed to coerce rival states in South China Sea', AP News, July 11, 2025

88 'Former US admiral says China "their own worst enemy" as tensions rise in South China Sea', ABC News, September 12, 2021

89 ' "Peacemaker" Trump can end Africa's biggest war, former White House advisor says' Fox News, July 12, 2025

90 'US cancelled military talks with Taiwan', *Financial Times*, July 30, 2025

91 'Donald Trump blocks Taiwan's President Lai Ching-te from New York stopover', *Financial Times*, July 29, 2025

92 'Briefing: There will be no next Taiwan election, mainland scholar warns', BBC Monitoring, May 28, 2025

93 'Trump says Xi told him China will not invade Taiwan while he is in office', *Guardian*, August 16, 2025

94 Interview with the author

95 'China displays military strength in parade on eightieth anniversary of World War Two', Politico, September 2, 2025

96 'Hot mic catches Xi and Putin discussing organ transplants and immortality', BBC News, September 3, 2025

97 'China rules out participating in denuclearisation talks with US and Russia', CBS, August 27, 2025

98 'Remarks: Donald Trump holds a bilateral meeting with Karol Nawrocki of Poland', Roll Call, September 3, 2025

Afterword: A Still-Unravelling World?

1 'Senate committee considers nominations for Central Command, European Command', DOD website, June 24, 2025

2 'Poland is at its closest to open conflict since World War II, PM says', Reuters, September 10, 2025

3 'Leaders call for national resilience as war risk grows', Radio Prague International, September 23, 2025

4 'Press conference with NATO commander and Lithuanian defence minister', DRM News, September 11, 2025

5 'Estonia says it summoned Russian diplomat after helicopter violated airspace', Reuters, September 8, 2025

6 Interview with the author

7 'Full speeches: Trump, Hegseth address military leaders', Face the Nation, September 30, 2025

8 'Every time they are making progress, it seems like he bombs someone', *Politico*, September 11, 2025

9 'Leaders in Middle East and Europe welcome Trump Gaza peace plan', BBC, September 30, 2025

10 'Vance: "I don't care if strike on Venezuelan drug boat is war crime"', *Daily Telegraph*, September 7, 2025

11 interview with the author

12 'Pakistan soldiers killed in border clashes with Afghanistan', *Financial Times*, October 12, 2025

13 'Ukraine war and Taiwan worries drive push for faster, cheaper weapons', Reuters, September 19, 2025

14 'Russia's hybrid war is only the beginning, warns Danish PM', *Financial Times*, October 1, 2025

15 'Moldova's pro-EU party wins pivotal election setback for Russia', Reuters, September 29, 2025

16 'Some Europeans fear Trump aids want a far right takeover', *New York Times*, September 20, 2025

17 'Political bias on social media', Global Witness, March 27, 2025

18 'How Russia is helping China prepared to seize Taiwan', RUSI, September 26, 2025

19 'Taiwan to build their defence dome', BBC, October 10, 2025

20 'Taiwan unveils first missile jointly developed with American arms company', CNN, September 18, 2025

21 Taiwan steps up sea cable patrols', Reuters, September 11, 2025

22 'Japan spots Chinese aircraft carrier sailing for first time in the East China Sea', Stars and Stripes, September 12, 2025

23 'Philippines, China trade accusations over South China sea vessel clash', Reuters, October 12, 2025

24 'No clarity on TikTok sale after Trump-Xi phone call', *Politico*, September 19, 2025

25 'Western companies Wall of China rare earth supply chain chaos', *Financial Times*, October 14, 2025

26 Interviews with the author

27 'Chinese kindergartens in crisis', *Financial Times*, July 25, 2025

28 'Yamaha looks for sax appeal among China's ageing population', *Financial Times*, May 9, 2025

29 'China surges ahead as global robotics powerhouse', *China Daily*, July 29, 2025

30 Interviews with the author

31 US allies must come first amid Trump dealmaking: ex-China ambassador', Nikkei Asia, October 11, 2025

32 'Hegseth NATO-bound, allies fret', Politico, October 7, 2025

33 Interviews with the author

34 'AUKUS survives Pentagon review', Nikkei Asia, September 30, 2025

35 Ibid

36 'US Army tank unit arrives in Estonia', ERR, October 14, 2025

Index